THE CONFIDENCE GAP

THE CONFIDENCE GAP

BUSINESS, LABOR, AND GOVERNMENT IN THE PUBLIC MIND

SEYMOUR MARTIN LIPSET
AND
WILLIAM SCHNEIDER

Studies of the Modern Corporation
Graduate School of Business
Columbia University

THE FREE PRESS
A Division of Macmillan, Inc.
NEW YORK

Collier Macmillan Publishers
LONDON

The Free Press
A Division of Macmillan, Inc.
866 Third Avenue, New York, N.Y. 10022

Collier Macmillan Canada, Inc.

Library of Congress Catalog Card Number: 82–70720

Printed in the United States of America

printing number

2   3   4   5   6   7   8   9   10

Library of Congress Cataloging in Publication Data
Lipset, Seymour Martin.
    The confidence gap.

    (Studies of the modern corporation)
    Includes index.
    1. Corporations—United States—Public opinion.
2. Trade regulation—United States—Public opinion.
3. Trade-unions—United States—Public opinion.
4. Politicians—United States—Public opinion.   5. Public
opinion—United States.   I. Schneider, William.
II. Title.   III. Series.
HD2785.L53   303.3′8′0973   82–70720
ISBN 0–02–919230–7   AACR2

STUDIES OF THE MODERN CORPORATION
Graduate School of Business, Columbia University

The Program for Studies of the Modern Corporation is devoted to the advancement and dissemination of knowledge about the corporation. Its publications are designed to stimulate inquiry, research, criticism, and reflection. They fall into three categories: works by outstanding businesspeople, scholars, and professionals from a variety of backgrounds and academic disciplines; annotated and edited selections of business literature; and business classics that merit republication. The studies are supported by outside grants from private business, professional, and philanthropic institutions interested in the program's objectives.

RICHARD EELLS
Director

Contents

List of Tables   xi

List of Figures   xv

Preface   xix

Acknowledgments   xxi

Introduction   1

PART I   Confidence in Institutions: General Patterns

CHAPTER 1   *Confidence in Institutions*   13

    The Rise and Fall of Confidence
    Confidence in Government: Trends
    Confidence in Business: Trends
    Comparison of Anti-Business and Anti-Government
        Sentiment

Contents

Attitudes Toward Industries and Firms
Attitudes Toward Labor Unions
Conclusion

CHAPTER 2   *The Generality of the Trends*   41

Confidence in Institutional Leaders: The Harris and
    NORC Surveys
Trends of Confidence in Institutional Leadership
Another Perspective on the Trends
Confidence in Institutions: The Gallup and ORC
    Surveys
Confidence and the Economy

CHAPTER 3   *How Confidence Ratings Compare*   67

The Confidence Rankings of Institutions
Confidence and Ethical Practices
The Perception of Size
Conclusion
Appendix: The Effects of Variations in Question
    Wording

CHAPTER 4   *The Correlates of Confidence in
                 Institutions*   97

A General Index of Confidence
The Influence of Education and Socioeconomic
    Status
The Influence of Politics and Ideology
The Influence of Psychological Factors
Confidence: General and Specific

CHAPTER 5   *Personal Satisfaction and Confidence in
                 the Nation*   126

Satisfaction with Self and Nation
Personal Views of the Past, Present, and Future
The Impact of the Economy
Conclusion: What Explains the Decline in
    Confidence?

Contents

PART II Business, Labor, and Government

CHAPTER 6 *Business: Productive but Unpopular*　163

Report Card for Business
The Role of Morality and Self-Interest
Business, Labor, and Political Leaders
Disdain for Money-Making
Attitudes Toward Profits
Public Perceptions of Industries

CHAPTER 7 *Labor Unions: Necessary but
　　　　　　Unpopular*　199

Public Attitudes Toward Unions
Union Power: A Source of Concern
Unions and Workers
The Effect of Unions on Inflation
The Public's Perception of Union Leaders
Conclusion

CHAPTER 8 *Government Regulation*　221

A Short History of Public Attitudes
Regulation in Particular Industries
Wage and Price Controls
The Limits of Regulation and Deregulation
The Costs of Regulation
Regulation to Protect Consumers
Conclusion

CHAPTER 9 *Government Intervention and Free
　　　　　　Enterprise*　257

Divestiture
Nationalization
Alternative Forms of Government Control of
　　Business
The Productivity Problem: A Cross-National
　　Comparison

The Legitimacy of Free Enterprise
Conclusion

CHAPTER 10 *The Social and Political Bases of
Attitudes Toward Business, Labor,
and Government* 291

The 1970s: Continuity and Change
Business, Labor, and Government: Attitude Scales
Socioeconomic Status and Attitudes Toward
    Business, Labor, and Government
The Political Bases of Attitudes Toward Business,
    Labor, and Government
Summary
A Further Inquiry into Political Trust

PART III   Causes and Consequences

CHAPTER 11 *The Effects of "Malaise"* 337

Consequences for Government
Consequences for Labor
Consequences for Business

CHAPTER 12 *Is There a Legitimacy Crisis?* 375

Concern about Legitimacy
Optimism about the System
Causes of Alienation and Cynicism
The Impact of National Decline

Index of Poll Results 413

General Index 419

About the Authors 433

List of Tables

2-1   Confidence in Leaders of Ten Institutions, 1966–81   48

2-2   Confidence in Institutions, 1973–81   57

2-3   Confidence in Institutions, 1975–81   60

2-4   Confidence in Leaders of Institutions: Correlation Coefficients over Time   63

2-5   Effects of Unemployment and Inflation on Confidence in the Leaders of Institutions   64

3-1   Average Percentage Expressing "A Great Deal of Confidence" in the Leaders of Ten Institutions, 1966–81   68

3-2   Rank-ordering of Ratings on "Confidence" and "Ethical and Moral Practices" for Various Institutions and Groups   78

3-3   Confidence in Selected Institutions and Groups   82

3-4   Perceptions of Power and Influence   87

3-5   Three Versions of the Confidence-in-Institutions Question   94

4-1   General Index of Confidence in Institutions by Partisanship and Ideology   106

List of Tables

4-2   Correlates of Confidence in Specific Institutions, 1973–77   123

5-1   Average Ladder-Scale Ratings of "Your Life," "the Situation of the Country," and "the State of the Economy," Five Years Ago, at the Present Time, and Five Years from Now, Plus Unemployment and Inflation Rates, 1959–81   142

5-2   Effects of Inflation and Unemployment on Mean Ladder-Scale Ratings, 1959–81   144

5-3   Percentage of "Optimists," "Temporary Crisis" Types, and "Pessimists" Concerning "Your Life," "the Situation of the Country," and "the State of the Economy," 1974–81   146

5-4   Effects of Inflation and Unemployment on Ladder-Scale Response Patterns, 1974–81   148

6-1   Perceptions of the Extent of Bribes and Payoffs   174

6-2   Industry Rankings: Concentration of Power and Favorability   186

7-1   Ratings of Labor Unions, 1936–81   203

7-2   Evaluations by AFL-CIO Members of Union Services   205

7-3   Evaluation of the Influence of Unions and Workers in American Life and Politics   210

7-4   Sentiments Toward Unions   219

8-1   Attitudes Toward Regulation of Business and Labor, 1961–62   225

8-2   Attitudes Toward Regulation, 1978–80   227

8-3   Personal Effects of Regulation, 1966–81   228

8-4   Correlates of Attitudes Toward Regulation   229

8-5   How the Public Rates Consumer Protection Activities by the Federal Government   232

8-6   Attitudes Toward Specific Regulations, by General Attitude Toward Regulation   233

8-7   Attitudes Toward Government Regulation: Sources of Variation   240

List of Tables

8-8	Costs vs. Benefits of Regulation	243
8-9	Attitudes Toward Consumer Regulation, 1970–81	254
9-1	Attitudes Toward Divestiture in the Oil Industry, 1976–80	259
9-2	Agreement with Arguments for and against Divestiture in the Oil Industry	260
9-3	Anticipation of Price Increases by Attitude Toward Divestiture	263
9-4	Education and Opinion Concerning Price Increases with Divestiture	264
9-5	Alternative Forms of Government Control of Business	271
9-6	Steps Government and Business Should Take to Improve Economic Growth	278
9-7	Attitudes Toward Nationalization of Railroads, Banks, and the Munitions Industry, 1936	284
9-8	Statements about the American Economic System	286
9-9	Comparisons Between Business and Federal Agencies: Four Criteria	288
10-1	Confidence in the Leaders of Major Companies and Organized Labor by Education, Occupational Status, Partisanship, and Ideology	293
10-2	Confidence in the Leaders of Major Companies and Organized Labor by Education, Occupational Status, and Partisanship, Controlling for Age	298
10-3	Public Approval of Large Companies, by Education, Occupation, and Age	300
10-4	Attitudes Toward Government, by Education	304
11-1	Trust in Government and the Tax Revolt, 1978	344
12-1	Factors Making America Great	388
12-2	Expectations for Carter, Reagan, and "Any President"	394
12-3	Political Efficacy by Media Use, Controlling for Education, 1968	404

List of Figures

1-1   Confidence in Government, 1958–80   17

1-2   Internal and External Efficacy, 1952–80   21

1-3   Perceived Responsiveness of Government, 1964–80,
       and Citizen's Duty, 1952–80   25

1-4   Attitudes Toward Business, 1959–81   30

1-5   Average Trends in Anti-Business and Anti-Govern-
       ment Sentiment, 1958–81   33

1-6   Industry and Company Familiarity and Favorability
       Ratings   36

2-1   Trends of Confidence in Institutional Leadership,
       1966–81   50

2-2   Confidence in Institutional Leadership, Six Periods   54

2-3   Relationship Between Confidence in the Executive
       Branch and in the Press, 1966–81   56

3-1   Groups and Institutions, Rank-ordered by Com-
       bined Scores on "Ability to Get Things Done"
       and "Honesty, Dependability, and Integrity"   75

List of Figures

4-1   Average Factor Scores, General Index of Confidence in Institutions, by Ideology and Partisanship   102

4-2   General Index of Confidence in Institutions, by Personal Trust, Personal Satisfaction, and Education   121

5-1   "Your Life" at the Present Time, Five Years Ago, and Five Years from Now: Average Ladder-Scale Ratings, 1959–81   131

5-2   "Your Life" at the Present Time, Five Years Ago, and Five Years from Now: Average Ladder-Scale Ratings, 1959, 1975 (4th Quarter), and 1980 (4th Quarter)   133

5-3   "The Situation of the Country" at the Present Time, Five Years Ago, and Five Years from Now: Average Ladder-Scale Ratings, 1959–81   136

5-4   "The Situation of the Country" Five Years Ago, at the Present Time, and Five Years from Now: Average Ladder-Scale Ratings, in 1959, 1975 (2nd Quarter), and 1979 (1st Quarter)   138

6-1   Trend of Anti-Business Sentiment, 1968–81   183

6-2   Industry Rankings: Two Dimensions   197

9-1   Perceived Responsibility for Low Productivity: A Comparison among Five Nations   276

9-2   Attitudes Toward Government Bail-Outs of Corporations   280

10-1   Attitudes Toward Business, Labor, and Government, by Education   311

10-2   Attitudes Toward Business, Labor, and Government, by Occupational Status   313

10-3   Attitudes Toward Business, Labor, and Government, by Ideology   317

10-4   Perceived Influence of Specific Business and Labor Groups, by Ideology   320

List of Figures

10-5   Attitudes Toward Government, by Ideology   323

10-6   Attitudes Toward Business, Labor, and Government, by Ideology and Partisanship   325

10-7   Confidence in Government, the Political System, and the Ford Administration, by Partisanship and Ideology   331

10-8   Trust in Government Index by Party Identification, 1958–78, and by Liberal-Conservative Index, 1964–76   333

12-1   Ladder-Scale Ratings, Your Financial Situation and the State of the Nation's Economy, February 1981   397

Preface

THIS study of the American public's attitudes toward key institutions is an outgrowth of our larger interest in locating, analyzing, and comparing the results of the myriad of public opinion polls conducted by academic and commercial survey research organizations since the Gallup Poll began in 1935. Although some polling organizations, notably the Gallup Poll, the National Opinion Research Center of the University of Chicago, and the Survey Research Center and Center for Political Studies of the University of Michigan, have presented many of their findings over the years in printed volumes, it is not easy to recover the data collected by most other survey organizations. The reports that are available are usually limited to the work of a single research organization and typically show results from one survey on a specific subject.

Our experience with poll data convinces us that no single survey can be taken as definitive or authoritative, and few specific survey results withstand the test of time. Indeed, much of the value of the information gathered by the pollsters lies in the fact that some of them have been reporting public attitudes on the same topics for over four decades. It is possible, therefore, to trace changes in public opinion over time and to examine the effects of timing, question-wording, and context from one poll to another. As we wrote a few years ago:

Preface

> To obtain a reasonably valid interpretation of what public opinion is on any given issue, one must undertake a systematic comparison of questions asked with different wordings, in different contexts, in different polls, and at different times—with no presumption that any single pollster's approach is necessarily more accurate.[1]

Thus, the data presented in this book are drawn almost entirely from surveys carried out by other researchers for their own purposes. We attempt to offer new and, we hope, illuminating interpretations based on the juxtaposition of diverse—and often divergent—research findings. The basic attitudes of the American public cannot be gauged from any single question or even a battery of questions. Rather, various scraps of evidence must be assembled like a mosaic and reexamined over time in order to get even a vague sense of the public's basic predispositions on any given issue. We believe that this approach helps to compensate for the notorious "softness" and instability of survey data. We believe that readers should never fully accept any single poll's results, but should rather compare the findings of many surveys, through which they can get a reasonably accurate sense of the social reality under examination.

This book focuses on issues related to business, government, and labor. It is our intention to apply the same approach to the analysis of public attitudes on other issues. Specifically, we are planning to carry out similar studies of attitudes toward women, blacks, Jews, and other minority groups. Our limited explorations have demonstrated to us that there is a wealth of data on these and other topics lying almost unnoticed and unanalyzed. We have made a start, and, if others join us, the results may eventually add up to a comprehensive record of the history and dynamics of American public opinion.

SEYMOUR MARTIN LIPSET
WILLIAM SCHNEIDER
Stanford, California
January 1983

[1] Seymour Martin Lipset and William Schneider, "Polls for the White House and the Rest of Us," *Encounter* 49 (November 1977), p. 25.

Acknowledgments

A number of people associated with survey organizations have cooperated by providing data or reviewing our analyses. These include Richard Baxter of the Roper Organization, George Gallup, Jr., of the Gallup Poll, John Gorman of Cambridge Reports, Inc., Madelyn Hochstein of Yankelovich, Skelly & White, Inc., I. A. Lewis of the *Los Angeles Times* Poll, Harry O'Neill of the Opinion Research Corporation, Roy Pfautch of Civic Service, Inc., and Scott Taylor of Louis Harris and Associates. Everett Ladd, the Director of the Roper Center at the University of Connecticut, and Karlyn Keene, Managing Editor of *Public Opinion* magazine, have also provided useful information.

Chauncey G. Olinger, Jr., the Consulting Editor to the Program for Studies of the Modern Corporation at the Graduate School of Business of Columbia University, has been our editor and has done much to make this book more readable. Appreciation is also due to John B. Seiberling, who typed the tables, and to Rebecca P. J. Sargent, who assisted with the editing of the manuscript.

Steven Markowitz and Lynn Foster of the Continental Group have given us advice and encouragement. Jeanne Fleming, a graduate research assistant at Stanford, has assisted us greatly in various research tasks. Finally, Brenda McLean of the Hoover Institution has managed, with remarkable patience, to shepherd this manuscript through countless revisions, maintaining order

Acknowledgments

and sanity despite the best efforts of two wandering authors to create chaos.

Work on *The Confidence Gap* has been supported by financial assistance from the Business Roundtable, the Institute for Educational Affairs, the William and Flora Hewlett Foundation, and the Hoover Institution on War, Revolution, and Peace. The content and conclusions of this book are the sole and exclusive responsibility of the authors.

S.M.L.
W.S.

Introduction

THE 1960s and 1970s were decades of introspection for Americans. Our political and economic systems were severely tested by the conflicts and reversals of those years. First students and intellectuals, then leaders, and eventually the public itself became concerned over the gap between the promise and the performance of our major institutions, particularly government and business. In large measure this concern was produced by the waves of mass protest that arose in the United States and then swept across the entire Western world (and Japan) during the late 1960s. While the demands for racial justice in the early 1960s had broken the surface calm of national self-approbation, the Vietnam War was the catalytic event that led to the wide diffusion of a sense of alienation and protest and to pressures for women's, minority, and homosexual rights, environmental renewal, restraints on nuclear power, educational reform, and a host of other goals. The breadth of these concerns attested to what some observers saw as a real crisis of authority in our society.

A genuine crisis of authority is characterized by a breakdown in the mechanisms of social control, by widespread protest against diverse forms of authority, and by a deepening of radical sentiment. In a letter to John Adams, his wife Abigail pointed out in strong terms that the challenge to authority during the American Revolution was stimulating feminist protest. "If particular care

1

and attention are not paid to the ladies," she threatened, "we are determined to foment a rebellion, and will not hold ourselves bound by any laws in which we have no voice or representation." John Adams vividly described the extensiveness of such a crisis in his reply, which was couched in terms that recall the Shakespearian concern with "the great chain of being" and the anarchy that is let loose when authority is in dispute:

> We have been told that our struggle has loosened the bonds of government everywhere, that children and apprentices were disobedient; that schools and colleges were grown turbulent; that Indians slighted their guardians, and negroes grew insolent to their masters. . . . [Now we have the] intimation that another tribe [women], more numerous and powerful than all the rest, were grown discontent.[1]

That first general crisis of authority in American history wound down at the end of the Revolution without much changing the status of the various socially disadvantaged groups. The active phase of the most recent crisis, which occurred in the 1960s and early 1970s, appeared to decline as the Vietnam War ended. Protesters in the United States, and then in other developed countries, gradually returned to the normal routines of their usual occupations. The host of organizations and publications that promoted the amorphous "movement" slowly dissolved and disappeared. The crisis of authority seemed to end, leaving in its wake major changes in social values bearing on personal behavior, sexual practices, and minority rights. A generation of the college-educated and of young professionals—relatively conservative strata in the past—had been liberalized or even radicalized. Many continued to believe in and put into practice the new values they had assimilated during the protest era. Citizen action organizations emerged for the purpose of furthering social reform through—for the most part—conventional political methods of supporting candidates, lobbying, writing, and petitioning.

Universities, the centers of militant activism, remained in the 1970s much more liberal institutions than they had been in the 1950s. Students, largely the scions of middle- to upper-class families, still held predominantly liberal views, though somewhat less

---

[1] Charles Francis Adams, ed., *Letters of John Adams Addressed to His Wife*, Vol. 1 (Boston: Charles C. L. Little and James Brown, 1841), pp. 96–97.

fervently than those of the classes of the late 1960s and early 1970s. But for the most part, a "great calm" descended on the campus. Undergraduates studied hard, prepared for careers, took part once again in the myriad of social and athletic events that had been typical of their pre-movement predecessors. The casual observer of the American scene could be forgiven for concluding that the protest era had passed without leaving much of a residue.

Even if there is little behavioral evidence of continuing discontent, opinion polls taken regularly by commercial and academic organizations report that the era of alienation did not end with the close of the Vietnam War. Survey after survey reveals that the sharp increase in negative feelings about the performance of the major institutions of American society, which first became evident during the late 1960s, did not reverse during the 1970s and early 1980s. When queried by pollsters, Americans today voice sentiments more like those expressed ten years ago than twenty years ago. Social scientists analyzing these surveys continue to perceive in them alienation, distrust, lack of confidence, and the attribution of low levels of legitimacy to social and political institutions.

The loss of public faith in America's leaders has had a noticeable impact on their concerns. Two presidents and a host of politicians have expressed anxiety about the decline of confidence among their fellow citizens. Outside of government, leaders of business, labor, education, science, and various professions have also been seriously disturbed by their loss of popular support. Many groups have commissioned opinion surveys designed to uncover the sources of the criticism, while developing elaborate public relations campaigns to improve their image. However, the *generality* of the confidence trends calls into question the assumption behind these efforts, namely, that confidence in a particular institution and its leaders can be increased by such narrow and contrived campaigns. As the evidence in this book will show, the public did not lose confidence in different institutions at different times. Rather, the data reveal a widespread loss of faith in the leadership of business, government, labor, and other private and public institutions at more or less the same time. The question that should be addressed, therefore, is not "What's wrong with business?" or "What's wrong with Congress?" but "What's wrong with the functioning of the entire institutional order?"—at least as the public perceives that order.

Given the general nature of the decline of confidence, one may ask whether the United States is suffering from a crisis of legitimacy, a loss of faith in "the capacity of the system to engender and maintain the belief that the existing political institutions are the most appropriate ones for the society."[2] Are Americans beginning to question the soundness of the country's institutional arrangements—the Constitution, the structure of authority, political parties, and elections—in short, the formal and informal arrangements that underlie the give-and-take of democratic struggle?

The subject of "legitimacy" is not an academic one, although much of the discussion of it is by scholars. How a nation reacts to a crisis of political effectiveness—a period in which powerholders are not able to provide what people want—depends, in large part, on the degree of legitimacy that its political institutions sustain. Perhaps the most telling example of such a crisis of effectiveness is the Great Depression of the 1930s. That crisis resulted in dramatically different political outcomes that varied according to the level of legitimacy of each country's institutional order. Although the German and Austrian republics were not accepted as legitimate by large and powerful segments of their populations in the 1920s, their apparent effectiveness provided them with a fair degree of political stability. But the effectiveness of those governments broke down during the economic crisis of the 1930s. In nations such as Germany and Austria (and Spain, which became a republic in 1930), discontent with economic policy was transformed into opposition to the regime itself.

Those democratic societies that were high on the scale of legitimacy maintained stable polities. The United States, which entered the Great Depression with highly legitimate political institutions, suffered no less from the economic crisis than Germany and Austria and, in fact, more than most industrialized nations. Yet this country emerged from the Depression without having to endure a major challenge to its basic institutions. In spite of high rates of unemployment that continued for the entire decade, our two-party political system and capitalist economic system came through the 1930s largely intact. This past success, however, does not imply that our system will be able to withstand such pressures again. If

[2] Seymour Martin Lipset, *Political Man: The Social Bases of Politics*, expanded ed. (Baltimore: The Johns Hopkins University Press, 1981), p. 64.

the prolonged loss of confidence in American institutions since 1965 has in fact produced a significant loss of legitimacy, the chances that the country can withstand a future crisis of effectiveness may be much reduced.

To address these issues, we will examine in some detail the findings of the many public opinion polls that have dealt with the way Americans view their major institutions, particularly business, government, and labor. Survey organizations have repeatedly asked cross sections of the population to express their confidence in these and other institutions. Pollsters have often inquired about Americans' view of the functioning of our democracy and the capability of the nation's leaders. Polls have also examined what Americans think of our society's two most powerful nongovernmental institutions, business corporations and labor unions, and how they contribute to solving or exacerbating our society's problems. More fundamentally, pollsters have queried the public about its basic valuation of our democratic political order and our free enterprise economic system—and its preference for possible alternatives.

In using polls, we acknowledge the "soft," volatile, and highly subjective nature of such data. We assume that no poll or question can grasp the essence of these issues. What sets this study apart from most public opinion research is that it is not based on the results of a single poll or a series of polls conducted by one research organization. Rather, we compare results from many polls and survey agencies and identify trends as reported by the whole range of available sources.

As the body of this book will make clear, the great majority of Americans still adhere to views that can be traced back to the Founding Fathers and to events surrounding the creation of the Republic. The public remains antagonistic to concentrations of power, whether it is in the hands of public or private institutions. People are suspicious of the motives of those in positions of authority. They assume that everyone is basically self-interested and that power-holders will seek to use their authority to maximize their private ends at the expense of the public welfare. We discover, therefore, a fundamental paradox of the American belief system: Americans hold their political and economic institutions in high esteem and realize that it is the exercise of competitive self-interest that makes those institutions work. But at the same time, they do not admire self-interested behavior and look with suspicion on anyone who has succeeded in acquiring political or economic power.

The result is that Americans tend to separate the basic legitimacy of the institutional order from the question of confidence in particular leaders. The public is predisposed to turn against their leaders when things go wrong and to assume that more honest or competent power-holders could make a fundamentally sound institutional structure work. Those who voice the severest attacks on government, business, and labor usually do so in terms of abuses of power and betrayals of the public trust. But even they, like most Americans, are well aware of the positive and indispensable contributions these institutions make to the society as a whole and to their own lives. In other words, criticisms are usually leveled at the behavior of power-holders and not at the underlying structure and functions of the institutions themselves.

Americans reconcile their fears and concerns about concentrations of power through a continuing faith in a system of checks and balances, that is, in the principle of countervailing power. They approve of conflict within and among their major institutions. They want to see power divided among antagonistic units and organized in as small segments as feasible. Thus, they prefer that political authority be divided between different parties and that large firms be broken up into smaller competitive units. While the public increasingly regards government as inefficient and costly, they still want it to keep a watchful regulatory eye on business and labor. They also regard the institutionalized tension between business and labor as beneficial to the larger society.

This leads to another paradox. People value the functions of institutionalized conflict, but they do not like the kind of behavior associated with it. Americans prefer cooperation to polarization and antagonism. They abhor the spirit of partisanship and want business and labor, and business and government, to "get along together." If conflict must take place, then it should be contained within clearly defined boundaries of consensus; business, labor, and government should not "go too far" in pursuing their self-interest. The evidence we shall examine suggests that this is exactly what the public perceived as having happened in the late 1960s and early 1970s: conflict and polarization went "too far." The result was that the public became cynical and mistrustful of the willingness of their leaders to recognize the boundaries of hitherto consensual norms. This widespread perception is what underlay the general collapse of confidence, and nothing that happened during the latter part of the 1970s served to restore a prevailing sense of public trust.

Some general questions this study seeks to answer are these:

1. How real is the decline in confidence or the growth of "malaise" in the United States? What is its source? How pervasive is it? To what developments in American society, our political system, our economy, and the behavior of the media can changing levels of confidence be related?

2. Does the decline of confidence in most American institutions, which the opinion polls have reported since the late 1960s, portend any general breakdown in the perceived legitimacy of the country's economic and political systems?

3. Why do Americans express generally positive evaluations of their social and political system and of their own personal experiences with major institutions while, at the same time, expressing generally negative opinions about the institutions themselves and the people who run them?

4. What explains the relative esteem of different institutions? Why have labor, government, and business in recent years always been ranked lowest in public trust, while medicine, education, science, the military, and religion have usually ended up at the top of confidence orderings?

5. What are the practical consequences of declining confidence? Is the public merely expressing a ritualistic dissatisfaction with power-holders, or are developments such as declining participation in elections, the tax revolt, continued support for regulation of business, and the fall-off in trade union membership expressions of this general public mood of dissatisfaction?

This book consists of three parts. Part I, "Confidence in Institutions: General Patterns," which includes Chapters 1 to 5, reports detailed evidence of the decline of public confidence in institutions to a level that raises questions about the legitimacy of our major social and political order. This development remains with us in the early 1980s. In 1981, as in most years in which a President has taken office, Americans initially believed that the new occupant of the White House would turn the situation around by providing the leadership necessary to solve the basic problems of the society, but many had lost this faith by the end of the year. This first section also seeks to identify the economic and social correlates of changing levels of confidence and to specify the reasons for varying degrees of trust in different institutions and their leaders. It includes an analysis of confidence trends as well as an investigation of the rank-ordering of specific institutions. We discover that confidence *trends* tend to be parallel for different institutions and appear to have the same general causes, while *patterns* of trust in different institutions tend to be highly specific and to have disparate causes.

In order to explain confidence trends, we look at the impact of objective economic conditions—inflation and unemployment—as well as purely subjective psychological factors (personal trust, optimism, happiness). The data show that people make a sharp demarcation between the functioning of the society at large and the way things are going in their own personal lives. A striking characteristic of the decline of confidence is that it is almost entirely related to events beyond people's own personal experience: conflicts, scandals, protests, and failures that affect their own lives indirectly, if at all. Thus, Americans repeatedly express optimism and confidence about their own lives and their personal futures, even while decrying the terrible mess the country is in.

The book then turns to a detailed examination in Part II, "Business, Labor, and Government" (Chapters 6 to 10), of specific attitudes toward business, labor, and government, their leaders, and the perceived relationship between the private and public sectors. Both opponents and supporters of the American system see the conduct and role of business at the heart of it. Hence we have given considerable attention to identifying and interpreting public attitudes concerning business-related issues. These include the following:

1. What are the social and ideological roots of sentiment toward business? How do they compare with the sources of feelings about labor and government?

2. What are the public's expectations concerning the ethical behavior and social responsibility of business?

3. What is the public's view of the magnitude and role of profits? Does an exaggerated perception of profits produce anti-business sentiment—or is it the reverse?

4. What accounts for the relative ranking in public esteem of different industries and firms? Why do banks, for instance, almost always rank at the top in confidence polls, and oil companies at the bottom? How consistent are these rankings over time?

5. How far does the public go in accepting government regula-

tion of business? What support is there for more radical measures such as divestiture and nationalization?

In Chapters 6 and 7, we explore why business and labor, institutions that are felt to be essential for a free and productive country, are nevertheless held in disdain by many Americans. The opinion data suggest that the public feels the need to place limits on the activities of both. The nature of these limits is discussed in Chapters 8 and 9, which focus on sentiments toward government involvement in the economy. In Chapter 10, we return to a broader examination of the social and political factors that determine attitudes toward business, labor, and government.

Part III, "Causes and Consequences" (Chapters 11 and 12), discusses the general causes of the confidence gap in terms of people's perceptions of the way the institutional order is functioning—and in terms of the media that shape those perceptions. The final chapter seeks to assess the question of legitimacy and to evaluate whether the changes in public sentiment documented in this book are likely to affect the performance of our major institutions. We address the question recently raised by no less than a President of the United States, Jimmy Carter—whether the public's profound "malaise" is a cause or a consequence of ineffective leadership.

Finally, we do not assume that an analysis of public opinion will in and of itself give substantive answers to the problems of our society, but it should yield greater understanding of how the American people view themselves, their basic institutions, and their society at the beginning of the 1980s. The substantive answers must come from public policy research and political ingenuity, not from polls. But the first step in solving any problem is to find out what the problem is—or, in the case of social and political problems, what people *believe* the problem is. Why is there a confidence gap in the public mind, and what kinds of experiences will it take to close that gap? What exactly do people expect of their institutions? Can government, business, and labor take positive steps toward restoring public trust, or is "malaise" an inherent condition of modern American life unlikely to be affected by policy decisions and pronouncements? By presenting a detailed analysis of how the public feels and why it feels that way, we hope to clarify the issues and define both the possibilities and the limits of creative leadership.

Part I

Confidence in Institutions: General Patterns

1

Confidence in Institutions

On July 15, 1979, President Carter delivered a dramatic television address to the American people on the subject of the energy crisis. Shortly into his remarks he broadened his topic and drew attention to "a subject even more serious than energy or inflation . . . a fundamental threat to American democracy." That threat, he said, was a "crisis of confidence . . . that strikes at the very heart and soul and spirit of our national will." He pointed to "a growing disrespect for government and for churches and for schools, the news media and other institutions . . ." and emphasized that "the gap between our citizens and our government has never been so wide. . . ."

Jimmy Carter thus became one—albeit the most prominent—of many commentators who have noted and expressed concern over the declining confidence shown by the American public in their political, social, and economic institutions and leaders. The evidence of this decline appears in many public opinion polls; they indicate that a sharp downturn in public confidence in a wide variety of institutions began in the mid-1960s and continues to the present. Political scientist Jack Citrin of the University of California, writing in 1974, foreshadowed a point to be reiterated five years later by Jimmy Carter, then still unknown: "The current

13

decline in trust in government and the public's seeming loss of confidence in a wide range of social institutions are expressions of a pervasive sense of malaise."[1]>

What, then, is the evidence for this decline, and what are its characteristics? To answer this, we will first document the extent to which confidence in government and in business has been lost; feelings about labor unions will also be noted and discussed more fully in Chapter 7. How much have anti-business and anti-government sentiment grown? Does the timing of these two trends suggest a common underlying cause? Data will be examined on issues related to business and government generally and to specific branches and segments of each in order to assess how *pervasive* the decline of confidence has been. The analysis will then be extended to a number of additional institutions in order to establish how *general* the trends have been. Finally, data on the economy will be brought in to determine whether there is a link between confidence in institutions and prevailing economic conditions.

The Rise and Fall of Confidence

In 1965 and 1966, Robert Lane, a political scientist at Yale University, published two articles in which he discussed public attitudes toward American social and political institutions from the late 1930s—when scientific polling began—down through the early 1960s. He found that, on a number of different indicators, Americans had become more positive about the operation of their society in general and of their political system in particular. From a relatively low point during the 1930s in the midst of the Great Depression, Americans became increasingly affirmative about their society, until by 1965 the great majority of those interviewed by various pollsters were giving consistently positive evaluations. Lane interpreted the growth of favorable replies as a function of increasing affluence and higher levels of education. As he noted, with the end of the Depression and continuing prosperity on the one hand, and with an increase in the proportion of the population that had completed high school or had gone on to college on the other, more

[1] Jack Citrin, "Comment: The Political Relevance of Trust in Government," *American Political Science Review* 68 (September 1974), p. 987.

and more Americans said they liked their society and believed its political system was honest, effective, and responsive.[2]

As it happened, the early 1960s turned out to be a high-water mark in the history of the American public's attitudes toward their key social, political, and economic structures. The explosion of protest against U.S. participation in the Vietnam War, as well as other conflicts stemming from the rise of militant social movements concerned with the status of women and various minority groups—blacks, Hispanics, and American Indians—apparently changed the prevailing perception that Americans had of their country. One public opinion survey after another registered a steady decline in the public's confidence in the country's institutions and in the people running them. As one major pollster, Daniel Yankelovich, noted in 1977:

> We have seen a steady rise of mistrust in our national institutions. . . . Trust in government declined dramatically from almost 80% in the late 1950s to about 33% in 1976. Confidence in business fell from approximately a 70% level in the late 60s to about 15% today. Confidence in other institutions—the press, the military, the professions—doctors and lawyers—sharply declined from the mid-60s to the mid-70s. More than 61% of the electorate believe that there is something morally wrong in the country. More than 80% of voters say they do not trust those in positions of leadership as much as they used to. In the mid-60s a one-third minority reported feeling isolated and distant from the political process; by the mid-70s a two-thirds majority felt that what they think "really doesn't count." Approximately three out of five people feel the government suffers from a concentration of too much power in too few hands, and fewer than one out of five feel that congressional leaders can be believed. One could go on and on. The change is simply massive. Within a ten- to fifteen-year period, trust in institutions has plunged down and down, from an almost consensual majority, two thirds or more, to minority segments of the American public.[3]

Confidence in Government: Trends

It is not difficult to find examples of Yankelovich's generalization from a variety of poll sources. One of the most widely reported

[2] Robert E. Lane, "The Politics of Consensus in the Age of Affluence," *American Political Science Review* 59 (December 1965), pp. 874–75; and "The Decline of Politics and Ideology in a Knowledgeable Society," *American Sociological Review* 31 (October 1966), pp. 649–62.

[3] Daniel Yankelovich, "Emerging Ethical Norms in Public and Private Life" (Unpublished ms., University Seminar, Columbia University, April 20, 1977), pp. 2–3.

shifts has been the level of political trust expressed by the American public. The Survey Research Center (SRC)—since 1970, the Center for Political Studies (CPS)—of the University of Michigan has been asking a series of "trust in government" questions in its biennial national election surveys since 1958. The trend lines for four of these questions are shown in Figure 1-1. (In each case, the figures show the percentage giving the "distrusting" response.)

Political Trust

Trust in government changed little between 1958 and 1964. Over that six-year period, the average increase in "mistrust," as measured by the four questions in Figure 1-1, was 5 percent. During the subsequent six years, from 1964 to 1970, there was a virtual explosion of anti-government feeling. Mistrust on the four items increased by an average of 17 percent during this period, up 8 percent between 1964 and 1968 and another 9 percent from 1968 to 1970.

Those years were, of course, a period of intense political controversy and polarization in the United States. The 1964 presidential election was an unusually sharp ideological confrontation, with charges of extremism raised against the Republican candidate. The era of student protest began with the Free Speech Movement at the University of California at Berkeley in September 1964, followed in short order by President Johnson's decisive escalation of the Vietnam War in February 1965, the first racial disorder in Watts, California, in July 1965, and the Gulf of Tonkin crisis in August 1965. From 1964 to 1970, the percentage of Americans saying that "people in the government waste a lot of money we pay in taxes" rose from 47 to 59; those replying that "the government is pretty much run by a few big interests looking out for themselves" rather than "for the benefit of all the people" increased from 29 to 50 percent; and the proportion who felt that "you can trust the government in Washington to do what is right only some of the time" or "none of the time," rather than "just about always" or "most of the time," went up from 22 to 44 percent.

However, political cynicism did not increase very much during this period on the fourth SRC political trust question. The proportion who believed that "quite a few of the people running the government are a little crooked" (rather than "not very many" or "hardly any") changed only slightly, from 29 percent in 1964 to 32

16

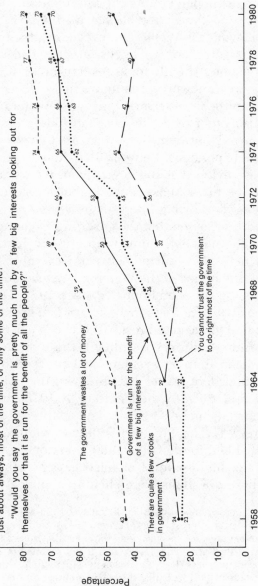

FIGURE 1-1
Confidence in Government, 1958–80

Questions asked in survey:

"Do you think that people in the government waste a lot of money we pay in taxes, waste some of it, or don't waste very much of it?"

"Do you think that quite a few of the people running the government are a little crooked, not very many are, or do you think hardly any of them are crooked at all?"

"How much of the time do you think you can trust government in Washington to do what is right—just about always, most of the time, or only some of the time?"

"Would you say the government is pretty much run by a few big interests looking out for themselves or that it is run for the benefit of all the people?"

The government wastes a lot of money

Government is run for the benefit of a few big interests

There are quite a few crooks in government

You cannot trust the government to do right most of the time

Source: Warren E. Miller, Arthur H. Miller, and Edward J. Schneider, *American Election Studies Data Sourcebook, 1952–78* (Cambridge, Mass.: Harvard University Press, 1980), pp. 257–59. 1980 figures are from Center for Political Studies, University of Michigan, 1980 American National Election Study (Wave C-3), distributed by Inter-University Consortium for Political and Social Research, Ann Arbor, Michigan.

17

percent in 1970, an increase hardly comparable to the enormous increase in cynicism measured by the other items. By 1972, the attitude that most government officials are crooked had increased a bit more, to 36 percent. As one might guess, the Watergate affair soon corrected the noticeable lag in this political trust item. By 1974, following the Watergate revelations, the proportion who felt that most government officials are crooked had risen to 45 percent. It then declined slightly to 42 percent in 1976 and 40 percent in 1978. By 1980, however, the figure had reached 47 percent, even higher than the level recorded just after Watergate.[4]

As for the other three "distrust" attitudes, the marked increases that occurred between 1964 and 1970 were sustained by the Watergate experience. Between 1970 and 1974, the percentage of the public saying that the government wastes a lot of tax money rose from 69 to 74; those replying that the government is run for the benefit of a few big interests grew from 50 to 66 percent; and the proportion saying that the government cannot be trusted to do what is right most of the time went up from 44 to 62 percent. Most of these increases occurred between November 1972 and November 1974, the period of the Watergate revelations.

Nor has the situation improved since 1974. The level of distrust remained about the same in 1976 as it had been in 1974. Between 1976 and 1978, despite President Carter's election pledge that he would restore faith in government, the indicators of mistrust increased again from an average of 61 percent to an average of 63 percent. President Carter's alarm about the public's loss of confidence was justified by the fact that, by 1978, the level of mistrust had reached its highest point to date on three of the four indicators in Figure 1-1. The President's dire warnings, however, had no apparent effect: in the fall of 1980, every one of the four indicators showed the highest level of mistrust since the series began in 1958. These questions were eliciting a cynical response from an

[4] There is one additional question included by the Michigan Center for Political Studies in its "political trust" series: "Do you feel that almost all of the people running the government are smart people, or do you think that quite a few of them don't seem to know what they are doing?" This item is not reported in Figure 1-1 because its evaluative content is less clear than that of the other four questions. Some respondents have offered the cynical reply that the people running the government "know exactly what they are doing," and it is not clear how these responses were coded in the earlier surveys. This question is the item least strongly intercorrelated with the other four in the series. However, it does show the same general trend as the others, i.e., increasing mistrust after 1964. See Arthur H. Miller, "The Institutional Focus of Political Distrust" (Paper presented at the Annual Meeting of the American Political Science Association, Washington, D.C., August 31–September 3, 1979), Figure 1, p. 6.

average of 67 percent—two out of every three Americans—just before Jimmy Carter was turned out of office.

On the other hand, it must be kept in mind that most of the increase occurred long before Jimmy Carter took office. The Michigan Center for Political Studies computes its own "Trust in Government" index, which includes the four questions from Figure 1-1. According to the Michigan index, trust in government fell from +42 in 1964 (i.e., a net trusting attitude) to +2 in 1970 and 1972. The drop between 1972 and 1974 was again severe, from +2 to −26 (net mistrusting). After 1974, things did not get much worse, but they did not get any better either; the Michigan index was −31 in 1976 and −33 in 1978.[5]

Political Efficacy

The Michigan Survey Research Center (SRC)/Center for Political Studies (CPS) has tracked a number of additional items related to political trust since the inception of its biennial election surveys in 1952. Several of these are described as measures of "political efficacy," or "subjective competence." These indicators relate to respondents' estimation of their own personal capacity to comprehend and influence political events. The factor differentiating these items from the pure "political trust" questions described above is that the efficacy questions focus on the self. The key phrase, "people like me," recurs in the standard "agree/disagree" efficacy tests and draws attention to the strongly subjective content of these measures: "*People like me* don't have any say about what the government does"; "Voting is the only way that *people like me* can have any say about how the government runs things"; "I don't think public officials care much what *people like me* think"; "Sometimes politics and government seem so complicated that *a person like me* can't really understand what's going on." [Emphasis added.]

Political efficacy is strongly correlated with education. This fact was demonstrated cross-nationally in Gabriel Almond and Sidney Verba's "Five Nation Study," and it has been confirmed in the Michigan series.[6] As the level of formal education increases, so

[5] Warren E. Miller, "Crisis of Confidence II—Misreading the Public Pulse," *Public Opinion* 2 (October/November 1979), p. 11.

[6] Gabriel Almond and Sidney Verba, *The Civic Culture* (Princeton: Princeton University Press, 1963) pp. 204–8, and Philip E. Converse, "Change in the American Electorate," in Angus Campbell and Philip E. Converse, eds., *The Human Meaning of Social Change* (New York: Russell Sage Foundation, 1972), pp. 322–37.

does the sense of efficacy or subjective competence. In other words, the better educated the individual, the more likely he or she is to *disagree* with each of the four statements above. Philip Converse, for instance, has shown in an analysis of the 1966 SRC survey that the percentage agreeing with the statement, "I don't think public officials care much what people like me think," declined steadily with education; acceptance ranged from 77 percent among those with no formal education to 68 percent among those with some grade school education, 53 percent among those who had completed grade school, 48 percent among those with some high school education, 32 percent among high school graduates, 16 percent among those with some college education, and 10 percent among college graduates.[7] Apparently education raises a person's "subjective competence" by raising his or her self-esteem.

If a sense of political efficacy is truly imparted by the educational process, then one would expect the efficacy level of the American population to rise as its level of formal education goes up. As the population becomes better educated, more people should feel "efficacious." Alternatively, if perceived efficacy is not developed in the educational process but is a product of the status system, then the overall level of efficacy should remain fairly constant over time, as *relative* positions in the status order and the political influence system do not change. Converse describes these two hypotheses as the "education driven" model and the "pecking order" model of efficacy. Each yields an empirical prediction: the first, that the sense of efficacy will rise with education, and the second, that efficacy will remain constant as education improves.[8]

What actually happened is not predicted by either model. The trends from 1952 to 1980 for the four efficacy items noted above, plus two others, are shown in Figure 1-2. Figure 1-2-A traces agreement with the three "internal efficacy" measures, as they are labeled by CPS. Figure 1-2-B shows agreement with what CPS calls measures of "external efficacy." In all cases, agreement with the statement is assumed to indicate a *low* sense of efficacy.

Between 1952 and 1960, the four original efficacy measures show a slight negative trend, where declining agreement signifies an increasing sense of efficacy. The evidence over this eight-year period is consistent with the "education-driven" model. But three

[7] Philip E. Converse, "Change in the American Electorate," Table 2, p. 326.
[8] Converse, pp. 326–27.

FIGURE 1–2
Internal and External Efficacy, 1952–80

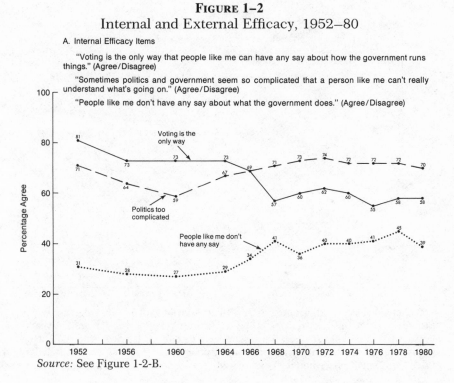

A. Internal Efficacy Items

"Voting is the only way that people like me can have any say about how the government runs things." (Agree/Disagree)

"Sometimes politics and government seem so complicated that a person like me can't really understand what's going on." (Agree/Disagree)

"People like me don't have any say about what the government does." (Agree/Disagree)

Source: See Figure 1-2-B.

of the four measures reverse direction beginning in 1964. Agreement with the statements that "people like me don't have any say about what the government does," that public officials don't "care much what people like me think," and that politics and government are sometimes "so complicated that a person like me can't really understand what's going on" all *increased* beginning in 1964; that is, the sense of political efficacy in the aggregate declined, despite rising levels of education. (The percentage of respondents who had gone to college rose from 15 percent in the 1952 survey to 22 in 1960, 25 in 1970, and 37 in 1980.) The American public's sense of political efficacy fell after 1960 for reasons apparently independent of education.

Those reasons are probably the same ones underlying the declining levels of political trust in Figure 1-1. In that figure, political trust fell by an average of 4 percent from 1958 to 1964 and 17 percent from 1964 to 1970. In Figure 1-2, the average decline in political efficacy was 3.5 percent between 1956 and 1964 and 8

21

FIGURE 1–2

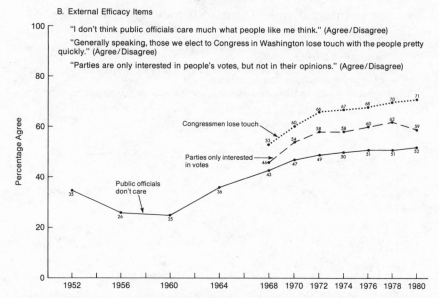

B. External Efficacy Items

"I don't think public officials care much what people like me think." (Agree/Disagree)

"Generally speaking, those we elect to Congress in Washington lose touch with the people pretty quickly." (Agree/Disagree)

"Parties are only interested in people's votes, but not in their opinions." (Agree/Disagree)

Source: Warren E. Miller, Arthur H. Miller, and Edward J. Schneider, *American Election Studies Data Sourcebook, 1952–78* (Cambridge, Mass.: Harvard University Press, 1980), pp. 259–61. 1980 figures are from Center for Political Studies, University of Michigan, 1980 American National Election Study (Wave C-3), distributed by Inter-University Consortium for Political and Social Research, Ann Arbor, Michigan.

percent between 1964 and 1970. The political efficacy items seem to be, in Converse's terms, both "cognitive" and "affective." They involve a perception and an evaluation of both the *self* and the *system.* Thus, when a respondent is offered the statement, "People like me don't have any say about what the government does," his answer reflects the respondent's opinion of (a) people like himself and (b) what the government does. It is the cognitive component that rises with education. The evaluative one is mostly a response to events and conditions. If "what the government does" seems to bear no relation to how people feel, then more and more people will agree that they have no say.

The most explicitly evaluative efficacy measure, "I don't think public officials care much what people like me think," showed the strongest increase from 1964 to 1970: 11 percent, from 36 percent agreement in 1964 to 47 percent in 1970. On the other hand, the most cognitive efficacy indicator, "Sometimes politics and government seem so complicated that a person like me can't really understand what's going on," moved up by only 6 percent.

The fourth efficacy measure, "Voting is the only way that people like me can have any say about how the government runs things," changed in the opposite direction from the other measures. Agreement with this "internal efficacy" indicator actually fell, from 73 percent in 1964 to 60 percent in 1970. Converse argues that this item "has pulled out of line rather markedly in response to phenotypic events" and should not be included with the other items in an efficacy scale.[9] More and more Americans disagreed with the view that "voting is the only way that people like me can have any say," even though their sense of political efficacy was declining according to the other indicators. This viewpoint seems to reflect the growth in more active forms of political participation, particularly protest, during the 1960s. Notably, disagreement with this item—the view that people like me have ways other than voting of influencing what the government does—increased much faster among better educated Americans than among the poorly educated. The "voting" indicator is an efficacy measure that focuses primarily on "inputs" (what citizens do). The other items, which relate more directly to "outputs" (what the government does, whether public officials care), all share a trend of declining trust.

That trend continued into the 1970s. Reactions to the "voting is the only way" and to the "politics is too complicated" statements did not change much between 1970 and 1980. These two measures are, as noted, the most cognitive and the least output-related items. But support for the comment, "People like me don't have any say about what the government does," rose from 36 percent in 1970 to 45 percent in 1978, in tandem with acceptance of the statement that public officials "don't care much what people like me think," which increased from 47 to 51 percent over this same period. In 1980, however, the latter figure remained high at 52 percent, while the view that "people like me don't have any say . . ."

---

[9] Converse, p. 329. However, Warren E. Miller of the Center for Political Studies continues to include the "voting" item in his "internal efficacy" scale. See Miller, "Crisis of Confidence," p. 12. But William M. Mason, James S. House, and Steven S. Martin reach the same conclusion as Converse, "Dimensions of Political Alienation in America: Theoretical and Empirical," (Unpublished paper, University of Michigan, Department of Sociology, February 1981): "The voting item is 'double-barreled' in its manifest content and reflects a mixture of different dimensions of alienation. Thus it is most appropriately dropped from consideration in future work on political alienation in America" (p. 65).

declined a few points, to 39 percent, from the high figure reached in 1978.

The Michigan Center for Political Studies added two new measures of "external efficacy" beginning with their 1968 survey (see Figure 1-2-B). Both are explicitly evaluative and showed steadily increasing levels of agreement from 1968 to 1980: "Generally speaking, those we elect to Congress in Washington lose touch with the people pretty quickly" (53 percent agreed in 1968, 71 percent in 1980), and "Parties are only interested in people's votes, but not in their opinions" (46 percent agreed in 1968, 59 percent in 1980). Thus, Warren E. Miller of the Michigan CPS has argued that "internal efficacy" hardly changed during the 1970s, while "external efficacy" ("how much others—public officials, congressmen, and the political parties—care about what 'people like me think' ") has declined along with trust in government.[10]

Perceived Responsiveness of Government

An additional battery of questions asked by CPS since 1964 also shows declining confidence in government. These, dubbed "perceived responsiveness of government" indicators by CPS, are shown in Figure 1-3-A. They deal with how responsive political institutions are seen to be to "what people think." These measures involve no self-perception and are, therefore, not cognitive in nature: "Over the years, how much attention do you feel the government pays to what the people think when it decides to do something—a good deal, some, or not much?" The proportion saying "a good deal" declined from 32 percent in 1964 to 11 percent in 1974, while those replying "not much," increased from 24 to 28 percent. Similar trends can be observed from 1964 to 1974 in responses to questions dealing with how much "political parties help to make the government pay attention to what the people think," how much "having elections makes the government pay attention to what the people think" and how much attention "most Congressmen pay . . . to the people who elect them when they decide what to do in Congress." In each case, the proportion answering "a good deal" fell (by an average 19 percent over the ten-year period), while the number replying "not much" rose (by an average of 7 percent).

[10] Warren E. Miller, "Crisis of Confidence," pp. 12–13.

FIGURE 1–3

Perceived Responsiveness of Government, 1964–80,
and Citizen's Duty, 1952–80

A. Perceived Responsiveness Items

"Over the years, how much attention do you feel the government pays to what the people think when it decides what to do—a good deal, some, or not much?"

"How much do you feel that political parties help to make the government pay attention to what the people think—a good deal, some, or not much?"

"And how much do you feel that having elections makes the government pay attention to what the people think—a good deal, some, or not much?"

"How much attention do you think most Congressmen pay to the people who elect them when they decide what to do in Congress—a good deal, some, or not much?"

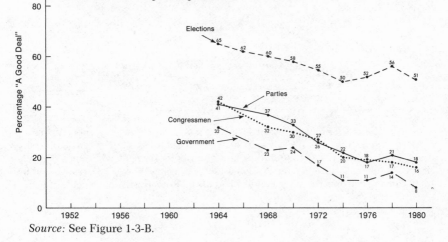

Source: See Figure 1-3-B.

Like the trust measures, these "responsiveness" indicators remained about the same between 1974 and 1976. However, between 1976 and 1978, the data show a slight gain in the "perceived responsiveness of government" for all subjects except Congressmen. This is the best evidence that Jimmy Carter's election accomplished something in the direction of restoring confidence in government. By 1980, however, the effect had worn off and perceived responsiveness reached an all-time low on three out of the four measures in Figure 1-3-A.

Similar findings were reported by Cambridge Reports, Inc., in response to the statement: "Most politicians don't really care about people like me." Sentiment for this view increased from 56 percent in late 1974 to 63 percent in late 1975. The trend then reversed to 59 percent agreeing in 1976 and 55 percent in 1978.

25

FIGURE 1–3

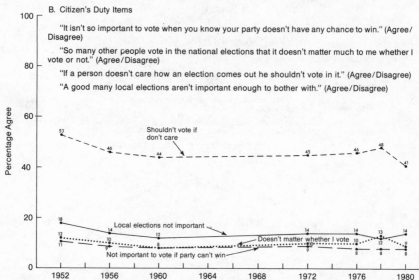

B. Citizen's Duty Items

"It isn't so important to vote when you know your party doesn't have any chance to win." (Agree/Disagree)

"So many other people vote in the national elections that it doesn't matter much to me whether I vote or not." (Agree/Disagree)

"If a person doesn't care how an election comes out he shouldn't vote in it." (Agree/Disagree)

"A good many local elections aren't important enough to bother with." (Agree/Disagree)

Source: Warren E. Miller, Arthur H. Miller, and Edward J. Schneider, *American Election Studies Data Sourcebook, 1952–78* (Cambridge, Mass.: Harvard University Press, 1980), pp. 261–64. 1980 figures are from Center for Political Studies, University of Michigan, 1980 American National Election Study (Wave C-3), distributed by Inter-University Consortium for Political and Social Research, Ann Arbor, Michigan.

Citizen's Duty

Finally, Figure 1-3-B indicates almost no change from 1952 to 1980 in the "citizen's duty" items asked by the Center for Political Studies. The vast majority of respondents in 1980, as in 1952, rejected the views that "it isn't so important to vote when you know your party doesn't have any chance to win" (87 percent disagreed in 1952, 92 percent disagreed in 1980), "so many other people vote in the national elections, it doesn't matter much to me whether I vote or not" (87 percent disagreed in 1952, 91 percent disagreed in 1980), and "a good many local elections aren't important enough to bother with" (81 percent disagreed in 1952, 86 percent disagreed in 1980). The public continued to be divided over the statement, "if a person doesn't care how an election comes out, he shouldn't vote in it" (53 to 45 percent agreement in 1952, 58 to 41 percent *dis*agreement in 1980). Thus, there is no evi-

26

dence of increasing cynicism about democracy or the citizen's role in it.

Confidence in the Political System

Nor does it appear that the public has lost its basic confidence in the American political system. In the 1976 CPS survey, several questions dealt with the basic soundness of our political system, as distinct from attitudes about political leaders and public officials. Where trust in the latter two remained quite low (see Figure 1-1), belief in the soundness of the political system was very high. For instance, respondents were offered a choice between two statements: "I am proud of many things about our form of government," or "I can't find much in our form of government to be proud of." Over three quarters (76 percent) said that they were proud of our form of government, while 19 percent chose the negative response. To be sure, these answers were slightly more negative than they had been in 1972, when CPS asked the question for the first time. In 1972, this question was put to respondents in the pre-election wave of interviewing; the first option (". . . proud of many things . . .") was chosen over the second (". . . can't find much . . . to be proud of") by 82 to 15 percent. The choice was presented to most of the same interviewees again in the post-election wave, and the margin was about the same (83 to 13 percent). Since the 1972–76 period included the Watergate scandals, it is not altogether surprising that the number of Americans who said they could not find much in our form of government to be proud of had grown by a few points. But they were still outnumbered four to one by those who said they were proud of many things about our system.

A question asked by the Roper organization revealed a positive trend in attitudes toward the political system during the 1970s. In June 1974, at the peak of the Watergate controversy, Roper asked respondents to select one of four characterizations of "our political system": "basically sound and essentially good," "basically sound but needs *some* improvement," "not too sound, needs *many* improvements," or "basically *un*sound, needs fundamental overhauling." Fifty percent said that our political system is "basically sound" (8 percent "basically sound and essentially good" and 42 percent "basically sound but needs some improvement"). Roper repeated the question in February 1977. In the latter poll, the proportion saying that our political system is "basically sound" had grown by fully twenty points, to 70 percent (13 percent "basically sound and essentially good," 57 percent "basically sound but needs some improvement"). Those replying that the political system is "not too sound, needs many improvements" fell from 28 to 20 percent between 1974 and 1977, while the proportion choosing the most negative response, "basically unsound, needs fundamental overhauling," declined sharply, from 19 to 7 percent. February 1977 was the first month of Jimmy Carter's Presidency, and the effect of his election appeared to show up in the replies to this question as well as to the other items reported above. The new President alleviated the intensity of Watergate-induced cynicism.

The four years of the Carter Administration and the election of Ronald Reagan had little effect on these attitudes. If anything, positive feelings declined slightly. When Roper presented the same question to a national cross section in February 1981, 67 percent replied "basically good," (14 percent "basically sound and essentially good" and 53 percent "basically sound but needs some improvement"). The percentage who felt that the political system is "not too sound" was 20, of whom 8 percent chose the "basically unsound" response. Seemingly, neither the Carter "malaise" nor the promises associated with a new President affected the public's assessment of the "soundness" of the political system. In any case, that assessment remained relatively high.

The 1976 CPS survey also included the following query: "Some people believe a change in our whole form of government is needed to solve the problems facing our country, while others feel no real change is necessary. Do you think a big change is needed in our form of government, or should it be kept pretty much as it is?" About one quarter of the respondents (24 percent) said that we need a "big change" in our system of government, while an additional quarter (26 percent) replied that we need "*some* change" (the latter response was coded on the original questionnaire forms, presumably as a volunteered answer). Almost half (44 percent) felt that the system should be kept pretty much as it is.

The 50 percent of the sample who said that at least some changes were needed was then asked, "What kinds of changes in our form of government are you thinking of?" The answers most frequently given were criticisms of government waste and inefficiency ("let's streamline the system," "run government like a business," "too much spending," etc., mentioned by 11 percent of those who wanted a change); changes in the types of people involved in politics ("need more blacks in politics," "get different people in," etc., indicated by 4 percent); and criticisms of present-day politicians as untrustworthy and insincere (made by 4 percent). Thus, the reforms in the "system" that critics wanted were mostly changes in leadership and in the way the system is run, not changes in the underlying institutional structure. It appears that the trend of declining trust in góvernment is focused on the performance of government and the behavior of public officials, and not on the system itself or the institutions and norms associated with it.

Confidence in Business: Trends

What was happening to attitudes toward business as trust in government was declining? Were government and business perceived by the public as naturally adversary forces, so that as faith in the one declined, confidence in the other went up? Or did they both share the general trend of declining trust in institutional leadership?

One polling organization, the Opinion Research Corporation (ORC), has been tracing attitudes toward business for about as long as the Michigan CPS has been dealing with trust in government, that is, since the late 1950s. ORC has administered a battery of six questions concerning *large companies* every two years since 1959. No other series of questions about business has been asked so regularly over such a long period of time. Two of the statements in the ORC series are worded favorably to business and four are worded unfavorably. Figure 1-4 shows the trends in the percentages agreeing with each statement.

The trend lines indicate that there was no significant increase in anti-business sentiment in the early 1960s. Indeed, there is evidence of a slightly pro-business trend between 1959 and 1965, as agreement with the two positive statements rose: "Large companies are essential for the nation's growth and expansion" (from 60 percent in 1959 to 67 percent in 1965), and "The profits of large companies help make things better for everyone who buys their products or services" (from 82 percent in 1959 to 88 percent in 1965). The period 1961 to 1965 also witnessed a slight decrease

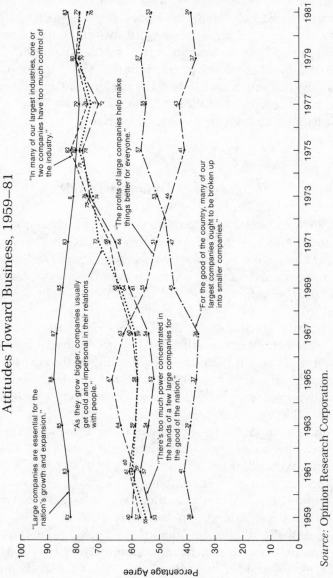

FIGURE 1-4
Attitudes Toward Business, 1959–81

"In many of our largest industries, one or two companies have too much control of the industry."

"Large companies are essential for the nation's growth and expansion."

"As they grow bigger, companies usually get cold and impersonal in their relations with people."

"The profits of large companies help make things better for everyone."

"There's too much power concentrated in the hands of a few large companies for the good of the nation."

"For the good of the country, many of our largest companies ought to be broken up into smaller companies."

Percentage Agree

1959 1961 1963 1965 1967 1969 1971 1973 1975 1977 1979 1981

Source: Opinion Research Corporation.

in the expression of anti-business sentiment on the four negative indicators.

The period from 1965 to 1975, however, was one of enormous growth in anti-business feeling. Every biennial ORC survey during this period saw a significant increase in the percentage of the public agreeing with each of the anti-business statements. By 1973, a majority of the public had come to feel that "for the good of the country, many of our largest companies ought to be broken up into smaller companies." And, in 1975, about 80 percent agreed with statements that "in many of our largest industries, one or two companies have too much control of the industry," "as they grow bigger, companies usually get cold and impersonal in their relations with people," and "there's too much power concentrated in the hands of a few large companies for the good of the nation." In 1965, by contrast, these same statements met with agreement from only 52–58 percent of the public. The two positive statements about business showed a corresponding trend of declining agreement. This was particularly true in the case of the statement that "the profits of large companies help make things better for everyone," where agreement fell from 67 percent in 1965 to 41 percent in 1975.

The year 1977 saw a bit of relief from the post-1965 anti-business trend. For the first time in ten years, i.e., in five sequential polls, the percentages expressing anti-business attitudes declined, albeit only slightly (about 5 percent). Other survey questions about business, for which the trend lines do not go back as far as those in Figure 1-4, also reveal a positive shift around 1977; the evidence on these questions will be considered below. This modest recovery appears to parallel the slight improvement in sentiments about government in 1977, the first year of Jimmy Carter's presidency, as documented above. But as the 1979 ORC data reveal, the recovery did not persist. The slight increases in public support for business between 1975 and 1977 were reversed in 1979, and in most cases attitudes were more negative than they had been in 1975.

Ronald Reagan's first half year in office was associated with a second improvement in attitudes toward business, but the recovery in 1981 was even more modest than in 1977, an average decline in anti-business sentiment of 3 percent. Thus, the view that "the profits of large companies help make things better for everyone" gained 2 percent support between 1975 and 1977, lost 6 percent between 1977 and 1979, and then regained 2 percent in 1981. Backing for the opinion that "there's too much power concentrated in the hands of a few large companies for the good of the nation" went down 6 percent from 1975 to 1977, moved up 8 percent between 1977 and 1979, and subsequently fell off 3 percent in 1981.

Comparison of Anti-Business and Anti-Government Sentiment

With the data that are available, it is possible to compare anti-business and anti-government trends. An index of anti-government sentiment was calculated by taking the average percentage expressing such attitudes on the four SRC/CPS questions shown in Figure 1-1. (These four trust-in-government questions were asked by SRC/CPS in 1958, 1964, 1968, and in every even-numbered—i.e., federal election—year thereafter.) An index of anti-business feeling was developed by taking the average anti-business percentage for the six ORC items in Figure 1-4. For the two items expressing views favorable to business, the percentage disagreeing was used. For the four negative statements, the anti-business response was to agree. (The ORC questions were asked every two years, in odd-numbered years, from 1959 through 1981.) The resulting trends are shown in Figure 1-5.

This figure illustrates how anti-business and anti-government sentiment have been rising together for fifteen years. Massive increases in hostility toward both institutions began to appear in the 1960s. As indicated earlier, anti-government sentiment rose sharply between 1964 and 1970 and then moved up slightly in 1972. The Watergate period witnessed another burst of hostility between 1972 and 1974. The anti-government trend leveled off in 1976, then rose a bit in 1978 and quite a bit more in 1980, to reach an all-time high of 67 percent.

Anti-business sentiment in Figure 1-5 tends to lag just behind anti-government sentiment. Attitudes toward business were, as noted, improving slightly until 1965. They fell a bit in 1967 and then became substantially worse after that. Anti-government feeling reached 62 percent in 1974, the year of Watergate; anti-business feeling peaked a year later, in 1975, during the mid-decade recession. The leveling-off of antipathy to government in 1976 was

FIGURE 1–5

Average Trends in Anti-Business and Anti-Government Sentiment, 1958–81

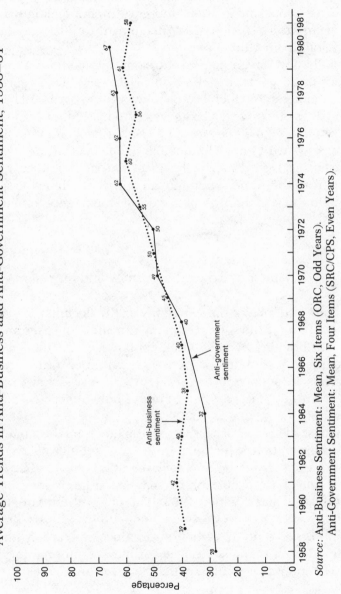

Source: Anti-Business Sentiment: Mean, Six Items (ORC, Odd Years).
Anti-Government Sentiment: Mean, Four Items (SRC/CPS, Even Years).

33

matched by a modest recovery in attitudes toward business in 1977. Both effects quickly wore off in 1979 and 1980, as inflation intensified. In 1979, anti-business sentiment was at its highest level since 1959. And in 1980, anti-government feeling was higher than at any time since 1958. Antagonism to business, however, fell off slightly in 1981.

Overall, anti-government sentiment climbed from an index number of 28 percent in 1958 to 67 in 1980. That represents a 139 percent rate of increase over twenty-two years. The rise in anti-business feeling was less severe, from an index number of 39 percent in 1959 to 58 percent in 1981, a 49 percent rate of growth over twenty-two years. The notable parallelism in the two trends suggests that feelings about business and government may have been part of the same syndrome, an apparently broad loss of confidence in the leadership of our major political and economic institutions.

Attitudes Toward Industries and Firms

Further evidence of the generality of the decline may be found in the shift in attitudes toward many specific industries and major firms. Historically, levels of public confidence have tended to differ considerably from industry to industry and from firm to firm; but the trends in support over the last two decades have moved in tandem with the larger changes in the public mood that we have just examined.

The best evidence of this comes again from the Opinion Research Corporation, which has been doing regular polls on corporate and industry reputations for over twenty years. The biennial ORC studies have been probing company reputations since 1957 and industry images since 1965. The eleventh survey, taken in 1977, included data on thirty-two industries and sixty-nine companies. Respondents were first given a pack of cards with names of industries on them (aerospace, airline, aluminum, automobile, etc.). The interviewers then made the following request:

> You probably know some of these industries better than others. Would you sort them on this card according to how well you feel you know each industry. In making your choice, take into account any of the ways you may have learned or heard about the industry.

The alternatives included "know very well," "know a fair amount," "know just a little," and "know almost nothing." A second request was then made of the respondents:

> Now I'd like to know how favorable or unfavorable your opinions or impressions are of each industry. Would you please sort the cards here according to your overall impression of each industry. Take into account any of the things you think are important. Keep in mind we want your overall opinion.

Responses were coded "very" or "mostly" favorable, "very" or "mostly" unfavorable, "half and half," or "no opinion."

Finally, the same two requests were made about the considerably larger group of companies: how familiar the respondent was with each company, and whether respondents felt favorable or unfavorable, on the whole, toward each one. The only difference between the company and the industry inquiries was that the response, "never heard of the company," was allowed, and those totally unfamiliar with a company were not asked their favorability toward it. The results are shown in Figures 1-6-A, 1-6-B, and 1-6-C.

Eight industries were included in virtually every ORC poll from 1965 to 1977: aluminum, automobile, chemical, electrical equipment and appliances, food and food products, oil and gasoline, steel, and tire and rubber. Similarly, ORC has inquired about twenty-two companies on a regular basis from 1959 to 1977, including the following major national firms: Alcoa, American Telephone and Telegraph, Amoco, Dow Chemical, du Pont, Exxon, Ford, General Motors, IBM, Mobil, Sears, Shell, Texaco, and Union Carbide.

Figure 1-6-A shows the *average* familiarity with and favorability toward these eight industries and twenty-two companies in each survey. The most striking impression from this figure is the sharp decline in popularity of both industries and companies after 1965. Average favorability toward the eight industries fell from 68 percent "very" or "mostly" favorable in 1965, to 62 percent favorable in 1967, 59 percent in 1969, then a steep decline to 46 percent favorable in 1971 and 35.5 percent in 1977. Fully one-third of the public, or half of those favorable to these industries in 1965, had lost confidence by 1977.

Since sentiment toward companies can be traced back further,

Figure 1-6
Industry and Company Familiarity and Favorability Ratings

A. Average Familiarity and Favorability Ratings: 8 Industries and 22 Companies, 1959-77*

Familiarity question:

"You probably know some of these (industries/companies) better than others. Would you sort them on this card according to how well you feel you know each (industry/company). In making your choice, take into account any of the ways you may have learned or heard about the (industry/company)." (Know very well/know a fair amount/know just a little/know almost nothing) Familiar = "Know very well" + "Know fairly well"

Favorability question:

"Now I'd like to know how favorable or unfavorable your opinions or impressions are of each (industry/company). Would you please sort the cards here according to your overall impression of each (industry/company). Take into account any of the things you think are important. Keep in mind we want your overall opinion." (Very favorable/mostly favorable/half and half/ mostly unfavorable/ very unfavorable) Favorable = "Very favorable" + "mostly favorable"

*Industries: Aluminum, Automobile, Chemical, Electrical Equipment and Appliances, Food and Food Products, Oil and Gasoline, Steel, and Tire and Rubber. Companies: Amoco, Dow, du Pont, Eastman Kodak, Exxon, Ford, General Electric, General Motors, Goodyear, Gulf, IBM, Mobil, Monsanto, RCA, Reynolds, Sears, Shell, Texaco, Union Carbide, U.S. Steel, and Westinghouse.

Source: See Figure 1-6-C.

to 1959, the timing of the loss of confidence in them can be more precisely specified. Approval of the twenty-two companies referred to above remained high for the first four biennial surveys: 69 percent "favorable" in 1959, 70 percent in 1961, 70 percent in 1963, and a high of 73.5 percent in 1965. The decline began after 1965: 70.5 percent positively inclined in 1967, 69.5 percent in 1969, 59.5 percent in 1971 (a drop of ten points), 58 percent in 1973, 48 percent in 1975 (another ten-point decline), and then a slight increase to 50 percent favorable in 1977.

Thus, a significant loss of faith in industries and companies took

36

place between 1965 and 1975—precisely the same years when anti-business attitudes, as shown in Figure 1-4, and political distrust, as shown in Figure 1-1, were increasing most rapidly. The collapse of confidence in business appears to have been quite broad; it applied to business in general and to every major part of the business community.

The familiarity trends in Figure 1-6-A show a surprising decline between 1965 and 1971 in the percentages of the public who claimed to know the average industry and company "very well" or "a fair amount." It suggests that familiarity is partly a "confidence" measure. The decreasing sense of acquaintanceship on the part of the public may indicate an increasing sense of *remoteness* from business and industry. Knowing little or nothing about a firm or industry may be a result of increasing disfavor, not a cause of it.

It is no accident that the trend line showing average favorability toward companies in Figure 1-6-A is always higher than the line showing average positive feeling toward industries. The public tends to be more sympathetic toward specific firms than toward industries as a whole, as Figures 1-6-B and 1-6-C show. Thus, in 1977, 25 percent of the public felt positively toward the oil indus-

FIGURE 1–6

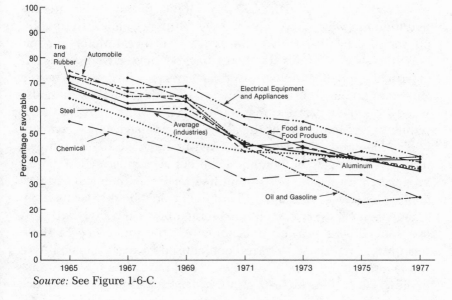

B. Industry Favorability Ratings, 1965-77

Source: See Figure 1-6-C.

37

FIGURE 1-6

C. Company Favorability Ratings, 1959-77

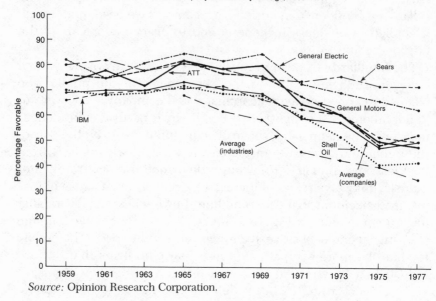

Source: Opinion Research Corporation.

try. But 39 percent expressed positive attitudes toward Amoco, 40 percent toward Texaco, 41 toward Exxon, 42 toward Shell Oil, and 43 toward Mobil and Gulf. The favorability rating of the automobile industry was 37 percent in 1977. But over half of the public, 53 percent, had a positive impression of General Motors and 54 percent felt the same way about the Ford Motor Company. The electrical appliance industry won a 41 percent favorability rating; the comparable figures for General Electric and Westinghouse were 63 and 61 percent, respectively. Thirty-nine percent of the public were positive about the aluminum industry, but 47 percent liked Alcoa and 52 percent approved of Reynolds. The chemical industry was near the bottom of the popularity list in 1977, with 25 percent favorable; but the figures for Dow Chemical (45 percent), Monsanto (49), and du Pont (51) were about twice as high.

Since almost every one of these companies had been heard of by over 90 percent of the public in 1977, the difference in these reactions is not likely to have been caused by the exclusion from the favorability ratings of those who had never heard of the companies. These figures testify to the *generality* of the confidence

38

phenomenon. It does not seem that negative experiences with specific companies have produced bad feelings about entire industries and about business in general. Such a causal ordering would require that favorability be lowest in the case of specific firms; that is clearly not the case. Instead, the more general the category, the lower the level of approval.

Although specific companies tended to be more popular than their respective industries, the fall-off in support over the period studied was still universal. Texaco, Shell, Exxon, Amoco, and Sunoco all went down 20–30 percent in the favorability ratings between 1967 and 1977. General Motors, Ford, and Chrysler lost 15–25 points. General Foods, Quaker Oats, Campbell's Soup, and Kellogg's declined 12–20 percent. Such familiar trade names as IBM, Xerox, Westinghouse, and General Electric fell by 15–22 percent. Such less familiar ones as Allied Chemical, Monsanto, and Union Carbide also lost favor, by 15, 10, and 17 percent, respectively. Even "Ma Bell," AT&T, saw its positive rating drop by 31 points between 1967 and 1977, while its minor competitor, General Telephone, also went down in public esteem by 24 percent. The company that usually was the most highly regarded firm on the list—Sears, Roebuck—fell from 81 percent favorable in 1965 to 72 percent favorable in 1977. *Not a single industry out of twenty-five and not a single firm out of fifty actually improved its public reputation between the late 1960s and the late 1970s.*

Attitudes Toward Labor Unions

There is some evidence to indicate that labor also shared in these trends. Unfortunately, no survey organization has regularly asked a large battery of questions concerning the labor movement comparable to those asked about government and business over the past twenty years. Four polls, those of Gallup, Harris, National Opinion Research Center, and Opinion Research Corporation, have inquired from time to time about approval or disapproval of labor unions and about confidence in labor leaders. These surveys show a by-now familiar drop-off in support after 1965. The Gallup question is: "In general, do you approve or disapprove of labor unions." Approval declined continually from 71 percent in 1965 to 55 percent in 1981, while the proportion disapproving rose from 19 to 35 percent (see Table 7-1). Those expressing "a great deal of confidence" in the leaders of organized labor in twenty-four Harris and NORC surveys taken between 1966 and 1981 fell from 22 percent in 1966 to 12 percent in 1981. On the average, labor leaders ranked lower in the Harris-NORC surveys than leaders of all the other major institutions (see Table 2-1).

Conclusion

The evidence examined so far reveals a sharp decline of public faith in government, business, and labor since the mid-1960s. The marked parallelism of the confidence trends indicates that the loss of faith occurred most rapidly between 1964 and 1975 and that it applied very broadly to all three institutions and their leaders. Nor has the situation improved significantly since 1975. The business recovery and the election of Jimmy Carter in 1976–77 seemed to lift public spirits a bit, but only temporarily. Negative feelings resumed at the end of the decade as hyperinflation set in. By 1981, anti-government, anti-business, and anti-labor sentiment had all reached record high levels.

Public criticism appears to be directed at the performance of these institutions and their leaders: their competence, trustworthiness, and integrity. There is no evidence of any serious downturn in people's evaluation of their own political competence ("internal efficacy") or any loss of faith in the structure and norms of the political system as a whole ("civic duty," confidence in the political system). The business data suggest that people's hostility is directed at the performance of institutions generally (large companies and industries) rather than specific companies and firms. Thus, the decline of confidence appears to be general in nature but not fundamental or systemic: the system is good, but it is not performing well because the people in charge are inept and untrustworthy.

How general has the confidence gap become? The next chapter broadens the investigation to other institutions besides business, government, and labor. Does the trend of growing cynicism apply to all social structures, or has it been limited to these three most powerful and visible institutions?

40

2

The Generality of the Trends

In seeking to evaluate the confidence Americans show in their major institutions, the various survey organizations have dealt with almost all of them. Unfortunately, many of their findings are not useful for comparative or trend analysis, since the institutions inquired about vary from one study to another, as do the instruments used to gauge confidence. Some, for example, ask about confidence in the leaders of institutions, while others assess feelings toward the institutions directly.

Confidence in Institutional Leaders: The Harris and NORC Surveys

The best comparative evidence comes from a sequence of polls administered by Louis Harris and Associates and by the National Opinion Research Center (NORC) at the University of Chicago. In February 1966, the Harris poll for the first time asked a question about confidence in the leaders of different institutional structures: "As far as the people running [various institutions] are concerned, would you say you have a great deal of confidence, only some confidence, or hardly any confidence at all in them?"

The question was asked for seventeen different institutions in 1966. It may be argued that this question is phrased in such a way as to discourage favorable responses, since the only positive answer available is "a great deal." Nevertheless, in 1966, a majority of the public said they had a great deal of confidence in the people running "medicine," "the military," "education," "major companies," and "the U.S. Supreme Court." Over 40 percent reported that they had a great deal of confidence in those in charge of "the Congress," "organized religion," and "the executive branch of the federal government." "The press" and "organized labor" were at the bottom of the list with 19 and 22 percent, respectively, expressing a great deal of confidence in their leadership. For the leaders of the ten institutions just named (most of which were repeated in subsequent polls), the average percentage of the public expressing a great deal of confidence in 1966 was 47.5. Harris asked the question again a year later, in January 1967, to a sample of electoral participators (those who had voted in one of the last four federal elections or were registered to vote). In the 1967 poll, the average level of confidence in the leaders of these same ten institutions was slightly lower: 42 percent.

The Harris poll did not repeat the question for four years. Then, in August 1971, when it was once again asked of a national adult sample, the average percentage expressing a great deal of confidence in people controlling these ten institutions had fallen to 28. Confidence had declined in the leadership of every institution named in the surveys. Thus it appears that the trend identified for business and government in Figure 1-5 was extremely general. In the latter part of the 1960s, as the Vietnam War became a hopeless quagmire and as racial violence and protest movements erupted all over the country, Americans became increasingly mistrustful of the leadership of all the major institutions of their society, including those seemingly remote from social and political turmoil.

The decline in the percentage of the public expressing a great deal of confidence in the leaders of ten institutions averaged 20 points between the 1966 and the 1971 polls (both asked of national adult samples). Political, educational, military, and business leaders experienced the most severe loss over this five-year period. Credence in military leaders—the target of considerable antiwar sentiment—fell the fastest of all, 35 percent, from 62 percent expressing a great deal of confidence in military leaders in 1966 to a mere 27 percent in 1971. Faith in "the Congress" declined from 42 to 19 percent, while "the executive branch" moved down from 41 to 23. Even "the U.S. Supreme Court" suffered a significant loss of prestige, from 50 percent expressing a great deal of confidence in our highest judicial body in 1966 to 23 percent in 1971. Another institution that was the focus of controversy during the late 1960s, "education," lost substantial support for its leaders between 1966 and 1971, going from 61 to 37 percent. The findings in the case of business are consistent with the evidence presented earlier. Confidence in the people running "major companies" (as the item describing business is phrased in this series) fell from 55 percent in 1966 to 27 percent in 1971.

Leaders of two institutions that were highly regarded in 1966 continued to be so, relatively speaking, in 1971. Belief in the leaders of "medicine" remained strong, although it did decline from 72 to 61 percent. The leaders of "science" (included in the 1966 and 1971 polls but not regularly thereafter) fell from 56 to 46 percent. These two groups were at the top of the list in both years. "Medicine" and "science" were remote from the social strife of the late 1960s, and confidence in their leaders showed the smallest loss of public credibility, although neither entirely escaped the prevailing trend. Leaders of "organized religion" had been somewhat less well regarded in 1966 (41 percent expressed a great deal of confidence in this group); their favorability rating went down to 27 percent in 1971.

Finally, confidence in the leaders of two institutions that were not highly regarded to start with, "the press" and "organized labor," declined even further: high confidence in leaders of "the press" fell from 29 to 18 percent and in union leaders from 22 to 14 percent. Both were at the bottom of the list in 1971, as they had been in 1966. In fact, the overall rank-ordering was approximately the same in both years, the major difference being that "the Supreme Court," "the Congress," and "major companies" all fell below "organized religion" in the 1971 poll. Again, the main point is the generality of the trend, the fact that it was not a period of declining confidence in just business, or government, or labor, but a loss of faith in institutional leadership generally: a trend of public alienation, in varying degrees, from the leaders of all major institutions.

Harris was the only pollster who asked about confidence in the leaders of a large number of institutions during the 1960s. The Harris series continued into the 1970s: in 1971, as reported above, and at least once a year since then. The subject was picked up by several other research groups in the 1970s. Beginning in 1973, the Gallup poll inquired about confidence in a varying list of eight to twelve institutions every two years, plus an additional inquiry in 1980, while the Opinion Research Corporation asked about confidence in fifteen institutions in 1975, 1977, 1979, and 1981. The National Opinion Research Center asked the same question as Harris's in its annual General Social Surveys from 1973 through 1978 and again in 1980. Like the Harris question, the NORC question refers to "the *people running* these institutions" (emphasis in questionnaire). The response categories (beginning in 1974, listed on a card handed to respondents) were also the same: "a great deal of confidence," "only some confidence," or "hardly any confidence at all." Only the first of the three responses can be considered positive. In the Harris polls on this subject between 1971 and 1981, the number of institutions inquired about varied between six and thirty-seven; the average was seventeen, the same number asked about in 1966 and 1967. NORC included the same twelve institutions every year, plus "banks and financial institutions" beginning in 1975.[1]

The leadership of ten institutions was asked about in all NORC polls and almost all Harris polls during the 1970s and early 1980s; these were "major companies," "organized religion," "the executive branch of the federal government," "the press," "medicine," "the U.S. Supreme Court," "the Congress" (or, in one poll, "the U.S. House of Representatives"), "the military," "organized labor" (or, in two polls, "labor unions"), and either "education," "higher education," or "higher educational institutions." (The variations in descriptors in the case of "organized labor," "the Congress," and

---

[1] Tom W. Smith has written a comprehensive analysis of the Harris and NORC polls on this subject: "Can We Have Confidence in Confidence? Revisited," in Denis F. Johnston (ed.), *Measurement of Subjective Phenomena* (Washington, D.C.: U.S. Department of Commerce, Bureau of the Census, Special Demographic Analysis, CDS-80-3, issued October 1981), pp. 119–89. Smith's report includes a comparison of Harris and NORC results and trends. He also provides an exhaustive analysis of the effects of question-wording, ordering of institutions, placement in questionnaire, contextual effects, and other methodological problems.

"education" appear to have had a minor impact on the results.[2])
Responses to questions about confidence in the leadership of these
ten institutions can be used to describe *trends* in confidence from
1966 to 1981.

Trends of Confidence in Institutional Leadership

Twenty-four surveys taken between 1966 and 1981—seventeen
by Harris and seven by NORC—were used in this study to trace

[2] Thus, the Spring 1975 NORC poll showed 10 percent of the public expressing a
great deal of confidence in "organized labor." In April 1975, a Harris survey found
13.5 percent voicing a great deal of confidence in "labor unions." Then Harris used
the term "organized labor" in August 1975 and obtained a response of 18 percent
expressing high confidence.

A great deal of confidence in "Congress" was expressed by 23.5 percent in the
Spring 1975 NORC General Social Survey. In September 1973, the comparable figure
for "the U.S. House of Representatives" was 30 percent in a Harris poll. Eight other
institutions that had the same descriptors in both polls showed an average increase of
2 percent in the high confidence figure between the spring and fall. In December
1973, when Harris used the term "Congress," the percentage with a great deal of
confidence dropped to 17. Other items declined an average of 2 percent between
September and December.

The use of varying institutional descriptors of "education" may have had a measurable effect. Until 1973, both Harris and NORC used the term "education." Beginning
in 1973, Harris used either "higher education" or "higher educational institutions,"
while NORC continued to use simply "education." The following table compares the
mean percentage expressing "A great deal of confidence" in either "education" (NORC)
or "higher education" (Harris) during four periods between 1973 and 1980:

Mean Percentage Expressing "A Great Deal of Confidence"

Period	"Education" (NORC)		"Higher education" (Harris)	
Watergate (1973–74)	43	(1 poll)	45	(2 polls)
Recession (1974–76)	34	(2 polls)	38	(6 polls)
Early Carter (1977)	41	(1 poll)	41	(1 poll)
Late Carter (1978–80)	29	(2 polls)	37	(3 polls)

"Higher education" appears to receive a slightly higher rating in the first two periods
and a significantly higher one in 1978–80. Both trends, however, follow the same
pattern—down between the Watergate period and the mid-decade recession, then up
in President Carter's first year in office, then down again more recently.

Because the differences were not great until the last few polls, the trends were
similar, and the NORC surveys with the variant wordings were intermixed throughout
the time series, we retained both sets of items as a single time series in our analysis.
This was *not* done, however, in the case of "television" and "television news." NORC,
which used the term "television," always showed significantly lower confidence ratings than Harris.

trends. Ten polls conducted during this period were not included in the analysis, either because they were missing five or more of the ten institutions listed above or because they were asked of special samples (e.g., employed persons). In addition, a Harris poll dated February 1976 was found in a methodological analysis by Tom W. Smith of NORC to be significantly discrepant from others taken at about the same time. Since other Harris and NORC surveys were available for early 1976, the discrepant Harris poll was not included in our time series.[3]

The last column in Table 2-1 is the average percentage in each survey expressing "a great deal of confidence" in the leaders of all ten institutions. (Estimated values for the missing data are interpolated from the nonmissing data in computing averages.) Figure 2-1 shows the trend in this cross-institutional average derived from the twenty-four surveys. The trend for high confidence in the leaders of major companies is also shown in Figure 2-1.

The most pronounced and consistent shift, as noted above, occurred between the 1966 and the 1971 Harris polls, when the leadership of every one of the ten institutions lost popular support. This downward trend during the late 1960s is consistent with the evidence in Figure 1-5. That figure shows anti-government and anti-business sentiment rising steadily, year by year, from the mid-1960s through the early 1970s. Only one poll in the Harris-NORC series was taken during the five-and-a-half-year interval between February 1966 and August 1971; that was Harris's survey of electoral participators in January 1967. The 1967 poll showed the

---

[3] The discrepant Harris survey is discussed by Tom W. Smith, "Can We Have Confidence in Confidence? Revisited," pp. 156–57 and 166–67. Smith found that this one survey (Harris 2521) accounted for most of the "house differences" between Harris and the NORC: "In sum, there appears to be some tendency for Harris to find less confidence than NORC but with the exception of Harris 2521 this difference is small" (p. 153).

Our time series in Table 2-1 does include two Harris surveys in which the samples were restricted to "electoral participators" (January 1967 and October 1972). In 1967, the sample was defined as those twenty-one and older who were registered to vote *or* who had voted in any one of the last four federal elections. In 1972, the sample included those eighteen and older who were registered to vote, *or* who had voted in 1968 or 1970, *or* who had been too young to vote in previous elections (Smith, p. 120). The population of "electoral participators" is sufficiently broad that the results of these two polls were consistent with the trend shown by the rest of the data (see Figure 2-1). Finding no significant discrepancies, we decided to retain these two surveys in the time series. Two other samples of electoral participators (June and July 1976) were excluded because too few institutions were dealt with in the confidence question.

average confidence level a few percentage points lower than it had been one year earlier. This bit of evidence, too, suggests that the decline during the late 1960s was gradual rather than abrupt.

Compared with the 20-point drop from 1966 to 1971, changes during the 1970s were neither pronounced nor regular. The average confidence level for twenty-one polls taken between 1972 and 1981 was in the relatively narrow range of 23 to 34 percent, never approaching the 40-percent-plus level observed in the mid-1960s. With the exception of the leadership of "organized religion," no institution in Table 2-1 received a rating anytime after 1971 that matched its standing in 1966. For instance, both "the executive branch of the federal government" and "the Congress" secured a high confidence rating of just over 40 percent in 1966. From 1971 on, neither received over 30 percent in any poll. The best evaluated institution in 1966, "medicine," was given a great deal of confidence by 72 percent of the public that year. After 1971, the comparable figure never went above 60 percent. The leaders of "major companies," rated high in confidence by 55 percent in 1966, were never given a rating higher than 31 percent in the 1970s. Thus, it appears that only small-scale changes have occurred since 1971. The occasional increases in confidence have never been sustained for a long enough period of time to suggest that the country has entered the upward phase of a cycle.

The changes that did occur from survey to survey probably reflect a combination of sampling variations and responses to short-term events. These differences were fairly consistent for the leaders of the ten institutions in Table 2-1; that is, trust in all of them tended to rise and fall together. The confidence trend over time for each institution correlated positively with every other institution's trend. Factor analysis reveals that a single factor accounts for 66 percent of the variation in confidence from survey to survey for the leaders of all ten institutions. ("The press" showed the weakest correspondence with other institutions. Faith in the press correlated .43 with the general confidence trend, while the other nine factor loadings ranged between .69 and .93.)[4] It appears justified

---

[4] If one excludes the early (1966 and 1967) surveys, the general confidence trend accounts for 43 percent of the variance in confidence over time for all institutions. Thus, a good part of the consistency across institutions is attributable to their common decline between 1966 and 1971. But there was still a substantial consistency of trends during the 1970s. Factor analysis of the 1971–80 data reveals a general confidence trend, plus a separate factor defined by "the executive branch" (.80) and "the Congress" (.55) versus the press (−.68).

TABLE 2-1

Confidence in Leaders of Ten Institutions, 1966–81

"As far as the *people running* [various institutions] are concerned, would you say you have a great deal of confidence, only some confidence, or hardly any confidence at all in them?" (Emphasis added by NORC.)

Period	Date	Survey Organization	Medicine	Education	Military	Organized Religion	Supreme Court	Major Companies	Press	Executive Branch	Congress	Organized Labor	Average of All
			Percentage with "A Great Deal of Confidence" in Leaders of . . .										
Mid-Sixties	Feb 1966	Harris	72	61	62	41	50	55	29	41	42	22	48
	Jan 1967*	Harris	60	56	56	40	40	47	26	37	41	20	42
	Average		66	59	59	41	45	51	28	39	42	21	45
Early Seventies	Aug 1971	Harris	61	37	27	27	23	27	18	23	19	14	28
	Oct 1972*	Harris	48	33	36	29	28	27	18	27	21	15	28
	Mar 1973	NORC	54	37	32	35	32	29	23	29	24	16	31
	Average		54	36	32	30	28	28	20	26	21	15	29
Watergate	Sep 1973	Harris	58	44	40	36	33	30	30	19	30	20	34
	Dec 1973	Harris	60	46	—	29	—	28	28	13	17	16	31
	Mar 1974	NORC	60	49	40	44	33	31	26	14	17	18	33
	Average		59	46	40	36	33	30	28	15	21	18	33

48

Recession	Aug 1974	Harris	49	39	34	32	40	22	25	28	18	17	30
	Sep 1974	Harris	48	39	31	32	35	16	26	18	16	18	28
	Mar 1975	NORC	50	31	35	24	31	19	24	13	13	10	25
	Apr 1975	Harris	43	36	24	32	29	20	26	13	14	14	25
	Aug 1975	Harris	54	37	30	36	28	20	28	16	12	18	28
	Mar 1976	Harris	—	—	36	—	32	22	21	16	18	—	28
	Mar 1976	NORC	54	38	39	31	35	22	28	14	14	12	29
	Jan 1977	Harris	42	37	28	29	29	20	18	23	16	14	26
	Average		49	37	32	31	32	20	24	18	15	15	27
Early Carter	Mar 1977	NORC	52	41	36	40	36	27	25	28	19	15	32
	Nov 1977	Harris	55	41	31	34	31	23	19	23	15	15	29
	Average		54	41	34	37	34	25	22	26	17	15	30
Carter "Malaise"	Mar 1978	NORC	46	28	30	31	28	22	20	13	13	11	24
	Aug 1978	Harris	42	41	29	34	29	22	23	14	10	15	26
	Feb 1979	Harris	30	33	29	20	28	18	28	17	18	10	23
	Mar 1980	NORC	52	30	28	35	25	27	22	12	9	15	26
	Nov 1980	Harris	34	36	28	22	27	16	19	17	18	14	23
	Average		41	34	29	28	27	21	22	15	14	13	24
Reagan	Sep 1981	Harris	37	34	28	22	29	16	16	24	16	12	23
	Total average		50	39	39	32	32	25	24	21	19	15	29

Source: 24 Harris and NORC surveys.

* Electoral participators only.

— = not asked.

49

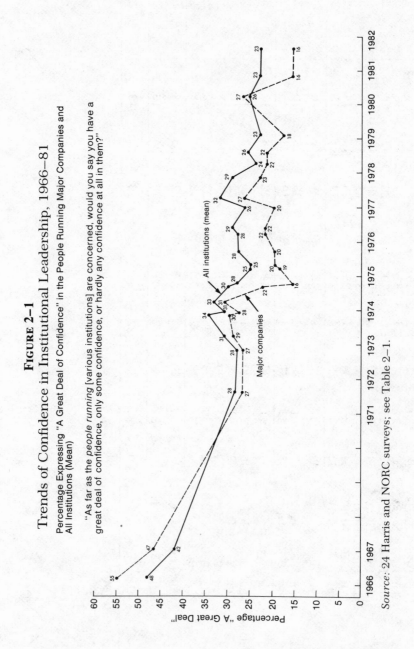

FIGURE 2–1

Trends of Confidence in Institutional Leadership, 1966–81

Percentage Expressing "A Great Deal of Confidence" in the People Running Major Companies and All Institutions (Mean)

"As far as the *people running* [various institutions] are concerned, would you say you have a great deal of confidence, only some confidence, or hardly any confidence at all in them?"

Source: 24 Harris and NORC surveys; see Table 2–1.

50

to speak of a common confidence trend for the leaders of all institutions, such as the average line in Figure 2-1. The correspondence between this overall trend and the trend line for confidence in the leaders of "major companies" in Figure 2-1 is obviously quite strong.

Periods of modestly increasing and declining faith in our institutional leadership between 1971 and 1981 can be observed in Figure 2-1. The early 1970s seem to have been a period of rising trust. The average confidence level for leaders of the ten institutions rose from 28 to 34 percent between August 1971 and September 1973. It remained above 30 percent through the first half of 1974. This increase was apparently associated with the winding down of the Vietnam War and the reelection of President Nixon during a period of relative prosperity.

What is surprising is that this modest increase persisted through the Watergate era. A close inspection of the data shows, however, that the Watergate revelations did affect trust in "people running the executive branch of the federal government." The percentage expressing a great deal of confidence in the executive branch was 27 in October 1972, just before Richard Nixon's landslide reelection, and 29 in the spring of 1973, shortly after Nixon's second inauguration and just when the Watergate revelations were beginning to appear. By September of that year, trust in "the executive branch" had dropped 10 points, to 19 percent. The figure fell further, to 13–14 percent, in the winter of 1973 and the spring of 1974, as the Watergate scandal came to dominate the national news. Finally, in a Harris poll taken in August 1974, just after Nixon's resignation and Ford's accession to the Presidency, confidence in "the executive branch" went back up to 28 percent.

The interesting finding is that support for other institutions was rising in 1973–74 as trust in "the executive branch" and "the Congress" was going down. Faith in nonpolitical institutional leadership rose: 2 percentage points for "major companies," 3 for "the press" and "organized labor," 5 for "medicine," 6 for "organized religion," 8 for "the military," and 10 for "education." Apparently the impact of the Watergate scandals was concentrated on "the executive branch" and other political institutions, but not on leaders outside of government.

A general downturn was delayed until Gerald Ford took office in 1974. Note in Table 2-1 that while confidence in "the executive branch," "the Congress," and "the Supreme Court" all increased in August 1974, just after Nixon's resignation, trust in the leaders of nonpolitical institutions fell. The improvement for political leaders was short-lived, however. In September 1974, after Ford's pardon of his predecessor, faith in "the executive branch" had slipped once again by 10 points, while confidence in "the Congress" and "the Supreme Court" had also begun to decline. The general trust level remained low for the rest of Ford's presidency, a period that included the most severe recession the nation had experienced since the 1930s.

The first poll conducted after Jimmy Carter took office in 1977 (the Spring 1977 NORC General Social Survey) showed an increase in trust compared to a year earlier. As one would expect, the improvement was especially marked in the case of "the executive branch," confidence in which rose from 14 to 28 percent between the Spring 1976 and Spring 1977 General Social Surveys. The overall level of public trust in institutional leaders slipped a bit but continued to be relatively high in a Harris poll taken at the end of 1977. Then, about a year into his administration, the "Carter effect," if that was what was involved, appears to have worn off in tandem with the finding in many polls of a sharp decline in the President's approval rating in 1978 and 1979. In the Spring 1978 NORC General Social Survey, trust in "the executive branch" was as low as it had been in 1974 (Watergate) and 1975–76 (the recession). Confidence in the leaders of every other institution also fell between 1977 and 1978, although none so much as "the executive branch."

This generally low level persisted through the August 1978 and February 1979 Harris polls (there was no 1979 NORC General Social Survey). By February 1979, a few months before the President's "crisis of confidence" speech, the average percentage of the public expressing a great deal of confidence in the leaders of the ten institutions had reached 23, the lowest point recorded in this series. Things looked up only slightly in the Spring 1980 NORC General Social Survey, which showed an average of 26 percent high confidence.

The final confidence survey of the Carter era was taken by Harris in November 1980, just after the presidential election. Overall confidence had fallen once again to a low of 23 percent. Although the ratings of the executive branch and Congress were up a bit from their record lows earlier in the year, the gains made by the military, business, and medicine had all vanished. The entire last three years of the Carter Administration (1978–80) seem to be aptly characterized by the President's own description: a period of national malaise.

Ronald Reagan's succession to the presidency seemingly contributed to greater confidence in the executive branch, which moved up from 17 percent to 24 percent high confidence in the September 1981 poll. But, unlike 1977, the increase did not carry over to other institutions, since the average percentage for all ten institutions remained at 23 percent, identical with the all-time low level of Carter's last year. In spite of Congress' record of cooperation with the new President, the proportion expressing a great deal of confidence in its leadership fell from 18 percent in 1980 to 16 percent in 1981. Major companies remained constant at 16 percent, while organized labor declined two points, down to 12 percent. Thus, Ronald Reagan seemed less able than his predecessor to raise the national morale during his first eight months in office.[5]

Another Perspective on the Trends

To simplify inspection of the data, the 1966–81 Harris and NORC surveys have been grouped into seven periods, as shown in Figure 2-2.

The 1966 and 1967 polls reveal the relatively high level of trust during the mid-1960s (average of 45 percent expressing "a great deal of confidence" in the leaders of the ten institutions). The three polls from the early 1970s (August 1971 through March 1973) show a much lower level, 29 percent. The three surveys taken during the Watergate period (September 1973 through March 1974) indicate, as noted, a higher confidence level for all but political institutions. The next group of eight polls was taken dur-

---

[5] The Spring 1982 NORC General Social Survey revealed a slightly more positive mood, with an average of 26 percent expressing a great deal of confidence in leaders of the ten institutions, up 3 percent from September 1981. This modest improvement seems to have had nothing to do with the President, however, since trust in the executive branch fell five points between Fall 1981 and Spring 1982. By the Fall of 1982, when unemployment reached a 42-year high, confidence in institutions was at an all-time low, averaging just 21 percent in a Harris poll taken in late October and early November. Confidence in eight out of ten institutions had dropped from the levels recorded in Harris's 1981 poll, with the White House experiencing the sharpest decline (eight points). Only the military and major companies showed slight improvements in their ratings, three points and two points, respectively.

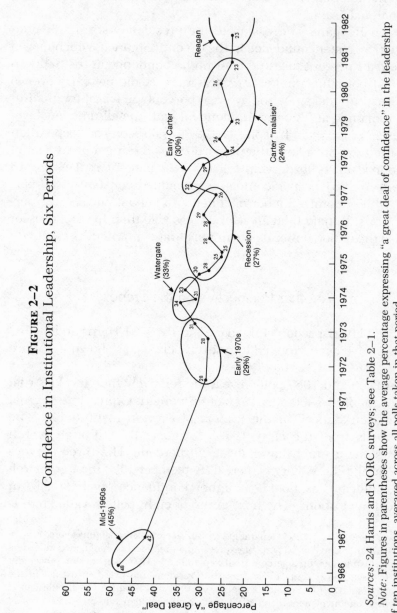

Figure 2-2

Confidence in Institutional Leadership, Six Periods

Sources: 24 Harris and NORC surveys; see Table 2–1.

Note: Figures in parentheses show the average percentage expressing "a great deal of confidence" in the leadership of ten institutions, averaged across all polls taken in that period.

ing the Ford Administration (August 1974 through January 1977) and reflect the lack of faith associated with the mid-decade recession (average of 27 percent expressing high confidence). Trust rose in 1977, the first year of Carter's presidency (average of 30 percent in two polls), and then fell to record low points in 1978, 1979, and 1980, as inflation rose and criticism of the President's leadership became widespread (average of 24 percent expressing high confidence in five surveys).

The negative relationship between feelings about the press and the executive branch deserves special comment. Excluding the two Harris surveys taken during the 1960s, trust in "the press" and "the executive branch" showed a moderately negative correlation during the 1970s ($-.31$). This was especially noticeable during the Watergate period, when confidence in the executive branch dropped from 26 to 15 percent while confidence in the press went up from 20 to 28 percent. When the country regained faith in the executive branch in 1977, trust in the press went down slightly. Carter's subsequent decline in 1978 and 1979 was accompanied by rising trust in the press. Positive views of both fell off, however, in March 1980. But shortly after the Presidential election in November, the executive branch had moved up a bit and the press had moved down. And in September 1981, Harris found that trust in the executive branch increased by 7 points while the press fell off by 3. (See Figure 2-3.)

This modest but noticeable see-saw relationship between "the executive branch" and "the press" suggests that the public has become conscious of a kind of adversary relationship between the two. To a limited extent, it appears that a downturn for the President boosts public faith in the press. In the 1970s, at least, the public tended to reward rather than punish the messenger when it brought bad news.

Confidence in Institutions: The Gallup and ORC Surveys

Faith in institutions was also the subject of inquiries by Gallup and the Opinion Research Corporation during the 1970s although not so frequently as in the case of the Harris and NORC polls. Since the other organizations' questions differed from the one used by Harris and NORC, it is difficult to make precise comparisons;

FIGURE 2-3

Relationship Between Confidence in the Executive Branch and in the Press, 1966–81

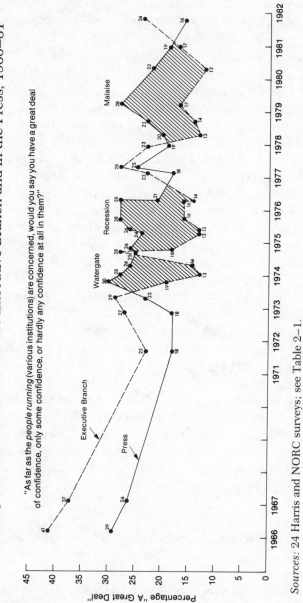

Sources: 24 Harris and NORC surveys; see Table 2–1.

but one may use the different polls to confirm the shifts and patterns during the decade.

The Gallup poll used a different approach from that of Harris and NORC, asking people to report their confidence in the "institutions" themselves, rather than the people running them, and giving respondents four rather than three options to describe their level of trust: "a great deal," "quite a lot," "some," or "very little." By offering respondents two positive choices ("a great deal" and "quite a lot"), as distinct from the one positive choice offered by Harris and NORC ("a great deal"), Gallup has always reported a higher level of confidence than the other two organizations. It asked its question every two years from 1973 through 1981 (and also in October 1980) for a somewhat varying list of institutions.

The Gallup results for those institutions that were regularly included, shown in Table 2-2, combine the two positive responses. These results show very little change from survey to survey. Between 1973 and 1975, when the Harris and NORC polls indicated

TABLE 2–2

Confidence in Institutions, 1973–81

"I am going to read you a list of institutions in American society. Would you tell me how much confidence you, yourself, have in each one—a great deal, quite a lot, some, or very little?"

Institutions	1973	1975	1977	1979	1980	1981
	Percentage Saying "A Great Deal" or "Quite a Lot"					
The church, or organized religion	66	68	64	65	66	57
The public schools	58	56	54	53	51	40
The U.S. Supreme Court	44	49	46	45	47	52
Congress	42	40	40	34	34	35
Organized labor	30	38	39	36	35	28
Big business	26	34	33	32	29	37
Average of the six institutions above	44	47.5	46	44	44	41.5
The military	—	58	57	54	52	53
Medicine	—	80	73	—	—	—
Newspapers	39	—	—	51	42	37
Television	37	—	—	38	33	23
Free enterprise	—	54	51	50	—	—
Banks and banking	—	—	—	60	60	51

Source: Gallup Poll, 1973–81.

trust generally declining, the Gallup results revealed a slight decline in confidence for "Congress" and the "public schools," and an increase for "religion," "the Supreme Court," and "big business." The gain from 26 to 34 percent positive in the case of "big business" is especially surprising, since 1975 was the worst year of the recession. In 1977, when Harris and NORC found a general rise in confidence, the Gallup results showed a very small decline. The Gallup data for 1979 point to another small decrease, a result consistent this time with the Harris and NORC findings. There was no difference between 1979 and late 1980 in the average response in the Gallup data, a finding paralleling that of Harris. (NORC's Spring 1980 General Social Survey did report a small increase in confidence, a result that may have been either a chance variation or a reflection of the resurgence of patriotic feelings in reaction to the hostage crisis.) Since the Gallup survey shifts are quite small over this seven-year period, it would be safer to conclude that these polls basically show little change at all between 1973 and 1980.

The Gallup Poll administered the confidence question again in July 1981 when a mood of optimism associated with Ronald Reagan's first months in office seemed to prevail. In this case too, that buoyancy did not appear to rub off on the public's assessment of the country's major institutions. The Gallup Poll found the lowest level of confidence ever in its confidence surveys, an average positive response of 41.5 percent for the six institutions included on all its surveys, down from 44 percent in 1979 and 1980. Most surprising is the fact that big business moved up from 29 to 37 percent, while organized labor fell from 35 percent to 28. These results may have reflected a growing conservative mood in the first year of the Reagan Administration. But challenging this interpretation is the fact that religion fell from 66 percent positive in 1980 to 57 percent positive in 1981.

Some indication that the fall-off of confidence in the Gallup Poll was not idiosyncratic is contained in the results of two national surveys taken by CBS News and the *New York Times* in June 1981 and by ABC News and the *Washington Post* in September. Both used the Gallup version of the confidence question. The CBS/*New York Times* survey included seven of the institutions listed in Table 2-2, while the ABC News/*Washington Post* poll inquired about the same ten institutions dealt with by Gallup in July. The findings of the three survey organizations were strikingly similar.

The average positive rating in the ABC News/*Washington Post* survey for the six institutions regularly inquired of by Gallup was 41.3 percent, practically identical with Gallup's average of 41.5 percent, which, as noted, was lower than that obtained by it in all earlier confidence ratings. The evidence from these three 1981 studies suggests that the "good feelings" surrounding the President during his honeymoon period did not restore a *general* sense of confidence in other institutions. These conclusions are reinforced by the results of the September 1981 Harris survey discussed earlier.

The Opinion Research Corporation asked a "confidence in institutions" question in 1975, 1977, 1979, and 1981. ORC uses a seven-point scale, from "complete trust and confidence" in the institution (point 7) to "no trust and confidence at all" (point 1). The results for fourteen institutions are shown in Table 2-3, which groups the responses into categories labeled "high" (6 or 7 points), "medium" (3, 4, or 5 points), and "low" (1 or 2 points). The ORC data, like those of Gallup, show a slight decline in the percentage expressing "high" confidence between 1975 and 1977, the period when Harris and NORC polls were showing an increase. According to ORC, trust in thirteen out of the fourteen institutions, including business ("large companies"), went down between 1975 and 1977, despite the recovery from the 1975 recession. The ORC data are consistent with the Harris and NORC results in one respect: faith in "the President" went up sharply, from 30 percent "high" in 1975 to 43 percent "high" in 1977, while the percentage giving "the President" a low rating fell by half between 1975 and 1977.

ORC results, however, are consistent with Harris and NORC in showing a decline from 1977 to 1979. The fall-off was greatest in the case of "the President," who plummeted from 43 percent "high" on the ORC seven-point scale in 1977 to 21 percent "high" in May 1979. "Large companies" remained about the same: 15 percent "high" in 1977, 16 percent "high" in 1979. The "medical profession" was the only institution to increase noticeably between 1977 and 1979, from 42 to 48 percent "high."

The results of ORC's 1981 survey, taken in September, parallel those of Harris and Gallup. Government institutions, particularly the presidency, improved their ratings. The President moved up to 34 percent "high," though still below the 43 percent of Jimmy Carter's first year. Most of the private institutions, however, de-

TABLE 2-3

Confidence in Institutions, 1975–81

"I would like your opinion on how much trust and confidence you have in some institutions." (Interviewer hands respondent an exhibit card with a seven-point scale on it.)

"This card gives you a series of choices ranging from 'I have complete trust and confidence in them' to 'I have no trust and confidence at all in them.'"

"You can position your opinion at any point in that range (1 through 7); just give me the number please."

	High (6–7)				Position on 1–7 Scale — Medium (3–5)				Low (1–2)			
	1975	1977	1979	1981	1975	1977	1979	1981	1975	1977	1979	1981
					Percentage							
Churches	63	61	57	57	27	30	35	37	10	8	8	6
Banks	60	51	48	36	35	43	45	56	5	6	6	8
The Armed Forces	47	44	38	36	43	45	51	53	8	10	10	10
Colleges and universities	46	43	44	38	47	52	47	55	6	5	7	6
The President	30	43	21	34	48	45	50	46	22	11	28	20
Medical profession	55	42	48	41	39	47	44	52	6	11	7	7
Supreme Court	39	33	29	33	44	50	54	56	16	17	16	10
News reporting on radio, TV, and in newspapers	34	31	30	31	50	56	53	58	15	13	16	11
Small companies	33	26	26	31	59	67	64	63	7	7	10	5
Legal profession	26	23	24	23	58	59	59	66	15	18	16	11
Labor unions	22	21	19	19	48	52	47	53	28	26	31	27
Congress	20	16	10	12	60	64	66	73	18	20	23	14
Large companies	18	15	16	13	60	68	56	69	21	17	28	17
Stock market	10	10	10	9	63	66	61	68	24	23	24	19
Average of the fourteen institutions above	36	33	30	29.5	49	52	52	57.5	14	14	16	12

Source: Opinion Research Corporation, 1975–81.

clined. The medical profession, for example, dropped from 48 percent "high" in 1979 to 41 percent in 1981, while banks fell from 48 percent to 36 percent.

Thus, our four-period version of the ORC series suggests a straight decline from 1975 to 1981, with no general revival in the "honeymoon years" 1977 and 1981 beyond those for "the President" himself and other major institutions of government. Nevertheless, the shift over time in the ORC data, as in Gallup's, was small—there was little change in the "low" confidence ratings in Table 2-3.

Most of the variations reported by Harris, NORC, Gallup, and ORC during the 1970s and early 1980s were small enough to have been the product of random factors occurring between one poll and another, and there is no evidence of any dramatic trend during the decade. Overall, what the data suggest is a continuing low level of confidence from the mid-1970s to the early 1980s. The change in the country's political mood associated with the election of Ronald Reagan and a conservative Congress does not seem to have had any effect on the trend, other than a modest surge of confidence in the presidency.

Confidence and the Economy

The state of the economy is one possible explanation for the decline in public confidence from the mid-1960s through the early 1980s. The 1960s, a period of relative prosperity, were succeeded by a decade of rampant inflation as well as the worst recession in forty years. The inflation rate between 1960 and 1964 averaged 1.2 percent per year; between 1965 and 1969, however, it averaged 3.4 percent per annum. From 1970 to 1975, it rose to a mean of 6.6 percent per year, reaching a height of 11 percent in 1974, in the wake of the Arab oil embargo, and then 9.1 percent in 1975. After a temporary decrease in 1976 and 1977 to about 6 percent per year, inflation once again soared; the rate was 8.8 percent in 1978, 13.3 percent in 1979, 12.7 percent in 1980, and 10.4 percent in 1981.

The story is similar in the case of unemployment. The annual unemployment rate averaged 5.7 percent between 1960 and 1965 and 3.8 percent between 1965 and 1969. It increased to 4.9 percent in 1970 and averaged 5.5 percent from 1971 through 1974. Unemployment rose sharply again in 1975, to 8.5 percent. The rate dropped gradually from 1975 to 1979, when it reached 5.8 percent. But the spring of 1980 saw unemployment rise once again to almost 8 percent in May, June, and July—one of the few recessions to be initiated during a Democratic administration. Unemployment moved beyond the 8 percent figure in the fall of 1981, as a recession took hold at the end of Reagan's first year in office.

In order to test the relationship between confidence in the leaders of institutions and the state of the economy, the unemployment and inflation rates were measured for each month in which a Harris or NORC confidence poll was taken between 1966 and 1980. (The "unemployment rate" was defined as the percentage of the civilian labor force unemployed the month of the poll. The inflation rate was defined as the percentage increase in the consumer price index for the quarter preceding the poll as compared with the immediately prior quarter, projected to an annual rate.)

Table 2-4 shows the correlations between confidence in institutional leadership, unemployment, and inflation for 23 surveys in the Harris and NORC series. In addition, the third column in Table 2-4 reports the relationship between confidence levels and Gallup's measure of presidential popularity (the percentage of the public approving the job the President was doing at the time of each survey). Table 2-4 correlates unemployment, inflation, and presidential popularity with separate confidence measures for each of the ten institutions regularly inquired about by Harris and NORC, as well as with the mean confidence level for all institutions.

As might be expected, there is a strong negative correlation between confidence in the leaders of institutions and the unemployment rate ($-.68$ correlation with the mean confidence level for all ten institutions). The correlation with unemployment is significantly negative for nine of the ten institutions—all except the press. The impact of inflation, however, is a good deal weaker. The inflation rate shows a moderately negative ($-.36$) but significant link with the general level of confidence. Inflation seems to be more specific in its impact than unemployment. There are significant negative correlations between the inflation rate and trust in "the executive branch," "Congress," "the military," and "major companies." But all the other correlations with inflation are insignificant.

It is interesting to note that presidential popularity is not related to trust in institutional leadership, either generally or specifically, with the obvious exception of "the executive branch of the federal

TABLE 2–4
Confidence in Leaders of Institutions:
Correlation Coefficients over Time

Correlation with Confidence in People Running:	Unemployment Rate	Inflation Rate	Presidential Popularity
Medicine	−.48	(−.31)	(.15)
Education	−.63	(−.26)	(.00)
Military	−.62	−.41	(.15)
Organized religion	−.39	(−.07)	(.22)
U.S. Supreme Court	−.49	(−.24)	.39
Major companies	−.72	−.38	(.16)
Press	(−.26)	(.18)	(−.22)
Executive branch	−.54	−.51	.64
Congress	−.68	−.47	(.19)
Organized labor	−.60	(.00)	(.10)
All institutions (mean)	−.68	−.36	(.23)

N = 23 Harris and NORC surveys, 1966–80.
Coefficients in parentheses are not significant at p = .05.
Notes:
"Unemployment rate": percentage of the civilian labor force unemployed for the month of the poll.
"Inflation rate": percentage increase in the consumer price index for the quarter preceding the poll as compared with the immediately prior quarter, projected to an annual rate.
"Presidential popularity": percentage approving the job being done by the President at the time of each survey, according to the Gallup Poll.

government" (correlation of .64 with presidential popularity) and the less obvious exception of "the U.S. Supreme Court" (correlation of .39). Presidential popularity does show a slightly negative correlation with confidence in "the press" (−.22), the only institution that correlates negatively with presidential popularity. This provides additional evidence that the press is the chief institutional rival of the presidency; when approval of the President declines, the prestige of the press tends to rise.

Inflation and unemployment show a negligible correlation with each other (.02) over these twenty-three points in time. If one enters both variables into a regression equation, the effect of each can be determined, controlling for the other. These effects are shown in Table 2-5.

Overall, the results indicate that much of the decline in institutional confidence can be attributed to adverse economic conditions. Unemployment alone accounts for 48 percent of the variance;

TABLE 2–5
Effects of Unemployment and Inflation
on Confidence in the Leaders of Institutions

Y Confidence in Leaders of:	Constant	Regression Coefficients:		R^2
		X_1 Unemployment Rate	X_2 Inflation Rate	
Congress	52.9	−4.1	−1.1	69%
Major companies	61.6	−4.5	−1.0	65%
Executive branch	49.4	−3.2	−1.2	60%
Military	66.1	−3.9	−1.0	54%
Education	63.8	−3.3	(−0.5)	43%
Organized labor	23.4	−1.3	(0.1)	37%
Medicine	74.2	−2.8	(−0.8)	29%
U.S. Supreme Court	47.2	−2.0	(−0.4)	29%
Organized religion	44.1	(−1.8)	(−0.0)	19%
Press	26.2	(−0.6)	(0.2)	6%
All institutions (mean)	51.0	−2.8	−0.6	58%

N = 23 Harris and NORC surveys, 1966–80.
Coefficients in parentheses are not significant at p = .05.
Notes: Unemployment and inflation rates are the same as in Table 2-4.

inflation adds an additional 10 percent. Every one percent increase in unemployment, with no change in inflation, tends to lower the general confidence level by 2.8 percent. Every one percent increase in inflation, with no change in unemployment, tends to lower the confidence level by 0.6 percent. Each factor—unemployment and inflation—has an effect independent of the other.

Four major institutions, "the executive branch," "Congress," "major companies," and, curiously, "the military" bear the brunt of public disaffection (as indicated by R^2) when economic trends take a turn for the worse. Confidence in each of these four organizations is affected by both unemployment and inflation. "Education," "organized labor," "medicine," and "the Supreme Court" are hurt by unemployment but not significantly by inflation. (The effect of inflation on confidence in the leadership of "medicine" is not quite significant, but it may become so as medical costs skyrocket. The public, it will be shown later, is aware that medical costs have risen faster than other consumer prices.) One interesting finding is that attitudes toward "organized labor" are only weakly affected by economic conditions, especially when compared with feelings about business and government. The principal reason is that confidence in organized labor has been consistently low and relatively invariant throughout the period covered by these polls. Finally, confidence in the leadership of two institutions, "organized religion" and "the press," is not particularly responsive to economic conditions at all. Both "religion" and "the press" can be interpreted as "guiding" institutions, outside the normal political and economic order, and to some extent "critics" of that order.

These results suggest that a good deal of the decline in confidence can be attributed to adverse economic conditions. The overall level of trust seems to be particularly sensitive to the unemployment rate. Some of the reasons have been pointed out by Douglas Hibbs:

> It is no mystery why people are averse to high and rising unemployment rates—after all, unemployment is a real quantity representing lost real output and underutilized human resources. Remember too that the measured unemployment rate is just that—a *rate*—and a far larger fraction of the labor force experiences bouts of actual unemployment over any given time interval than the average percentage numbers might suggest. In any given 12-month period the fraction is likely to be about three times the average "official" rate. Moreover, in addition to households touched directly by some form of unemployment or underemployment, an even larger number will be aware of unemployment among relatives, friends, neighbors and, of course, workmates.[6]

Americans tend to be especially sensitive to, and fearful of, unemployment, probably as a result of this country's experience during the Great Depression. Inflation, a relatively newer experience, seems to have a weaker and less consistent effect on faith in institutions. This result is compatible with economic analysis to the effect that "the aggregate wage and salary income share is not ended by inflation and that rising prices have no dramatic effects on the size distribution of income."[7] Unemployment, rather than inflation, is the great American trauma.

This conclusion is sustained by the findings of two Cambridge Reports, Inc. (CRI) polls taken during the inflation-ridden fall and winter of 1979. CRI inquired:

> In recent months the government has devoted most of its economic efforts to fighting the problem of inflation. Some of these programs to

[6] Douglas A. Hibbs, Jr., "The Mass Public and Macroeconomic Performance: The Dynamics of Public Opinion Toward Unemployment and Inflation," *American Journal of Political Science* 23 (November 1979), p. 713.

[7] Hibbs, p. 712.

fight higher prices actually made a recession more likely. If we get into a recession, do you think the government should go on fighting inflation, even if the policies make the recession worse, or try to fight recession problems, like unemployment, even if it means less effort against fighting inflation?

In both surveys, pluralities replied that they preferred government policies devoted to fighting unemployment rather than inflation if trade-offs are involved (46–31 percent in the fall of 1979 and 42–33 percent in the winter of 1979). Not surprisingly, higher income people were more inclined to concentrate on fighting inflation (46–42 percent in the winter of 1979 among people earning $35,000 a year or more). Lower-income individuals gave priority to unemployment (42 percent for fighting recession and 24 percent for concentrating on inflation among those earning less than $7,000 a year).

Nevertheless, the results in Table 2-5 confirm the fact that inflation does have an independent impact on confidence. Surging inflation in 1978–79 saw confidence levels erode to an all-time low. With inflation reaching 18 percent in early 1980 and the onset of a recession shortly thereafter, and with interest rates continuing to rise in 1981, it is hardly surprising that this record low in institutional confidence was sustained through the 1980 campaign and continued through the first year of the Reagan Administration.

In summary, the analysis indicates that unemployment and inflation have a clear, negative impact upon people's trust in major institutions. Business and government bear the brunt of public disaffection as economic trends take a turn for the worse. They are the core of "the system" and are held most directly accountable for its malfunctions. Other institutions are more weakly affected by "bad times," and the press in particular seems to be set apart from the others, with a certain degree of counter-institutional influence.

3

How Confidence Ratings
Compare

ALTHOUGH levels of confidence in institutions tend to move up and down in tandem with each other, the long-term rank-ordering of institutions is fairly stable and permits a specification of the activities Americans see as more or less worthy of trust. In this chapter, we first examine the hierarchy of confidence in institutions and then explore the factors associated with varying levels of trust.

The Confidence Rankings of Institutions

Chapters 1 and 2 examined the trends in confidence in institutions from 1966 through 1981. Let us look at the overall ranking of confidence in institutions as reported by the various polling organizations.

The Harris and NORC Polls

Table 3-1 shows the relative rankings of the ten institutions inquired about in the twenty-four Harris and NORC surveys taken during those years. The mean for each institution is the percentage of the public expressing "a great deal of confidence" in its leaders, averaged across all the surveys.

Table 3–1

Average Percentage Expressing "A Great Deal of Confidence"
in the Leaders of Ten Institutions, 1966–81

Ranking	Institution	Mean	Standard Deviation
		Percentage	
1	Medicine	50.5	9.7
2	Higher education	39.3	7.8
3	The military	34.3	9.0
4	Organized religion	32.0	6.3
5	U.S. Supreme Court	31.8	5.8
6	Major companies	25.3	9.2
7	The press	23.6	4.1
8	Executive branch	20.5	7.9
9	Congress	18.8	8.3
10	Organized labor	15.3	3.2
	Average of the ten institutions above	29.1	7.1

Source: Harris and NORC, 24 surveys.

Medicine, higher education, the military, organized religion, and the U.S. Supreme Court, in that order, fell in the upper half of the rank-ordering, while major companies, the press, the executive branch of the federal government, Congress, and organized labor placed towards the bottom all below the mean confidence rating.

Major companies showed the second highest standard deviation of any institution listed in Table 3-1. This means that confidence in the leaders of major companies varied more from survey to survey than did confidence in the leaders of any other institution except medicine. One reason is that trust in business fell more rapidly over these years than the average trust level for all institutions. The ratings for business, which were above the mean in 1966 and 1967, were slightly below average from 1971 to 1974 and then significantly below average once the recession took hold in 1974 (see Figure 2-1). During the Carter "malaise" of 1978–80, the gap between business and other institutions narrowed, but not because business was more positively rated; other institutions simply fell as low as business.

If businesspeople feel aggrieved at the public's declining faith in them, they may find solace in the fact that the consistently least popular institution in the Harris and NORC surveys has been organized labor. Confidence in labor leaders has generally been in the teens, averaging 14 percent below the mean for all institutions.

Labor leaders, it may be noted, suffered a lesser fall-off after 1966 largely because they had started out so low: 22 percent expressed "a great deal of confidence" in them in 1966, a figure that eventually declined to 12 percent in September 1981.

Leaders of government, particularly of Congress and the executive branch of the federal government, have also been less popular than the average, although their scores have tended to fluctuate in response to political events. Their mean scores, 20.5 percent high confidence in the case of the executive branch and 19 percent in the case of Congress, have placed them lower than major companies (25 percent) but above organized labor (15 percent). The executive branch varied from last place during the aftermath of Watergate to sixth place during the first year of the Carter administration. Congress went from sixth in the mid-1960s, to eighth in the early 1970s, to ninth from 1974 on. Whereas in the mid-1960s, Congress was rated twice as high as organized labor (42 percent expressing "a great deal of confidence" in Congress, 21 percent in labor), after 1974 the two were close to each other at the bottom of the list.

Two governmental units, the U.S. Supreme Court and the military, have done relatively well in the polls, possibly because they are perceived as "above politics." The Supreme Court placed close to or just above the mean in the twenty-four surveys, ending up with an average high confidence rating of 32 percent. The military suffered severely during the Vietnam War and then regained support once American participation in the fighting had diminished. From 1973 to 1978, military leaders generally scored in the 30–40 percent range, almost always above the mean in each survey. The 1979–81 figures show some slippage for the military, to just under 30 percent. The average rating for the military, at 34 percent, was five points above the mean for all institutions in all polls.

The press, at 24 percent "high" confidence, has consistently placed below the mean, but the trend has been one of increasing relative esteem. The press ranked ninth among the ten institutions during the mid-1960s and the early 1970s. Press ratings rose substantially during the Watergate period, promoting the press to the seventh-ranked position. Beginning with Watergate, the secondary pattern noted earlier appears in the data: the press and the executive branch move in opposite directions.

The public seems to hold disparate views about television and the press. The Harris and NORC surveys included a confidence rating of either "television" or "television news," but these were not included in Table 3-1 because the responses varied considerably depending on which term was used. In nine of the polls, respondents were asked about their confidence in people in charge of running "television"; the average percentage expressing "a great deal of confidence" in this group was 20. In these same nine surveys, trust in leaders of "the press" averaged slightly higher, 24 percent. In the other ten surveys, the term "television news" was used. On the average, 33 percent voiced "a great deal of confidence" in the leaders of "television news." In these surveys 24 percent gave a comparable rating to the press. "Television," which to most people probably means entertainment, ranked below the press in confidence eight out of nine times. But television *news* was always evaluated higher than the press. If "the press" signifies "newspapers" to most people, then it seems that people put more credence in television as a source of news than they do in newspapers.

The consistently top-rated institutions have been medicine, organized religion, and higher education (as well as science, in the occasional polls where it has been included). The most esteemed institution, medicine, is the only one in which a majority of Americans, on the average, has expressed "a great deal of confidence." In most polls taken between February 1966 and March 1974, three fifths or more exhibited such faith in medicine. But even that figure fell to 42–46 percent in 1978 and then down to 30 percent in early 1979, when higher education, at 33 percent, topped the list. This drastic fall-off for medicine in the Harris poll is difficult to explain; it did not occur in either the ORC or Gallup results for 1979. The March 1980 NORC poll suggested that medicine, at 52 percent high confidence, had made a complete recovery, so to speak. But in fact, the problem turns out only to have gone into remission. At the time of the 1980 Presidential election, the rating for medicine in the Harris polls had fallen back down to 34 percent, moving up only slightly to 37 percent in 1981.

The Gallup Polls

The Gallup surveys on confidence, which were taken every two years between 1973 and 1981 and also in 1980, came up with a roughly consistent rank-ordering of institutions. As noted in Chapter 2, eleven institutions were included by Gallup in at least two of these polls (See Table 2-3). Whenever Gallup inquired about them, higher than average confidence ratings were given to medicine, the church or organized religion, banks, the military, and the public schools, in that order. Until 1981, about three quarters expressed positive feelings about medicine and two thirds were favorable to organized religion, while the military and the public schools fell into the 51–58 percent range, with little variation across the five surveys. In 1981, however, organized religion fell to 57 percent positive, while public schools declined to 40 percent; these changes did not affect the relative position of the first, but they placed schools just below the average.

Like Harris and NORC, Gallup found the U.S. Supreme Court to be the highest-ranked governmental institution, with a positive rating of 44–52 percent, at or above average for the ten institutions. Congress, on the other hand, was 6–10 percentage points below the average confidence level. Gallup asked about newspapers and "television" four times, first in 1973 and again in 1979, 1980, and 1981. In each case, newspapers placed higher than television, a result that confirms the Harris and NORC pattern reported above.

Generally, Gallup's results have tended to agree with those of Harris and NORC, showing the least popular institutions to be business, labor, and government ("Congress" in the Gallup polls). But whereas "major companies" almost invariably did better than labor and government in the Harris and NORC surveys, "big business" in the Gallup polls came out worse than the other two, except in 1981. Banks, on the other hand, did much better than business, labor, and government, a finding consistent with all other surveys in which banks are rated. In 1981, however, banks declined sharply from 60 percent to 51 percent, a fall-off that may have reflected a negative response to higher bank interest rates.

The effect of the wording used to describe an institution may be seen in the strikingly different results that Gallup obtained when it varied the formulation for business. In 1975 and 1977, Gallup inquired about "free enterprise" as well as "big business." Confidence in "free enterprise" was significantly higher than confidence in "big business." In 1975, "free enterprise" received a 54 percent positive rating, compared to 34 percent favorable for "big business." In 1977, the positive evaluations were 51 percent for "free enterprise" and 33 percent for "big business." The substantially higher endorsement shows that the public clearly distinguishes "free enterprise" from "big business." This suggests that for big business to wrap itself in the mantle of free enterprise when under attack would lack credibility. "Free enterprise" implies a vigorously competitive system, while big business's problem, as we shall see, is that it tends to be identified with monopolistic power and is, therefore, viewed as antithetical to free enterprise.

The varying reactions to different types of business may also be seen in the responses Gallup obtained in 1975 when he asked separate questions about confidence in "business," "large companies," "small companies," and "the company or business you work for." "Large companies" were rated about the same as "big business": 35 percent positive, as compared with 34 percent in the case of "big business." The term "business" with no qualifying adjective secured a significantly higher vote, 48 percent. "Small companies" did even better, with a favorable response of 57 percent, while "the company or business you work for" elicited positive sentiments from fully 67 percent of the respondents. Clearly, it is *bigness* more than *business* that draws a negative reaction when the public is asked its feelings about "big business," whether the descriptive adjective is "big" for business or "large" for companies. "Business" alone draws an intermediate level of confidence, while considerable enthusiasm is shown for "small" business, for the respondent's own employer, and for the free enterprise system as a whole.

The ORC Polls

The rank-ordering of institutions in the surveys conducted by the Opinion Research Corporation in 1975, 1977, 1979, and 1981 was similar to those just reported (see Table 2-3 for the ORC results). Churches were at the top of the four ORC lists, with about 60 percent expressing "high" confidence in them each time. Banks followed, although their high confidence level fell from 60 to 48 percent between 1975 and 1979, dropping further to 36 percent and third place in 1981. The medical profession came in third in 1975 and 1977 and second in 1979 and 1981. The next group of institutions, with percentages in the 36–49 percent range, included "the armed forces" and colleges and universities. Below these, in the low 30 percent range, came the Supreme Court and the news media.

The institutions at the bottom of the ORC list also corroborate previous findings: the low-ranked ones pertained to business ("small companies," "large companies," "the stock market"), labor ("labor unions"), or government ("Congress"), plus the legal profession. "Small companies" were the most popular of this less esteemed group. The use of the term "small companies" rather than "small business" probably kept this institution from rising higher on the list, since a "company" is usually regarded as a business of at least modest size. In the ORC polls, labor unions ranked slightly higher than Congress. Congress, in turn, placed slightly above "large companies," in 1975 and 1977 but fell behind them in 1979 and 1981. The stock market was at the very bottom of the list on each occasion, with only 10 percent of the public expressing high confidence in that notoriously unstable institution.

An SRC Poll

In 1973, the Survey Research Center sought to evaluate the attitudes of a national sample of Americans to fifteen institutions by asking them to rate the overall job being done for the country by each. Respondents were asked to give each institution a rating on a scale running from 0, which meant a "very poor job," to 8, indicating a "very good job." The intermediate positions were labeled 2 ("poor"), 4 ("fair"), and 6 ("good"). The average rating for the fifteen institutions was 4.65 on the 0–8 scale, or just above "fair." The relative judgments corresponded, by and large, to those of the other studies. The three highest-rated institutions, in terms of their performance "for the country as a whole," were the military, colleges and universities, and churches and religious organizations, much as in the Harris, NORC, Gallup, and ORC surveys. Small businesses placed fourth, with an average score of 5.20, well above the mean, while large corporations ranked near the mean, with an average of 4.70. The public schools, the news media, and the U.S. Supreme Court scored somewhat higher. Political institutions, including Congress, state governments, the courts, the federal government, and the President and his administration, all came out well below average in performance. Labor unions ranked third from the bottom, with an average score of 4.26. Here, as in other surveys, nonprofit and non-"interest group" organizations tend to be rated the highest. Small business was the notable exception, far outranking large corporations in public esteem.

Confidence and Ethical Practices

A number of surveys have dealt with public perceptions of the attributes of various institutions; these help to explain the rank-orderings just described.

The Honesty and Efficiency Contrast

Samples of over 6,000 heads of households were surveyed in 1975 and 1977 by the marketing department of *U.S. News and World Report*. These polls probed attitudes toward twenty-six different institutions and groups in 1975, and a somewhat different list of twenty-five in 1977, including a variety of governmental units, the Republican and Democratic parties, politicians, the military, organized religion, business defined in several different ways, and various media. Respondents were asked to evaluate each using a scale that ran from one ("low") to seven ("high"). Institutions were evaluated twice, once for "honesty, dependability, and integrity" and a second time for "ability to 'get things done,' " i.e., efficiency. The average ratings on both scales for 1975 are shown in Figure 3-1.

The institutions tended to fall into three groups:

1. Some were judged high on both dimensions; banks and the medical profession, for instance, were at the top of both lists in 1975. In the 1977 study, "science and technology" was included and joined medicine at the top of the two lists; banks were not included in the 1977 survey. Small business, organized religion, educators, and the Supreme Court also received high ratings in both years; all ranked somewhat higher on honesty, dependability, and integrity than on ability to get things done.

2. Corporate business ("business executives," "large business," and "advertising agencies") received relatively high evaluations on their ability to get things done but were rated low on honesty, dependability, and integrity. The same was true for labor leaders, lawyers, the media, and, to a lesser extent, the military.

3. Political units were in a class by themselves—and a very bad class, indeed. Ten of the eleven governmental institutions listed on the questionnaire—all except the Supreme Court—were placed low on both dimensions. In fact, the only institutions considered neither honest nor efficient were the political ones.

The Supreme Court was the only organ of government that re-

FIGURE 3–1
Groups and Institutions, Rank-ordered by Combined Scores on "Ability to Get Things Done" and "Honesty, Dependability, and Integrity"

"Below is a list of various groups and institutions, along with two qualities that each group possesses in one degree or another. For each of these qualities, please rate *each* of the groups by checking a score from 1 (the lowest rating) to 7 (highest)."

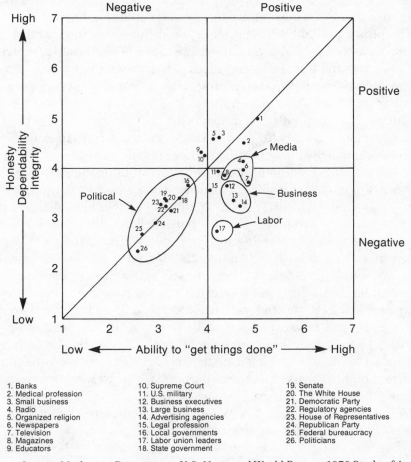

1. Banks	10. Supreme Court
2. Medical profession	11. U.S. military
3. Small business	12. Business executives
4. Radio	13. Large business
5. Organized religion	14. Advertising agencies
6. Newspapers	15. Legal profession
7. Television	16. Local governments
8. Magazines	17. Labor union leaders
9. Educators	18. State government

19. Senate
20. The White House
21. Democratic Party
22. Regulatory agencies
23. House of Representatives
24. Republican Party
25. Federal bureaucracy
26. Politicians

Source: Marketing Department, *U.S. News and World Report, 1976 Study of American Opinion,* Vol. 1—*U.S. Household Heads* (Washington, D.C.), pp. 250–58.
N = 6,277.

ceived a high rating. Interestingly, it is also the least competitive and least partisan branch of government. Two other groups that are commonly thought to serve "the truth," the legal profession and the media, were perceived by respondents as very much like business, i.e., relatively efficient but self-interested. Both law and journalism are highly competitive professions, and, possibly for this reason, they are seen as relatively low in standards of honesty (businessmen will do anything to make a profit, lawyers will say anything to win a case, journalists will do anything to get a story). The public probably views science, medicine, education, and religion as less competitive and, therefore, more honest. Banks, which show up at the top of this and many other surveys, are not seen as particularly competitive or profit-oriented. We shall see evidence below that banks are viewed these days primarily as service institutions that keep people's money safe, pay interest for the privilege, and lend money for good reasons—a far cry from their earlier popular image as citadels of monopoly capital.

The differences among the political institutions charted in Figure 3-1 are also revealing. The least popular political groups in 1975 as well as in 1977 were "politicians," the federal bureaucracy, and the two major political parties. Politicians and political parties seek votes, are intensely competitive, and thus are perceived to be primarily self-interested. While the federal bureaucracy is not particularly competitive, many would consider a "bureaucrat" no less self-interested than a politician. But a key characteristic of the federal bureaucracy is that it is *large and powerful,* and to most Americans, therefore, remote and impersonal. The importance of the perception of size can also be seen in the case of business-related institutions. Small business was one of the highest ranked sectors, particularly in terms of honesty, dependability, and integrity, where it ranked second only to banks. "Business executives," "large business," and "advertising agencies" connote larger organizations, and all were ranked significantly lower than small business in terms of honesty, dependability, and integrity, although they were still considered slightly more "efficient" than small business.

The Relationship between "Confidence" and "Ethical and Moral Practices"

Evidence of a direct relationship between confidence in institutions and evaluations of their ethical and moral practices may be found in the 1975, 1977, 1979, and 1981 ORC studies. Unfortunately, the scale ORC used in inquiring about confidence (a seven-point, high-to-low rating system) differed from that used to rate ethical practices. The latter offered only four choices, "excellent," "good," "only fair," or "poor." ORC also varied the objects inquired about in the two questions; "confidence" was gauged for banks, the medical profession, and large companies, etc., while "ethical and moral practices" were measured for their respective *practitioners,* e.g., bankers, physicians, and corporate executives. In spite of these differences, a comparison between confidence in institutions and the ethical and moral practices of their practitioners suggests that there is a relationship between the two sets of judgments.

Table 3-2 displays the rank-orderings on both dimensions, using the average scores for all four surveys.

The top-ranked groups in terms of ethical and moral practices were physicians, small business proprietors, "average workers" (a group that probably comes closest to the public's conception of itself), and scientists. Near the middle of the list were professors, news reporters, one business group (bankers), lawyers, and a few political authorities (the President, the military, and the Supreme Court). At the bottom of the list—and separated by a considerable gap—were the corporate business groups (corporate executives, stockbrokers, and advertising executives) and politicians and bureaucrats (Senators, Representatives, and state, local, and federal government officials). Labor union leaders were rated last in terms of their ethical and moral practices. In other words, most groups associated with business, labor, and government were given poor ratings on ethical and moral practices, with a few by now predictable exceptions: small businessmen, bankers, the President, the military, and the Supreme Court.

Moreover, groups rated high on ethical and moral practices tended to show up near the top of the list of institutions ranked by confidence (churches, banks, medicine, universities, the military, the Supreme Court). Small business was the one anomaly. "Small business proprietors" placed second on ethical and moral practices, while "small companies" were ninth in terms of confidence. The designation "small business proprietors" probably has a somewhat more positive connotation—smaller, more personal—than the term "small companies." Once again, at the bottom of the trust and confidence list one finds business (large companies, the stock market), labor unions, and government (Congress).

Table 3–2
Rank-ordering of Ratings on "Confidence" and "Ethical and Moral Practices" for Various Institutions and Groups

"How much trust and confidence do you have in . . . How would you rate the ethical and moral practices of . . . ?"

Trust and Confidence		Ethical and Moral Practices	
Institutions	Percentage "High" (6 or 7)	Institutions	Percentage "Excellent" or "Good"
1. Churches	59.5	1. Physicians	73
2. Banks	49	2. Small business proprietors	71
3. Medical profession	46.5	3. Average workers	71
4. Colleges and universities	43	4. Scientists	67
5. Armed forces	41	5. Bankers	58
6. Supreme Court	33.5	6. College professors	58
7. The President	32	7. Newspaper, radio and television news reporters	55.5
8. News reporting on radio, television, and in newspapers	31	8. The President	55
9. Small companies	29	9. Military leaders	51
10. Legal profession	24	10. Supreme Court	48
11. Labor unions	20	11. Lawyers	45
12. Large companies	15.5	12. U.S. Senators and Representatives	34.5
13. Congress	14.5	13. Corporate executives	33
14. Stock market	10	14. Stockbrokers	32
		15. Advertising executives	30
		16. State and local government officials	29
		17. Federal government officials	24
		18. Labor union leaders	22

Source: Average of ORC Studies in 1975, 1977, 1979, and 1981.

The similarity of the rank-orderings on the ORC questions suggests that confidence in institutions tends to follow the public's perceptions of the ethical and moral practices of their leaders.

The same conclusions can be drawn from 1976, 1977, and 1981 Gallup surveys in which respondents were asked to rank different professions in terms of their "honesty and ethical standards." Ten occupational groups were listed in the first survey, twenty in the second, and twenty-four in the third. Those rated highest on honesty and ethical standards were clergymen, doctors, engineers, and college teachers—all practitioners of some form of science or learning, presumably thought by the public to be above the fray of competition. Only one economic group was ranked above the mean on honesty and ethical standards, namely, bankers.

All those placing below average were in one of the three categories of business, labor, or government. Low ratings for honesty and ethical standards were given to U.S. Senators and Representatives, local and state officeholders, business executives, building contractors, insurance salesmen, real estate agents, advertising practitioners, and, at the very bottom, labor union leaders and car salesmen.

Similar results were obtained in a 1978 Yankelovich, Skelly & White survey, which found "big businessmen" and "union leaders" rated lowest in terms of acting in a "morally ethical" manner: 29–30 percent called them "morally ethical," but 55–56 percent said their behavior was "morally unethical." Environmentalists, consumer advocates, and, notably, small businessmen were perceived by majorities of over three to one as "morally ethical in their behavior," while less than half of the respondents said the same thing about state and local officials (48 percent) and federal officials (41 percent).

Variations in confidence in institutions appear to be based in large part on variations in the *perceived ethical standards* of those involved in each institution. Ethical standards are considered high in the "service" professions (education, science, medicine, religion, the military) and low in most areas of the economy and government, including business, labor, politics, and the bureaucracy. There is an interesting anomaly in this finding. Americans certainly value the freedom and competitiveness of both our economic system ("free enterprise") and our political system ("democracy"). But they do not seem to approve of the behavior that is most characteristic of both systems, namely, competition for power and profit motivated primarily by self-interest. Perhaps the public is responding to reports of corruption and malfeasance in high places, that is, *abuses* of free enterprise and democracy. But to some extent, one gets the impression from these data that the public feels negatively about the *normal* patterns of conduct associated with economic and political competition. What is it that the public finds specifically objectionable?

Self-Interest and Power

The principal difference between the positively regarded professions and the negatively evaluated ones would appear to be the varying importance of self-interest. Medicine, science, education, and military service are all "altruistic" professions; they are occupations that serve the needs of others, or of the public. Whatever economic rewards accrue to these professions—and, with the exception of medicine, the economic rewards are probably not perceived as particularly great—they are seen as incidental to the true goal of these activities, which is to serve others. Those involved in business and labor, on the other hand, are essentially concerned with furthering their own self-interest through making as much money as possible. Whatever public good these activities may serve—creating material prosperity, stimulating economic growth, generating employment, and the like—these are regarded as incidental to the goals and motivations of those involved. Americans undoubtedly recognize the social value of commercial activity, for they continue to praise the free enterprise system. But they have reservations about the kind of behavior that makes it work, namely, the pursuit of self-interest.

In this connection, politics and government seem to be an interesting exception. Politicians, like scientists, military leaders, and educators, claim to be serving the public good. But many people apparently believe that those who go into public life do so in order to serve their private self-interest, either by benefiting economically or by obtaining power. *What our political system has in common with our economic system is competitiveness.* It is, indeed, competitiveness that makes both democracy and free enterprise work, and Americans would have it no other way. But this does not mean that Americans admire the activities and values inherent to competition.

Joseph Schumpeter argued in his classic work, *Capitalism, Socialism, and Democracy* (1942), that the functions an economic system serves—the production and distribution of goods—are incidental to the motivations that lead people to participate in it. Individuals do not engage in economic and commercial activity to "produce and distribute goods" for the benefit of the larger society; they do so to make money so that they can survive and live well, i.e., for their own personal good.[1] The public seems to be aware of

[1] Joseph Schumpeter, *Capitalism, Socialism, and Democracy* (New York: Harper, 1942).

the distinction between the functions served by the economic and political systems, on the one hand, and the motivations of the people who participate in them, on the other. The poll evidence shows that Americans understand and appreciate the functions while distrusting the motivations. Moreover, the public probably has rather idealistic notions about the motivations that lead people into science, education, or medicine, and about the apparently public-spirited and noncompetitive behavior associated with these "altruistic" activities.

The Perception of Size

The size of an institution appears to be a second source of distrust. As noted above, large and powerful institutions—the federal bureaucracy, large corporations—are less well regarded. Indeed, Americans display an exceptional degree of hostility toward "bigness." One report on attitudes toward economic growth noted "a public fear of all very large institutions and a belief that it is always harmful to concentrate power in a few hands."[2] Whenever surveys have dealt with different size levels of the same institution, they have found greater hostility to the "big" or "large" versions than to smaller ones. Thus, a 1975 Procter & Gamble survey showed a systematic relationship between the public's confidence in an institution and its perceived "bigness": favorable attitudes decline as power ("bigness") increases (see Table 3-3). For instance, 20 percent of those sampled expressed a great deal of confidence in "business," and slightly fewer, 18 percent, expressed the same feeling about "business leaders." But only 12 percent said they had a great deal of confidence in "big business." Conversely, some 7 percent expressed no confidence in "business"; this increased to 14 percent in the case of "business leaders" and 26 percent for "big business."

Comparable results were obtained in five Roper polls taken between 1978 and 1981 that inquired separately about "your opinion of *most big* business corporations" and of "*most small* business companies" (emphasis in original questions). Big corporations were given highly favorable ratings by 10–16 percent, while the percentages having such positive feelings about small business com-

[2] *The Vital Consensus: American Attitudes on Economic Growth* (New York: Union Carbide Corporation, 1980), p. 20.

Table 3–3
Confidence in Selected Institutions and Groups

"I am going to name several institutions and groups in our country. And for each of them I would like you to tell me whether you have a great deal of confidence, a moderate amount of confidence, or no confidence in it. For example, the first is _____. Would you say that you have a great deal of confidence, moderate amount of confidence, or no confidence in _____?"

	Percentage Expressing "A Great Deal of Confidence"	Percentage Expressing "No Confidence"
A. Business	20	7
B. Business leaders	18	14
C. Big business	12	26
A. Organized labor	21	26
B. Union leaders	12	25
C. Big labor	7	27
A. Government	20	16
B. Federal government	16	15
C. Big government	6	32

Source: Procter & Gamble Survey, 1975.
Sample A: N = 121; Sample B: N = 122; Sample C: N = 121.

panies ranged from 35 to 46 percent. About a third of the respondents in the five surveys gave big business corporations either not-too-favorable or unfavorable ratings, compared to the one twentieth who evaluated small companies in a negative light. The adjective "big" appears to have similar effects on judgments of trade unions. In the Procter & Gamble poll, "big labor" was much less positively evaluated than "organized labor" (Table 3-3).

Evaluations of governmental bodies generally show the same pattern. The Procter & Gamble survey found a decline in favorability marking the progression from "government" to "the federal government" to "big government." Harris, in a 1973 study of attitudes toward government conducted for a subcommittee of the U.S. Senate, inquired separately about confidence in the people running "the executive branch of the federal government," "state government," and "local government." The percentages expressing "a great deal of confidence" were 50 for local government, 27 for state government, and 17 for the federal executive.[3] Gallup

[3] Louis Harris and Associates, *Confidence and Concern. Citizens View American Government* (Washington, D.C.: U.S. Government Printing Office, 1973), Vol. III, pp. 43, 45.

reported a similar pattern in 1980 using a somewhat differently worded question: "How much confidence do you, yourself, have in these American institutions to serve the public's needs—a great deal of confidence, a fair amount, or very little?" The percentages saying a "great deal" ranged from 19 for local government to 17 for state to 14 for national government. The proportions responding negatively ("very little" or "none") varied from 36 percent for the national government to 28 percent for the state and 27 percent for the local. Harris found comparable variations in seven surveys conducted between 1967 and 1981 in response to a question dealing with law enforcement at different levels of government: "How would you rate the job done by law enforcement officials on the (local, state, federal) level—excellent, pretty good, only fair, or poor?" Positive evaluations (excellent or pretty good), ranged from 59 percent for local law enforcement officials to 55 percent for those at the state level and 47 percent for those at the federal level.

The data also reveal that institutions are more popular than their leaders. Thus, Table 3-3 shows more confidence in "business" than in "business leaders" and more confidence in "organized labor" than in "union leaders." The same Procter & Gamble sample also gave higher approval ratings to "medicine" than to "doctors," to "established religion" than to "ministers and other religious leaders," to "the military" than to "military leaders," and to "colleges" and "the educational system" than to "professors." Only judges and pollsters seemed to escape this rule, possibly because they were not identified as "leaders": "judges" were more highly regarded than "the judicial system," and "pollsters" came out better than "public opinion polls."

Several explanations may be suggested for the distrust of bigness.

1. Those who wield authority in big institutions tend to be remote from the experience of most people and therefore distrusted. Most people have less personal contact with "business leaders" than with "small businessmen" or "bankers." The latter, as noted, are usually given high marks in the polls. A 1976 Harris survey asked whether each of twenty-five industries did a good or poor job "in serving customers." The sample rated banks higher than all the others, with 41 percent saying banks did a good job and only 8 percent, a poor one. "Small shopkeepers" received the next highest service rating, 30 percent good to 6 percent poor. "Car manufacturers" were viewed negatively, with a 7 percent good to

36 percent poor vote. Banks, presumably, are seen as more like shopkeepers, i.e., as competitive retail "service" institutions. Banks actually pay people for the services they offer, while interest on loans is probably not perceived as profit or markup.

In the public mind, big business, as compared with small business, is less likely to fulfill either individualistic or social values. Big business "management" has very little to do with most Americans' notion of hard work and individual achievement. Moreover, big business is viewed as impersonal and, therefore, insensitive to social needs, even though big business may be efficient and produce important social benefits.

As noted in Chapter 1, ORC's battery of statements concerning large corporations (Figure 1-4) shows a discrepancy in public opinion between the perceived contribution of big business to the overall economy, presumably because of greater efficiency, and concern for the dysfunctional effects of size, including bureaucratization. Thus, in eight polls between 1961 and 1979, about four fifths always responded positively to the statement, "Large companies are essential for the nation's growth and expansion." But a growing majority, from three fifths to three quarters of the same samples, agreed that "as they grow bigger, companies usually get cold and impersonal in their relations with people."

In a 1977 Harris poll, people said they would rather work for a small company than for a large one, 37 to 25 percent, with 31 percent perceiving no difference. Union members and blacks were the only population groups that preferred to work for large companies, no doubt for reasons related to the interests and experiences of these groups. Respondents were also asked whether, from a number of specific standpoints, they preferred that a large company or a small one build a plant in their community. From the standpoint of economic gains, people tended to prefer a large unit; large companies were considered better for "keeping a steady number of people employed," "hiring minorities," "exerting political influence in the community," and "paying a fair share of taxes." However, people chose small companies over large ones when the following criteria were specified: "caring about community needs," "caring about the young people in the community," and "caring about the environment." *Caring*, in other words, is associated with small business.

Some evidence that these judgments are related to actual experience is contained in the report of a Fall 1980 Roper survey.

Respondents were asked to say which among fourteen possible improvements in job conditions "would make you work harder." The *Roper Report* notes:

> There is some indication that people who work for small organizations (less than 50 employees) feel closer to management and happier in their work than people who work for medium size organizations (50 to 499 employees) and large organizations (500 or more employees). . . . Small firm employees named far fewer things that would make them work harder (1.8 on average) than medium-size firm employees (2.0 on average) and large-size firm employees (2.7 on average).[4]

The only possible change that a larger percentage of small firm employees felt might cause them to work harder was higher pay. On the other hand, there was a strong relationship between larger firm size and the tendency to cite employee treatment (mentioned by 24, 20, and 11 percent of large, medium-size, and small firm employees respectively). The same held true for "more feeling of accomplishment and satisfaction." Apparently, the smaller the company one works for, the more likely employees are to feel that the firm cares for its employees and provides them with interesting tasks.

2. The public no doubt suspects that political and economic strength is associated with corruption. People may feel that some businessmen become "big businessmen" by being less honest than "small businessmen" and that federal politicians and officials are more corrupt than state and local politicians; obtaining political power almost always involves raising a lot of money, which may require payoffs to special interests. Moreover, the public can keep better watch over small businessmen and local officials. When the 1977 *U.S. News and World Report* survey asked about honesty, dependability, and integrity, the ratio of "good" to "poor" responses was 9 percent to 25 percent in the case of large business, 10 to 21 percent for "business executives," and 27 to 8 percent for "small business"; it was 3 to 43 percent good-to-poor in the case of the "federal bureaucracy" and 8 to 27 percent for "state and local government."

The Opinion Research Corporation also reported substantial differences in evaluations of "the ethical and moral practices" of "small

---

[4] *Roper Reports,* 80-9 (New York: Roper Organization, 1980), p. X.

business proprietors" and "corporate executives" in 1975, 1977, 1979, and 1981. An average of 71 percent in the four polls rated the ethical and moral practices of the former as excellent or good, while the percentage who felt the same way about the latter averaged only 33.

A 1976 Cambridge Reports study revealed an interesting contrast in the responses to two questions. "Do you think, in general, that larger companies or smaller companies are more likely to be honest in their dealings with people like you?" Here a majority, 51 percent, said that smaller companies would be more honest; 33 percent that the two would be the same, while only 10 percent chose larger companies. Then respondents were asked to choose between two opinions: "Big corporations are more likely to engage in criminal activities than little ones," or "Little businesses are just as likely to be criminal as big ones." This time a majority—54 percent—felt that "little businesses are just as likely to be criminal as big ones," while 31 percent thought that big corporations were more likely to be criminal.

Why did these two questions produce different responses concerning the relative morality of big business and small business? The first question asks which type of company is more likely to be honest "in their dealings with *people like you*." The second query, on the other hand, makes no reference to dealing with individuals, only to general "criminal activities." People do not see small business as especially more inclined to obey the law than big business, but they seem to feel that the personal factor is a form of control over small business that does not exist for big business. Small business is regarded as more honest only when this personal element is taken into consideration. Big business will be less honest in dealing with "people like me," it would seem, because of the feeling that there is no way "I" can influence it; in short, to the large corporation, the individual counts for nothing.

3. Since the public is already negatively disposed toward the motives of those who participate in political and business life— "They're only in it for themselves"—people may feel that power in the hands of the self-interested will naturally be abused. Nothing better can be expected of "big business" or "big labor."

Concern about the excessive power of big institutions was revealed in Roper polls taken in 1973, 1974, and 1977. People were asked to look at a list of groups and institutions and indicate whether each had "too much power" or not enough power in our society.

The rank-ordering of the responses in the three surveys changed somewhat between 1973–74 and 1977. In the first two years, "big business corporations" headed the institutions with too much power, a feeling shared by two out of three respondents. Labor unions followed (55 percent said "too much power" in 1973 and 58 percent in 1974); then the executive branch of the federal government ("the President, the White House staff, the Cabinet"), which was seen as too powerful by 45 percent in 1973 and 41 percent in 1974; and then the press, called too powerful by 31 percent in 1973 and 36 percent in 1974. At the other end of the list, "small business companies" stood out as "not having enough influence or voice in our society today." Four years later, in 1977, labor unions climbed to the top of the list (65 percent), while "big business corporations" fell to second position (59 percent). Strikingly, fear of excessive power in the executive branch dropped considerably between 1974 and 1977, down to 28 percent; this may reflect the differences in attitudes toward the imperial presidency during the Watergate period and during the first few months of the Carter Administration. Small business companies remained the least distrusted institution, with only 2 percent saying their power was too great. The comparison between small business and big business was indeed dramatic, as Table 3-4 reveals.

TABLE 3–4

Perceptions of Power and Influence

"Turning now to another subject, there is talk from time to time about how much power or influence various groups in our society have. Here is a list of some different groups. (Card shown respondent.) Would you read down that list and call off those groups, if any, you think have too much power and influence in our society today? Are there any groups on that list that you think don't have *enough* influence or voice in our society today? Which ones?"

	Percentage Saying:	
	"Too Much Power"	*"Not Enough Influence"*
Big business (1973)	66	1
Big business (1974)	68	2
Big business (1977)	59	2
Small business (1973)	1	46
Small business (1974)	2	41
Small business (1977)	2	44

Source: Roper Organization
1973: N = 1,263; 1974: N = 2,000; 1977: N = 2,004.

In fact, more people perceived small business as not having enough power than any other group tested by Roper, including consumer protection groups, farmers, religious leaders, and educators. Americans are acutely aware of the powerlessness of small business, and that perception seems to make small business more likeable.

4. Finally, competition, for whatever motives, is seen as essential to the preservation of democracy and free enterprise; monopoly power is antithetical to the functioning of both the political and economic systems. Many clearly believe that the concentration of power destroys competition. In October 1979, the Roger Seasonwein poll asked a national cross section whether the increased power of corporations, labor unions, and the federal government "helps the American economy or hurts it." In each case, many more replied that greater power is bad for the economy than good for it. The power of labor unions was perceived to hurt the economy most (56 percent "hurts," 23 percent "helps"), followed by the federal government (54 percent "hurts," 20 percent "helps") and corporations (45 and 27 percent).

The public regards business leaders, as well as labor leaders and political leaders, as essentially self-serving. Hence, they must be influenced—even controlled—if they are to serve the public interest. The bigger the leaders are, the less susceptible they are to control—and the greater the potential for abuse of the public interest. Thus, a 1974 ORC survey offered respondents the following choice: "Some people say that the bigger a company gets the worse it uses its power. Others say that the bigger it gets the more it tries to serve the public. Which comes closer to your point of view?" The sample felt, by 53 to 29 percent, that the bigger a business gets, the more it will abuse its power and the less it will serve the public.

Conclusion

In sum, the evidence indicates that confidence in institutions generally has remained low throughout the 1970s and that the three most powerful sectors—business, government, and labor—have been held in particular disdain. These sectors will be examined in more detail in subsequent chapters. Those chapters will explore the paradox noted above: that the public is highly critical of the behavior and motivations of people associated with each of these "self-serving" institutions, while at the same time it recognizes the indispensable functions those institutions perform. How does the public resolve this dilemma? The answer is that a free enterprise economy and a democratic polity do not require that people show deep-seated trust in either business, or government, or labor alone; rather, the system must show a proper counterbalancing of interests among the three.

Appendix: The Effects of Variations in Question Wording

Typically, different survey organizations report varying levels of confidence in institutions. Harris and NORC, for example, almost always show a preponderance of negative sentiment. In Gallup surveys, on the other hand, positive feelings about institutions usually outnumber negative ones. As indicated in Chapter 2, these discrepancies can be accounted for by differences in wording between the Harris-NORC and Gallup versions of the confidence question. Nevertheless, the press often follows the lead of the pollsters in reporting the absolute results as if they were generally valid ("only 15 percent of the public has confidence in Congress"). Similarly, one might be dismayed by the fact that, on the average, only 29 percent of Americans have expressed positive sentiments about their institutions in all the Harris-NORC surveys since 1966 (Table 2-1). Since Harris's polls have been the ones most frequently administered and cited on the subject of confidence in institutions, the overall impression that the nation is suffering a "crisis of confidence" may be to some extent an artifact of that poll's methodology. Exactly how much difference does question-wording make?

The Number of Answers and the Characterization of Institutions

The Harris-NORC question, "How much confidence do you have in the people in charge of running [various institutions]?" allows one positive response—"a great deal"—and two negative ones— "only some" or "hardly any." Gallup poses his question as follows:

89

> I am going to read you a list of institutions in American society. Would you tell me how much respect and confidence you, yourself, have in each one—a great deal, quite a lot, some, or very little?

Thus Gallup allows two positive responses ("a great deal" or "quite a lot"), one response that may be regarded as neutral ("some," certainly a more positive option than the "only some" in the Harris-NORC formulation), and only one negative choice ("very little"). A second difference between the questions is that Gallup inquires about the institutions themselves, while Harris and NORC ask about the leaders of institutions, i.e., "the people in charge of running" each of them.

Not surprisingly, Gallup and Harris-NORC supply very different impressions of the attitudes Americans hold toward their institutions. Gallup's respondents are invariably more positive than either Harris's or NORC's. Thus, in the case of organized labor, Harris's early 1977 confidence figure was 14 percent positive, while Gallup's was 39. For medicine, the confidence estimate was 43 percent positive for Harris and 73 for Gallup. The military received a positive rating of 23 percent from Harris and 57 from Gallup. It is not possible to make a direct comparison of the Harris and Gallup findings concerning business since the two polls use different terms to describe that institution. Harris, who regularly inquires about "major companies," found 20 percent positive in early 1977. Gallup used two different terms and reported 51 percent with "a great deal" or "quite a lot" of confidence in "free enterprise," while 33 percent expressed comparably positive views about "big business."

The variation between the results of the two major pollsters is not minor. Both Harris and Gallup have inquired about seven institutions for which the same descriptive word is used. In early 1977, Harris found a mean of 26 percent expressing "a great deal" of confidence in the leaders of these institutions, while 60 percent, on the average, indicated that they had "only some" or "hardly any" confidence in them. On the other hand, Gallup reported an average of just over half of his respondents—a figure twice as high as Harris's—voicing "a great deal" or "quite a lot" of confidence in the same seven institutions. Only 17 percent, on the average, chose Gallup's negative options of "very little" or "none," while the relatively neutral middle response, "some confidence," averaged 28 percent. Apparently, most people do not want to say they have "a great deal" of confidence in the leaders of major institutions, even when the alternative choices open to them are not really positive ("only some" and "hardly any"). But many leap to express confidence when Gallup offers *two* positive choices, the lesser of which is "quite a lot"; and only a small minority chooses clearly negative options when, in addition to two favorable choices, they are allowed to pick the ambiguous term, "some."

The Civic Service Poll: An Experiment

In order to estimate the effects of these variations in question-wording, three different versions of the confidence question were included in a national survey carried out by Civic Service, Inc., in February 1980. The total sample of 1,611 respondents was divided randomly into three subsamples of approximately equal size. Each subsample (A, B, and C) was asked a different version of the question. The questions varied in two respects: whether confidence was gauged for the institution itself or for its leaders, and in the number of response categories offered.

• Format A employed the Harris-NORC question. Respondents were asked about "the people running" various institutions and three response choices were offered, "a great deal of confidence, only some confidence, or hardly any confidence at all."

• Format B was the Gallup format. This version asked about institutions directly, and four response categories were defined, "a great deal, quite a lot, some, or very little."

• Format C also used the four Gallup response categories, but the Gallup question was modified to inquire about "the people running" each institution rather than the institution itself.

Thus the contrast between versions A and C shows the effect of response coding—two positive categories, as in C, or one, as in A. The contrast between versions B and C reveals the effect of asking about institutions directly (B) rather than their leaders (C), while keeping the same response coding. Since the Harris-NORC version (A) and the Gallup version (B) differ on both characteristics, it is difficult to determine which factor is mainly responsible for discrepancies in their results.

In the Civic Service test, all interviews were administered at the same time, in person, by the same research organization, and the confidence question was located in the same place in all three versions of the questionnaire. These potential sources of variation were therefore kept under control. The same seven institutions, in the same order, were inquired about in all three versions: "big business," "the military," "Congress," "organized labor," "the executive branch of the federal government," "major companies," and "the press." The inclusion of both "major companies" and "big business" showed whether varying these terms, one of which is standard for Gallup and the other for Harris and NORC, produces a systematic difference in the public's reaction. Results of the experiment are shown in Table 3-5.

Results

The contrast between versions A and C reveals the sharp discrepancy created by the number of responses allowed. In version A—the Harris-NORC format—an average of 20 percent gave the positive response, "a great deal." In version C (Gallup, modified to specify leaders), only 10 percent said they had "a great deal of confidence" in the leaders of the same seven institutions, on the average. An average of 20.5 percent gave the second positive response, "quite a lot." Combining the two favorable responses in version C, one finds an average of 31 percent giving positive evaluations of institutional leaders.

Thus, when only one positive response is allowed in version A, only one in five Americans appears to approve of the leadership of the country's principal institutions. In version C, with two positive answers, approval increases to almost one in three. The discrepancy also applies to each institution separately: the percentage saying they have "a great deal of confidence" is always higher in version A, where it is the only positive response, but the two positive responses always combine to a higher figure in version C. The second positive response in version C, "quite a lot of confidence," appears to draw some respondents who would have said "a great deal" and some who would have said "only some" in version A. It seems reasonable to consider these people as basically positive in their views, since they chose not to give the neutral answer "some," which was available in version C. Thus, many of them appear to be negative ("only some") in version A simply because they refuse to endorse the *strongest possible* answer, "a great deal."

Note that at the negative end of the scale, the discrepancy between versions A and C is much less. In version A, an average of 26 percent said "hardly any" confidence. In version C, an average of 28 percent said "very little" or volunteered "none." Some of the negative feeling in version A was apparently absorbed by the mildly negative intermediate response, "only some."

The contrast between versions B and C indicates that it makes almost no difference whether people are asked their feelings toward the institutions themselves or the people running them. Version B, which followed the Gallup format of asking about institutions directly, showed averages of 11 percent saying "a great deal of confidence," 22 percent "quite a lot," 40 percent "some," 22 percent "very little," and 5 percent "none" (volunteered). Version C, which asked about the leaders of the same institutions, showed, on the average, 10 percent saying "a great deal," 21 percent "quite a lot," 41 percent "some," 23 "very little," and 5 volunteering "none." The only institution that displayed a significant discrepancy between the two formats was the military. In version B, 53 percent gave positive responses about "the military," whereas in version C, the percentage positive toward military leaders was 46. Fourteen percent were negative toward the military, while 19 percent felt the same way about military leaders. In several other cases—big business, major companies, Congress, and organized labor—there was a slight tendency in the same direction, that is, for people to give more positive answers about the institution itself than about its leaders. Only in the case of the press was there any suggestion that people were more approving of the "people in charge" than of the institution itself, although the difference was very small.

Conclusions

Generally, it appears that the distinction between institutions and the people running them is not very salient. Specifying the institution itself may raise confidence ratings a bit, particularly in the case of a security-related institution like the military. But by far the stronger effect has to do with the number of responses offered. The single positive choice presented by Harris and NORC —"a great deal"—results in a low estimate of the degree of confidence that Americans have in their institutions. It produces the finding that negative sentiments outweigh positive ones. In Table 3-5, version A (Harris-NORC) shows 26 percent giving negative responses, on the average, while 20 percent are favorable. Indeed, the 54 percent who give the invidious sounding middle position, "only some," might also be seen as negative. But versions B and C

TABLE 3–5
Three Versions of the Confidence-in-Institutions Question

Version A (Harris and NORC Wording)

"I am going to name some institutions in this country. As far as the *people running* these institutions are concerned, would you say you have a great deal of confidence, only some confidence, or hardly any confidence at all in them?" (Institutions named)

Institution	+ A Great Deal	0 Only Some	– Hardly Any, None (Volunteered)	
		Percentage		
The military	33	53	14	= 100
The press	24	53	23	
The executive branch of the federal government	19	55	26	
Congress	15	58	27	
Big business	16	53	31	
Major companies	15	55	30	
Organized labor	16	49	35	
Average of the seven institutions above	20	54	26	= 100

Version B (Gallup Wording)

"I am going to read you a list of institutions in American society. Would you tell me how much confidence you, yourself, have in each one—a great deal, quite a lot, some, or very little? How much confidence do you have in . . . ?" (Institutions named)

Institution	+ A Great Deal, Quite a Lot	0 Some	– Very Little, None (Volunteered)	
		Percentage		
The military	53	33	14	= 100
The press	33	40	27	
The executive branch of the federal government	31	46	23	
Congress	28	45	27	
Big business	32	35	33	
Major companies	27	44	29	
Organized labor	27	37	36	
Average of the seven institutions above	33	40	27	= 100

How Confidence Ratings Compare

Version C (Variant Gallup Wording)

"I am going to read you a list of institutions in American society. As far as the *people running* these institutions are concerned, would you tell me how much confidence you, yourself, have in them—a great deal, quite a lot, some, or very little? How much confidence do you have in the *people running* . . .?" (Institutions named)

Institution	+ A Great Deal, Quite a Lot	0 Some	– Very Little, None (Volunteered)	
		Percentage		
The military	46	35	19	= 100
The press	34	40	27	
The executive branch of the federal government	31	45	24	
Congress	27	43	30	
Big business	29	40	31	
Major companies	25	45	30	
Organized labor	23	40	37	
Average of the seven institutions above	31	41	28	= 100

Average of Versions A, B and C

Institution	+ Positive	0 Neutral	– Negative	
		Percentage		
The military	44	40	16	= 100
The press	30	45	25	
The executive branch of the federal government	27	49	24	
Congress	23	49	28	
Big business	26	42	32	
Major companies	22	48	30	
Organized labor	22	42	36	
Average of the seven institutions above	28	45	27	= 100

Source: Civic Service, Inc., February 1980.
Version A: N = 527; Version B: N = 507; Version C: N = 580.

both show a slight preponderance of *positive* over negative sentiments toward the same institutions—33 to 27 percent positive in version B, 31 to 28 percent positive in version C. Moreover, the middle category in versions B and C, "some confidence," would not usually be considered negative. To a large extent, then, the widely reported negative findings of the confidence series most frequently administered, those of Harris and NORC, are an artifact of the question format.

The rank-ordering of the seven institutions is fairly stable across all three formats, however. In all three versions, the military is the top-ranked institution and organized labor ends up at the bottom. Fairly positively regarded, but at some distance behind the military, are the press and the executive branch; the latter achieve virtually identical ratings in versions B and C, although the executive branch is somewhat lower than the press in version A, the Harris-NORC format. The last three institutions, "big business," "major companies," and "Congress," come out in all three versions between the press and the executive branch on the one hand, and organized labor on the other. Sentiment toward these institutions might be described as moderately negative.

There seems to be little difference between ratings of "big business" and "major companies." "Big business" averaged 26 percent positive and 32 percent negative, while "major companies" averaged 22 percent positive and 29 percent negative. Thus, on balance, public sentiment was 6 percent more negative than positive toward "big business" and 7 percent more negative than positive toward "major companies." The only hint of a difference is that "big business" obtains a larger volume of both positive and negative responses, while the neutral category is larger for "major companies." Thus, it may be that opinion is more polarized toward "big business," but the overall balance of sentiment is about the same whichever term is used.

The discrepancies in responses to different question-wordings give warning that one should not treat the answers to any given poll as showing the "real" distribution of public attitudes on an issue. Nevertheless, these findings do not undermine our efforts to analyze trends, to locate relative positions high or low, and to identify the correlates of confidence. The evidence for a long-term, general decline in confidence and for the stability of the relative standings of different institutions remains convincing.

4

The Correlates of Confidence in Institutions

H<small>AVING</small> identified a significant drop in public confidence in our major institutions and their leadership, we turn now to analyze the social, political, and psychological factors associated with evaluations of institutions generally, and of business, government, and labor in particular. Do such factors help explain the sharp and apparently quite broad decline in trust that occurred between the mid-1960s and the early 1970s? Is confidence in institutions higher among certain groups in American society? Or does the pattern of confidence vary institution by institution?

Our analysis will examine the relationship between "public" and "private" confidence, that is, between confidence in social, political, and economic institutions, on the one hand, and personal satisfaction, optimism, and alienation, on the other. We will consider whether personal dissatisfaction accounts for public distrust, or whether both are related to certain underlying changes in the political and economic environment.

A General Index of Confidence

Is it possible to speak of confidence in institutions as a general phenomenon? Chapter 2 revealed a notable degree of consistency in the trends for different institutions. Thus, negative feelings about business, government, and labor all intensified between 1964 and 1974. The Harris poll found a decrease in confidence for every one of seventeen institutions tested between 1966 and 1971. The upswings and downswings of the 1970s also displayed considerable uniformity from institution to institution.

Similarity in confidence trends does not demonstrate, in and of itself, that the trends reflect the same underlying cause. It is possible for diverse phenomena to show parallel responses to disparate underlying events. If church attendance and psychiatric disorder both increase, this does not mean that the two are rising because of, say, an economic depression; rather one may be moving up because of a short-term economic depression and the other because of a long-term deterioration of family structure. The similarity of trends merely suggests the possibility that confidence in different institutions may be linked.

To obtain more direct evidence, we looked at the interrelationships among the different confidence measures, using data from the combined NORC General Social Surveys from 1973 through 1977.[1] The correlation matrix revealed that confidence in the leadership of every institution was associated with confidence in the leadership of every other institution. All relationships (correlation coefficients) were positive. Confidence in the leaders of Congress and of the Supreme Court showed a positive correlation of .40, the highest in the matrix. This means that, on the average in these five surveys, respondents who expressed confidence in Congress also tended to express faith in the Supreme Court. Those who were more positive toward religious leaders were also more positive toward the leaders of science (.16). Faith in the people running major companies was associated with confidence in those running organized labor (.12). In addition, separate correlation matrices were calculated for each of the five surveys, 1973 through 1977. There was not a single negative correlation between confidence measures in any survey.

These findings suggest the possibility of constructing a "general index of confidence in institutions," reflecting the fact that people who express high confidence in the leaders of any one institution tend to be favorable toward leaders of all institutions, while those

[1] The number of people interviewed each year varied between 1,484 and 1,530. The five surveys were, therefore, given equal weights of 1,500 each to eliminate this slight disparity.

with low confidence in any one set of institutional leaders are prone to give negative ratings to all. It must be noted, however, that while all the correlations were positive, they were fairly small in magnitude. In the matrix combining all surveys, the coefficients ranged from .08 (for science and organized labor) to .40 (for Congress and the Supreme Court, as noted). The average correlation was a modest .21. Thus, while the correlations indicate a consistent pattern, it is not a strong one.

To create a general index of confidence, we carried out a factor analysis of the replies to the twelve questions in the NORC surveys.[2] A single factor accounted for 28 percent of the variance in the responses; that is, between a quarter and a third of the variance could be attributed to a common, underlying "general confidence" factor. There is clearly *some* common content to these questions, but a considerable amount of variance remains distinct for each of the institutions tested.[3] What accounts for the tendency of people to give similar confidence ratings to all institutions?

The Influence of Education and Socioeconomic Status

Education, or socioeconomic status, may be relevant. Let us consider two contradictory hypotheses. On the one hand, it might be supposed that better educated and higher-status individuals have had more "success," have been more highly rewarded, and are, therefore, more likely than the less fortunate to express faith in the country's institutions. Moreover, those higher in status tend to compose the stratum from which institutional leaders are recruited, and the Harris and NORC questions ask specifically

[2] The first principal component was extracted from the correlation matrix for all surveys. All twelve confidence questions correlated positively with this principal component, with loadings varying between .43 (labor) and .65 (Congress).

[3] Additional factors were extracted in order to determine whether there might be more than one "general confidence" factor. Only one additional factor with any general meaning (eigenvalue greater than 1.00) could be extracted. The second factor was defined by two media questions: confidence in the press and in television. This factor was negatively associated with confidence in major companies and in the executive branch of the federal government. The second factor thus corresponds to the second factor extracted from the time series data reported in Chapter 2. Both analyses suggest a distinct pattern for the *media* as opposed to other institutions. The media factor was felt to be insufficiently general, however, to justify the inclusion of a second factor. In the cross-sectional data, as in the time series, the media questions did correlate with the general index of confidence (.46 in the case of the press, .48 in the case of television).

whether respondents have confidence in the people running our major institutions. An alternative hypothesis would hold that lower status and more poorly educated Americans are likely to give less sophisticated responses, that is, to express a naive belief that those who run our major institutions know what they are doing. The better educated may be more knowledgeable and more cynical about how things are run. In addition, the poorly educated may be more susceptible to "response set," that is, the tendency to repeat a pattern of positive (or negative) responses for every institution.

In fact, the data indicate no relationship whatever with either education or socioeconomic status. The correlations between the general index of confidence and education, occupational status, and family income all turn out to be approximately zero. To illustrate, those respondents with factor scores at least half a standard deviation above the mean were classified as "high" on the confidence index; they constituted 30.5 percent of the five combined samples. When broken down by educational attainment, the proportions expressing "high" general confidence were as follows: 31 percent among those with a grade-school education, 30 percent for those with some high school, 32 percent for high school graduates, 28 percent for those with some college, and 29 percent for those with a college degree.

The relationship with occupation was also weak and irregular, although there was a very slight tendency for general confidence to be higher among those at lower status levels. Nor did any pattern emerge when respondents were classified by family income.[4] Thus, neither hypothesis appears to work. Those high in status and those low in status are not significantly different in their tendency to express confidence in the performance of our institutions *generally*.

Again, one might expect blacks to express lower confidence in the country's institutions because of punitive historical experi-

---

[4] The proportions expressing "high" general confidence were 30 percent of those in professional positions, 30 percent of those in managerial occupations, 29 percent in the clerical-sales category, 30 percent of skilled workers, 32 percent among semi-skilled and unskilled workers, and 32.5 percent of those in service jobs. Given the large sample, respondents could be classified into twelve income categories with at least 140 respondents in each. The categories ranged from under $1,000 at the bottom to over $25,000 at the top. Here is what happened to the level of "high" confidence as income increased, category by category: 39 percent among the poorest respondents, 29.5 percent, 32, 35, 29, 30, 35, 31, 30.5, 31, 27, and, finally, 29 percent among those in the highest income category.

ence. But once more, no relationship appears. Among whites, 31 percent expressed "high" general confidence. The figure for blacks was 29 percent. To check for differences at the low end of the scale, we classified those respondents whose general index scores were half a standard deviation or more below the mean as "low." The percentage "low" for blacks and whites was exactly the same: 30.

A rather different hypothesis might be suggested in the case of age. As a rule, older people tend to identify more strongly with institutions simply because they have been tied to them for a longer period of time. Thus, research in the United States and elsewhere has shown that identification with political parties increases with age under normal circumstances because older voters have had a longer period to "conserve" their party loyalty. The same process leads older people to develop stronger identification with a local community because they usually have lived there longer.[5] Thus, we should expect older Americans to show more faith in institutions generally. The relationship between age and confidence in institutions, however, turns out to be inconsistent. Confidence varies from 30 percent "high" among people who were under 30 years old when they were interviewed by NORC, to 28 percent for those aged 30 to 44, 33 percent among those 45 to 60, and 31 percent for those over 60 at the time of the interview.

The Influence of Politics and Ideology

It may be that feelings of confidence are more political than sociological in origin. Historically, the left has been more critical of the American system, its institutions, and its leaders, while conservatives have usually been more defensive of the status quo. Since the New Deal, however, conservative activists have become increasingly alienated from what they regard as a left-leaning establishment running most major institutions in this country. Thus, there is reason to suspect that anti-institutional sentiment may show up on the right as well as on the left.

Figure 4-1-A breaks down factor scores on the general index of confidence by ideology (seven categories, from extremely liberal

[5] See the discussion by David Butler and Donald Stokes, *Political Change in Britain,* Second College Edition (New York: St. Martin's Press, 1976), pp. 36–43.

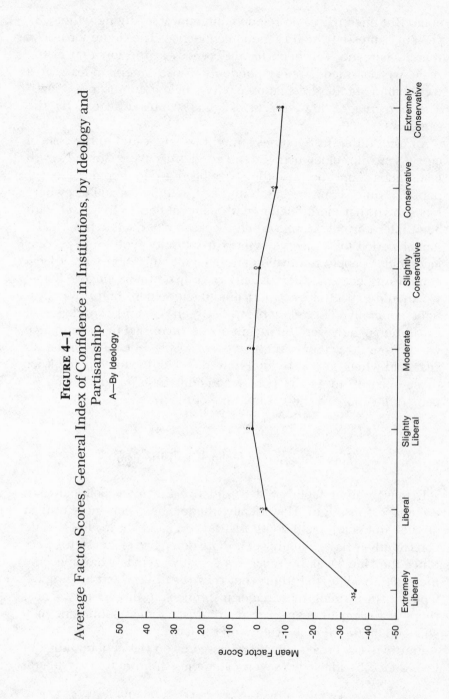

FIGURE 4–1

Average Factor Scores, General Index of Confidence in Institutions, by Ideology and Partisanship

A—By Ideology

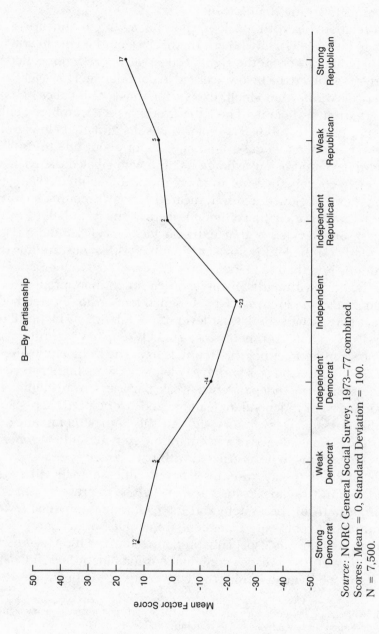

B—By Partisanship

Source: NORC General Social Survey, 1973–77 combined.
Scores: Mean = 0, Standard Deviation = 100.
N = 7,500.

to extremely conservative), while Figure 4-1-B breaks them down by self-described partisanship (seven categories, from strong Democrats to strong Republicans).

The relationship with ideology shows a weak curvilinearity, as suggested above. Those who put themselves on the left (liberal or extremely liberal) or on the right (conservative or extremely conservative) tended to be below average in confidence. However, the differences were quite small, except for those who called themselves "extremely liberal." The latter group, which numbered only 2 percent of the combined sample, was substantially below average in confidence (average score of − 35, or about one third of a standard deviation below average). Those who labeled themselves "extremely conservative," also 2 percent of the sample, averaged − 8, or slightly below the overall mean. Ideology accounts for very little of the variation in confidence across the population. Still, there is some evidence that extreme ideological self-definition, particularly on the left, is associated with a critical posture toward institutions and their leaders.

The relation with partisanship shows a much more pronounced curvilinearity (see Figure 4-1-B). Independents who rejected both political parties had the lowest level of confidence in institutions generally. Positive sentiments rose steadily as party identification became stronger in either the Republican or the Democratic direction. Thus, Independents with party leanings were higher in confidence than true Independents, weak partisans were higher in confidence than Independent leaners, and strong partisans—both Republicans and Democrats—showed the highest confidence of all. There is no evidence of a left-right difference. Rather, general confidence seems to be associated with partisanship per se.

It is difficult to say whether party loyalties actually increase confidence in the causal sense. It may well be the reverse, that is, declining faith in the system and its leaders may produce lower commitment to political parties. The trend of lessening party identification, which was especially pronounced after 1964, seems to be tied in with the broader confidence trends identified in Chapters 1 and 2.[6] Evidence from the University of Michigan election

---

[6] Nie, Verba, and Petrocik show that the erosion of party commitment, as measured by self-described "independence," vote switching, and alienation from political parties, accelerated rapidly between 1964 and 1972. Norman H. Nie, Sidney Verba, and John R. Petrocik, *The Changing American Voter* (Cambridge, Mass.: Harvard University Press, 1976), pp. 281–83.

surveys suggests that the decline of trust in government during the 1960s and 1970s could be detected in all partisan groups, among highly committed Democrats and Republicans as well as Independents. Partisan affiliation only delayed the decline. Thus it would be hard to argue that the decline of confidence might be reversed through a revival of partisan feeling. More likely, voters turned away from political parties after 1964 for the same reasons that they soured on business, government, and labor: because things were not going well and no institution seemed to be functioning soundly. While the answer to the question of causality must be left ambiguous, the relationship between confidence and partisanship does suggest that something real is being measured by the general index of confidence, namely, a form of institutional trust and identification that applies to political parties as well as to the other twelve institutions regularly tested by NORC.

Partisanship and ideology are moderately correlated (gamma = .21), since Democrats tend to be relatively liberal and Republicans, conservative. The relationships in Figures 4-1-A and 4-1-B become clearer when we look at the effects of partisanship controlling for ideology, and of ideology controlling for partisanship. Table 4-1 does this by showing the average score on the general index of confidence for all cross-classifications of partisanship and ideology in the combined 1974–77 NORC General Social Surveys. (The 1973 survey did not include an ideology question.)

Reading across the table, one finds that the partisan pattern of Figures 4-1-A and 4-1-B holds up within every ideological group. With a few minor exceptions, the level of confidence falls as it approaches the center of the table (true Independents) from either the left (strong Democrats) or the right (strong Republicans). At the bottom of each party column, a simple average is presented for the seven ideological groups. These show the effect of partisanship correcting for ideology, since they are calculated as if the distribution by ideology were the same for each party column. The curvilinear pattern holds up well. Only "Independent Republicans" are slightly out of line; in several cases, their level of confidence is higher than that of weak Republicans. As a rule, however, confidence is lowest among Independents and highest among strong partisans.

The ideology pattern is clarified somewhat by controlling for partisanship. Confidence exhibits a tendency to decline as it moves

TABLE 4–1

General Index of Confidence in Institutions by Partisanship and Ideology

Ideology	Partisanship							Average
	Strong Democrats	Weak Democrats	Independent Democrats	Independents	Independent Republicans	Weak Republicans	Strong Republicans	
Extremely Liberal	13	−34	−47	−113	(−38)	(100)	(84)	−45
Liberal	7	3	−19	−19	−17	15	22	−1
Slightly Liberal	15	8	−15	−18	−2	8	14	−1
Moderate	13	7	−16	−13	14	7	17	4
Slightly Conservative	18	4	−2	−25	6	−4	−1	−1
Conservative	21	−2	−8	−32	−9	−16	−3	−6
Extremely Conservative	52	−23	−35	−65	−21	−41	16	−16
Average	20	−5	−20	−41	−5	−5	12	0

Source: NORC General Social Surveys, 1974–77.

N = 5,549.

Note: Figures show *average* score on the general index of confidence for respondents within each cross-classification of partisanship and ideology (thus, extremely liberal strong Democrats averaged 13 on the general index of confidence, etc.).

Averages in parentheses are for fewer than 100 respondents.

from the middle row (moderates) toward "extreme liberals" and "extreme conservatives."[7] This negative curvilinearity shows up most clearly where party loyalty is weak. Among true Independents, where partisanship is totally absent, the effect of ideology is quite pronounced. Trust is lowest, for instance, among extreme liberals and conservatives who have no party ties—in other words, radicals of the left and right. Partisanship tends to blur the effect of ideology. Among strong partisans, ideology has no clear effect at all.

The impact of ideology may be summarized as follows: when partisanship is weak or nonexistent, belief in institutions tends to fall as one goes toward either the far left or the far right. Extreme liberals are usually lower in trust than extreme conservatives. Partisanship, however, generally overrides the effect of ideology. Strong party supporters are relatively high in confidence no matter what their ideological inclination. Thus, ideology appears to have an impact mostly at the extremes and in the absence of partisanship. Generally speaking, partisanship entails attachment to the system, while ideology, at least at the extreme levels, has anti-institutional connotations.

---

[7] The evidence on partisanship suggests that people with stronger institutional ties and greater communal involvement may also be higher in trust. The data give some support to this hypothesis, but the relationships are weak. Thus the general confidence level rose slightly as respondents' organizational memberships increased, from 28 percent "high" among those with no memberships to 34 percent "high" for those with six or more memberships. Persons who attended religious services regularly were somewhat higher in confidence (33 percent "high") than those who said they never attended (22 percent). Individuals who described their religious preferences as strong were a bit more trusting (34 percent "high") than those who said their views were "not very strong" (29 percent).

Voter participation, however, seemed to make very little difference. Using the combined 1973–77 surveys, the data showed no difference between eligible electors who recalled having voted for President in the 1972 election and those who said they did not go to the polls. In the 1977 survey, those who reported having voted in the 1976 Presidential election showed slightly more confidence (36 percent "high") than those who acknowledged abstaining (32 percent).

Media involvement was also weakly related to trust. Belief in institutions was slightly greater among those who watched six hours or more of television on an average day (35 percent "high") than among those who spent two to five hours a day in front of a television set (29 percent), or who watched television less than one hour per day (26 percent). People who indicated they read a newspaper every day scored 30 percent "high" on the confidence scale, compared with 28 percent "high" for those who read newspapers irregularly and 24 percent for those who said they never read a newspaper. Overall, there may be some validity to the hypothesis that involvement increases trust, but it does not appear to be an important explanatory factor.

The Influence of Psychological Factors

Confidence is really as much psychological as sociological or political. Perhaps those who exhibit strong trust in others and a high degree of personal satisfaction carry this optimism over to their evaluations of institutions.

Both psychological conditions, trust in others and personal satisfaction, have external and internal components. People's sense of well-being, happiness, and satisfaction with their jobs and incomes are partly personality characteristics, but they also reflect the objective environment. When there is widespread economic or physical insecurity—a depression, a war, a period of social upheaval—one would expect the aggregate level of personal satisfaction to decline, since everyone is threatened and everyone is likely to suffer. Similarly, trust in others is partly a personality characteristic, an "outlook on life." Certain types of people—the better educated, for instance—find the world less threatening. They say that others try to be fair and helpful, that people care about each other and can be counted on, that things have been getting better, not worse, and that one can look with hope to the future. But these attitudes, too, are sensitive to the external environment. If things are going badly, if people feel challenged by economic insecurity and social disruption, then their outlook on life may sour. In those instances, trust in others should go down and assessments of the present and future grow more pessimistic.

Is there any evidence that the decline of confidence coincided with a comparable decline in personal satisfaction, trust in others, or optimism? Can one argue that a loss of *personal* confidence is responsible for the loss of *public* confidence? Alternatively, is there any indication that personal and public confidence both declined in response to the same external conditions?

The first step in answering these questions is to determine whether there are any discernible trends in the data on personal trust and satisfaction. Some of the questions relating to personal trust, and many of those dealing with satisfaction, have been asked repeatedly over the years, although variations in question-wording and response-coding sometimes make precise comparisons difficult.

108

Personal Trust

Three of the questions on personal trust were included in most of the biennial national election surveys administered by the University of Michigan Survey Research Center between 1964 and 1976, in the SRC's 1971 Quality of American Life survey, and the 1973 Spring Omnibus survey. The trends for all three questions reveal a slight decline in trust from the 1960s to the 1970s. In 1964 and 1968, between 37 and 38 percent of the public, on the average, chose the less trusting answers: that most of the time people are just looking out for themselves (rather than trying to be helpful); that most people would try to take advantage of you if they got the chance (rather than be fair); and that you cannot be too careful in dealing with people. The average percentage giving mistrusting responses rose to 41 in 1971 and 45–56 in 1972, 1973, and 1974. It then fell slightly, to 42 percent, in 1976.[8]

NORC included these same questions in its annual General Social Surveys between 1972 and 1980 (with the exceptions of 1974 and 1977). The results differed somewhat from those obtained by SRC, but both polls show a lower level of trust in the 1970s than was found by SRC in the 1960s. For instance, the SRC surveys taken in 1964, 1966, and 1968, reported, on the average, 13 percent more support for the view that "people try to be helpful" than for the opinion that "people are mostly just looking out for themselves." In the SRC polls for 1971 through 1976, on the average, positive responses outweighed negative responses by only 6 percent. In the six NORC polls between 1972 and 1980, positive responses averaged 7 percent higher.

On the question of whether most people "try to be fair" or "would try to take advantage of you if they got the chance," the 1964 and 1968 SRC polls indicated an average margin of 38 percent in favor of the positive ("fair") view: 67 to 29 percent in 1964, 67 to 30 percent in 1968. This difference shrank to an average of 22 percent in the six 1972–80 NORC polls. Finally, in 1964, 1966, and

[8] For trends on these items, see Philip E. Converse, Jean D. Dotson, Wendy J. Hoag, and William H. McGee III, *American Social Attitudes Data Sourcebook 1947–1978* (Cambridge, Mass.: Harvard University Press, 1980), pp. 28–33. Trends on a composite "Trust in People Index" are reported on pp. 34–37. The authors report that "interpersonal trust suffered something of a decline in the early 1970s, by comparison with its values in the 1960s. Whether 1976 has represented a significant rebound or not remains to be seen with subsequent updates of these series" (p.2).

1968, the SRC data revealed that more Americans felt "most people can be trusted" than said "you can't be too careful in dealing with people." The average margin was 10 percent in favor of the "trusting" response. In the 1971 through 1974 SRC surveys, more people chose the "mistrusting" alternative, by a mean difference of 6 percent. Two years later, the "trusting" response won again, but only by 5 percent. In each of the six NORC polls between 1972 and 1980, the "mistrusting" response prevailed, by an average margin of 9 percent.

None of the other trust questions, including those designed to measure people's sense of "anomia" (social isolation or disorientation), was administered to a national sample during the 1960s. Anomia, as measured in NORC surveys, was, however, quite high during the 1970s. On the average, a 72 percent majority agreed with the view, "These days a person doesn't really know whom he can count on" in polls taken in 1973, 1974, and 1976. Majorities of between 56 and 58 percent said that "the lot of the average man is getting worse, not better" (1973, 1974, 1976, 1977, and 1980), and that "most people really don't care what happens to the next fellow" (1973, 1974, and 1976). An average of 42 percent endorsed the despairing sentiment, "You sometimes can't help wondering whether anything is worthwhile any more" (1973, 1974, and 1976). And 41 percent, on the average, felt that "it's hardly fair to bring a child into the world with the way things look for the future" (1973, 1974, 1976, 1977, and 1980). Agreement—the "anomic" response —rose between 1973 and 1974, stayed about the same in 1976, fell in 1977, and increased in 1980.

Thus there is evidence of a modest decline in personal trust from the 1960s to the 1970s, although it was hardly as sharp as the loss of confidence in institutions and leaders. Since the level of mass education has been gradually rising, the fall-off in trust is especially noteworthy. The sense of optimism in the American public —the tendency to express hopeful feelings and faith in others— has obviously not grown apace with education.

Sense of Alienation

There is additional evidence of increasing alienation in the American public. The Harris poll has used a battery of items to measure alienation almost every year since 1966. These ask people whether they feel that: "What I think doesn't count any more,"

"The rich get richer and the poor get poorer," "The people running the country don't really care what happens to me," "Most people with power try to take advantage of people such as myself," and whether the respondent feels "left out of things" going on around him or her. The average percentage expressing disaffection on these items increased from 29 percent in 1966 to 59 percent in 1977 and 62 percent in 1978 and 1980. Most of this increase took place between 1966 and 1972, when the average level of disaffection rose 20 points—in tandem with deteriorating confidence in institutions. But the movement upward continued into the 1970s, with alienation increasing an additional 17 points between 1972 and 1978. On the average, alienation rose 3 percent each year between 1972 and 1978 and then leveled off between 1978 and 1980.

The Harris alienation items have a strong evaluative component. They express alienation *from* something, namely, an external environment that is seen as hostile or indifferent: "the people running the country," "people with power," "the rich," "things going on," etc. There is also a significant evaluative component to the SRC–NORC trust items. Most of them involve perceptions of prevailing social conditions: "the lot of the average man," "the way things look for the future," and whether "most people" care about others, try to be helpful, can be counted on, try to be fair, or can be trusted. These questions are not simply cognitive or expressions of personality; they involve a view of reality, namely, that things are not going well, that the present is not good and the future does not look much better. The results suggest that the American people, though increasingly well educated, feel increasingly powerless.

Happiness

Is there any evidence that Americans are less happy than they used to be? Relevant data have been gathered by different survey organizations, all of which have given their respondents three choices: "Taken all together, how would you say things are these days—would you say that you are very happy, pretty happy, or not too happy?" This question was first asked in 1957, by the University of Michigan Survey Research Center; the results showed 35 percent "very happy," 54 percent "pretty happy," and 11 percent "not too happy," or a 24 percent margin of positive over negative responses. The same question was included in Gallup polls in 1963, 1964, and 1965. Gallup's results show between 30 and 38 percent of the public in the early 1960s saying "very happy"; the average figures were 33 percent "very happy" and 16 percent "not too happy." The margin of positive over negative responses, now 17 percent, had fallen slightly since the 1957 poll.

Both NORC and SRC continued asking this question in the 1970s. In the eight annual NORC General Social Surveys taken between 1972 and 1980, the percentages describing themselves as "very happy" again varied between 30 (1972) and 38 (1974), with an average of 34. The mean figure for "not too happy" was 13 percent. The SRC polls (one in 1971, two in 1972, and two in 1976) averaged lower at both ends of the scale: 28 percent "very happy" and 10 percent "not too happy." Overall, the SRC polls from the 1970s averaged an 18 percent positive margin, while the favorable margin for the NORC polls during this same period was 21 percent. At the other end of the scale, the mean percentage of the public describing themselves as "not too happy" was 16 in the 1963–65 polls and 12 in the 1972–80 surveys. Thus there is no evidence of any sharp decline in self-described happiness between the early 1960s and the 1970s. The distribution of responses in each period was just about the same, one third of the public claiming to be "very happy," just over half claiming to be "pretty happy," and about one in seven describing himself as "not too happy."

A few Gallup polls taken earlier did obtain somewhat higher percentages describing themselves as "very happy." For instance, in a 1956 poll, 54 percent called themselves "very happy." In a 1963 poll, 47 percent chose that response. However, in these earlier Gallup polls, the response categories were slightly different. The middle category was "fairly happy" rather than "pretty happy," as in the later Gallup and NORC questions. It is likely that respondents treated "fairly happy" as a more negative assessment than "pretty happy." When "fairly happy" was the second alternative, some respondents on the borderline probably said they were "very happy." In 1977, Gallup repeated the happiness question using the earlier specification, i.e., "very happy," "fairly happy," or "not too happy." The results showed 42 percent choosing "very happy," where NORC the same year reported 35 percent "very happy" when, as usual, "pretty happy" was the second alternative.

The same type of wording effect can be seen at the negative end of the scale. In the early Gallup versions of the happiness question, the proportions choosing the least happy responses were relatively small: 5 to 7 percent. But these responses were strongly negative: "not very happy" (1956) and "not happy" (1963). In the more recent questions, a less drastic negative category was used, "not too happy." With this phrasing, the negative response attracted between 10 and 17 percent of the public. Here, as in other cases mentioned earlier, the subtleties of question-wording have an impact on the distribution of replies. Results can be compared only where response categories remain exactly the same. As noted, such a comparison reveals no important trend in self-described happiness between the early 1960s and the 1970s.[9]

Job Satisfaction

Nor does there appear to be any major shift in the area of job satisfaction. The Gallup Organization dealt with job satisfaction as far back as 1950: "How much pleasure and satisfaction do you get from your work—a lot, a fair amount, or very little?" A majority, 56 percent, replied "a lot," while 32 percent said "a fair amount," and 10 percent "very little." The two positive responses summed to 88 percent. Between 1963 and 1971, Gallup asked a similar question but with only two choices: "On the whole, would you say that you are satisfied or dissatisfied with the work you do?" The percentage satisfied ranged between 82 and 90 in every poll, av-

[9] For this same reason, no direct comparison can be made between a University of Michigan question used to gauge "life satisfaction" in 1968–72 and a similar question asked by the Opinion Research Corporation in 1973–77. The Michigan SRC question asked: "In general, how satisfying do you find the way you're spending your life these days? Would you call it completely satisfying, pretty satisfying, or not very satisfying?" About two-thirds of the public consistently chose the middle response, "pretty satisfying." In four polls taken between 1968 and 1972, the responses averaged 21 percent "completely satisfying," 67 percent "pretty satisfying," and 12 percent "not very satisfying." The ORC question allowed four responses: "All in all, how satisfied are you with the kind of life you currently have—very satisfied, fairly satisfied, fairly dissatisfied, or very dissatisfied?" The averages across three ORC polls taken in 1973, 1975, and 1977 were 41 percent "very satisfied," 46 percent "fairly satisfied," and 10 percent "fairly" or "very" dissatisfied. The responses for 1973 and 1977 were similar, but the percentage "very satisfied" declined to 35 in 1975, most likely because of the recession. Note that, even with four available responses, the percentage of the public classifying themselves in the most positive category, "very satisfied," was quite high (between 35 and 46 percent). This is significantly higher than the percentage in the top category of the University of Michigan question (21, on the average). The explanation is probably that "completely satisfying" in the Michigan version is a more extreme response than "very satisfied" in the ORC question.

eraging 86 percent overall. An average of 9 percent claimed to be dissatisfied with their work.

The question about work posed by NORC in the 1972–80 General Social Surveys allowed four responses: "very satisfied," "moderately satisfied," "a little dissatisfied," or "very dissatisfied." The percentage giving positive answers—"very" or "moderately" satisfied—averaged 86, while 14 percent said they were dissatisfied in some degree. The slight increase in negative replies (from 9 to 14 percent) is probably due to methodological differences between Gallup and NORC. The Gallup polls averaged 5 percent "don't know" responses, while less than 1 percent were coded "don't know" by NORC. Also, the NORC question allowed people to say they were "a little dissatisfied" with their work; this option undoubtedly produced a larger volume of negative assessments. NORC had asked their four-response version once before, in 1966. The results—87 percent "satisfied," 13 percent "dissatisfied"—were almost exactly the same as those obtained in the 1972–80 series. Finally, SRC reports almost no change in job satisfaction between the 1950s, when the question was asked twice (1953 and 1957), and the 1970s, when it was included five times (1971–76). The margin of satisfaction over dissatisfaction averaged 79 to 8 percent in the 1950s and 78 to 9 percent in the 1970s, with 12–13 percent in both periods giving neutral or ambivalent answers.

Thus, whenever the question has been asked, an overwhelming majority of Americans—usually 80 to 90 percent—have said they are satisfied with the work they do. To some extent, this is because a positive answer serves to reduce dissonance in people's self-image: "I must be satisfied with the work I do, or else why would I be doing it?" In any case, there is no evidence of any decline in job satisfaction over the years. In fact, the trend may be toward greater satisfaction. In the 1966 NORC poll, 40 percent described themselves as "very satisfied" with their work. That figure rose to between 47 and 54 percent in the 1970s.[10]

Financial Satisfaction

There is, however, a negative trend in the area of financial satisfaction. This finding is not surprising, given the deterioration of

[10] For charts reporting on changes in job satisfaction from 1949 to 1981 in various polls, see "Satisfaction with Work Remains High," *Public Opinion* 4 (August/September 1981), pp. 29–30.

the economy between the 1960s and the 1970s. The same question on the subject was asked by SRC every two years from 1956 to 1964, by NORC every year from 1972 to 1980 (except 1979), and by Cambridge Reports, Inc., every quarter since mid-1974: "So far as you and your family are concerned, would you say that you are pretty well satisfied with your present financial situation, more or less satisfied, or not satisfied at all?" The percentage of respondents "pretty well satisfied" averaged 41 in the 1956–64 SRC polls. The average was 32 percent in the 1972–80 NORC surveys. The same average was obtained in the twenty quarterly CRI studies beginning in mid-1974. At the other end of the scale, an average of 19.5 percent said they were "not at all satisfied" with their financial situation in the 1956–64 period. That percentage rose to an average of 24 in the 1972–80 NORC polls and 29 in the 1974–79 CRI ones. According to the quarterly CRI results, the proportion "not at all satisfied" grew to as much as one third of the public during the recessionary period, 1975–77.

The evidence of declining satisfaction is somewhat weaker with respect to *changes* in people's financial situation. A question posed by SRC every two years between 1956 and 1964 and by NORC in the 1972–80 General Social Surveys inquired: "During the last few years, has your financial situation been getting better, getting worse, or has it stayed the same?" The data show very little change between the 1956–64 and the 1972–80 series. In the earlier SRC polls, the averages were 38 percent "getting better" and 19 percent "getting worse," a margin of 19 points. In the later NORC ones, the averages were 38 percent "getting better" and 21 percent "getting worse," a difference of 17. The data just presented from these two organizations revealed a decline in people's assessment of their current financial positions (less satisfaction). But there is no comparable falloff in people's perceptions of changes in their financial situations.

SRC has also used a slightly different question in polls taken almost every year since 1947: "Would you say that you and your family are better off or worse off financially now than you were a year ago?" This version differs from the "change" question just reported in two ways: the reference is to the situation "a year ago" rather than "during the last few years," and therefore measures a shorter-term trend, and the option "stayed the same" is not offered in this question (although it was always coded). This latter version was also asked by the Opinion Research Corporation every two years between 1961 and 1979 (except 1971) and by Cambridge Reports, Inc., quarterly since 1974.

In the thirty-four-year SRC time series, the percentage claiming to be better off financially than a year ago has not varied a great deal. In thirteen polls taken between 1947 and 1959, that figure averaged 34 percent. The mean response was 35 percent during the 1960s (9 polls) and also 35 percent during the 1970s (8 polls). The ORC surveys show almost exactly the same results: an average of 34 percent felt better off from 1961 to 1969 and an unchanging 34 percent felt better off between 1973 and 1979. Two SRC polls taken in October 1980 and 1981, however, do report a drop down to 32 percent in the first survey and 31 percent a year later.

However, the number claiming to be *worse off* financially compared with a year ago has shown significant variation. In the SRC time series, that response averaged 30 percent between 1947 and 1959. It fell to only 20 percent during the prosperous 1960s and then went back up to 31 percent in the economically distressed 1970s. The ORC findings confirm this pattern. They show an average of 18 percent saying they felt "worse off" in the 1960s, a figure that increased to 29 percent in the 1970s. The quarterly CRI polls are consistent with the others taken during the 1970s: 31 percent, on the average, claimed to be "worse off" than a year before. The two SRC surveys of 1980–81 report an average of 39 percent saying "worse off."

It is clear from this evidence that the 1970s were a period of greater economic dissatisfaction than the 1960s. The SRC time series suggests that the 1970s were about the same as the 1950s. During the 1950s, the figure for those responding "better off" averaged 4 percent higher than the figure for those responding "worse off." In the 1960s, this difference increased to 15 percentage points. In the 1970s, the margin went back down to 4 points. The 1960s appear to have been an interlude of perceived high prosperity. The 1980s, however, begin with a larger percentage, 8, answering "worse off" than "better off," or worse than was the case in the 1970s. Seemingly, the combination of high prices, high interest rates, and growing unemployment are deepening the negative mood among the public.

The SRC data also reveal a diminishing difference in perceived financial well-being by race prior to the 1980s. Before 1970, blacks were consistently more negative than whites in evaluating their financial progress. After 1970, the difference between blacks and whites almost disappeared. Thus, from 1947 through 1959, blacks averaged 15 percent more negative than whites. In the 1960s, the average racial disparity was 10 percent. In the 1970s, blacks were only 2.5 percent more negative than whites in assessing their financial well-being. The prosperity of the 1960s, accompanied as it was by a revolution in race relations, clearly had a powerful impact on black Americans' sense of progress and optimism. However, a difference between the races (6 percent) appeared in polls taken just before the 1980 election and became even more marked in one conducted in 1981, when blacks were 21 percent less optimistic about their economic prospects than whites. The economic adversities of the 1980s have heightened the racial disparity in perceptions of economic well-being. That disparity appears to have grown larger under the Reagan Administration.

Thus, the data indicate that any decline in satisfaction between the 1960s and the 1970s has been limited to the financial realm, with no evidence of a decline in work satisfaction or in general happiness. And within the financial realm, the evidence of dissatisfaction is highly specific. During the 1970s, people were somewhat less pleased with their financial situations and somewhat more inclined to say that things had gotten worse in the past year. But financial satisfaction still tended to outweigh dissatisfaction, and people's longer-range assessment of their economic position —what has been happening "during the past few years"—showed no marked fall-off after the early 1960s. The sense of grievance with the economy was highly specific and does not seem to have spilled over into a general feeling of personal discontent. A private versus public distinction may apply here: "my life is going well, but the conditions prevailing in the country are not good and they are having a bad effect on my financial situation." The trouble, in other words, appears to be with things "out there."

Personal Satisfaction, Trust, and Confidence in Institutions

The relationship between psychological attitudes and general confidence in institutions turns out to be strong and consistent. For instance, in the NORC data:

- Those who described themselves as "very happy" were higher in confidence (37 percent "high") than those who felt "pretty happy" (27 percent) or "not too happy" (25 percent).

- People who were "pretty well satisfied" with their present financial situation scored higher on the confidence scale (36 percent "high") than those who were "more or less satisfied" (29 percent). The least confident were those "not satisfied at all" with their economic condition (26 percent).

- Those whose financial situation was "getting better" were above average in confidence (34 percent), while those whose situation had "stayed the same" were in between (30 percent, or exactly average). Confidence was low among those who said that their financial situation was "getting worse" (25 percent with "high" confidence scores).

- There was a moderately strong relationship between belief in institutions and job satisfaction. Respondents in the NORC surveys were asked every year to describe themselves as either "very satisfied," "moderately satisfied," "a little dissatisfied," or "very dissatisfied" with their work. As job dissatisfaction increased, the level of confidence in institutions fell, from 35, to 27, to 24, to 23 percent scoring "high" on the confidence index.

These four measures of personal satisfaction were combined into a single index of personal satisfaction. Respondents in the 1973–77 surveys were classified into five categories, from "very low" to "very high" in terms of personal satisfaction, each group constituting one fifth of the combined sample. As might be expected, confidence in institutions rose steadily as satisfaction increased. Among persons grouped as "very low" in satisfaction, 24 percent expressed a high level of confidence in institutions. The percentage "high" was 25 for those "low" in satisfaction, 30 for those in the middle category, 34 for those in the "high" category, and 41 among those "very high" in satisfaction. Thus, there appears to be a link between belief in institutions on the one hand and people's satisfaction with their lives, their work, and their financial situations on the other.

A second set of psychological factors was also related to confidence in institutions. These had to do with optimism and trust in others:

- "Would you say that most of the time people try to be helpful, or that they are mostly just looking out for themselves?" Confidence scores were higher among those who said that people try to be helpful (32 percent "high" confidence) than among those who felt that people mostly look out for themselves (24 percent "high" confidence).

• "Do you think that most people would try to take advantage of you if they got a chance, or would they try to be fair?" Among those who believed that people would try to take advantage of you, the percentage "high" in confidence was 23.5. It rose to 31 percent among those who thought others would try to be fair to them.

• "Generally speaking, would you say that most people can be trusted or that you can't be too careful in dealing with people?" Individuals who felt that "most people can be trusted" scored 32.5 percent "high" on the general index of confidence, while those who said "you can't be too careful" came out only 24 percent "high."

The three trust questions and the four "anomia" items discussed earlier, all of which were positively intercorrelated, were combined into a personal trust scale.[11] Again, respondents were classified into five equal categories, from those "very low" to those "very high." Here too, confidence in institutions rose as personal trust increased. Twenty-four percent of those "very low" in trust were "high" in confidence. That figure increased to 26 percent among those "low" in personal trust, 33 percent in the middle and "high" categories, and 37 among those in the "very high" category.

Thus, the data do reveal a relationship between personal and institutional trust. People who trust others, who think that most individuals try to be fair and helpful, and who express a sense of optimism about the present and the future also voice higher confidence in those running our major institutions. Favorable sentiments toward institutional leaders are consistently lower among those who tend to be mistrustful of others, suspicious, and pessimistic in their personal outlook.

Personal satisfaction and personal trust both seem to raise the level of confidence in institutions. They also correlate moderately with each other ($r = .29$) and with education: $r = .33$ for education and trust, $r = .14$ for education and satisfaction. As education increases, so does trust in others and personal satisfaction. Using

[11] Each statement was included in at least three of the four surveys (1973, 1974, 1976, and 1977). One additional anomia statement showed a very high correlation with the general index of confidence: "Most public officials are not really interested in the problems of the average man." The average confidence factor score was -13 among those who agreed with this statement and $+37$ among those who disagreed. This item was left out of the trust index, however, because it was felt to be too close in meaning to confidence in institutions. Unlike the other anomia statements, this one involved the evaluation of leaders of a particular institution, namely, government (public officials).

multiple regression analysis, it is possible to relate all three variables simultaneously to the general index of confidence. The results show that personal trust and satisfaction both have a modest but significant impact on confidence in institutions, controlling for each other and for education.

Moreover, the impact of education becomes a bit more negative, and significant, when trust and satisfaction are controlled. There appears to be some validity to the argument that the less well educated and the less sophisticated are more likely to express a "naive faith" that the people running our major institutions know what they are doing. Those at higher educational levels are less likely to say that they have "a great deal of confidence" in the people running things. This relationship did not show up at first because the better educated also show higher personal satisfaction and greater trust in others. These factors increase confidence in institutions and therefore counteract the negative effect of education. Figure 4-2 reveals that, when all three variables are taken into consideration simultaneously, each has a distinct impact: education (negative), and personal satisfaction and trust (both positive). Thus, there apparently is a link between personal optimism and state of well-being, on the one hand, and evaluations of institutions, on the other.

In sum, the general sense of confidence does not appear to be strongly rooted in social groups, since most social and economic variables show no correlation with it. Political factors have a mixed effect: partisans on both sides tend to be somewhat higher in trust, while ideologues of the left and right are, in the absence of strong partisan influences, relatively negative in their assessment of our major institutions. The strongest correlates, however, are *psychological:* a general feeling of confidence in institutions seems to derive from a personal outlook of optimism, satisfaction, and trust. Nevertheless, these psychological factors, while interesting, still cannot explain the situation of declining confidence in institutions after the mid-1960s. Personal optimism, satisfaction, and trust show no evidence of having deteriorated very markedly during the same period when confidence in institutions was collapsing.

Confidence: General and Specific

The index of confidence that we have been examining is indeed general. It combines feelings about twelve quite disparate insti-

FIGURE 4–2
General Index of Confidence in Institutions, by Personal Trust, Personal Satisfaction, and Education

Figures show percentage "High" on general index of confidence (overall 30%).

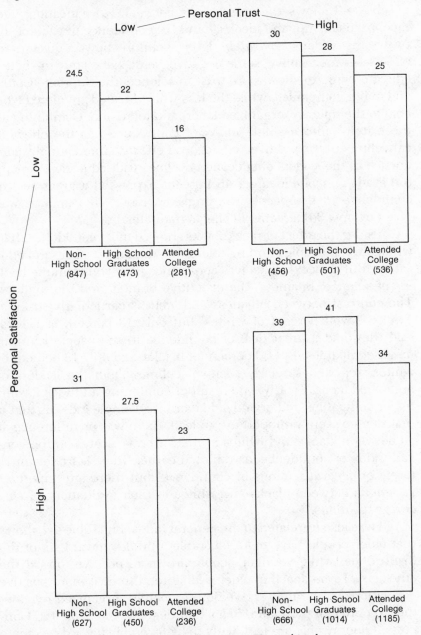

Source: NORC General Social Surveys, 1973–77, combined.

tutions. That is one problem in explaining it sociologically and politically. If feelings about two institutions have opposite correlates, those effects will be canceled out in the general index. Table 4-2 reveals that this is precisely what happens.

Table 4-2 shows the correlations between (a) education, age, race, partisanship, and ideology and (b) confidence in each of the twelve institutions *separately*. Every column shows a diversity of effects—some positive, some negative, some zero. Thus the better educated tend to show more trust in science, the Supreme Court, and major companies, while the less well educated are more favorable to the military, organized labor, and television. Combining all these items into a single index of confidence has the effect of canceling out the positive and negative effects. (Interestingly, confidence in the leaders of education declines with education. Among the grade school-educated, 45 percent expressed a great deal of confidence in the people running education. That answer was given by only 34 percent of college graduates.)

Consider the effect of race. Blacks showed more confidence than whites in the people running television, organized labor, and education. But they exhibited less confidence than whites in the leaders of science, business, the executive branch, and the military. The contrast between business and labor is particularly striking. Twenty-seven percent of whites, but only 13 percent of blacks, said they had a great deal of confidence in the people running major companies. But 20 percent of blacks, and only 13 percent of whites, reported similarly positive feelings about the leaders of organized labor. Clearly, one result of combining attitudes toward major companies and organized labor into a single index is that it makes race seem unimportant; indeed, there was no difference at all between blacks and whites in their average scores on the general index of confidence, as reported earlier. Race is irrelevant in terms of *general* feelings of confidence, but there are important variations between blacks and whites in their evaluations of *specific* institutions.

Age was also unrelated to the general index, but Table 4-2 shows that older people have more favorable attitudes toward six of the institutions, while younger people are more positive toward the other six. To be specific, older people tend to give more positive evaluations of the military, major companies, organized religion, the executive branch, and, to a slight degree, education and Congress. Older people are less likely to be favorable toward medicine

TABLE 4-2
Correlates of Confidence in Specific Institutions, 1973–77

Confidence in People Running:	Correlations with:				
	Education +more; -less	Age +older; -younger	Race +black; -white	Partisanship +Republican; -Democrat	Ideology +conservative; -liberal
Scientific community	+.27	-.09	-.40	+.07	-.01
U.S. Supreme Court	+.12	-.05	-.06	+.00	-.07
Major companies	+.08	+.12	-.29	+.14	+.17
Medicine	+.03	-.15	.00	+.04	-.01
Executive branch of the federal government	.00	+.08	-.14	+.14	+.10
Press	-.01	-.04	-.04	-.14	-.14
Congress	-.03	+.02	-.02	-.12	-.05
Organized religion	-.05	+.12	+.02	+.01	+.07
Education	-.07	+.03	+.19	-.07	-.04
Television	-.14	-.02	+.24	-.10	-.06
Organized labor	-.15	-.04	+.21	-.21	-.12
Military	-.21	+.12	-.10	+.02	+.17

Source: Five annual NORC General Social Surveys (1973–77).

1. N = 7,507 respondents interviewed in five surveys. For the ideology correlations, N = 6,003 (four surveys, 1974–77). Because the number of respondents interviewed varied each year between 1,484 and 1,530, an equalizing weight was applied to give each annual survey the same weight.

2. Figures are gamma coefficients.

3. Institutions are ordered according to their correlation with education.

(for reasons that are not difficult to imagine) and science (possibly because they are less well educated). Older people are also slightly less well disposed toward the Supreme Court, the press, organized labor, and television. Thus, trust in some institutions goes up with age, while faith in others goes down. Confidence in all of them combined shows no relationship at all with age.

Partisanship and ideology are similar in their effects. Republicans and conservatives have higher confidence in people running major companies, while Democrats and liberals are more favorable to the leaders of organized labor. Military leaders receive stronger support from conservatives than from liberals; 41 percent of the former, but only 31 percent of the latter, said they had a great deal of confidence in military leaders. There was almost no difference, however, between Democrats and Republicans in their evaluations of the military; 40 percent of Republicans and 39 percent of Democrats expressed a great deal of confidence in military leaders.

The executive branch was in the hands of the Republicans throughout most of the period of these surveys. Therefore, conservatives and Republicans tended to be more favorable toward it. (In the 1977 and 1978 NORC surveys, which took place during a Democratic Administration, Democrats and liberals were more positive toward the executive branch.) Congress, which was under the control of the Democratic Party throughout, received higher ratings from liberals and Democrats. Liberals were slightly more approving of the Supreme Court (38 percent expressed high confidence in it, compared with 33 percent of conservatives), but there was no partisan difference over the Court.

Conservative-liberal and Democratic-Republican differences showed up quite clearly in the case of the press. Thirty-two percent of liberals, 25 percent of moderates, and only 21 percent of conservatives said they had a great deal of confidence in the people running the press. This view was expressed by 29 percent of Democrats, 25 percent of Independents, and 19 percent of Republicans. Thus there is some evidence that the press is regarded as liberal and Democratic in its biases. Alternatively, since the presidency was under the control of the Republicans throughout most of this period (which included Watergate), and since evidence presented earlier indicates that the press is perceived as a countervailing institution to the presidency, these correlations may simply be artifacts of the timing of the surveys. In 1977, however, when the Democrats were in the White House, the press continued to be more favorably regarded by Democrats and liberals. Then in 1978, when the Democratic President came under increasing criticism, the normally higher Democratic support for the press vanished, although liberals continued to be relatively favorable. This attenuation of partisan differences gives a bit of support for the second hypothesis. It is likely that both hypotheses have some validity: the press is normally seen as liberal and Democratic in its inclinations, but the by-now virtually institutionalized opposition between the press and the White House causes the press to lose some Democratic support when a Democratic President is under attack.

The point is that each institution has its own social and political bases of support. Different groups tend to support business as opposed to labor, the executive branch as opposed to the Congress, the press as opposed to the military, and so forth. There is no social location of "confidence" per se. Our earlier analysis suggested that shifts in confidence *over time* tend to be broad, general, and responsive to events in the external environment. On the other hand, we find that patterns of support for institutions *across the population* tend to be specific and distinct for each institution.

5

Personal Satisfaction
and Confidence
in the Nation

In seeking to identify the causes of the decline of Americans' confidence in their major institutions and leaders, it would be reasonable to argue that attitudes toward institutions are related to people's satisfaction with their own lives. But as we shall see in this chapter, such an assumption is not borne out by the evidence. Indeed, it is contradicted by the finding that most of the 1970s were characterized by negative feelings toward institutions and positive feelings about personal well-being. Let us look at the evidence.

Satisfaction with Self and Nation

The distinction between people's personal well-being and their assessment of the situation in the country as a whole comes across dramatically in many surveys. Three times in 1979—in February, in July (just at the time of President Carter's "malaise" speech), and again in November—the Gallup poll asked two related questions: "In general, are you satisfied or dissatisfied with the way things are going in the U.S. at this time?" and "In general, are you satisfied or dissatisfied with the way things are going in your personal life?" People's satisfaction with their personal lives was very high in all three surveys. In February, personal satisfaction outweighed dissatisfaction by 77 to 21 percent. In July, the margin was only slightly less, 73 to 23 percent, while in November it was up again, 79 to 19 percent. The poll outcome reversed, however, when people described the way they felt things were going in the country. In February, people were more dissatisfied than satisfied with the state of affairs in the country, 69 to 26 percent. By July, when the President drew attention to the "crisis of confidence," the outlook on the country was overwhelmingly negative, 84 to 12 percent, a sentiment that attenuated slightly in November to 79 to 19 percent.

Another 1979 poll, taken by NBC News and the Associated Press in November, found comparable disparities in the public's evaluation of personal and national conditions over "the last 10 years." A plurality, 43 percent, replied that their "own life" was better now than ten years ago, while only 28 percent thought the United States "is a better place to live than it was ten years ago."

NORC reported large differences in respondents' sense of personal well-being and their assessments of the society and polity. As noted in Chapter 4, eight General Social Surveys taken annually from 1972 to 1980 (except 1979) found an average of 87 percent reporting that they were "very happy" or "pretty happy." Those interviewed by NORC also expressed satisfaction with their jobs (an average of 86 percent), with "the city or place you live in" (an average of 66 percent), with their "family life" (an average of 86 percent), and with their "present financial situation" (an average of 76 percent). Curiously, the responses varied very little from year to year, although it may be noted that satisfaction with both job and financial situation went down slightly between 1978 and 1980, from 87 to 82 percent for the former and from 76 to 73 percent for the latter. Responses to the question, "During the last few years, has your financial situation been getting better, getting worse, or has it stayed the same?" were somewhat more erratic. In each of the eight surveys, however, the overwhelming majority said their financial situation had been getting better (39 percent, on the average) or had stayed the same (also 39 percent). The proportion saying "worse" moved up in the economically troubled years 1975 and 1980, from 22 to 28 percent between 1974 and 1975, and from 19 to 25 percent between 1978 and 1980.

These respondents who were so positive and optimistic about their personal situations were characteristically much more negative when evaluating the society and polity. An average of 58 percent in five surveys (1973, 1974, 1976, 1977, and 1980) agreed with the statement, "In spite of what some people say, the lot (situation/condition) of the average man is getting worse, not better." And in the same five polls, the "agree" response to the assertion, "Most public officials (people in public office) are not really interested in the problems of the average man" came out to 64 percent, on the average.

Comparable differences have been reported by the Roper Organization in eight surveys conducted at year's end between 1971 and 1980 (except 1972). Roper asked the respondents at the start of the interview, "Do you expect [next year] . . . to be a better year for you than [this year] . . . , about the same, or not as good as [this year] . . . ?" He then inquired at the end of the session, "Thinking about the country as a whole, what kind of year do you think [next year] . . . will be for the nation—better than [this year] . . . , about the same, or not as good as [this year] . . . ?" The percentage of those who replied "better" for themselves ranged from 34 to 52, for an average of 44 percent. Pessimistic answers ("not as good") varied from 5 to 24 percent, averaging 12 percent. But each year, those queried were much less optimistic about what the following year would mean for the nation. The range of those replying that the country as a whole would have a better year ran from 12 percent to 47 percent, for an average of 30 percent, while between 12 and 62 percent said the next year would be "not as good" for the country, for a mean response of 27 percent.

Similar discrepancies can be seen in the results of other surveys conducted during the 1970s. In 1978, Gallup asked people how they felt about a number of subjects relating to the nation and their own personal lives. Respondents were asked to rate items on a scale from 0 to 10, with 10 representing extreme satisfaction. Only one third, 32 percent, expressed high satisfaction (scale scores 8 to 10) with "the way democracy is working in this country." But much larger proportions were highly positive about their "family life" (79 percent), their "health" (67), their "neighborhoods" (61), their "housing" (60), "this country as a place to live" (57), and their "life overall" (49). In other words, the broader and more general the subject, the less positive the evaluation.

In 1972, the Survey Research Center of the University of Michigan inquired of a national cross section how satisfied they felt with "the way our national government is operating," with "life in the United States today," with "yourself," with "your own family life," and with "your job." Almost two thirds, 65 percent, professed to be "delighted" or "pleased" with their jobs. Nearly as many, 63 percent, were positive about their "family life," and close to half (48 percent) felt this way about their general life situation ("yourself"). But only 29 percent said they were "delighted" or "pleased" with the state of the country generally, and only a tiny minority, 9 percent, reported the same feelings about "the operation of the national government" at that time. Or, to look at the same picture negatively, two thirds of the public, 66 percent, had ambivalent or critical feelings about the government; one third, 32 percent, were uncertain or unhappy about "life in the United States"; one fifth, 21 percent, had a comparable reaction to their personal state generally; less than a fifth, 17 percent, felt neutral or negative about their job; and only 9 percent gave such an assessment of their family life.[1]

In November 1979, the CBS News/*New York Times* poll asked people whether they thought "the economy is getting better, getting worse, or staying about the same." The question was then repeated with respect to "the financial situation in your household." The public's assessment of the national economy was considerably more pessimistic than people's judgment of their own financial situations. Seventy percent felt that the economy was getting worse, while only 33 percent thought their own financial situation was getting worse. Five percent believed the economy was getting better, but that view was held by 17 percent in reference to their own financial situation.

Here is how the research firm of Yankelovich, Skelly & White reported the findings of a survey taken in the winter of 1974–75, when the recession was becoming severe:

> Despite national economic and financial stress, the large majority of men and women report their *own* families are still doing well. A remarkable 83 percent report that their families are in good shape, but an equal number (79) feel that things are going badly in the country. Undoubtedly this sense of family well-being is an important ballast in these times of uncertainty, and fortunately, this sense of family prevails among diverse income and age groups, and is shared by other family members as well.[2]

[1] Frank M. Andrews and Stephen B. Withey, *Social Indicators of Well-Being* (New York: Plenum Press, 1976), pp. 249–68.
[2] *The General Mills American Family Report 1974–75* (New York: Yankelovich, Skelly, and White, 1975), p. 35.

Personal Views of the Past, Present, and Future

If personal dissatisfaction is not especially high, where does the public get the idea that the system as a whole is not functioning properly? We can approach this question more systematically by examining people's assessment of their own lives and of the national situation over many years. The best evidence on these trends comes from the "self-anchoring ladder scale" first developed by Hadley Cantril, F. P. Kilpatrick, Lloyd A. Free, and William Watts of the Institute for International Social Research.[3] The "ladder scale" originally applied to people's judgments about their lives. Respondents were shown a picture of a ladder, with steps numbered from 0 at the bottom (the worst possible situation) to 10 at the top (the best possible situation). They were then asked the following question:

> Here is a ladder representing the "ladder of life." Let's suppose the top of the ladder represents the *best* possible life for you; and the bottom, the *worst* possible life for you. On which step of the ladder do you feel you personally stand at the present time? On which step would you say you stood *five years ago*? Just as your best guess, on which step do you think you will stand in the future, say about *five years from now*? (Emphasis in original)

Responses were reported in the form of the mean, or average, rating given by the public to their own lives "at the present time," "five years in the past," and "five years in the future."

Evaluations of People's Own Lives

The same question was asked by the Institute for International Social Research in 1959 and 1964 and, beginning in 1971, by the Gallup poll on behalf of Potomac Associates.[4] Since 1974, Cambridge Reports, Inc. (CRI) has been administering the ladder scale quarterly to a national cross section. Figure 5-1 traces the mean ratings the public has given to their lives "at the present time," "five years in the past," and "five years in the future," from 1959

---

[3] See William Watts and Lloyd A. Free, *State of the Nation III* (Lexington, Mass.: Lexington Books, 1978), pp. 3–6.

[4] Watts and Free, *State of the Nation III*, pp. 203–8.

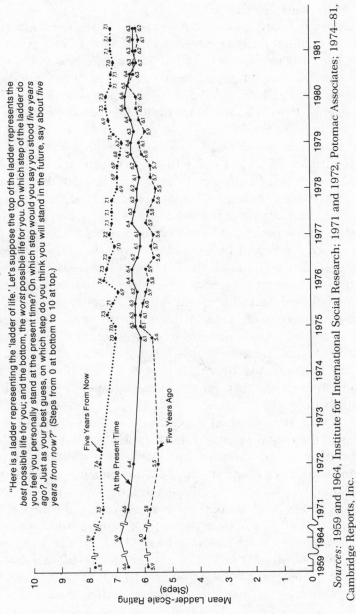

FIGURE 5-1

"Your Life" at the Present Time, Five Years Ago, and Five Years from Now: Average Ladder-Scale Ratings, 1959–81

"Here is a ladder representing the 'ladder of life.' Let's suppose the top of the ladder represents the *best* possible life for you; and the bottom, the *worst* possible life for you. On which step of the ladder do you feel you personally stand at the present time? On which step would you say you stood *five years ago?* Just as your best guess, on which step do you think you will stand in the future, say about *five years from now?*" (Steps from 0 at bottom to 10 at top.)

Five Years From Now

At the Present Time

Five Years Ago

Mean Ladder-Scale Rating (Steps)

Sources: 1959 and 1964, Institute for International Social Research; 1971 and 1972, Potomac Associates; 1974–81, Cambridge Reports, Inc.

131

to 1981. (The data for 1959 and 1964 are from the Institute for International Social Research surveys. The data for 1971 and 1972 are from the Potomac Associates polls. Beginning in 1974, the quarterly CRI polls are used.)

Figure 5-1 suggests that Americans' ratings of their own lives have remained fairly constant over the past fifteen years. During the period between 1964 and 1974, people's evaluations of their past, present, and future lives tended to decline. Average expectations for the future fell from 7.9 in 1964 to 7.0 in the third quarter of 1974. The mean rating for people's lives "at the present time" dropped from 6.9 in 1964 to 6.1 in 1974. And the average ladder position assigned to people's lives five years earlier went down from 6.0 in 1964 to 5.6 in 1974. Figure 5-1 also reveals that the three ratings converged during the late 1970s. Estimates of life "at the present time" have gone down slightly since 1974. Average evaluations of the near future have fallen a bit more. But ratings of the past have improved markedly.

During the period between 1959 and 1972, the three lines in Figure 5-1 were parallel: the decline in ratings occurred similarly with respect to past, present, and future. The future was rated 1.1 steps better than the present, on the average, while the present was considered 0.8 steps better than the past. Since 1974, the gaps between perceptions of past, present, and future have narrowed. Across the five surveys taken in 1980 and the first quarter of 1981, the future averaged only 0.7 steps above the present, while the present was, on the average, rated an insignificant 0.1 steps better than the past.

The year 1980 marked a significant shift in the relative evaluations of the past, present, and future. Until 1980, one pattern was consistent: on the average, the public saw the present as better than the near past and the near future as better than the present. In other words, the prevailing tendency was one of optimism; things had become better in the recent past and were expected to get better still in the near future. (Of course, this does not mean that everyone saw things this way. The trends in Figure 5-1 are averages. In other words, there were more people who saw things as improving than as getting worse.) In 1980 that pattern changed. For the first time, Americans did not rate their lives "at the present time" more favorably than their lives "five years ago." Optimism regarding the future remained, but in the last three quarters of

132

1980 and the first three quarters of 1981, Americans believed their lives had not improved over the past half decade.

Figure 5-2 slices across Figure 5-1 at three points in time: 1959, when the ladder ratings were first measured; in 1975, at the depth of the mid-decade recession; and in 1980, after almost two years of hyperinflation. The upward slope of the lines from the recent past to the present to the near future indicates that optimism was the prevailing pattern at each point. But optimism regarding the future declined from 7.8 in 1959 to 6.9 in 1975 (4th quarter) and 7.0 in 1980 (4th quarter). The fourth quarter of 1980 also marked the first and only time—to date—that people rated their own lives at present as *worse,* on the average, than they had been five years earlier.

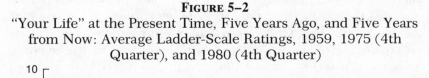

FIGURE 5–2

"Your Life" at the Present Time, Five Years Ago, and Five Years from Now: Average Ladder-Scale Ratings, 1959, 1975 (4th Quarter), and 1980 (4th Quarter)

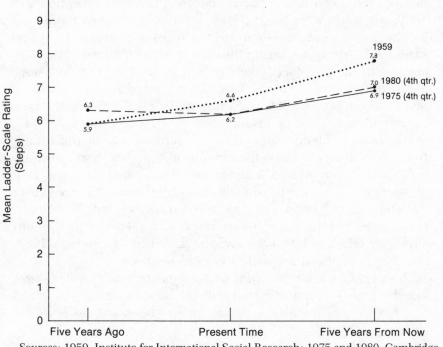

Sources: 1959, Institute for International Social Research; 1975 and 1980, Cambridge Reports, Inc.

Evaluations of the Situation of the Country

In all of these polls, the ladder question was asked a second time with reference to the country as a whole rather than to "your own life":

> Looking at the ladder again, suppose the top represents the *best* possible situation for our country; the bottom, the *worst* possible situation. Please show me on which step of the ladder you think the United States is at the present time. . . . five years ago. . . . five years from now.

The public tended to rate personal well-being and personal expectations for the near future in much more positive terms than they did the state of the nation. In every survey except the first, the mean judgment for "your own life" at present was higher than people's view of the situation in the country. On the average, across all thirty-three polls Americans put their own lives 1.5 steps higher than the situation in the country. (The only exception was 1959, when two were about the same—6.6 for "your own life," 6.7 for the country.) At the depth of the recession, in late 1974 and early 1975, and again during the double-digit inflation of late 1979 and 1980, people placed their own lives at least two full steps above the country's rating. The gap narrowed in the first three quarters of 1981, possibly reflecting initial confidence in the new President's economic program.

The same tendency showed up in anticipations for the future. In every poll, people rated their own future higher than the country's, by an average of 1.5 steps. The discrepancy between estimates of people's own future and that of the country grew to over two steps in 1979 and 1980, as inflation accelerated. This difference decreased, however, to an average of 1.4 steps in the four CRI polls taken in late 1980 and the first three quarters of 1981, i.e., the year following Ronald Reagan's election.

This evidence is consistent with the data presented earlier showing the gap between personal and public satisfaction. As Watts and Free wrote in their most recent report on the *State of the Nation*,

> Americans express a sharp dichotomy between views about their personal lives, which have remained uniformly positive and essen-

tially unchanged over the years since 1959, and their far more sober views of the state of the nation.[5]

Figure 5-3 displays the mean ladder ratings for the country from 1959 to 1981. The trends are a good deal more erratic than those for people's personal lives. The evaluations of the country show a steep decline from 1959 to the mid-1970s. In 1959, the mean for the country "at the present time" was a strongly positive 6.7. By 1971, the mean rating had fallen to a barely positive 5.4. In 1974 and 1975, when the recession hit, the average for the country fell as low as 4.3. With economic recovery in 1976 and 1977, the country's rating began to rise, reaching a peak of 5.2 in early 1977. But it began to move down again with the inflationary crisis of 1978 and 1979, falling to an average of 4.3 in 1980. As with the other evaluations, the rating for the country at present moved up slightly, to an average of 4.8, in the first three quarters of 1981.

Changes in the Pattern of Optimism

The earliest national ladder scales show the same pattern of optimism for the country as for people's personal lives; that is, the country's present was evaluated as better than its recent past, and its near future was rated higher than its present. A shift occurred sometime between 1964 and 1971. As early as 1971, the public was judging the nation's past as better than its present; this negative assessment of the present in comparison with the past did not appear in the case of people's personal lives until the end of 1980. As estimates of the present situation declined, particularly during the recession, assessments of the recent past rose. People believed things were much worse "now" than they had been before. With economic recovery in 1976 and 1977, the rating for the present went up and that for the past moved down. The two lines crossed in 1977, and it looked as if the old optimistic pattern (the present better than the past) might again emerge. But the two lines have diverged once again since 1978, and by mid-1980, the gap between ratings of the present and the past averaged nearly two steps on the ladder scale. The nation's recent past once again looked better than its present. This pattern continued into 1981, although the gap diminished after Ronald Reagan's inauguration.

[5] Watts and Free, *State of the Nation III,* p. 204.

FIGURE 5–3

"The Situation of the Country" at the Present Time, Five Years Ago, and Five Years from Now: Average Ladder-Scale Ratings, 1959–81

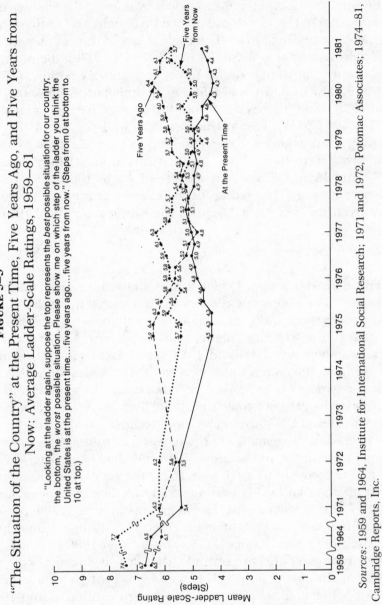

"Looking at the ladder again, suppose the top represents the *best* possible situation for our country; the bottom, the *worst* possible situation. Please show me on which step of the ladder you think the United States is at the present time....five years ago....five years from now." (Steps from 0 at bottom to 10 at top.)

Sources: 1959 and 1964, Institute for International Social Research; 1971 and 1972, Potomac Associates; 1974–81, Cambridge Reports, Inc.

One type of optimism, however, can be detected throughout this twenty-year period. The public has almost always said—even during the mid-decade recession and the inflation of the late 1970s—that the country's future will be better than its present. Generally, assessments of the present and the near future have moved in tandem. As people see the current situation getting worse, they also see the future as bleaker. That tendency has been particularly noticeable since 1977. Beginning that year, assessments of the future of the country began to fall rapidly—more quickly, in fact, than evaluations of the present.

In February and March of 1979, an unprecedented shift occurred: for the first time in this series of polls, Americans rated the near future of the United States as likely to be *worse* than the present (ratings of 4.6 for the future, 4.7 for the present). The situation improved, but only slightly, in surveys taken in the spring and summer of 1979, when assessments of the future moved just above evaluations of the present. Was the negative pattern of early 1979 a fluke, perhaps the product of sampling error or a biased sample? Apparently not, because the same relationship had been discovered a few months earlier in a study conducted by the Roper Organization for the Department of Labor. This poll, carried out in June, 1978, asked the ladder-scale question for the nation and compared the results with previous national ladder ratings. The 1978 survey showed a mean rating of 5.8 for the recent past, 5.4 for the present, and 5.3 for the near future. As the authors, Albert H. and Susan D. Cantril, noted in their analysis,

> What is new . . . and alarming is the finding that, unlike all previous measures, the public feels things are not going to get any better in the future. . . . It is the first time since these scale ratings have been obtained that the U.S. public has not looked toward some improvement in the future. In all previous measures people have tended to feel the nation would recover much of the ground lost in declines from the past to the present.[6] (Emphasis in original)

The distinctiveness of this pattern can be seen in Figure 5-4, which, like Figure 5-2, slices across the time series at three points: in 1959, 1975 (2nd quarter), and 1979 (1st quarter). The pattern for 1959 is optimistic; the slope is upward from the recent past to

---

[6] Albert H. Cantril and Susan D. Cantril, *Unemployment, Government, and the American People* (Washington, D.C.: Public Research, 1978), pp. 16–17.

FIGURE 5–4

"The Situation of the Country" Five Years Ago, at the Present
Time, and Five Years from Now: Average Ladder-Scale Ratings in
1959, 1975 (2nd Quarter), and 1979 (1st Quarter)

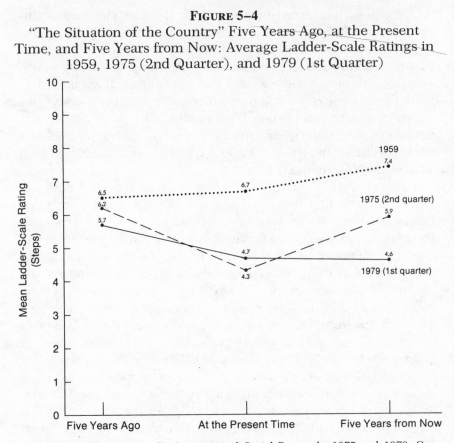

Sources: 1959, Institute for International Social Research; 1975 and 1979, Cambridge Reports, Inc.

the present to the near future. The new pattern that began to
appear sometime between 1964 and 1971 shows up clearly in
1975. It is a "V"-shaped configuration, with the present rated considerably below the recent past, but the near future rated higher
than the present. Patrick Caddell has called this a "temporary
crisis" outlook, namely, that affairs in the country are at a temporary low from which recovery will take place.[7] The shift to a predominant "temporary crisis" outlook, which occurred between the
mid-1960s and the early 1970s, represented a major change in
public attitudes toward the nation. It is this pattern that pre-

[7] Patrick H. Caddell, "Crisis of Confidence I: Trapped in a Downward Spiral,"
Public Opinion 2 (October/November 1979), p. 4.

138

vailed throughout most of the 1970s. (The "V" is not usually symmetrical, however. When times are bad, as during the 1974–75 recession and the 1978–79 inflation, the past looks better than the future. During periods of recovery, as in 1976–77, the future looks better than the past.)

The winter 1979 data show the "pessimistic" pattern that Caddell and the Cantrils found so alarming: a downward slope, with the present worse than the past and the future worse than the present. These findings marked the second major stage of deterioration in public attitudes concerning the nation. The CRI 1979 results portrayed in Figure 5-4 describe the situation that President Carter was referring to in his July 15th "malaise" speech, when he said that "for the first time in the history of our country, a majority of the people believe that the next five years will be worse than the past five years."

Ironically, given the importance President Carter assigned to the early 1979 survey results, as interpreted for him by his personal pollster, the negative pattern changed in the second half of 1979. Expectations for the country "five years from today" moved ahead of evaluations of the present, 5.0 to 4.6, in a survey taken in August and September; the margin of expectations for the future over the present improved even further, 5.3 to 4.6, in a November-December survey. During 1980 and the first three quarters of 1981, estimates for the future of the country once more moved sharply ahead of those for the present, resulting in an average difference of 0.9 steps in the seven polls. These findings compare with differences of only 0.1 steps between judgments of the present and the near future in polls taken in late 1978 and early 1979. The President had called attention to a real deterioration of public confidence, but it was apparently a temporary condition that improved within a few months.

The Impact of the Economy

So far, our interpretation has suggested that ratings of the country may be closely tied to the economic situation. Can this hypothesis be tested directly? The CSI polls have, quarterly since 1974, included a third set of ladder ratings along with those for people's perceptions of their personal lives and of the country. Respondents were also asked to rate the economic condition in the United States "at the present time," "five years ago," and "five years in the future." Evaluations of the economy correlated very closely with evaluations of the country. Across twenty-nine surveys taken between 1974 and the beginning of 1981, the correlation between mean ratings for the economy and those for the country "at the present time" was .88. Ladder positions for the economy and for the country were also strongly associated in the past and in the future: .93 for the past and .97 for the future. When Americans consider the current state of the nation, its past, and its future, their evaluations depend substantially on their views of the economy.

Ratings for personal lives and ratings for the country were less closely associated. Expectations for the future of "your own life" and the future of the nation correlated at .82. Perceptions of one's own life in the past and the country's past were less strongly linked (.66). And the correlation between personal and national ratings "at the present time" was a moderate .44.

Finally, evaluations of the economy and of people's personal lives were also only moderately associated. For the past, the correlation was .60; for the future, .54. Oddly, the relationship between evaluations of the present condition of the economy and "your own life" was negative (− .35).

All three sets of ladder ratings—for people's own lives and for the country since 1959 and for the economy since 1974—are displayed in Table 5-1. The ratings for the economy followed the same pattern as those for the country. The "temporary crisis," or "V"-shaped, pattern has prevailed since 1971, with the exception of the early 1979 poll when the "pessimistic" configuration appeared. The principal difference is that the economy was always rated slightly below the country as a whole (0.5 steps lower for the present and 0.4 steps lower for the future, on the average).

The Effects of Inflation and Unemployment

Table 5-1 also includes data on inflation and unemployment rates. The unemployment rate is for the quarter immediately preceding the survey. The inflation rate was calculated as the percentage increase in the Consumer Price Index over the two quarters preceding the survey (annualized). These data allow analysis of the relationship between each of the nine ladder-scale ratings and the economic situation at the time of each survey. Table 5-2 shows

140

the effects of inflation and unemployment on the public's mean ladder-scale ratings of their own lives, the country, and the economy, past, present, and future, across the time period of Table 5-1.

Table 5-2 reveals that inflation and unemployment affect people's ratings of their own lives, the country, and the economy in a similar manner. Inflation and unemployment both tend to depress views of the present. As either the inflation or the unemployment rate goes up, respondents offer a more negative assessment of the current state of their own lives, of the situation in the country, and of the economy. People also rate the recent past in more positive terms as the inflation rate goes up. Unemployment apparently does not relate significantly to evaluations of the past.

The inflation rate has a particularly strong impact on perceptions of the future. A high rate of inflation appears to lower the public's expectations for the future in all respects: for their own lives, for the country as a whole, and for the economy. Unemployment, on the other hand, does not appear to affect people's view of their own personal futures or of the future of the country. In fact, the economic ratings suggest that, as unemployment goes up, expectations for the future of the economy tend to improve ("things will get better").

Thus, the consequences of inflation and unemployment are in some respects parallel and in some respects divergent. Both create negative feelings about the current state of affairs, but inflation has a uniquely depressing effect on assessments of the future. These findings confirm the interpretations offered earlier of the trend lines in Figure 5-4. The effect of the 1974–75 recession was to create an extremely negative view of the way things were going in the country at that time. But ratings of the near future were only slightly affected. The inflation crisis of 1978–80 had a notably different impact. It tended to lower people's assessment of the present somewhat, but inflation had a drastic effect on people's expectations for the future. *Inflation more than anything else created the infamous, albeit temporary, "malaise" of 1979.*

Optimism and Pessimism

So far, we have examined the mean ladder-scale ratings for the entire sample. Another way of looking at the ladder ratings may clarify these relationships. The public can be divided into subgroups

TABLE 5–1

Average Ladder-Scale Ratings of "Your Life," "the Situation of the Country," and "the State of the Economy," Five Years Ago, at the Present Time, and Five Years From Now, Plus Unemployment and Inflation Rates, 1959–81

Question on "Your Life":

"Here is a ladder representing the 'ladder of life.' Let's suppose the top of the ladder represents the *best* possible life for you; and the bottom, the *worst* possible life for you. On which step of the ladder do you feel you personally stand at the present time? On which step would you say you stood *five years ago?* Just as your best guess, on which step do you think you will stand in the future, say about *five years from now?*" (Steps from 0 at bottom to 10 at top.)

Question on "the Situation of the Country":

"Looking at the ladder again, suppose the top represents the *best* possible situation for our country; the bottom the *worst* possible situation. Please show me on which step of the ladder you think the United States is at the present time . . . five years ago . . . five years from now."

Question on "the State of the Economy":

"Now once more but this time the top rung represents the best possible economic condition for the United States. The bottom rung represents the worst possible economic condition for the United States. Now I would like you to tell me on which rung you think the country is today . . . where it was five years ago . . . and where it will be five years from now."

Year	Quarter	Your Life			Country			Economy			Unemployment Rate	Inflation Rate
		5 Years Ago	At the Present Time	5 Years From Now	5 Years Ago	At the Present Time	5 Years From Now	5 Years Ago	At the Present Time	5 Years From Now		
1959	—	5.9	6.6	7.8	6.5	6.7	7.4	—	—	—	5.5	1.5
1964	—	6.0	6.9	7.9	6.1	6.5	7.7	—	—	—	5.2	1.3
1971	—	5.8	6.6	7.5	6.2	5.4	6.2	—	—	—	5.9	4.3
1972	—	5.5	6.4	7.6	5.6	5.5	6.2	—	—	—	5.6	3.3
1974	4	5.6	6.1	7.0	5.9	4.5	5.7	6.1	4.6	5.6	5.3	11.3
1975	1	6.1	6.3	7.0	6.4	4.3	5.4	6.6	4.2	5.2	8.4	12.8

Year	Q											
1975	2	6.1	6.3	7.3	6.2	4.3	5.9	6.6	4.0	5.8	8.4	7.3
1975	3	6.0	6.3	7.1	6.1	4.6	5.6	6.5	4.2	5.5	8.6	6.3
1975	4	5.9	6.2	6.9	5.8	4.6	5.4	6.1	4.2	5.2	8.6	7.3
1976	1	5.8	6.4	7.4	5.6	4.8	5.8	6.1	4.6	5.7	7.7	5.1
1976	2	5.9	6.4	7.3	5.6	4.9	5.8	5.8	4.6	5.6	7.5	3.4
1976	3	5.6	6.2	7.2	5.2	5.0	5.9	5.4	4.6	5.8	7.7	6.0
1976	4	5.7	6.1	7.0	5.1	4.9	6.0	5.3	4.5	5.7	7.8	5.1
1977	1	5.6	6.1	7.2	4.8	5.0	6.3	5.2	4.5	6.0	7.6	4.3
1977	2	5.9	6.4	7.1	5.1	5.1	5.8	5.4	4.8	5.5	7.1	8.9
1977	3	5.8	6.3	7.1	5.1	5.2	5.7	5.3	5.0	5.4	6.9	6.9
1977	4	5.6	6.2	7.1	5.1	5.1	5.7	5.2	4.9	5.5	6.8	5.0
1978	1	5.5	6.1	6.9	5.2	4.9	5.4	5.3	4.7	5.0	6.2	5.6
1978	2	5.7	6.2	6.9	5.4	4.9	5.3	5.5	4.7	5.0	6.0	7.9
1978	3	5.7	6.4	6.9	5.3	4.8	5.1	5.4	4.5	5.0	6.0	11.0
1978	4	6.0	6.4	6.8	5.7	4.9	5.0	5.8	4.6	4.8	5.8	8.7
1979	1	6.1	6.3	6.7	5.7	4.7	4.6	5.8	4.4	4.3	5.7	7.8
1979	2	5.9	6.4	7.1	5.8	4.9	5.0	5.8	4.5	4.7	5.7	11.9
1979	3	6.1	6.4	6.9	5.9	4.6	5.0	5.8	4.4	4.9	5.8	14.0
1979	4	6.2	6.6	7.3	6.0	4.6	5.3	6.1	4.3	5.0	6.0	12.5
1980	1	6.2	6.6	7.3	6.1	4.3	5.0	6.0	3.9	4.8	6.1	13.7
1980	2	6.5	6.5	7.1	6.4	4.2	5.0	6.3	3.8	4.8	7.5	16.3
1980	3	6.3	6.4	7.1	6.1	4.3	5.2	6.1	4.0	5.1	7.6	12.0
1980	4	6.3	6.2	7.0	6.1	4.4	5.7	6.0	4.0	5.6	7.6	7.9
1981	1	6.2	6.3	7.1	5.7	4.6	5.7	5.6	4.0	5.5	7.3	10.5
1981	2	6.1	6.3	7.1	5.7	4.8	5.6	5.7	4.3	5.5	7.4	9.2
1981	3	6.2	6.4	7.2	5.7	5.1	5.9	5.7	4.6	5.8	7.2	11.4
Mean		5.9	6.3	7.1	5.7	4.9	5.7	5.8	4.4	5.3	6.8	8.3

Sources: 1959 and 1964, Institute for International Social Research; 1971 and 1972, Potomac Associates; 1974–1981, Cambridge Reports, Incorporated.

TABLE 5–2
Effects of Inflation and Unemployment on
Mean Ladder-Scale Ratings, 1959–81

Mean Ladder-Scale Rating of: Y	Effect of:		R^2
	Unem- ployment X_1	Inflation X_2	
Your Life (N = 32)			
Five years ago	(.20)	.59	39%
Today	−.37	(−.05)	14%
Five years from now	(−.18)	−.50	29%
The Situation of the Country (N = 32)			
Five years ago	(−.23)	.31	15%
Today	−.44	−.70	71%
Five years from now	(−.06)	−.72	53%
Economic Condition of the Country (N = 28)			
Five years ago	.48	.59	40%
Today	−.55	−.36	54%
Five years from now	.47	−.70	46%

1. Figures are standardized regression coefficients for equations including both variables.
2. Figures in parentheses were not significant at p = .05 (two-tailed test).

based on how people perceive the recent past, the present, and the near future. Cambridge Reports, Inc., classifies respondents into four types:

1. "Optimists"—those who see the present as better than the past and anticipate that the future will be even better than the present;
2. "Steady-staters"—those who see essentially no change from the past to the present and expect no change in the future;
3. "Temporary crisis" types—those who see the present as worse than the past, but anticipate that the future will be better than the present (the "V"-shaped pattern);
4. "Pessimists"—those who see the present as worse than the past and expect the future to be worse than the present.[8]

Table 5-3 presents the percentages of "optimists," "pessimists," and "temporary crisis" types classified by Cambridge Reports, Inc., in each of their quarterly polls since 1974. ("Steady-staters" are omitted.) Respondents are grouped separately according to their

[8] Caddell, "Crisis of Confidence I," p. 4.

views of their own personal lives, the country, and the economy. As can be seen in this table, optimism has consistently outweighed pessimism in people's evaluations of their personal situations. In fact, personal optimism has usually characterized close to half of the public. On the other hand, assessments of the country reveal a shifting balance between optimism, pessimism, and the perception of a "temporary crisis." During the recession, from 1974 through early 1976, the prevailing view was that we were in a temporary crisis. In late 1976 and 1977, optimism about the country was the dominant sentiment. Close to half the public (47 percent) was hopeful for the country at the beginning of 1977, when Jimmy Carter took office. As shown in Chapter 2, this was also a period of rising confidence in institutions. But in 1978, the prevailing pattern became pessimistic. In early 1979, when the mean rating for the future of the country dipped below the rating for the present, close to half of the public could be classified as pessimistic about the country. Not until the late summer of 1979 did the "temporary crisis" view surpass pessimism about the country. It then took over again as the dominant mood through 1980 and the first three quarters of 1981. Ronald Reagan clearly contributed to renewed optimism about the future of the country during his first eight months in office.

Ratings of the economy have, overall, been more negative than those of the country. Only once in the twenty-nine CRI polls has a plurality taken an optimistic view of the economy; that was at the end of 1977, when the optimistic view just barely outweighed the attitude that we were in a temporary crisis. Generally, the economic situation has been viewed as a "temporary crisis" except during a brief pessimistic period at the end of 1978 and in early 1979. As a rule, one can usually expect the public to be most optimistic about the way things are going in their personal lives, less so about the way things are going in the country as a whole, and least optimistic about the state of the economy.

Table 5-4 relates the inflation and unemployment rates to the percentages of "optimists," "pessimists," and "temporary crisis types" in each survey. The effect of inflation can be seen quite clearly: it decreases optimism and increases pessimism about people's lives, the country, and the economy. This is simply another way of expressing the finding from Table 5-2, that inflation has a powerful effect on the way people assess the future as well as the present. (Pessimism, it should be recalled, is defined as a

TABLE 5–3

Percentage of "Optimists," "Temporary Crisis" Types, and "Pessimists" Concerning "Your Life," "the Situation of the Country," and "the State of the Economy," 1974–81

Year	Quarter	Your Life			Country			Economy		
		Optimists	Temporary Crisis	Pessimists	Optimists	Temporary Crisis	Pessimists	Optimists	Temporary Crisis	Pessimists
1974	4	48	16	22	20	45	30	16	50	28
1975	1	41	23	25	12	55	30	6	59	32
1975	2	45	23	18	18	56	22	8	70	19
1975	3	43	21	23	21	43	31	9	60	28
1975	4	45	15	23	22	36	35	12	48	35
1976	1	49	20	18	29	38	30	18	51	28
1976	2	47	19	20	30	36	28	22	47	25
1976	3	48	19	19	35	32	26	28	40	24
1976	4	47	18	21	38	32	24	26	46	23
1977	1	48	22	16	47	27	21	32	42	21
1977	2	43	20	18	39	23	30	29	32	30
1977	3	46	19	19	38	22	31	29	28	33
1977	4	47	20	19	41	21	32	34	33	26

1978	1	48	18	20	32	25	34	24	30	36
1978	2	47	17	23	30	24	38	23	31	40
1978	3	45	17	24	24	28	39	20	36	36
1978	4	39	17	28	21	25	44	13	33	44
1979	1	38	17	32	16	28	48	13	30	50
1979	2	46	19	22	19	30	41	13	35	42
1979	3	43	16	27	17	40	38	14	45	36
1979	4	44	19	22	18	44	33	12	48	35
1980	1	41	22	24	12	49	34	10	51	35
1980	2	38	23	24	11	52	32	7	59	31
1980	3	42	23	21	15	51	28	10	59	27
1980	4	37	28	22	15	56	23	11	64	20
1981	1	42	23	20	23	49	23	15	59	20
1981	2	44	24	21	26	40	26	20	50	24
1981	3	42	23	20	34	34	26	24	48	23
Mean		44	20	22	24	37	31	18	46	30

Source: Cambridge Reports, Inc.

Note: For definition of "Optimists," "Temporary Crisis" types, and "Pessimists," see p. 144.

negative view of the future in relation to the present and of the present in relation to the past.) The attitude associated with rising unemployment is that of the "temporary crisis": unemployment produces negative assessments of the present, but not of the future.

Thus the view typical of a recession such as that of the mid-1970s is that things are very bad now, but will improve. Apparently, the view that things are fairly bad now and are likely to get worse arises during a period of high inflation. One possible explanation for this difference is that the public is aware of a solution for recession and unemployment, namely, economic expansion and government spending. At the very least, the public probably remembers the New Deal (if not World War II) as the solution to the Great Depression. We know how to "cure" recessions because we got ourselves out of the Depression and subsequent, less serious downswings. As will be demonstrated, prior to 1982, the public had no comparably clear sense of how to "cure" inflation.

This is not to say that unemployment is less serious or less consequential than inflation. The analysis in Chapter 2 revealed

TABLE 5–4

Effects of Inflation and Unemployment on
Ladder-Scale Response Patterns, 1974–81

Response Type: Y	Effect of:		R^2
	Unem-ployment X_1	Inflation X_2	
Your Life			
Optimists	(−.18)	−.61	34%
Pessimists	−.31	.35	29%
Temporary Crisis	.58	.35	33%
The Situation of the Country			
Optimists	(−.12)	−.74	50%
Pessimists	−.64	.69	42%
Temporary Crisis	.57	(.03)	54%
Economic Condition of the Country			
Optimists	−.30	−.70	44%
Pessimists	−.62	.54	41%
Temporary Crisis	.74	(.06)	58%

1. Figures are standardized regression coefficients for equations including both variables.
2. Figures in parentheses were not significant at $p = .05$ (two-tailed test).
N = 28.

148

that unemployment has a stronger effect than inflation in lowering confidence in the people running our major institutions. The notion of "confidence" may have a strong "at-the-present-time" orientation. If things are bad, it is because the people controlling things are corrupt or incompetent. The solution is to replace them.

There is evidence to confirm this assertion. In late October and early November 1979, CBS News and the *New York Times* asked the ladder-scale question in their poll. (Since the CBS News/*New York Times* ladder scale ran from one to ten instead of zero to ten, the results cannot be added to the time series in Table 5-1.) In their analysis, the CBS News/*New York Times* poll classified respondents as either optimists or pessimists based on their ladder-scale rating of the United States. Another question in the CBS News/*New York Times* poll asked, "Do you think things would improve by electing new people, or do you think that wouldn't change things much?" Pessimists about the country were more likely than optimists to say that electing new people would improve things (49 percent of pessimists, compared with 36 percent of optimists). The truly pessimistic response would have been to say that electing new people would not change things much, but that answer was actually more prevalent among optimists. Low confidence in the leaders of our major institutions may be the same kind of pessimistic reply, namely, one not without hope.

There is some direct evidence that lower-status groups, which often suffer from high unemployment, tend to have high expectations for the future. Young people (18 to 29), for instance, turned out in 1976 to be the most optimistic about their personal futures:

> The upward shift from the past to the present among them came to 1.5 steps on the ladder. . . . And the young were much more optimistic about the future: their present to future shift was a remarkable 2.2 steps on the ladder.

Even more notable is the fact that

> . . . blacks in the [1976] survey had at least as much sense of progress from past to present as whites: the upward shift from past to present ratings amounted to 1.1 steps of the ladder among blacks, compared to 1.0 among whites. And they were much more optimistic about their personal futures, foreseeing an upward shift from present to future of 1.6 compared to 0.9 for whites. In sum, while rating their present

149

position lower than that of whites, black Americans showed very marked feelings of progress and even greater optimism about the future.[9]

The Cantrils found the same thing with respect to national expectations in their 1978 study:

> Contrary to whites, blacks see the nation as having made progress from the past to the present and are optimistic about progress in the future. Whites and blacks do not differ in their assessment of the current well-being of the nation. Where they differ is on the trend perceived to be taking place.

Moreover, the Cantrils report that low-income respondents were more likely than others to hold the view that "things will get better" in the future.[10]

The greater sense of optimism expressed by blacks as compared with whites about their personal futures and the future of the country is perhaps the most surprising finding in these surveys. It is reinforced by the results of a national study of young blacks, aged 18 to 29, conducted for *Ebony* magazine in 1978 by the Roper Organization. As the *Ebony* report states,

> This new breed of blacks is optimistic about the future. Fully 58 percent of them say they will be *far* better off in terms of work and career ten years from now; another 32 percent feel they will be somewhat better off than they are today.

Their optimism also appeared in the responses to questions that asked for evaluations of "conditions for black people in this country . . . with regard to housing, education, job opportunities, social acceptance by whites," ten years ago, today, and ten years from now. Only 6 percent rated such conditions as good or excellent ten years ago, 39 percent said they were good or excellent at the time of the poll, and fully 69 percent thought they would be good or excellent ten years in the future. Almost two thirds were "sure they will earn more than their parents." They also seemed to espouse traditional American achievement values: "As to careers, young blacks prefer to develop and be responsible for and own their own businesses; 41 percent of them say that." As *Ebony*

---

[9] Watts and Free, *State of the Nation III*, p. 5.
[10] Cantril and Cantril, *Unemployment*, p. 17.

describes them, "economically oriented, they are an optimistic, pragmatic, and materialistic group."[11]

It must be noted, however, that the combination of high inflation, increased unemployment, and more importantly, Ronald Reagan's election, has reversed the pattern of black optimism. Blacks overwhelmingly opposed Reagan at the polls in November 1980. Fewer than 10 percent voted for him. And post-inaugural surveys conducted by Gallup and the ABC News/*Washington Post* poll in February 1981 indicated that the majority of blacks expected to be treated worse by Reagan's Administration than by Carter's. In tandem with these views, the proportion of blacks who reported that their current situation had improved relative to their status five years ago declined in the Gallup poll from 49 percent in 1980 to 30 percent in 1981. In the ABC News/*Washington Post* poll, blacks were more likely to feel that "the nation's economy is getting worse": 72 percent as compared with 52 percent of whites. At the same time, the majority of these blacks were still disposed to agree with the statement, "If blacks would try harder, they could be just as well off as whites," by 55 to 39 percent. But, as noted in Chapter 4, by October 1981, the proportion of blacks who told University of Michigan Survey Research Center interviewers that they were worse off than a year ago had risen to 62 percent, compared to 34 percent for whites.

Unemployment, Inflation, and Public Expectations

The indication in these data that unemployment does not diminish faith in the system or in the legitimacy of its major institutions is sustained by a 1976 survey of the labor force in the 150 largest metropolitan areas. This survey, conducted by Kay Lehman Schlozman and Sidney Verba, was designed "to assess the impact of joblessness" and therefore oversampled the unemployed.[12] The researchers were surprised to find that "in terms of commitment to the American Dream, there is little difference between working and unemployed members of the same occupational category." The following statements were taken as indicators of faith in the

[11] "The New Generation: A Statistical Study," *Ebony* 33 (August 1978), pp. 158–62.

[12] Kay Lehman Schlozman and Sidney Verba, *Injury to Insult: Unemployment, Class, and Political Response* (Cambridge, Mass.: Harvard University Press, 1979), pp. 139–60.

American Dream: "Hard work is the most important factor in getting ahead," "A worker's child has at least some chance to get ahead," and "The chances for success are distributed fairly." On each of these questions,

> . . . the unemployed do not differ from the employed in any consistent way. An unhappy encounter with the economic system—and the unemployed can clearly be said to have had such an experience—does not appear to reduce belief in the extent or fairness of opportunities in America.[13]

Schlozman and Verba differentiated between attitudes toward personal life and attitudes toward the larger system and concluded that, while

> . . . unemployment is associated with low levels of satisfaction with personal life, it does not seem to be accompanied by disenchantment with the class system, with opportunities offered by the system, or with the opportunities available to the jobless and their offspring.[14]

Two leading opinion analysts, Daniel Yankelovich and Bernard Lefkowitz, have also pointed out the differences in national expectations that accompany recessions and inflationary periods:

> Twenty years ago, when the United States went through a period of recession or a downturn in the economy, people generally retained their sense of optimism about the future. . . . That this has changed [during the inflationary late 1970s] is evident in the answers people give about their personal future and their expectations about the American economy.[15]

Evidence that unemployment has a more negative effect on evaluations of the present than of the future is also presented by Schlozman and Verba in their re-analysis of a 1939 Roper survey. That survey asked a national sample of whites to evaluate their own opportunities relative to those of their parents and to evaluate their children's opportunities relative to their own. Only 45 per-

---

[13] Schlozman and Verba, *Injury to Insult*, pp. 140–41.
[14] Schlozman and Verba, *Injury to Insult*, p. 150.
[15] Daniel Yankelovich and Bernard Lefkowitz, "The Public Debate on Growth: Preparing for Resolution" (Mitchell Award Paper, presented at the Third Biennial Woodlands Conference on Growth Policy, the Woodlands, Texas, October 28–31, 1979), pp. 15–16.

cent of those unemployed at the end of the Depression decade believed that their opportunities were better than those of their parents, but almost two thirds of the jobless, 64 percent, felt that their children would have better opportunities than they did. Variations among the employed members of the sample were in the same direction, but the difference between perceived opportunities for the current and future generations was much smaller, 66 percent positive for themselves, 70 percent positive for their children.[16]

Thus, it is not too surprising that recessions and unemployment produce low confidence in the present without diminishing hopes for the future. Or that when confidence in current leaders is low, anticipations concerning new leaders may be high. High expectations, the perception of a "temporary crisis," is probably a traditional American response to hard times. If so, then persistent inflation seems to have added an entirely new element to the situation, for the analysis here indicates that what inflation destroys is not so much confidence as hope, i.e., the expectation that plans for the future will be fulfilled.[17]

By the latter part of the 1970s, the public had lost confidence in the ability of the government to solve the problem of continually rising prices. In January 1977, the CBS News/*New York Times* poll reported that only 22 percent believed Jimmy Carter could prevent a steady increase in prices. And a poll taken by NBC News and the Associated Press in January 1980 found a large majority, 61 percent, saying it was not possible for *any* President—not just Jimmy Carter—to solve the nation's inflation problem, while only 32 percent felt that inflation could be solved. Subsequent surveys taken by the same organization and by the CBS News/*New York Times* poll during the 1980 campaign reported similar results.

Even the election of a new President, Ronald Reagan, whose campaign emphasized proposed changes in government policy to reduce inflation, did not convince Americans that a new administration—one committed to a major reduction in government spending—could affect the situation. When the CBS News/*New York Times* poll inquired in late January, 1981, "Do you think Ronald Reagan will or will not be able to keep prices from going up all the time?," only 25 percent replied that he would be able to

[16] Schlozman and Verba, *Injury to Insult,* pp. 150–55.

[17] For detailed evidence to this effect, see Yankelovich and Lefkowitz, "The Public Debate on Growth," pp. 18–21 and Table 2.

do so; 66 percent said he would not. And of the two thirds who thought Reagan would not stop inflation, fully three quarters answered a follow-up question by saying that no President could do it, that rising prices are "something beyond *any* President's control." Republicans, it may be noted, were almost as dubious as Democrats about the ability of Reagan, or any President, to end inflation.

Five months later, in mid-July 1981, as Congress was adopting the President's inflation-fighting package of cuts in taxes and spending, the NBC News/Associated Press poll asked: "Do you think an effective President would be able to control inflation, or is that something beyond any President's control?" Only one third, 33 percent, replied that an effective President could control inflation, while fully three fifths, 59 percent, said inflation was beyond control.

As a major recession hit the country in the fall of 1981 in the context of continued inflation and high interest rates, Americans grew even more pessimistic about the future of the economy. Asked by Harris at the end of October what they expected to happen "a year from now as a result of President Reagan's economic program," a majority, 56 percent, anticipated that "business bankruptcies will be increasing"; only 35 percent thought that "unemployment will be reduced to below where it is now"; and even fewer, 27 percent, believed that "the rate of inflation will have come down to below 10 percent," as in fact it did in 1982.

Conclusion: What Explains the Decline in Confidence?

This chapter and the preceding ones have examined trust in institutions and their leaders as a general phenomenon. A general index of confidence was created by combining the ratings of the leaders of twelve different institutions in the 1973–77 NORC General Social Surveys. This general index, however, was found to have weak demographic and political correlates. Instead, people who say they trust leaders of institutions generally are distinguished by certain psychological characteristics: they tend to be more optimistic in their outlook on life, more satisfied with their personal well-being, and more trusting of others.

But one cannot argue that a decline in personal trust and satisfaction caused the post-1965 decline of confidence in the institutions of the nation. There is no evidence of a massive increase in Americans' personal dissatisfaction or unhappiness. At most, the 1970s witnessed some growth in frustration with immediate financial situations—hardly surprising, given the economic dislocations of the past decade. But as the ladder-scale data show, the decline in people's estimates of their own personal well-being has been modest in comparison with the fall-off in evaluations of the country's well-being. And, as noted, Americans have consistently rated their own well-being and their own expectations for the future higher than their comparable judgments about the country. Overall, the data point to some deterioration in "private" confidence, but not nearly as much as the fall-off of confidence in the country and its institutions. It would be difficult to account for the latter in terms of the former.

The Economy as a Causal Factor

The time-series analyses in this chapter and in Chapter 2 revealed a relationship between faith in institutions and the condition of the economy. Rising inflation and unemployment depress trust in the people running various institutions and lower the public's estimate of the ways things are going in the country. Inflation in particular has a depressing effect on expectations for the future. Economic conditions also affect people's assessment of their own personal situations. The economy seems to be a shared causal factor accounting, in part, for the decline of confidence in individuals' own lives and in the nation as a whole.

It is interesting that people's assessments of their own lives seem less strongly affected by economic conditions than do their evaluations of the country. Inflation and unemployment together accounted for 14 percent of the variance over time in the mean estimates of "your own life today," but 71 percent of the variance in views of "the situation of the country today." The correct causal sequence would not appear to be that worsening economic conditions cause a declining sense of personal well-being, which in turn produces lower confidence in the country. Rather, it appears that a troubled economy primarily affects people's conceptions of how things are going in the country and only secondarily their sense of personal well-being. A recession, for instance, leads people to believe that "times are bad," even if they do not feel personally affected.

155

Thus the crisis of confidence in institutional leadership to a large extent reflects "bad times." Jimmy Carter's argument in his July 1979 speech, however, was that the national malaise was somehow a moral failing on the part of the American people and that the government could not act decisively unless confidence was restored:

> What can we do? First of all, we must face the truth and then we can change our course. We simply must have faith in each other. Faith in our ability to govern ourselves and faith in the future of this nation. Restoring that faith and that confidence to America is now the most important task we have.

The data, however, suggest that confidence is mostly a response to events, a reaction to the way things are going in the country. If anything, it is the failure of leadership that has caused the loss of confidence, and not the other way around. What the President did not appear to have noted is that confidence in the country rose in 1977, when he first took office, and declined sharply thereafter, when results were not forthcoming. People gave the President their confidence when they elected him and then waited to see if their faith would pay off.

The economy appears to be part of the reason for the decline of trust in institutions, but not the whole explanation. It is true that inflation and unemployment accounted for 58 percent of the variance over time in the mean level of confidence for all institutions (Table 2-5). And as Table 5-2 indicates, inflation and unemployment accounted for 71 percent of the variance from survey to survey in mean ladder-scale ratings for the country. *But most of the surveys in both time series were administered during the 1970s.* (Of twenty-three surveys in Table 2-5, only two were conducted in the 1960s. Of thirty-three surveys in Table 5-2, one was taken in 1959 and one in 1964; all others were taken between 1971 and 1981.) Thus the economic variables may explain changes mostly during the economically troubled 1970s.

Indeed, both regression equations underestimate confidence levels at the earlier time points. Thus:

• Using the regression associated with Table 5-2, one would have predicted a mean national ladder rating of 5.9 from the economic data for 1959; the actual mean ladder rating in 1959 was considerably higher, 6.7. The regression would have predicted a mean ladder rating of 6.0 in 1964; the actual ladder regression rating in 1964 was 6.5. But in 1971, the regression would have *over*estimated the rating of the country—5.5, as compared with an actual ladder-scale rating of 5.4.

• Using the regression associated with Table 2-5, one would have estimated a mean of 38 percent of the public expressing "a great deal of confidence" in all ten institutions in 1966, given the inflation and unemployment rates that year. In fact, the average confidence rating in 1966 was considerably higher: 48 percent. The same equation would have estimated an average of 39 percent high confidence from the 1967 economic data. The actual figure was 42 percent. But in 1971, when economic conditions would have predicted a mean of 31 percent high confidence, the true figure was lower (28 percent).

Thus, both regressions produce underestimates of confidence for time points prior to the 1970s and, in most cases, overestimates during the 1970s. Confidence in leaders and in the country during the 1950s and 1960s was higher than economic conditions would have led one to predict. In the 1970s, confidence was lower than could be accounted for by inflation and unemployment alone. This means the state of the economy does a rather good job of accounting for fluctuations during the 1970s, but it does not explain most of the substantial decline from the mid-1960s to the early 1970s. That was the period of sharpest fall-off for both the NORC-Harris confidence ratings and for the Institute for International Social Research/Potomac Associates/CRI ladder-scale evaluations. It was also a period of relative prosperity.

It has been suggested that inflation and unemployment do not demoralize the public by destroying people's sense of personal well-being. Personal well-being seems to be quite resilient. Instead, inflation and unemployment may function as a kind of "bad news," as potential threats in the external environment against which people must protect their personal situations. When the economy turns downward, what collapses most readily is the public's estimate of how things are going in the country and their faith in leaders, long before any sense of personal desperation sets in. This reasoning suggests a more general explanation for the decline of confidence—namely, that the sheer quantity of "bad news" increased rapidly beginning in the mid-1960s. Between the mid-1960s and the early 1970s, most of the "bad news" was noneconomic in nature—a disastrous foreign war, racial conflict, and social polarization. That was also true in the early 1970s, when the Watergate scandal cut short the country's effort to return to normal. Finally, beginning with the oil embargo of late 1973, "bad news" about the economy tended to monopolize the country's attention—albeit with a regular smattering of social conflict, foreign policy failures, and political scandal. Moreover, to a considerable extent, the "bad news" of the last fifteen years has been presented in the context of implicit or explicit criticism of the country's leaders and institutions. Not only have things not been going well, but it almost always seemed to be someone's fault—that of the President, or big business, or the press, or the military, or the Congress, or the oil companies.

Resiliency and Differentiation

Two general characteristics of confidence deserve special emphasis. One is the resiliency of the public's confidence. It appears that dramatic national crises such as the events of the late 1960s, the Watergate scandal, the mid-1970s recession, and the inflation of 1978–81 push confidence levels down. But in the absence of such crises, as in the early 1970s and the first year of Jimmy Carter's presidency, there appears to be a tendency for Americans to regain confidence as "good feelings" about the system resume. According to Figure 5-2, the public's trust in all institutions, with the notable exception of the executive branch, went up even during the Watergate crisis, only to be diminished again in the ensuing recession. Carter's accession to office occasioned a second modest spurt of confidence in 1977. This pattern is roughly paralleled by the trend line in Figure 5-3 showing the average ladder-scale ratings for "the situation in the country today." Estimates of the country's present situation rose noticeably in 1976 and 1977 as the country recovered from the recession. But the inflationary period that began in 1978 again depressed ratings of the present. Ronald Reagan's accession to the presidency in 1981 once again had a positive effect on the public's mood, as evidenced by the increase in the proportion of "optimists" in the first three quarters of 1981 reported in Table 5-3. However, as noted in Chapter 2, Reagan's "honeymoon" boosted public confidence in the executive branch but had little effect on other institutions. With continuing deterioration of the economy, the public seemed more wary than in the past.

The public is inclined to believe that the system works unless it receives compelling evidence to the contrary. Unfortunately, evidence of this sort has not been in short supply during the past fifteen years. Still, one is impressed by the resiliency of trust during the all-too-few noncrisis periods. Events and circumstances have prevented confidence levels from reaching the high points recorded in the late 1950s and early 1960s. That would apparently require a sustained period of "good news" far longer than the modest upswings experienced during the past decade.

The second notable characteristic of public trust is its differentiated quality. As noted, severe criticism of institutions has coincided with a high degree of satisfaction with personal and family situations and with optimism about the future. This finding helps to explain another anomaly, that Americans are able to combine a high level of criticism of their major institutions and low confidence in their leaders with a strong attachment to those institutions and to the system itself. Political scientist David Easton has argued that trust may be differentiated among three general objects: the incumbent political authorities, the "regime," or system of institutions and norms, and the overall political community.[18] Democratic procedures tend to direct discontent at the incumbent authorities, who may be thrown out and replaced, while insulating the system from opposition. The evidence indicates that this has so far been the case. The fact that such a long period of frustration has not resulted in a loss of legitimacy may account for the fact that increased conservatism, rather than leftist radicalism, was the predominant reaction in the late 1970s to the sense that things had been going badly. Americans want their traditional institutions to work better, to behave the way they used to; they do not want to change them in any fundamental way. Nevertheless, the possibility remains that "if the process of elections does not succeed in producing popular incumbents, the discontent generated by a series of distrusted authorities may accumulate and eventually be directed at the institutions of government."[19]

[18] David Easton, *The Political System* (New York: Alfred A. Knopf, 1965).

[19] Arthur H. Miller, "The Institutional Focus of Political Distrust" (Paper presented at the Annual Meeting of the American Political Science Association, Washington, D.C., August 31–September 3, 1979), p. 3.

Part II

Business, Labor, and Government

6

Business: Productive but Unpopular

On January 9, 1981, then President-elect Ronald Reagan took up the issue of confidence in business in the context of expressing concern about the growth of an "adversary relationship between the federal government and business," which he linked to the "steady decline in public confidence in business" as reflected in the public opinion polls.[1] But, as we have seen, the phenomenon of low confidence is not limited to business. As was shown in Chapters 1 and 2, anti-government and anti-business sentiment grew virtually in tandem with one another beginning in the mid-1960s. There was no evidence during the 1970s that either institution was declining in public esteem while the other was growing, although the 1981 surveys of Harris and ORC suggest that during Reagan's first year in office, confidence in the presidency moved up, while ratings for big business declined. The same principle applies to an even older adversarial relationship, that between business and labor. If confidence in organized labor did not fall quite so precipitously as trust in government and business, that is simply because, as indicated in Chapter 2, confidence in organized labor was very low to begin with.

What is it about business and labor in particular that disturbs so

[1] Ronald Reagan, "Government and Business in the '80s," *Wall Street Journal*, January 9, 1981, p. 18.

many Americans and causes these two private institutions to end up near the bottom of the list in most confidence rankings? This chapter will attempt to define the grounds on which the public criticizes business.

Americans have sharply contradictory feelings about both business and labor. On the one hand, people repeatedly acknowledge that business deserves much of the credit for the nation's high standard of living and for the steady growth in productivity that, until recently, has kept the United States in the forefront among industrial nations. The public also believes that trade unions have played a central role in improving the standard of living and the employment conditions of working people.

On the other hand, survey after survey has reported that most Americans are extremely critical of the *behavior* of business and labor organizations and give business and labor leaders low ratings for their ethical standards. The public sees itself at a disadvantage as consumers, employees, and union members because of the power exercised by large organizations and their leaders. This power is seen as inherently inimical to the public interest. The importance of power is seen repeatedly whenever the public is asked to characterize big and small institutions; small business, as noted earlier, is always evaluated more positively than big business, even though the public recognizes that the latter may be more productive and efficient than the former. This chapter and the next will examine closely the factors related to these ambiguous and sometimes divergent attitudes.

Report Card for Business

High Marks

One of the strongest themes running through the polls is an appreciation of the technical and economic accomplishments of business, including "big business." On four separate occasions between 1966 and 1978, the Harris poll asked Americans to give their "impression of the job American business is doing" in a long list of areas. The strongest positive evaluations were for its technological and economic performance: developing new products and services through research, improving the production process, developing new markets, and expanding growth opportunities. Just

164

behind these achievements came a number of accomplishments that aided employees: complying with federal standards for workplace safety, developing job openings for minorities, providing safe working conditions, furnishing steady jobs, and paying good wages and salaries.

In December 1976 and again two years later in December 1978, the Roper Poll asked Americans to evaluate the activities of business by reacting to a list of twelve "things people have said are or should be responsibilities of business in this country." Once again, the strongest positive evaluations in both surveys were for technological and economic achievements and for providing job opportunities. Thus, majorities gave business positive grades for meeting its responsibilities "fully" or "fairly well" with respect to "developing new products and services" (88 percent in December 1978), "hiring minorities" (74 percent), "providing jobs for people" (71 percent), "paying good salaries and benefits to employees" (69 percent), "producing good quality products and services" (66 percent), and "making products that are safe to use" (65 percent). Similar sentiments were expressed in three other Roper studies, in 1975, 1979, and 1981, which asked respondents to agree or disagree with various statements characterizing American business and industry. About four fifths in each year agreed that "American business and industry has been progressive in the development and introduction of new products." And in September 1981, Harris found 59 percent rated business positively ("excellent" or "pretty good") on "improving modern tools, machinery and plants to make the U.S. superior in technology and know-how again," while 39 percent evaluated it negatively ("only fair" or "poor"). Overall, Roper found 57 percent agreeing in May/June 1981 with the statement, "What's good for business is also good for the average person—the more money business makes the better off we'll all be," while only 20 percent felt that "what's good for business is bad for the average person . . . the more money business makes the worse off you and I are."

These Roper surveys inquired about "business" in general; a 1977 Harris poll asked Americans to rate "big business" on a similar list of goals. While the overall ratings came out a bit lower when the phrase "big business" was used, the public tended to recognize the same types of achievements. At the top, the public gave big business high ratings for technological development both in manufacturing processes and in new and better products (70–77 percent positive). Just below that, big business was marked high for "providing steady work," "concern for employee health benefits," and "concern for employee safety" (61–63 percent positive). The next set of items showed big business ranked positively by a margin that was smaller but still 50–59 percent favorable: "concern for the reputation of its products," "product safety," "management training," and several worker-related items ("insurance for employees," "high wages," "career opportunities for minorities," and "business expansion to provide more jobs").

An important conclusion from these Roper and Harris polls is that neither business in general nor big business in particular is seen as reactionary in dealing with employees. Most Americans do not believe that business exploits workers. One of the most striking findings is that the public gives business a relatively high rating for providing opportunities for minority groups. When asked by Harris to indicate whether business has or has not helped to solve a list of social problems, respondents in 1966, 1971, and 1972 felt that "eliminating racial discrimination" was a problem that business *has* helped to solve, a view endorsed by a margin of 50 to 33 percent in 1972. In 1975, National Family Opinion found that a majority of Americans agreed with the statement, "On the whole, big business no longer discriminates against minorities in hiring and advancements" (55 percent agreed, 24 percent disagreed). In 1978, a Yankelovich, Skelly & White poll found that 56 percent of the public felt business is "trying hard" to improve the situation of minorities, compared to 34 percent who said business was "dragging their feet" on the issue.

Americans also see a close link between business conditions and their own personal welfare. Thus, when Cambridge Reports, Inc., in a study conducted for Union Carbide in the spring of 1978, asked people to react to a number of possible consequences of business *not* making "enough profits," it found majorities predicting a number of adverse personal effects: "My standard of living will fall" (52 percent agreed, 32 disagreed); "The quality and amount of goods and services I will be able to choose from in our economy will decline" (64–20 percent agreed); and "My chances of having a job and job security will suffer" (63–23 percent agreed).

Low Marks

The same respondents, however, often complained about other ways "business" and "big business" behave. In the four 1966–78

Harris polls discussed above, business was given negative marks by a majority of respondents in the following areas: "producing better [as opposed to 'good'] quality products for the American people," "allowing people to use their full creative abilities," "helping to take care of workers displaced by automation," "really caring about the individual's well-being," "keeping profits at a reasonable level," "caring about the home living conditions of employees," and, worst of all, "keeping the cost of living down." Those polled by Roper in 1976 and 1978 voiced negative judgments when evaluating the role of business in "charging reasonable prices for goods and services" (67 percent negative in 1978), "advertising honestly" (66 percent negative), "paying their fair share of taxes" (60 percent), "keeping profits at a reasonable level" (58 percent), and "cleaning up their own air and water pollution" (55 percent). In 1975 and 1979 Roper surveys, majorities of 68–69 percent agreed that "American business and industry is far too often not honest with the public." These findings were supported by Roger Seasonwein polls in 1975 and 1978 that reported that majorities of 57 and 60 percent felt that major corporations do not "care enough about protecting the public from environmental and pollution problems." In 1980, Harris found that, when asked to rate the job both business and other groups were "doing to make our society acceptably safe," only 31 percent of the public gave business positive ratings, compared to 50 percent for consumer groups and 52 percent for environmental groups; however, the federal government, at 29 percent, was rated lower than business.

Although Ronald Reagan entered office with a positive view of business, the 1981 surveys do not suggest any decline in the public's disdain for business. As noted earlier, the confidence ratings for business institutions and leadership remained low or declined further. When Harris asked in September, "All in all, how would you rate the job American business is doing to solve our economic problems—excellent, pretty good, only fair, or poor?" only 30 percent chose the two positive responses, while over two thirds, 68 percent, judged it negatively. Reacting to eight possible ways that business might be dealing with economic problems, most respondents rated the record of business as "only fair" or "poor" on seven of them. According to Harris:

- A 73–24 percent majority [gave] business a negative rating on "helping to bring down the rate of inflation."
- By 66–29 percent, a majority [gave] business a negative rating on "plowing back profits to make the economy grow."

- By 66–28 percent, a majority [came] up with negative marks for business on "putting the interests of the economy ahead of short-term business gain."
- A 61–32 percent majority [was] negative about business efforts on "borrowing the capital needed for investment to provide more jobs and to make the economy grow."
- By 58–39 percent, most Americans [gave] business negative marks on "working with unions and employees to improve productivity."
- A 52–41 percent majority [was] negative on business "changing from being interested in short-term profits to being interested in long-term growth."

The only dimension on which business received more positive than negative judgments (59–39 percent) was on improving tools, machinery, and plants, mentioned earlier.

The public appears especially sensitive to the excessive power of *big* business. Thus, when Yankelovich, Skelly & White asked respondents in a 1977 survey to react to eight statements reflecting concerns about the role of big business, the one approved by the largest majority (62 percent) was "large companies are too powerful in politics." A majority, 54 percent, agreed that "large companies unfairly keep out smaller companies." Conversely—and curiously—only 19 percent felt that large companies were responsible for "inadequate opportunity to introduce something new because of a lack of competition" in their industry.

The national surveys conducted for *U.S. News and World Report* in 1975 and 1977 yielded a similar ambiguity in responses to questions asking people to rate various "functions of the American business system." As the report of the 1977 study notes:

> Business received a relatively high rating on its ability to develop new products and to provide products and services that meet people's needs. It also got good marks on the hiring of minorities and on paying good wages—in fact, the ratings for business improved in all of these areas compared to the . . . [1975] ratings.
>
> However, as in the previous study, business did not score well on conservation of natural resources, honesty in advertising, dealing with shortages, controlling pollution or helping solve social problems. In all of these areas, business scored as poorly [as] or worse than in . . . [1975].[2]

[2] Marketing Department, *U.S. News and World Report, The Study of American Opinion, 1978 Summary Report* (Washington, D.C.), p. 11.

The Role of Morality and Self-Interest

What differentiates the matters on which business is rated negatively from those on which it is rated positively? It is not simply that the negative areas have a significantly "moral" aspect. Business has received high marks for being concerned about product safety, employee health benefits, employee safety, humane working conditions, and the reputation of its products and services. It has also been rated high for promoting certain social values: eliminating racial discrimination and giving opportunities to minority groups, providing more jobs for people in the community, and promoting economic growth. In none of these areas is business considered socially oppressive or reactionary.

Yet on other moral considerations, business is given a low evaluation: protecting the environment, working for better government, improving the community, and upholding the law. Attitudes vary considerably depending on the exact issue: for providing humane working conditions, the rating is good; helping workers displaced by automation, the rating is bad; caring about its reputation, good; setting a moral example, bad; providing opportunities for minority groups, good; providing opportunities for the physically handicapped, bad; promoting economic growth, good; keeping down prices, bad.

These variations are not difficult to explain. The public believes that economic *self-interest* is the key motivation behind all business activity. The poll results show that the public feels business does a good job in areas that are in its economic self-interest and a poor job in areas that are not. It is thought to be in the economic self-interest of business to develop technology, promote economic growth, create humane working conditions, pay good wages, care about employee and product safety, provide more jobs, and create opportunities for minorities. But it is *not* in the economic self-interest of business, in any obvious way, to help workers displaced by automation, care about the customer or employee as an individual, protect the environment, promote good government, or hold down prices.

Americans are under no illusions about business practices. Business will give opportunities to minorities, not out of moral or social concern, but because it can use a larger supply of able workers. Handicapped people are not usually thought of as able workers—and, thus, people do not expect business to do anything on their behalf. One does not have to be a cynic to conclude that those areas where business is perceived as socially progressive have a striking tendency to coincide with its economic self-interest, while those areas where business is given low marks for moral and civic virtue happen to be those areas where there is little or no (apparent) advantage to be gained. This, we suggest, explains the public's tendency to see much of what business, and even big business, do as socially enlightened and morally praiseworthy, while still giving business low ratings for its ethical character in many other respects.

This view that the public sees businessmen as creatures driven by self-interest has been supported in many polls investigating conflicts between morality and self-interest in the business world. Cambridge Reports, Inc., offered respondents the following statement in 1975, 1976, and 1977: "Businessmen—big and small— put profit ahead of morality." A majority (51 percent) agreed with this statement in 1975 while a large minority (41 percent) rejected it. In the 1976 poll, the percentage agreeing rose to 60 and those disagreeing fell to 24 percent. By the fall of 1977, agreement had risen further, to 66 percent, while opposition had declined to only 20 percent. CRI found even stronger support for a statement describing the motives and behavior of big business: "Big business doesn't care whether I live or die, only that somebody buys what they have to sell." Between 69 and 79 percent agreed with this rather extreme proposition put forth in four surveys between 1975 and 1977, while a fifth or less disagreed with it.

Similar results were obtained by Peter D. Hart Research Associates in a survey conducted in 1975. The same overwhelming majority, 72 percent, voiced agreement with the statement, "Profits are the major goal of business even if it means unemployment and inflation," and gave business a negative rating with respect to "really caring about the individual." Almost as many, 68 percent, felt that "profits mainly benefit stockholders and management" compared to only 23 percent who said that "profits mainly improve the general economic prosperity of everyone." In December 1976, Harris found that, by 71 to 11 percent, the public agreed that "businessmen will do nothing much to help the consumer if that reduces profits—unless it is forced to do so."

In polls taken biennially from 1973 to 1981, the Opinion Research Corporation also found substantial majorities, from 65 percent in 1973 to 72 percent in 1979 (down to 69 percent in 1981), agreeing that "businessmen do everything they can to make a profit even if it means ignoring the public's need." When offered a positive statement, "Business today has a moral conscience—it is motivated by more than just the profit motive," almost half of a 1975 ORC sample *dis*agreed, while a smaller number, 41 percent, agreed.

The Roper Organization reported that large majorities, 64–65 percent, approved the statement, "American business and industry has lost sight of human values in the interest of profits," while 22–23 percent disagreed in surveys taken in 1975, 1979, and 1981.

According to a Roger Seasonwein poll taken in October 1979, 67 percent believed that during prosperous times, business uses its increased income for "higher profits, higher executive salaries, and fat expense accounts. The average person doesn't benefit very much." An identical two-thirds majority agreed that during economic downswings, "business keeps its profits high and cuts jobs and wages." When asked how higher business profits affect the standard of living of the average person, only 42 percent said that they produce an improvement, 35 percent saw no effect, while 20 percent thought they lower the average person's standard of living.

Roper inquired in August 1976 and again in August 1981 whether each of ten occupational groups "tend to act more in their own self-interest, or more in the public interest." "Business executives in large corporations" received the highest percentages replying "their own self-interest" both times—71 in 1976, 76 in 1981. Labor leaders were second (58 percent in 1976 and 62 percent in 1981). Senators, Congressmen, and government officials followed, with percentages in the high forties seeing them as primarily self-interested.

The results of these surveys showed little relationship with political ideology. In the 1977 CRI poll, liberals, moderates, and conservatives all felt about the same: 69 percent of the liberals, as compared to 65 percent of the conservatives, felt that businessmen "put profit ahead of morality," while 20 percent of the former and 23 percent of the latter disagreed. But the answer to this question did correlate very strongly with social status. Poorer and less well-educated respondents were much more likely to agree with the statement than were wealthier and better-educated respondents. About one third of those who had gone beyond college, for example, rejected it, as compared with 11 percent of those who had not completed high school.

Roper reported a slight relationship with ideology in 1979, 68 percent of the liberals and 61 percent of the conservatives agreeing that business and industry has "lost sight of human values in the interests of profits." As in the CRI surveys, Roper found a stronger class difference, with blue-collar workers less likely to disagree with the statement (20 percent) than business and professional people (34 percent).

Business, Labor, and Political Leaders

To be sure, the public is cynical about the values and behavior of labor and political leaders as well as business leaders. In Chapter 3, we noted that in surveys conducted for *U.S. News and World Report* in 1975 and 1977, business executives and labor leaders ranked low on "honesty, dependability, and integrity" (labor leaders below those of business), as compared with various professions, organized religion, small business, and the Supreme Court (see Figure 3-1). Political groups and institutions received disparate rankings; for instance, politicians came out at the bottom of the list, while local and state governments and the White House were rated slightly higher than large business companies. Similarly, in four polls taken by ORC in 1975, 1977, 1979, and 1981, labor leaders placed last among 18 occupational groups with respect to judgments about their "ethical and moral practices," while most categories relating to business and government were also located far below the average (Table 3-2).

In a Yankelovich, Skelly & White survey taken in 1978, "big businessmen" and "labor leaders" were the only groups from a list of sixteen to be judged by a majority as "generally immoral and unethical," 56 percent in the case of businessmen and 55 percent for labor leaders. A plurality, 44 percent, voiced the same opinion of "federal government officials," while between a tenth and a fifth viewed teachers, religious leaders, doctors, scientists, small businessmen, and television newscasters in an invidious light.

The Roper poll asked respondents in 1975 and again in 1977 to look at a list of ten words and phrases and indicate which ones "are descriptive of a good majority of the country's top *political* leaders; then review the list a second time and indicate which qualities are descriptive of the country's top *business* leaders; and then go down the list yet a third time and choose the terms which best describe the country's top leaders in *labor*." The most striking finding is the overall negative view of leaders in all three categories. The phrase most frequently chosen to describe all three types of leaders was "self-seeking"; the phrase least frequently chosen to describe all three was "high moral calibre." Clearly the moral cloud that hangs over business also hangs over government and labor.

But there were certain positive qualities that respondents associated more frequently with business leaders than with political or labor officials: "very intelligent," "able and competent," and "forward-looking and progressive." About 40 percent of the 1977 sample said that these qualities were descriptive of top business leaders, compared with between 23 and 37 percent who described political and labor leaders that way. There was one characteristic, however, on which the public scored business leaders unusually low: "sincerely interested in solving social problems." Only 10 percent said that such an interest was descriptive of business leaders, while 12 percent said it could be applied to labor leaders and 33 percent said it was true of political leaders.

In a November-December 1980 poll, Roper inquired into the public's reaction to the "Abscam scandals involving members of the United States Congress dealing with bribes." He asked people to evaluate the extent to which Congressmen, top business executives, and labor officials deal "in bribes and payoffs in return for favors." The results are reported in Table 6-1.

Given the fact that the media had recently reported the arrest and conviction of a number of Congressmen for receiving bribes, the belief that corruption was equally characteristic of top business executives and labor officials, if not more so, substantiates the public's serious doubts about the integrity of leaders of all three institutions. Business, labor, and political leaders are all regarded as self-seeking and frequently dishonest. Business leaders, as compared with labor and political leaders, have the advantage of being regarded as generally more competent and intelligent, but they are also considered less socially responsible.

Disdain for Money-Making

Attitudes toward making money also color beliefs about business. In an article published in 1976, Wilson C. McWilliams and

TABLE 6–1
Perceptions of the Extent of Bribes and Payoffs

"Do you think this dealing in bribes and payoffs in return for political favors that has been reported about some Congressmen is widespread throughout Congress, or that it's true of quite a lot of Congressmen but not most, or that it's true of just a few Congressmen? How about in the business world? . . . And how about among labor officials?"

	Congressmen	Top Business Executives	Labor Officials
		Percentage	
Widespread	33	35	46
True of a lot but not most	37	36	29
True of just a few	27	23	17
Don't know	3	6	8
	100	100	100

Source: Roper, November-December, 1980.
N = 2,004.

Henry A. Plotkin of Rutgers University pointed out that business-men have often been under attack in American history. "Religious and democratic ideals contested any claim to moral primacy, insisting that business justify itself in their terms."[3] Survey data support the contention that Americans show a certain degree of hostility to "making money" and to "profits." In 1976, a Cambridge Reports, Inc. (CRI) poll suggested that "corporations, in general, have four goals: producing products, making money, providing jobs, and serving the public interest. Which of the ones we list is most important to you? Which is second?" The two top choices were "producing products" (32 percent) and "providing jobs" (29 percent). Twenty-four percent chose "serving the public interest," leaving the last choice, "making money," far behind (15 percent). When first and second choices were added together, the results show over 50 percent of the sample choosing each of the top three goals as important: production, jobs, and serving the public interest. Only 33 percent of the respondents gave "making money" as either a first or second choice of what was most important to them.

In another question asked in 1976, CRI asked: "Here is a list of things corporations might be concerned about. For each item, please tell me how much attention a corporation should pay to it." Over 80 percent of the sample said that corporations should pay "a lot"

[3] Wilson C. McWilliams and Henry A. Plotkin, "The Historic Reputation of American Business," Journal of Contemporary Business 5 (Autumn 1976), p. 3.

of attention to "protecting the safety of employees." Over 70 percent said that a lot of attention should be paid to "minimizing costs of products to consumers" and to "paying employees well." Over 60 percent stressed "improving the quality of work for employees" and "protecting the environment." Just over half, 53 percent, said that corporations should pay a lot of attention to "making special efforts to hire unemployed, disadvantaged people." The goal that was seen as least important among the eight listed was "earning profits for owners and stockholders," which a bare majority, 52 percent, thought should receive "a lot" of attention by corporations.

A more recent CRI poll conducted in early 1979 again found Americans valuing consumer and public interests more than those of stockholders and workers. CRI asked: "Whose interests do you think a business should put first—the interests of the stockholders, the interests of the workers, the interests of the consumers, or the interests of the American people as a whole?" Put this way, only 9 percent placed the stockholders first, while even fewer, 7 percent, said the workers. Close to a third, 32 percent, emphasized consumers, while 35 percent replied that a corporation should be most concerned with the interests of the American people.

A more general question put by ORC to national cross sections in 1973, 1975, 1977, 1979, and 1981 found in each poll that two thirds or more of the public agreed with the statement: "Business has an obligation to help society, even if it means making less profit."

Liberals, moderates, and conservatives were very much alike in their feelings about the legitimacy of profits and moneymaking in both the 1976 and 1979 CRI surveys. Indeed, resentment of profits and moneymaking appears to be more of a populist (anti-elitist) than an ideological sentiment. A 1976 Cambridge Reports poll offered the following choice to respondents: "Some say that a business corporation's chief function is to provide goods and services to consumers at prices that also provide the owners and investors a fair profit. Others say corporations have broader responsibilities to help achieve certain social and economic goals in this society. Which do you think is the correct view?" Thirty-six percent said that providing goods and services is a corporation's chief function. Only 17 percent said that the achievements of social and economic goals "should be the main purpose of a business." But 37 percent insisted that *both* were the proper objective of business. Adding together those who said "social and economic goals" alone are the proper function of business and those who said business should concentrate on both goals, we find 47 percent of self-described conservatives, 58 percent of moderates, and 61 percent of liberals endorsing an emphasis on social responsibility.

McWilliams and Plotkin argue that what Americans admire about business is not moneymaking, but the "virtues and activities at least distinct from, and often at odds with, the norms and values of business per se," specifically, hard work and inventive genius, the qualities one associates with individuals as opposed to large organizations.[4] Men like Thomas Edison, John D. Rockefeller, and Andrew Carnegie were not admired because they made money or founded large corporations; they were admired for qualities separate from their business acuity: Edison's inventive genius and Rockefeller's and Carnegie's philanthropy. Making money in business is not considered a moral or a virtuous objective by most Americans, and business activities are widely regarded as having undemocratic and anti-Christian characteristics. McWilliams and Plotkin go on to state that "business is one of the few—if not the only—white collar professions in which money is not regarded as incidental. It is pejorative to say that a physician is 'merely a businessman.' Americans believe that doctors deserve a high income because they heal the sick; but there, respect for the work precedes and justifies the respect for income."[5]

In what McWilliams and Plotkin label the public's "pre-industrial" understanding of economic morality, business activity tends to be, by definition, immoral. For the public, business is justified only in terms of other values, which are of two types: *individualistic* values, whereby business rewards those who show talent, hard work, and achievement, and *social* values, in which business performs the social functions mentioned in the CRI poll: producing goods, providing jobs, and serving the public interest. Business is admired to the extent that it achieves these goals.

Attitudes Toward Profits

The Exaggerated Perception of Profits

The public's disdain for the "self-interested" behavior of business is reflected particularly in its attitudes toward profits. Over

[4] McWilliams and Plotkin, "Historic Reputation," p. 3.
[5] McWilliams and Plotkin, "Historic Reputation," p. 13.

the years, surveys have often revealed the public's exaggerated notion of their magnitude. Thus, when asked to judge how much profit "the average manufacturer" actually makes on each dollar of sales, estimates in polls taken from 1971 to 1981, according to Opinion Research Corporation surveys, have averaged between 25 and 32 cents (31 cents in 1981), while judgments as to what would constitute a reasonable profit have run four to six cents lower. The actual rate of profit for manufacturing companies in 1981, according to ORC, was much smaller, 4.9 cents per dollar of sales. Those queried by ORC in 1981 about profit margins per dollar of sales for specific, mainly nonmanufacturing, industries gave even higher estimates: 62 cents for the average oil company, 49 cents for the local electric utility company, 41 cents for the average automobile company, 49 cents for the telephone company, and 35 cents for the average food company. The actual rates for these five industries in 1981, according to ORC, averaged 5.9 cents (per dollar of sales) for oil companies, 10.1 cents for electric utilities, minus 4.0 cents for automobile companies, 8.9 cents for the telephone company, and 3.0 cents for food companies.

A survey conducted by the Roper Organization in August 1977 found similar results. Roper asked: "What profit do you think business as a whole makes as a percentage of sales?" Only 10 percent estimated profit as less than 10 percent, while almost two fifths said that it was over 30 percent. The other options, 10 to 20 percent and 20 to 30 percent, were each chosen by one fifth of the respondents.

In April 1975 and again in December 1979, Roper asked respondents to estimate how much the price of "a gallon of gas," "a car that now costs $6,000" and "a food order that now costs you $10" would be reduced if the oil companies, the automobile manufacturers, and the food chain supermarkets "were to pass *all* of their profits to the consumer in the form of lower . . . prices." The median profit estimates were quite high: for a gallon of gas, 13 cents in 1975 and 32 cents in 1979; for a $6,000 automobile, $749 in 1975 and $1,198 in 1979; and for a $10 food order, $1.99 in 1975 and $2.11 in 1979.

Given these evaluations of profit margins, it is hardly surprising that pluralities or majorities in different surveys have been convinced that profits are excessive and that business could get by earning a good deal less. Thus in 1975, a plurality, 42 percent, reported to National Family Opinion that "most companies in the

United States can afford to raise wages 10 percent without raising prices," as against 33 percent who felt this was not possible. Yankelovich, Skelly & White (YSW) found substantial majorities, between 77 and 85 percent, agreeing that "most businessmen could make a lot less profit and still be earning plenty" in four polls taken between 1977 and 1980. And when ORC asked in 1981, "Which do you think is the most practical way for workers to increase their standard of living—by all workers producing more, or by all workers getting more of the money companies are already making?" 44 percent preferred their getting more of what the companies earn, compared to 41 percent who thought workers had to produce more in order to earn more. These sentiments may underlie the reactions Roper and Cambridge Reports obtained in 1978 and 1979 to proposals for wage and price controls. Both organizations found much more support for freezing prices than for limiting wages. (See Chapter 8, pp. 234–36.) Presumably, many people favored controls on price increases to stop inflation while believing that excessive profits could be used to subsidize continuing wage increases.

The Public's Understanding of "Profits"

Although the public clearly believes that profits are unreasonable, most people do not have a very precise understanding of the term "profit." YSW found in 1976 that 70 percent of a national sample thought that profits were "what business has left over after it has paid all its taxes and expenses." But apparently without recognizing the difference, most respondents also felt that profits were "the excess of the price received over the price paid for goods sold," which is technically known as markup. This latter definition is probably closer to the way profit is generally understood by the public.

One consequence of the widespread acceptance of the second definition is the prevalence of the belief that a great many legitimate business costs are paid for out of profits. The 1975 and 1977 *U.S. News and World Report* studies took this belief into account by phrasing their profit-margin question somewhat differently: "Out of every sales dollar about how much of that sales dollar do you think the manufacturer is able to keep as profit, after all costs and taxes are paid?" This formulation elicited an average estimate of 14.4 cents profit in 1975 and 17 cents in 1977. By specifying profits *after costs and taxes,* and thereby correcting any misunderstanding of the term, the question cut the public's estimate of the size of profits in half.

The confusion about the meaning of profits was brought out even more explicitly in a 1973 General Electric survey that asked respondents to examine a list of "some things manufacturers pay for" and then indicate, for each, whether "you think of them as being paid for out of the percent profit or not." While 58 percent felt that "dividends to stockholders" were paid for out of profit and 46 percent said the same thing about "bonuses for top-level executives," 42 percent believed that profits were used to finance "construction of new buildings or plants," 35 percent stated that profits were used for "research to produce technological breakthroughs," 32 percent thought they were used for "creating new jobs," 29 percent for "retirement benefits," and 26 percent for "pollution controls."

Of those who estimated the level of profits correctly (under 10 percent), only 25 percent said that profits were used to finance research and development, while fully half of the high profit-estimators (those who said that profits amounted to over 30 percent of every sales dollar) believed that profits were used to support research. Only 18 percent of those with correct estimates said that profits were used for retirement benefits, while 45 percent of the high profit-estimators thought this was the case. The same pattern occurred in the case of "pollution controls," "construction of new buildings or plants," and "creating new jobs." Those who greatly overestimated profits were more likely to see each of these costs as paid for out of profit.

Moreover, a 1975 Procter & Gamble study revealed that profit estimates are related to judgments about their reasonability. After estimating the typical amount of profit per dollar of sales, each respondent was asked whether he or she felt that this amount was "about right," "too much," or "not enough." The percentage who said that business was making too much profit increased sharply with the estimated size of the profit. Of those who said profits were under 20 cents on the sales dollar, 24 percent thought this was too much. Of those who judged profits as between 20 and 39 cents, 46 percent felt that this figure was too high. Almost three quarters —71 percent—of those who estimated profits at 40 cents on the dollar or more stated that this level represented "too much profit." Thus, a critical attitude toward profits is associated with higher estimates of their magnitude.

The same study showed that, as profit estimates increased, so did the proportion of respondents who felt that there should be more federal regulation of business. But the percentage favoring more federal regulation of labor unions did not vary with profit estimates. Clearly, then, profit estimates and antibusiness attitudes are correlated. The Procter & Gamble study noted this correlation and concluded that "a concerted effort to improve public understanding of actual profit levels could be a key step—if not the single most influential step—in reducing pressures for federal regulation."

High Profit Estimation and Anti-Business Sentiment

This conclusion assumes a causal connection about which we have serious doubts. Do high profit estimates cause people to be antibusiness, or is it the other way around? Our guess—and it can only be a guess—is that, to a large extent, exaggerated profit estimates are *essentially the reflection of an attitude:* those who are anti-business express their ideological commitment by overestimating the size of profits. It is not likely that informing them of the fact that profits are actually much lower will change their antibusiness convictions.

This interpretation is reinforced by several surveys that have related perceptions of manufacturers' profits to political orientations, occupational status, education, and income. The higher the estimate of "profit out of a sales dollar," the more likely a person is to be a self-identified liberal or Democrat. Thus, of the *U.S. News and World Report* respondents in 1977 who believed the profit margin per dollar of sales was less than 10 cents, 20 percent were liberals, while of those who felt the profit margin was 50 cents or more, 39 percent were liberals. On the other hand, the proportion of conservatives declined from 70 percent among people who said that manufacturers earned less than 10 cents on the dollar to 37 percent among those who estimated profits at 50 cents or more. In 1979, ORC found that Democrats estimated the after-tax rate of profit at 35 cents per dollar, compared to 28 cents for Republicans.

National Family Opinion in 1975 reported striking relationships between profit estimates, on the one hand, and education and income, on the other. Among persons with less than $10,000 annual income in 1975, 21 percent perceived profit per sales dollar as 30 cents or more, while only five percent of those with incomes over $25,000 a year gave a comparably high estimate. The correlation between household income and profit estimates in the *U.S. News and World Report* poll was especially striking. The proportion of those judging profits as less than 10 cents on a sales dollar declined steadily from 65.5 percent among those earning at least $50,000 a year, to 53 percent of those in the $25,000 to $49,999 income range, 41 percent among those with a family income of $15,000–$24,999, 33 percent for the $10,000–$14,999 group, and 25 percent among those with an income of less than $10,000.

The difference by education in the National Family Opinion poll ran from 24 percent giving a high profit-estimate among those who did not graduate from high school to 10 percent among college graduates. In August 1979, ORC found a variation in estimates of profits ranging from 40 cents on the dollar among those who had not completed high school to 35 cents among high school graduates and 23 cents among people who had attended college.

Since the public tends to confuse profit with markup, it is not surprising that Americans interpret rising *prices* as a sign of rising *profits*. In a 1975 Procter & Gamble study, 56 percent of the public said that business profits were a major cause of inflation; only federal spending, cited by 69 percent, and oil prices, mentioned by 85 percent, were more frequently named. As will be shown below, business profits, together with high wage demands by labor unions, appeared high on the list of perceived causes of inflation in Roper polls taken between 1973 and 1978. The only item that outdistanced profits and wages was "increased fuel and energy costs." Hostility to profits is, in part, an expression of resentment of higher prices, since profit is seen as such a large portion of the sales dollar to begin with.

Trends in Attitudes Toward Profits

In Chapter 2, we noted that the decline of confidence in the leaders of "major companies" in the Harris and NORC surveys has been significantly greater than the average fall-off of confidence in the leaders of all the institutions tested, including government. This shift may have been related to a change in feelings about profits. An indication of this relationship may be found in several polls that show anti-profit sentiment growing concurrently with anti-business sentiment. The Opinion Research Corporation noted a dramatic change in reactions to a statement offered respondents repeatedly between 1967 and 1981: "The profits of large companies help make things better for everyone." Two thirds, 67 percent, agreed with the proposition in 1967, but two years later, those approving the comment dropped to 55 percent. By 1973, fewer than half, 46 percent, felt this way. In 1975, the proportion accepting the proposition had dropped to 41 percent. ORC reported a slight upswing in pro-profit sentiment in 1977 to 43 percent, but 1979 saw a drop to a new low of 37 percent, followed by a slight rise to 39 percent in 1981.

This pattern of increased disdain for profits is reiterated in other ORC questions. For instance: "In industries where there is competition, the government should put a limit on the profits companies can make rather than allowing companies to make all they can." The data show increases from 25 percent agreeing in 1962 to 33 percent in 1971, 40 in 1973, 55 in 1975 and 1977, and 60 percent in 1979; agreement then fell off sharply to 51 percent in 1981. One ORC anti-profit statement, perhaps the broadest of all —"Business as a whole is making too much profit"—did not benefit from the slight relaxation of anti-business sentiment that seems to have occurred in 1977. Where only one quarter of the public in 1971 thought that this last statement was true, the proportion jumped to 35 percent in 1973, 45 percent in 1975, 50 percent in 1977, and, as with the previous questions, it reached a high of 51 percent in 1979, where it remained in 1981—more than twice the 1971 percentage.

Yankelovich, Skelly & White found a comparable trend when the following statement was offered in their national surveys almost every year between 1968 and 1981: "Business tries to strike a fair balance between profits and the interests of the public" (see Figure 6-1). Agreement with this proposition essentially collapsed in the two-year period between 1968 and 1970. In the 1968 poll, 70 percent said they felt this fairly modest statement was correct. In 1969, only 58 percent agreed. By 1970, the percentage had fallen to one third. Agreement continued gradually downward for the next seven years: 32 percent in 1972, 34 percent in 1973, 19 percent in 1974 and 1975, and exactly 15 percent in 1976 and 1977—down 55 points in less than ten years! The percentage agreeing with the statement did move up slightly in 1978, 1979, and 1980, to 17, 19, and 23 percent respectively, but it declined in 1981 to 19 percent, figures far below the levels of the late 1960s and the early 1970s (see Figure 6-1).

Although the public usually identifies government spending as the single major cause of inflation, Americans are also strongly

FIGURE 6–1
Trend of Anti-Business Sentiment, 1968–81
"Business tries to strike a fair balance between profits and the interests of the public"

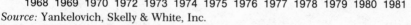

Source: Yankelovich, Skelly & White, Inc.

resentful of profits made by business and the wages won by labor unions. What disturbs people is that both appear, under conditions of high inflation, to be antithetical to the public interest, or at least to the interest of the vast majority of consumers who must pay for high profits and wages in the form of added costs.

Public Perceptions of Industries

Do general attitudes toward "business" or "big business" carry over to specific industries and firms? A closer inspection of the data on public favorability toward particular areas of business will allow us to identify the dimensions of judgment that people use when they express feelings about business.

Many surveys have asked respondents to evaluate different industries on the basis of a number of criteria. In order to examine the considerations underlying the public's ratings of individual industries, data from polls conducted by six survey organizations were factor analyzed.[6] Twenty-three questions were selected from fifteen surveys administered between 1976 and 1980. The number of industries about which the polls inquired varied considerably from question to question, from as few as six to as many as thirty-two, but a fairly constant core of thirteen major industries turned up repeatedly. Table 6-2 details the rankings of each of the thirteen industries on each question.

Certain patterns are discernible from the table alone. Oil companies were almost invariably considered the worst in terms of abuse of power, poor public service, and undue influence. Utilities (gas and electric power companies) were typically ranked high in terms of monopoly power but were not otherwise unpopular. The banking sector tended to draw the most favorable ratings, much as in the confidence surveys reported in Chapter 3.

The results of the factor analysis show that the twenty-three questions selected for analysis divide into two types:

1. Twelve of the questions rate industries in terms of *concentration of power*. We have listed these as Questions 1 through 12 in Table 6-2-A.
2. Eleven questions—1 through 11 in Table 6-2-B—measure the public's *favorability* toward individual industries.

These two factors seem to constitute the basic dimensions along which public perceptions of specific industries vary. Within each category of questions, the industry rankings are fairly consistent from one question to the next.

Concentration of Power

Three of the questions in the "concentration of power" category asked respondents to name industries too tightly controlled by a

---

[6] In this factor analysis, the twenty-three survey questions were the variables and the thirteen industries were the cases. A positive correlation between two questions indicated that the industries were rated similarly on both of them.

few large firms. Thus, Roper polls in 1976 and 1979 asked respondents to choose from a list those industries "where you think there is too little competition—where too few companies dominate the industry" (Questions 3 and 4 in Table 6-2-A). In 1977, Yankelovich, Skelly, and White asked a sample to pick the industries "you think of as consisting of companies that are too large and powerful" (Question 9). All three queries found that, when asked to identify industries where power rests in the hands of too few companies, a far larger proportion of people named oil and utilities than any others.

Three other questions dealing with the concentration of power related to efforts to break up the large firms that hold too much power. Question 2, from a 1977 Harris survey, asked, "How do you feel about breaking up major companies of the [specified] industry into smaller companies . . . ?" Yankelovich, Skelly & White asked in 1977, "Towards which, if any, of these industries do you believe a more vigorous antitrust stance on the part of the government is necessary?" (Question 7). Question 10 called for an opinion on the effects of antitrust action: "Would breaking up each of these industries improve competition in that industry and result in lower prices, or would it create inefficiency and result in higher prices?" (Cambridge Reports, Inc., 1976). Nearly two thirds of the respondents indicated their support for breaking up large firms in the oil and utilities industries, and almost half believed that such action would reduce prices. The drug, steel, and food industries were also considered good candidates for antitrust action.

Two questions falling into the power category identify popular targets for federal regulation. Both are from a 1976 Harris poll. Question 11 asked, "Do you favor federal regulation of the [specified] industry?" Not a single industry appeared on the list for which a majority of the public opposed government regulation. Drug, food, oil, and utility companies were considered prime candidates for regulation—in the case of the drug and food industries, one would guess, in order to protect the public health, and in the case of oil and utilities, to control monopolistic tendencies and hold down prices. Question 8 asked whether federal regulation should be increased, decreased, or maintained for each industry. The percentage favoring an *increase* in regulation averaged only half the percentage favoring regulation in principle: 34 as compared with 67 percent. The same industries as before were the top candidates for increased regulation: oil, drugs, and utilities, with food sub-

TABLE 6–2

Industry Rankings: Concentration of Power and Favorability

A. Concentration of Power

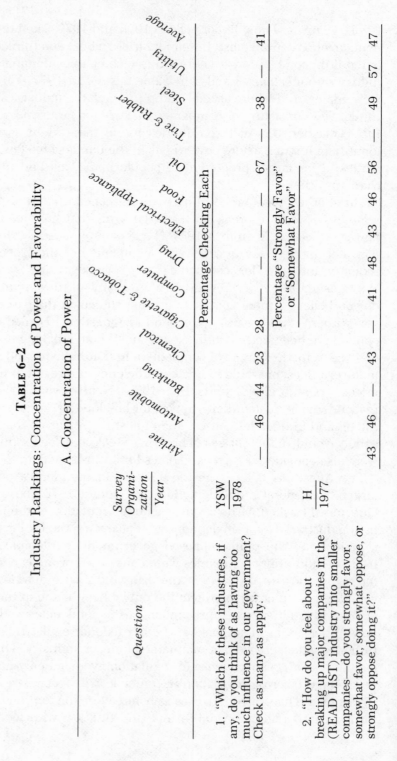

Question	Survey Organization / Year	Airline	Automobile	Banking	Chemical	Cigarette & Tobacco	Computer	Drug	Electrical Appliance	Food	Oil	Tire & Rubber	Steel	Utility	Average
		Percentage Checking Each													
1. "Which of these industries, if any, do you think of as having too much influence in our government? Check as many as apply."	YSW 1978	—	46	44	23	28	—	—	—	—	67	—	38	—	41
		Percentage "Strongly Favor" or "Somewhat Favor"													
2. "How do you feel about breaking up major companies in the (READ LIST) industry into smaller companies—do you strongly favor, somewhat favor, somewhat oppose, or strongly oppose doing it?"	H 1977	43	—	46	43	41	—	48	43	46	56	—	49	57	47

Percentage Choosing Each

3. "Now here is a list of some different kinds of industries. (Card shown respondent.) Are there any industries on that list where you think there is too little competition—where too few companies dominate the industry?"

R
1979

| 11 | 15 | — | 11 | — | 12 | 14 | — | 9 | 50 | — | — | 57 | 22 |

Percentage Choosing Each

4. Text of question same as 3 above.

R
1976

| 10 | 16 | — | 11 | — | 16 | 19 | — | 10 | 41 | — | — | 58 | 22 |

Percentage "Above Average"

5. "Now I'm going to call off some American industries. For each industry, tell me if you feel its profits during the last year have been above those of the average U.S. industry, or about the same as the profits of the average U.S. industry."

H
1976

| 32 | 45 | 47 | 43 | 49 | 42 | 59 | 29 | 34 | 76 | 35 | 47 | 57 | 46 |

Percentage "Absolutely Essential" or "Very Important"

6. "Now I'd like to ask you about several different industries, all of which are important to this country, to one degree or another. Using this card (card shown respondent), would you tell me just how important you feel the _____ industry is to this country?"

R
1978

| — | 77 | 89 | 85 | — | — | — | — | 96 | — | — | 92 | 97 | 89 |

187

Table 6-2 (Cont)

Industry Rankings: Concentration of Power and Favorability

A. Concentration of Power (Con't.)

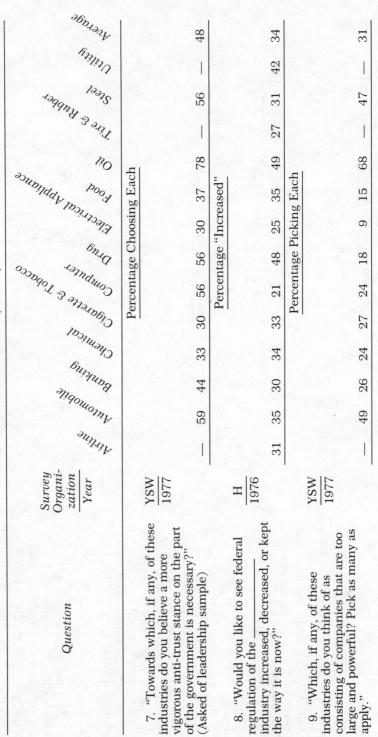

Question	Survey Organization / Year	Airline	Automobile	Banking	Chemical	Cigarette & Tobacco	Computer	Drug	Electrical Appliance	Food	Oil	Tire & Rubber	Steel	Utility	Average
7. "Towards which, if any, of these industries do you believe a more vigorous anti-trust stance on the part of the government is necessary?" (Asked of leadership sample)	YSW 1977	*Percentage Choosing Each*													
		—	59	44	33	30	56	56	30	37	78	—	56	—	48
8. "Would you like to see federal regulation of the ___ industry increased, decreased, or kept the way it is now?"	H 1976	*Percentage "Increased"*													
		31	35	30	34	33	21	48	25	35	49	27	31	42	34
9. "Which, if any, of these industries do you think of as consisting of companies that are too large and powerful? Pick as many as apply."	YSW 1977	*Percentage Picking Each*													
		—	49	26	24	27	24	18	9	15	68	—	47	—	31

Percentage Predicting "Lower Prices"

10. "Would breaking up each of these industries improve competition in that industry and result in lower prices, or would it create inefficiency and result in higher prices?"

CRI 1976													
—	36	34	—	—	32	43	—	42	44	33	40	45	39

Percentage Favoring

11. "Do you favor federal regulation of the ———— industry?"

H 1976													
67	64	66	68	63	54	80	62	73	73	64	66	71	67

Percentage Choosing a Negative Rating (0–4)

12. "I want to ask you about your overall attitudes toward some industries, and have you answer by giving me a number between zero and ten. A zero means that an industry does a very bad job of balancing the public interest and making a profit. A ten means it does a very good job in this area. In other words, the lower the number you give, the worse job you feel an industry is doing in terms of balancing the public interest and making a profit. In terms of balancing the public interest and making a profit, would you give ———— a zero, a ten, a seven, a three or what?"

RS 1979													
20	43	—	29	59	—	35	—	28	62	—	22	—	37

TABLE 6–2 (Cont)
Industry Rankings: Concentration of Power and Favorability

B. Favorability

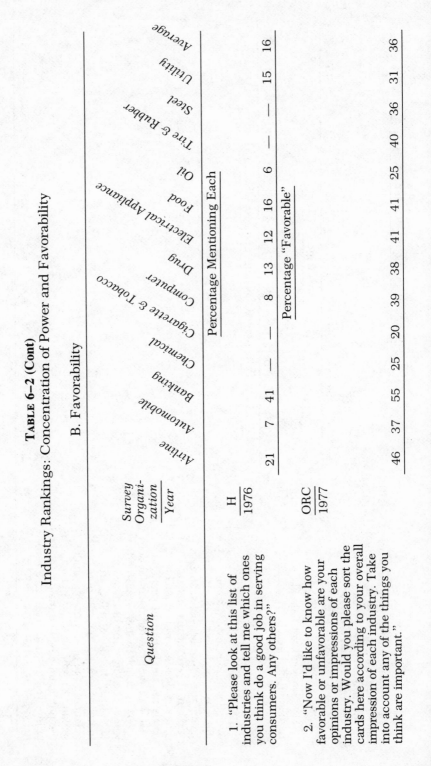

Question	Survey Organization / Year	Airline	Automobile	Banking	Chemical	Cigarette & Tobacco	Computer	Drug	Electrical Appliance	Food	Oil	Tire & Rubber	Steel	Utility	Average
		Percentage Mentioning Each													
1. "Please look at this list of industries and tell me which ones you think do a good job in serving consumers. Any others?"	H 1976	21	7	41	—	—	8	13	12	16	6	—	—	15	16
		Percentage "Favorable"													
2. "Now I'd like to know how favorable or unfavorable are your opinions or impressions of each industry. Would you please sort the cards here according to your overall impression of each industry. Take into account any of the things you think are important."	ORC 1977	46	37	55	25	20	39	38	41	41	25	40	36	31	36

190

ORC 1976 — "Which three or four kinds of companies do you think are best in their ethical and moral practices?"	—	5	56	4	—	8	20	—	18	5	5	4	15	14

Percentage "Very Favorable" or "Somewhat Favorable"

CRI 1979 — "I'd like you to tell me whether you have a very favorable, somewhat favorable, somewhat unfavorable, or very unfavorable opinion of each of these industries."	—	41	80	30	—	—	—	28	—	35	—

Percentage "Do Not Care Enough"

RS 1978 — "Generally, would you say that major corporations in this country care enough about protecting the public from environmental and pollution problems, or that they don't care enough? I'm going to read down a list of industries. As I do, please call off those, if any, you feel do *not* care enough about protecting the public from environmental and pollution problems."	22	43	46	51	—	30	27	42	38	37

Percentage "Favorable"

ORC 1979 — Text of question same as 2 above.	52	38	45	27	21	38	49	17	39	36	39	36

TABLE 6–2 (Cont)

Industry Rankings: Concentration of Power and Favorability

B. Favorability (Con't.)

Question	Survey Organization / Year	Airline	Automobile	Banking	Chemical	Cigarette & Tobacco	Computer	Drug	Electrical Appliance	Food	Oil	Tire & Rubber	Steel	Utility	Average
										Percentage "Almost Always" or "Usually"					
7. "I'd like to ask you about these groups. (Card shown respondent.) Do you think ____ is almost always open and frank about what it is doing and why, is usually open and frank, is only sometimes open and frank, or is almost never open and frank about what's going on inside?"	R / 1978	—	20	47	—	—	—	—	—	—	14	—	—	27	27
									Percentage "Highly Favorable" or "Moderately Favorable"						
8. "Using this card (card shown respondent), is your opinion of that industry highly favorable, or moderately favorable, or not too favorable, or rather *unfavorable*?"	R / 1980	46	—	—	—	32	—	54	—	59	20	—	59	—	45

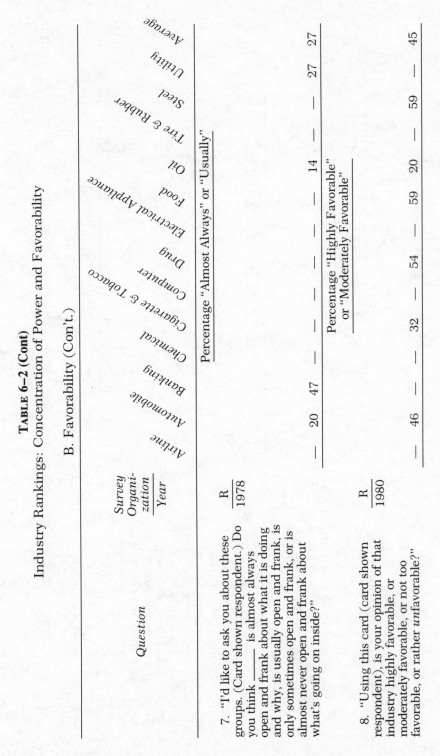

Percentage "Excellent" or "Pretty Good"

9. "How would you rate _____ on protecting the health and safety of the public in the products and services they offer—excellent, pretty good, only fair, or poor?"

	H 1977
	66 52 — 39 — 51 66 64 57 41 65 — — 56

Percentage "Very Interested" or "Moderately Interested"

10. "We'd like your impression as to how interested a few major industries are in the well being of their customers. (Card shown respondent.) Using this card, how interested would you say the _____ industry is in the well being of its customers?"

	R 1979
	— 53 — 44 — 57 64 20 — 45 47

Percentage "Highly Favorable" or "Moderately Favorable"

11. Text of question same as 8 above.

	R 1978
	— 56 — 56 — 55 60 40 — 43 51

CRI: Cambridge Reports, Inc.
H: Harris.
ORC: Opinion Research Corporation.
R: Roper.
RS: Roger Seasonwein.
YSW: Yankelovich, Skelly & White.
—:   Not asked.

193

stantially lower this time. However, there was no case where a majority of the public favored increasing regulation.

Question 1, from a 1978 poll by Yankelovich, Skelly & White, distinguishes another aspect of the concentration of power dimension: "Which of these industries, if any, do you think of as having too much influence in our government?" Of the six in the list shown to respondents, oil was chosen most frequently by far (by 67 percent). The chemical industry and, surprisingly, the tobacco industry were considered to have the least influence over the federal government (by 23 and 28 percent, respectively).

Question 5 also related to concentration of power, although it dealt with power only indirectly: "For each industry, tell me if you feel its profits during the last year have been above those of the average U.S. industry, below those of the average U.S. industry, or about the same as the average U.S. industry" (Harris, 1976). Three quarters of the public saw profits as above average in the case of the oil industry. Over half the public said that utilities and drug companies made above-average profits. Those least likely to be identified as making above-average profits were the electrical appliance, airline, food, and tire and rubber industries.

Interestingly, opinions about the importance of different industries correlate with the power dimension. A 1978 Roper survey asked respondents how important they felt various industries are to this country (Question 6). More people named oil and utilities as "absolutely essential" or "very important" than any other industry. The automobile industry was seen as least important of those about which the question was asked. All six industries on the list, however, were seen as at least "very important" by the great majority (an average of 89 percent).

Finally, respondents' ratings of industries in terms of "balancing the public interest and making a profit" are associated with the concentration of power (Question 12, administered in 1979 by Roger Seasonwein). Oil companies and the cigarette and tobacco industry were ranked negatively far more often than any other industries. People appear to believe that industries in which power is concentrated use that power to make profits, and do a poor job of balancing profits against the public interest.

These data suggest that several considerations contribute to the public's evaluation of the concentration of power within an industry. The industries Americans perceive as dominated by a few large companies are believed to make excessive profits at the expense of the public and to possess undue political influence. Consequently, the public supports federal regulation of monopolistic industries and efforts to break up the large firms that dominate these industries. People also believe, however, that the industries where power is concentrated are very important to the United States.

Favorability

The data also show that when Americans express approval or disapproval of specific industries, their evaluations depend on somewhat different considerations from those used to judge the concentration of power. Among the twenty-three questions selected for analysis, five asked directly for expressions of favorability (Questions 2, 3, 4, 8, and 9 in Table 6-2-B). Across the five questions, the oil industry and the cigarette and tobacco industry were consistently the least favorably rated (by an average of 24 percent for the tobacco industry and 26 percent for oil). Banking and the food industry were judged the most favorably: an average of 60 percent for banking and 52 percent for food.

The factor analysis helps to identify the characteristics that contribute to overall favorability ratings in the public mind.

Most closely associated with favorability is perceived service to consumers. Question 1, from a 1976 Harris poll, asked people to identify industries "you think do a good job in serving consumers." Twice as many respondents mentioned banking as any other industry. The oil, automobile, and computer industries were least often mentioned as serving consumers well.

Beliefs about an industry's concern for public health and well-being also correlate with expressions of favorability. Roger Seasonwein in 1978 asked a sample to name the industries "you feel do *not* care enough about protecting the public from environmental and pollution problems" (Question 6). The largest percentage of respondents named the cigarette and tobacco industry. Also frequently accused of not caring enough were the chemical, automobile, and oil industries. The public saw the airlines as the industry most concerned about environmental and pollution problems.

People also see airlines, along with the drug, tire and rubber, and food industries, as the most concerned with "protecting the health and safety of the public in the products and services they offer," according to responses to Question 9 asked by Harris in

1977. The cigarette and tobacco industry was not among the choices offered in this question, but, consistent with the previous ratings on concern for pollution, the chemical and oil industries were rated lowest. Oil was again rated lowest in Question 10: "How interested would you say the [specified] industry is in the well-being of its customers?" (Roper, 1979). The food and drug industries were judged most interested in their customers' well-being. Thus, perceptions of concern for the public in general and for customers in particular seem to play a major role in determining popular approval or disapproval of specific industries.

Responses to Question 3 suggest that perceptions of the ethical practices of industries also relate to favorability. Banks were mentioned as best in their "ethical and moral practices" nearly three times as often as any other industry in the question posed by the Opinion Research Corporation in 1976. The chemical, steel, automobile, oil, and tire and rubber industries were all named by 5 percent or less. Banking stands out again in the responses to Question 7, as the industry most often "open and frank about what it is doing and why . . ." (Roper, 1978). Oil was rated lowest among the choices given respondents.

The analysis shows that the favorability ratings for an industry relate to perceptions of the quality of service the industry provides, both to consumers of its products and services and to the public in general. Americans also take into account ethical considerations when judging individual industries.

Overall Ratings of Industries

By computing two factor scores for each industry—one for concentration of power and the other on the favorability dimension—we can observe the distribution of industries on the two dimensions simultaneously. This is shown in Figure 6-2.

The oil industry is by far in the worst position. It is at the top of the list in terms of concentration of power and near the bottom of the list in terms of favorability. The public sees utilities as almost as monopolistic as the oil industry, but utilities are not rated so unfavorably. The utilities are regarded as powerful concentrations meriting public control, but they are not "evil" monopolies, which is apparently the way the public sees the oil industry. The drug industry is a third area in which power is considered relatively concentrated. It is rated much more favorably than either oil or

FIGURE 6–2
Industry Rankings: Two Dimensions

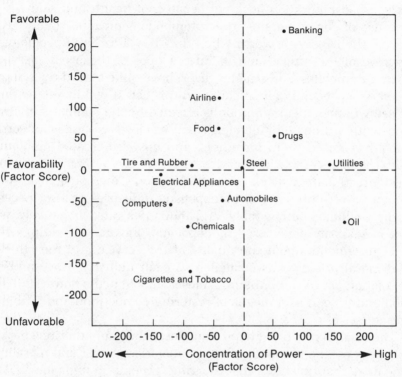

Source: See Tables 6–2-A and 6–2-B.

the utilities, however, since, as noted, drug companies are given higher marks for promoting the public health and safety.

The industry that stands out on the favorability dimension is banking. The perception of banks as providing good service and as being high in "ethical and moral practices" clearly lies behind their uniquely high favorability rating. But banks are also rated relatively high in terms of concentration of power. The banking industry is considered powerful but benign. The most recent evidence suggests that this view may be changing in reaction to the high interest rates of the early 1980s (see Table 2-3). The industry with the worst favorability rating is cigarette and tobacco, probably because it is associated with health hazards. Unlike the oil business—which is probably also perceived to be a source of pollution—the tobacco industry is not seen as particularly monopolistic.

It is interesting that the automobile industry is *not* ranked particularly low in terms of favorability, even though automobiles are a major cause of air pollution and accidental death. If automobiles have a bad reputation, it is not because of health and safety but because of consumerism—the automobile companies do not give people their money's worth when they buy a car, and people disapprove of the ethical and moral practices of those who service their automobiles. Airlines, however, have quite a good reputation for service, second only to banks on this list. It will be interesting to see whether this reputation is affected by the country's experience with airline deregulation, which has lowered prices for some trips, has raised them for others, and has also created problems with the quality of airline service.

Figure 6-2 thus displays the distinction Americans make between power and service. Monopolistic industries are not necessarily evaluated unfavorably, and industries rated negatively are not necessarily considered monopolistic. Favorability ratings reflect judgments about the quality of the service and the ethical and moral practices associated with each industry. Government regulation, on the other hand, is closely linked to the power dimension and is seen as a means of restoring competition and curbing the abuses of power.

The analysis in this chapter suggests that public criticisms of business can be grouped into two categories: power and morality. The next chapter shows that the same general grounds for dissatisfaction are raised against the main nongovernmental adversary of business: labor unions.

7

Labor Unions: Necessary but Unpopular

LABOR unions are something of a limiting case in the study of confidence. In almost every poll on the subject of public esteem, unions end up at, or close to, the bottom of the list. They are the least trusted major institution in American life, despite the fact that they have the largest mass membership of any organization in this country. Americans show an ambivalence toward unions similar to their contradictory feelings about a number of other institutions, that is, approval of their function accompanied by condemnation of their behavior. The public, as we shall see, views unions as necessary to protect workers from the arbitrary misuse of power by employers. People believe that without unions, workers would have to endure lower pay and worse employment conditions. But unions are also perceived as powerful, self-interested bodies working for their own advantage, and so they are automatically placed under suspicion. In addition, labor bears the special burden of having a leadership that is widely believed to be autocratic, corrupt, and contemptuous of the public interest. Thus, the public raises the same criticisms of labor as it does of business: too much power, too little morality. In the case of labor, however, the charge of unethical behavior seems to carry special weight.

Public Attitudes Toward Unions

√ Confidence

In the twenty-four evaluations of confidence in the leaders of institutions conducted by Harris and NORC between 1966 and 1981, the proportion expressing "a great deal" of confidence in the leadership of organized labor was 15.3 percent, lower than the figure for any other institution and only about half the average for all institutions together. The mean level of confidence for leaders of major companies was 25.3 percent in the same surveys. In the most recent poll in this series taken by Harris in September 1981, the confidence rating for labor leaders was 12 percent; for leadership of major corporations, 16 percent; and for the leaders of the ten institutions regularly inquired about, an average of 29 percent.

As indicated in Chapter 2, "labor unions" or "organized labor" did come out slightly ahead of "big business" in the Gallup confidence surveys taken between 1973 and 1980, only to fall behind in 1981 (Table 2-2). In the four ORC samplings of confidence in institutions taken between 1975 and 1981 (Table 2-3), the ratings of "labor unions" were more polarized toward the high and low ends of a seven-point scale than were those for "large business." Since the difference was much greater at the negative than the positive end of the scale, the ORC results seem more consistent with Harris' results than with Gallup's. In any case, all three sets of confidence polls agree that the evaluations of labor unions dropped off in 1981, putting them at or close to the bottom compared to all other institutions judged in these surveys.

A national poll conducted by the *Los Angeles Times* in September 1980 produced further evidence that labor stands lower in public regard than business, although still higher than government. When asked, "Which institution—business, government, or labor—do you have the most confidence in?" 41 percent replied business, 31 percent labor, and only 15 percent government. Similarly, in response to the question, "Which institution—business, government, or labor—has the best leaders?" 40 percent said business, 25 percent labor, and 22 percent government.

Labor placed below both business and the political sector in two Roper surveys taken in 1975 and 1977. An average of only 6.5 percent voiced a great deal of confidence in labor leaders in these two polls, compared to 12 percent for both business leaders and political leaders. More strikingly, 42 percent reported "not much confidence" in the heads of labor, while the comparable response for political leaders was 33 percent and for business leaders, 27.5. Labor also came out very poorly in 1974, 1977, and 1981 Roper polls when respondents were asked to assess the soundness of our political system, our system of business and industry, and our system of organized labor. Less than half of the respondents, 45.5 percent, rated the system of organized labor as basically sound, compared to substantial majorities giving the same response for our political system (62 percent) and our system of business and industry (63.5).

When the Roper Organization asked national cross sections for their opinion of people in eleven different occupations in 1976, 1977, and 1980, labor leaders were consistently near the bottom, followed only by politicians. Doctors headed the list with an average positive evaluation of 86 percent; business placed third, with 72 percent; advertising executives averaged 46 percent; federal agency and department heads were at 41 percent; labor leaders were evaluated positively by only 37 percent; and politicians, at 25 percent, were last on the list.

In view of these results, it is perhaps not surprising that the American people are reluctant to endorse the idea of a labor leader as president. When asked by Yankelovich, Skelly & White in April 1979: "Would it be good for the country or not good to have as President: a business executive, . . . a labor leader, . . . ?", respondents approved of having "a business executive" in the White House by a ratio of 59 to 25 percent, but rejected "a labor leader" by 53 to 30 percent. Surprisingly, blue-collar workers favored a business executive 55 to 29 percent but opposed a labor leader, 48 to 36. Democrats approved of someone from business by 56 to 29 percent but were unhappy about the suggestion of a union leader as head of the nation by 45 to 38 percent.

High Valuation

Clearly, the majority of Americans exhibits little confidence in organized labor or in its leaders. Nevertheless, when people are asked to assess the functions of labor unions, most reply that unions are essential and do more good than harm. The low level of trust in labor unions has not affected the public's positive judgments of their role and function in our socioeconomic system, a sentiment first expressed in Gallup polls as early as 1936.

On three occasions, in 1970, 1974, and 1975, the Harris survey asked whether unions are more helpful or harmful to the country; majorities of 56–58 percent consistently replied that they were more helpful, compared to 25–28 percent who called them harmful. In 1975, two National Family Opinion surveys found that exactly half the public agreed that "the only way for employees to get a fair shake in the average big company today is to belong to a union strong enough to stand up for them," while one third disagreed. A December 1976 Harris poll indicated that 85 percent of the public felt that "in many industries, unions are needed so the legitimate complaints and grievances of workers can be heard and action taken on them"; 59 percent said, "If there were no unions, most employers would quickly move to exploit their employees." Also in 1976, Cambridge Reports, Inc., found 58 percent agreement with the statement, "If it weren't for labor unions, management would take advantage of the workers," while 25 percent rejected it. The same survey found a comparable majority, 53 to 25 percent, agreeing that "unions are in the best interests of working people." The following year, in May 1977, a national cross section polled by Fingerhut/Granados agreed by a 59 to 34 percent margin that "most working people need labor unions to protect their rights." The same sample *dis*agreed, 54 to 35 percent, that "even if there weren't labor unions, big corporations would pay fair wages and give decent benefits to people who work for them."

Survey data gathered by Fingerhut/Granados in August 1977 indicated that three quarters of union members and those belonging to their immediate families felt that they or their relatives were "better off . . . as a result of being a union member." Only 4 percent thought they were worse off, while 17 percent said it made no difference. A similar question posed to those who had no personal or family involvement in unions yielded a plurality, 48 percent, replying that unionists were better off as a result of their membership, compared to 14 percent replying worse off and 19 percent saying that it made no difference. In the spring of 1978, Cambridge Reports, Inc., asked, "Which side—business or labor unions—do you think has more concern for the welfare of the average employee?" Not surprisingly, the public opted in favor of labor unions by over two to one, 52 to 23 percent.

Even though most Americans see labor unions as serving the interests of their constituency, approval of the institution has been moving in the same direction as other confidence trends—downward. That trend can be seen in a question asked by the Gallup

Poll twenty-one times over forty-three years: "In general, do you approve or disapprove of labor unions?" (see Table 7-1). This question appears to tap feelings primarily about the social function rather than the actual behavior of unions, and, as with the other questions on the role of unions reported above, the balance of sentiment has always remained strongly positive.

The Gallup question displays a series of peaks and declines. Approval was high during the New Deal 1930s, followed by a moderate decline during World War II and the early postwar years, possibly in reaction to wartime strikes and the subsequent high rates of inflation. The peak of union approval occurred during the "conservative" Eisenhower years, which were also a period of prosperity, low inflation, and generally high levels of confidence in all institutions. The steady falloff in support from 1965 to 1979 paralleled the general loss of faith in all institutions between the mid-

TABLE 7-1
Ratings of Labor Unions, 1936–81

"In general, do you approve or disapprove of labor unions?"

Year	Approve	Disapprove
	Percentage	
1936	72	20
1937	72	20
1939	68	24
1940	64	22
1941	61	30
1947	64	25
1949	62	22
1953	75	18
1957 (Feb.)	76	14
1957 (Sept.)	64	18
1959	68	19
1961 (Feb.)	70	18
1961 (May)	63	22
1962	64	24
1963	67	23
1965 (Feb.)	71	19
1965 (June)	70	19
1967	66	23
1973	59	26
1978 (April)	59	31
1979 (May)	55	33
1981 (August)	55	35

Source: Gallup, 1936–81.

1960s and the early 1980s. By 1979, approval of unions had fallen to an all-time low of 55 percent. But even then, in a double-digit inflation year, unions still won approval from a majority of the public, 55 to 33 percent.

There is some evidence that public support of unions may have begun to go up at the start of the 1980s. Two surveys conducted in March 1981 by Civic Service and the *Los Angeles Times,* which included the Gallup trade union approval question, came up with virtually identical results. Over three fifths, 62 percent in the Civic Service poll and 63 percent in the *Los Angeles Times* poll, voiced approval of labor unions, while only 26 percent in the first sample and 25 percent in the second indicated disapproval. These findings represent increases of 7–8 percent approval over Gallup's report for May 1979. The "feeling thermometer" evaluations conducted by the Center for Political Studies, as reported in Figure 2-3, also revealed an improvement in attitudes toward labor unions in its November–December 1980 test. As will be shown below (p. 213), evaluations of labor unions also improved in responses to questions dealing with power and with blame for inflation.

As can be seen in Table 7-1, however, an August 1981 Gallup poll found that only 55 percent approved of unions while 35 percent disapproved. The differences between the results obtained by the *Los Angeles Times* and Civic Services and those of Gallup may reflect variations in poll procedures or chance error, or they may point to an actual change in public attitudes. We are inclined to favor the latter interpretation. The earlier surveys were taken during a period of relative peace in labor relations, while Gallup's was conducted during a prolonged strike by the air controllers that severely inconvenienced large segments of the public and involved a clash between the labor movement and a new president at the height of his popularity.

Further evidence of the negative impact of the air controllers' strike on public attitudes toward unions may be found in a survey taken by Harris in August 1981, which focused on the "right to strike" of different groups of workers. Compared to polls taken in the mid-1970s, the 1981 results showed less support for the right of both public employees and private-sector workers to strike. Thus, between 1976 and 1981, the percentages endorsing the right to strike declined for public transportation employees (57 to 45), for sanitation men (51 to 45), postal workers (51 to 38), police officers (44 to 36), and, in the private sector, for automobile industry workers (70 to 65), truck drivers (66 to 63), airline industry workers (67 to 55), and railroad industry workers (66 to 55).

The Ambivalence of Union Members

Union members show some ambivalence about how well organized labor is serving their specific needs. A national survey of AFL-CIO members conducted for the labor federation in 1980 by Opinion Research Survey (ORS) asked them to evaluate how good a job their union was doing in providing eleven different services. Those interviewed were asked to rate their own union's performance in each area as either 4 (excellent), 3 (good), 2 (fair), or 1 (poor). (See Table 7-2.) Few judged any specific performance as excellent. The report submitted by ORS noted that "taking all of the services together, 13 percent of the respondents rated their unions as doing an excellent to good job [3–4], 54 percent thought their unions were doing a good to fair job [2–3], and 33 percent thought . . . [they were] doing a fair to poor job [2–1]."

It is difficult to evaluate these results in the absence of trend or comparative data. Each of the eleven services received an average

TABLE 7–2
Evaluations by AFL-CIO Members of Union Services

"I am going to read a list of services unions provide for their members, and for each one, I'd like you to tell me whether you think your union is doing an *excellent* job, a *good* job, only a *fair* job, or a *poor* job?"

	Mean Scores*
Increasing medical benefits	2.58
Improving health and safety on the job	2.56
Increasing wages	2.53
Representing member grievances	2.48
Improving working conditions	2.41
Supporting legislation in Congress for workers	2.33
Informing about voting records of Senators and Representatives	2.17
Increasing pensions	2.16
Increasing workers' compensation benefits	2.09
Supporting Congressional candidates	2.04
Protecting jobs against plant closings	2.01
Average Score	2.31

Source: Opinion Research Survey, July 1980.
N = 1,035.
 * Key: 4 = excellent, 3 = good, 2 = fair, 1 = poor.

score between fair and good. Union members were most positive about the ability of unions to secure direct payoffs to them with respect to medical benefits, higher wages, better and safer working conditions, and grievance representation. They were less content with the record of their unions in obtaining higher pensions, workmen's compensation, and, least of all, job protection against the threat of plant closings. Union political activities were also rated relatively low. In sum, AFL-CIO unions received a moderate vote of endorsement from their membership for improving wages, benefits, and job conditions but less approval for protecting their members from the economic consequences of job curtailments, retirement, or job related injuries.

It should be noted that more unionists in the 1980 poll felt that "unions in this country are getting weaker" than believed they were getting stronger. Thirty-three percent of all ORS respondents said that unions were getting stronger, 42 percent said they were getting weaker, and 14 percent thought they were staying the same.

Union Power: A Source of Concern

One source of public distrust of labor unions is revealed in polls that ask whether certain groups have too much or too little power. Consistently the most common response has been that unions are too powerful. In a 1965 Gallup survey, for example, 70 percent of the respondents affirmed that they approved of labor unions "in general," but at the same time, 57 percent felt that "unions have too much power in this country." In 1974, Harris found that 63 percent of those surveyed believed that unions had too much power, 22 percent replied that they had just the right amount of power, and 6 percent said too little. Even union members agreed that unions were too powerful, by 48 to 11 percent.

Two years later in 1976, the Center for Political Studies (CPS) asked whether "labor unions have too much influence, too little influence or about the right amount of influence on American life and politics today?" They reported that 64 percent answered "too much," 25 percent said "the right amount," and only 5 percent responded "too little." In September 1981, the CBS News/*New York Times* poll repeated the CPS question and found that hostility to unions had declined slightly, although the great majority, 60 percent, still felt they had too much influence, compared to 22 percent who said "the right amount" and 11 percent who answered "too little." Even among respondents who belonged to union members' families, 51 percent thought unions had too much influence in the country.

A majority of the public, 51 percent, told Cambridge Reports, Inc. (CRI) interviewers in 1976 that they favored "forbidding labor unions to engage in any kind of political activity," while 28 percent opposed such a prohibition. In 1978, CRI found 53 percent of a national cross section saying that "labor unions have too much political power," compared to 7 percent replying "too little" and 25 percent, "about the right amount." When asked in the same survey, "In general, which side do you think has more power—business or labor unions?" 50 percent answered labor unions compared to 33 percent for business. The CRI respondents also said, by 44 to 31 percent, that "the present labor laws . . . tend to favor labor unions [rather than business] in a dispute." In four polls conducted between 1977 and 1980, Yankelovich, Skelly & White reported that about 70 percent consistently agreed with the statement, "Unions are too powerful in our economy." In 1980, in a national survey focusing on the problems of the American economy, Penn + Schoen found that only 18 percent stated that "too much union power" was "not really a problem." Close to half the respondents thought it was a major problem, while 32 percent said it was a minor problem. Among the same national cross section, a majority, 53 percent, said they "would be more likely to vote for a political candidate who favored . . . reducing union power," compared to 35 percent who said they would be less likely to support someone who took such a position. Not surprisingly, union members backed the minority view: 53 percent of them said they would oppose an anti-union candidate; but still over a third, 36 percent, would favor such a candidate.

One of the most extensive comparisons of the public's assessment of institutional power was carried out by the Roper poll in December 1978. Roper inquired "whether you think the country would be better or worse off if certain groups had more influence and freedom to do what they think best." Labor unions obtained the most negative evaluation of the seven groups tested; over six times as many people said the country would be worse off rather than better off if labor had more influence (64 percent worse off, 10 percent better off). The public also disapproved of more influence and freedom for business and government, but by smaller margins: by two to one, people felt that the country would be worse off rather than better off if business had more influence, while majorities of three to one felt that more authority for Congress and the administration would be bad for the country. The public was only slightly negative toward the press (five to four), while it approved greater influence for scientists and "educators in the public schools" by roughly two to one.

In November 1981, Roper returned to the topic with a somewhat different wording, asking whether various groups and organizations had "too much influence, too little influence, or about the right amount of influence." At this point in the first year of the Reagan Administration, 53 percent replied that the federal government was too influential, 46 percent said labor unions were, while 32 percent credited corporations with excessive influence.

Though the public seems to view union power as more suspect than business power when queried about the two, people are less consistent in their views when asked to evaluate the power of unions compared with *big* business or *large* corporations. When faced with the latter choice, the public often, though not always, is more critical of the power of big business. As noted earlier, in Roper polls taken in 1973 and 1974, larger proportions said "big business corporations" had too much power than felt the same way about labor unions; but in a follow-up survey in 1977, fear of union power outweighed concern about big business. (See Chapter 3, p. 87). In 1980, Penn + Schoen found that 69 percent thought that "too much power" in the hands of large corporations was a major problem, compared with 46 percent expressing the same concern about labor unions. When Gallup asked, "Which of the following will be the biggest threat to the country in the future —big business, big labor, or big government?" in polls taken from the 1960s to the 1980s, there was no consistent pattern as between "big business" and "big labor." "Big government," however, was always seen as the greatest threat, with answers ranging from 39 to 49 percent. Larger percentages cited "big labor" (21–26) than "big business" (12–23) in surveys taken in 1967, 1968, and 1977. In 1979, however, 28 percent viewed "big business" as the greatest potential threat compared to 17 percent for "big labor." In a 1981 poll, the two institutions were tied, with 23 percent naming each.

The cue that seems to affect responses is the indication of size;

"big" institutions are generally seen as worse or more threatening. Thus, there is some indication that, in the case of labor as with government and business, the public sees large unions in much more negative terms than smaller ones. As noted earlier (see Table 3-3), the 1975 Procter & Gamble survey found that only 7 percent voiced "a great deal of confidence" in "big labor" compared to 21 percent in the case of "organized labor." When Cambridge Reports, Inc., inquired in 1976, "Can you tell me whether you favor or oppose breaking up national labor unions into smaller, less powerful groups?" 50 percent favored the suggestion, while 25 percent were opposed.

Unions and Workers

The fear of union power does not imply distrust of the unions' constituency, namely workers. In 1972 and 1976, the Center for Political Studies of the University of Michigan asked respondents to its national surveys whether various groups have too much, too little, or about the right amount of "influence in American life and politics." Among the groups inquired about were "labor unions" and "workingmen." The results for these two groups are presented in Table 7-3.

Clearly, Americans perceive labor unions as being too powerful, while "workingmen" are seen in opposite terms. Between 1972 and 1976, the percentage who said that unions have *too much* influence increased, while the proportion who felt that workingmen have *too little* influence went up during the same period. The public apparently differentiates between union power and workers' power. A comparable difference was evident in feelings about "workingmen" and "labor unions" as gauged by the CPS feeling thermometers (see Chapter 10, pp. 301–3, for further discussion). An extremely high proportion, 88 percent, were positive in their feelings about workingmen in the 1976 poll, compared to only 32 percent positive in the case of labor unions. CPS repeated the feeling thermometer question in 1980 and found 93 percent favorable toward "working men and working women" compared to 50 percent favorable in the case of labor unions.

The apparent tension between unions and workers in the public's view may be seen in the opposition of Americans to the idea of a union shop (i.e., the requirement that all workers must join a

209

TABLE 7–3
Evaluation of the Influence of Unions and Workers in American Life and Politics

"Some people think that certain groups have too much influence in American life and politics, while other people feel that certain groups don't have as much influence as they deserve. Here are three statements about how much influence a group might have. For each group I read to you, just tell me the number of the statement that best says how you feel: (1) Too much influence; (2) Just about the right amount of influence; (3) Too little influence."

	Percentage Describing Group as Having:			N
	Too Much Influence	Just about the Right Amount of Influence	Too Little Influence	
1972				
Labor Unions	56	33	4	2,166
Workingmen	3	49	44	2,161
1976				
Labor Unions	64	25	5	2,396
Workingmen	4	38	53	2,394

Source: Center for Political Studies, University of Michigan.

union). Gallup and ORC have repeated such questions a number of times since 1965. Gallup has asked: "Do you think a person should or should not be required to join a union if he or she works in a unionized factory or business?" In 1965, 44 percent said they should be so required, while 49 percent disagreed. By the spring of 1977, the percentage approving of a union shop had fallen to 31, while 63 percent were opposed to it.

A similar trend is evident in seven surveys taken by ORC between 1965 and 1980 that asked respondents:

> Which among these [three] arrangements do you favor for workers in industry?
> a. A man can hold a job whether or not he belongs to a union [open shop]
> b. A man can get a job if he doesn't already belong but has to join after he is hired [union shop]
> c. A man can get a job only if he already belongs to a union [closed shop].

Put this way, the proportion favoring the first alternative, the open shop, increased from 60 percent in 1965 to 68 percent in 1974 and 75 percent in 1976, and then held constant at 73 to 74 percent in 1977 and 1980. Very few, 4 percent or less, supported a closed shop while sentiment for the union shop declined from 32 percent in 1965 to 20 percent in 1980.

In 1978, Cambridge Reports, Inc., presented respondents with a statement that explained the case for the union shop:

> Some people say that if a majority of employees of a firm or factory want to have a labor union, then every employee should have to pay dues to the union since the union will be representing them. Do you agree with this idea or not?

Given this argument, 39 percent endorsed the union shop, but 46 percent still opposed the policy. Clearly most Americans do not approve of workers being required to join or pay dues to unions as a condition for employment, and the proportion opposed has been steadily increasing.

The public is less hostile to unions when asked to choose between them and business in a strike situation. Still, it may be noted that in two surveys taken four years apart, more people expressed support for business—described in the query as "a large company"—than for unions. The polls inquired: "When you hear of a strike by a union against a large company, and before you know of any of the details, is your first reaction to side with the union or to side with the company?" In August 1977, Roper found that a plurality, 32 percent, said they would side with the company, while 28 percent replied they would support the union. Another 21 percent volunteered the answer that their reaction would depend on the issues, the company, or the union involved, while 11 percent answered neither or both. Four years later in September 1981, the CBS News/*New York Times* poll repeated the Roper question with similar results, 40 percent for the company, 33 percent for the union, 10 percent for " it depends on the issues," and 8 percent for neither or both.

The Effect of Unions on Inflation

Organized labor, in the public mind, bears some of the responsibility for inflation. The survey data indicate that the public tends to see labor as a major source of inflation—more culpable than business, although considerably less to blame than government.

Both Gallup and ORC found this pattern in ten surveys taken between 1968 and 1979. These polls asked respondents to choose business, labor, or the government as the "most responsible for inflation." In a 1968 Gallup poll, for example, 46 percent blamed the government, 26 percent chose labor, and 12 percent, business. By 1978, ORC found 57 percent blaming the government, 29 labor, and 15 business. The results changed slightly in a mid-summer 1979 ORC survey, which showed 54 percent holding the government primarily responsible, with labor and business each blamed by 22 percent. The government was held responsible by the largest proportion in all ten polls, always followed (at a significant distance) by labor. Business was consistently in last place, except in the 1979 ORC poll.

The propensity of the public to hold labor more responsible for inflation than business was brought out even more strikingly in two polls conducted for *U.S. News and World Report* in 1975 and 1977. These surveys did not require respondents to select just one culprit, but rather asked for separate evaluations of several possible causes of inflation. Respondents were asked to agree or disagree with each of four statements: that "business is *mostly* to blame for inflation," "government is *mostly* to blame for inflation," "labor unions are *mostly* to blame for inflation," and "the general public is *mostly* to blame for inflation" (emphasis in questionnaire). While four separate responses were solicited, the context of the question was clearly comparative, given the emphasis on the word "mostly" each time.

In the results of these polls, the four attributions grouped quite clearly into two pairs. Government and labor were blamed by most people; the general public and business were not. Given the statement, "government is *mostly* to blame for inflation," 67 percent agreed and 22 percent disagreed in 1977. In the case of labor unions, agreement (blame) outweighed disagreement by 64 to 24 percent. The sample disagreed, however, 52 to 33 percent, that "the general public is *mostly* to blame for inflation." And when asked whether business was "*mostly* to blame," disagreement here too outweighed agreement by 57 to 30 percent. Overall, then, about two thirds blamed government and labor, while only one third held either the general public or business responsible.

Surveys taken by NBC News and by the *Los Angeles Times* in 1980 and 1981 suggest the possibility that Americans have changed their minds as to the relative degree of culpability of unions and business. NBC inquired in June 1978 and again in March 1980: "Who do you think is most responsible for inflation . . . the President, the Congress, unions, or consumers?" Unions headed the list in 1978 with 29 percent; political forces, the President and the Congress together, were second at 24 percent; industry was third at 22 percent and consumers fourth at 12 percent. By March 1980, the President and Congress led with 37 percent, industry was second at 14 percent, while unions and consumers tied for third, each chosen by 11 percent. In September 1980, the *Los Angeles Times* poll also found a slightly larger proportion saying that business was responsible for causing inflation (18 percent) than saying labor (15 percent). Still the majority of respondents, 52 percent, fixed the blame on government. Six months later, in March 1981, the same survey organization reported that 19 percent put primary responsibility on business, while only 13 percent cited labor; the government, at 47 percent, remained the most culpable institution.

It is difficult to reconcile the differences between the 1980–81 surveys and the earlier ones concerning responsibility for inflation. The most recent polls may reflect a real shift in the public's judgment, possibly reflecting the emphasis in election campaign rhetoric on the culpability of politicians, as well as the fact that prior to the air controllers' walkout, very few strikes in the 1979–81 period attracted media attention. But there is further evidence that the public's evaluation of labor unions may have been improving before the controllers' strike. As noted earlier, the proportion who approved of labor unions in the March 1981 *Los Angeles Times* poll was higher (63 percent) than that found by Gallup in 1979 (55 percent).

In 1980, the NBC News poll asked how much of the blame—a lot, some, or not much—each of several groups bore for the high rate of inflation. "Big business" was assigned "a lot" of blame by 53 percent, consumers ("Americans spending too much and saving too little") by 43 percent, Congress by 40 percent, labor unions by 32 percent, and President Carter by 20 percent. A 1981 poll by ABC News and the *Washington Post* inquired about each of five possible causes of higher prices. The results showed more frequent mention of "large corporations seeking maximum profits" as a major cause (47 percent) than "wage demands by large unions" (37 percent). "The price of foreign oil" and "spending by the federal government" were also cited by larger proportions than labor, over two fifths. The fact that business received more blame than labor unions in these two surveys is probably due to the fact that they inquired about "big business" and "large corporations," whereas most of the other surveys dealt with "business." As noted earlier, the public's comparative evaluation of business and labor varies considerably depending on whether or not the adjective "big" is used.

As with its attitudes toward business, the public repeatedly asserts its disdain for self-interested behavior, agreeing, for example, with the principle that organized labor "has a responsibility to do what is in the best interest of the whole nation—even if it means wage restraints over the next year." Overwhelming majorities, by ratios of five or six to one, approved of this statement in Roper surveys in 1975 and 1976. Asked by Cambridge Reports, Inc., in 1976 about the policies of trade unions, 81 percent replied that labor unions should be moderate in their wage demands and that large raises were bad for the country. Queried whether they thought "large labor unions generally considered the good of the country when making new wage proposals," almost three quarters, 73 percent, said they did not, while only 15 percent thought they did. In 1975 and 1977, when questioned by Roper as to what unions should do next in their contract negotiations, less than 10 percent of the public said that they should try to get the largest possible wage increases. A plurality in both years, 53 percent in 1975 and 45 percent in 1977, thought that unions should not look for any wage increases at all, while 31 percent in 1975 and 40 percent two years later felt they should ask for only "cost of living adjustments."

When asked to evaluate the institutions responsible for holding back economic growth, Americans tend to assign blame in the same way as in the case of inflation. Among the 51 percent of those interviewed by ORC in mid-summer 1979 who felt the "country is *not* making economic progress," 54 percent cited the government as most responsible for the lack of progress, compared to 28 percent who blamed labor unions and 16 percent, business. In a 1979 survey, Roger Seasonwein asked about various factors that might either help or hold down the nation's economic growth. "Government spending," at 62 percent, led the list of growth-inhibiting factors, followed by "the size of the federal government" (54 percent). Labor unions were viewed as anti-growth by 49 percent, while only 29 percent blamed "major corporations." Twenty-eight percent felt that unions *help* the nation's economic growth while 43 percent said the same thing about business. Thus, government and labor were seen as anti-growth forces, while major corporations were perceived as pro-growth.

The Public's Perception of Union Leaders

Antagonism toward labor leaders is greater than that towards unions. Roper inquired in 1975 and 1977, "In today's times, do you feel that most labor leaders are being responsible, that some of them are, or that very few of them are?" Put this way, only 11 percent in 1977 thought that "most union leaders" fit that description, down two points from the earlier survey. Forty-one percent replied in 1977 that very few labor leaders were reasonable and responsible, up from 36 percent in 1975.

The view that labor leaders are less likely than business leaders to consider the national interest has a long history. In a poll taken in 1941, Gallup asked, for labor union leaders and business leaders separately, whether each was "helping the national defense production program as much as they should." The public responded negatively about union officials by 78–12 percent, while it divided almost evenly in its judgment of business leaders, 42 percent "yes" to 41 percent "no."

Almost four decades later, in 1978, Cambridge Reports, Inc., inquired more generally whether "the average labor union leader" and "the average businessman" represents the interests of the American public or not. Once again, the proportion responding positively for businessmen was greater than that for labor leaders, 26 to 21 percent. But majorities—57 percent for unions, 54 for business—thought neither represented the public interest.

Given the fact that both labor and business are perceived as powerful, self-interested forces that do not have the public's interest at heart, why are labor organizations frequently held in greater disdain than business? The answer may lie in the *belief* that business does some good for everyone in society, even if only incidentally, while unions act primarily to benefit their members and leaders, and have only a negative impact on the rest of the public. Strikes, the most publicized activity of labor unions, inconvenience the public at large, and wage settlements are often seen as selfish and inflationary.

Part of the answer may also lie in the fact that the public has a much better impression of the personal qualities of business leaders than of labor officials. This judgment is suggested by the results of Roper surveys taken in 1975 and 1978, which invited respondents to choose from a list the two "qualities you think would help get a person ahead fastest in government, in business, and in the labor or union movement." Those most often selected for labor leaders had a more negative cast than those cited for government officials, while the qualities identified as important for business people were the most positive of all. Thus, the four qualities mentioned most often for labor leaders were "knowing the right people" (31 percent in 1975, 35 percent in 1978), "aggressiveness" (29 and 27 percent), "willingness to make deals and payoffs" (18 and 22 percent), and "playing the angles" (15 and 21 percent). For government, the important qualities were "knowing the right people (51 percent both years), "intelligence" (31 percent both years), "aggressiveness" (25 and 27 percent), and "courage to stand up for your beliefs" (31 and 20 percent). For business, the requisite qualities were first, "intelligence" (33 percent in 1975, 40 percent in 1978), "sheer hard work" (40 and 39 percent), "aggressiveness" (37 percent both years), and, tied for fourth place, "knowing the right people" (28 and 29 percent) and "creative ability" (27 and 29 percent).

In a 1981 Roper survey, only 50 percent of Americans expressed a great or fair amount of confidence in the ability of labor leaders to make real contributions to our society. Seventy-four percent had such confidence in both political and business leaders.

The negative feelings about unions may stem from the widespread belief that union leaders are personally corrupt, autocratic, and unrepresentative of their membership. Thus, in a 1957 survey in which Gallup found a very high figure—almost three quarters —voicing approval of unions, a plurality of the same respondents, 43 percent, said that "corruption and graft are pretty widespread in labor unions"; only 34 percent said these vices were limited to a few unions, while a mere 2 percent thought there "isn't any" corruption and graft.

This view of unions was reiterated when Gallup inquired in 1976, 1977, and 1981 about the honesty and ethical standards of people in different occupational groups (ten groups the first year, twenty in the second, and twenty-four in the third). He found that labor leaders were ranked at or near the bottom of the lists in all three surveys in terms of the proportions evaluating them favorably. In 1976, only 12 percent judged their ethical standards "high" or "very high," while 48 percent graded them "low" or "very low" and 38 percent saw labor leaders as having "average" standards. A year later, 13 percent rated them "high" or "very high," while 47 percent classed them as "low" or "very low." In 1981, 14 percent put them in the two highest categories and 48 percent placed them in the negative ones. In the first year, the other nine occupational groups, including business executives, building contractors, and engineers, scored well above labor leaders. Finishing in ninth position—just ahead of labor leaders—were Congressmen, whose ethical standards were judged "high" or "very high" by 14 percent and "low" or "very low" by 38 percent. In 1977, labor leaders placed eighteenth on the list of twenty. The only groups receiving a lower rating were car salesmen and advertising practitioners. All others—this time including insurance salesmen, realtors, undertakers, and local political officeholders—were judged by the public as having higher ethical standards than labor leaders. Business executives did considerably better than labor leaders, although they scored well below the clergy, medical doctors, engineers, college teachers, bankers, policemen, and journalists.

Four years later, only car salesmen had a higher proportion than union leaders saying their standards were "low" or "very low" (55 percent for car salesmen compared to 48 percent for union leaders). Less than a fifth, 19 percent, gave the same unfavorable rating to business executives. Building contractors (27 percent), realtors (30 percent), Congressmen (32 percent), insurance salesmen (36 percent), and advertising practitioners (38 percent) also had fewer respondents characterizing them negatively.

Similar findings were reported in two surveys conducted in 1975 and 1977 for *U.S. News and World Report,* which asked, as noted earlier, for evaluations of diverse groups with respect to their "honesty, dependability, and integrity." Only two of the twenty-five groups were rated "poor" in 1977 by a majority of respondents, "labor union leaders" (51 percent) and "politicians" (53 percent). As the data presented in Table 3-2 indicate, the Opinion Research Corporation came up with similar results in its 1975, 1977, 1979, and 1981 polls, all showing labor leaders at the very bottom of a list of eighteen occupations ranked by their "ethical and moral practices." Averaging the results of the four surveys indicates that only 22 percent rated union leaders "excellent" or "good," compared to 33 percent for corporate executives, 34 percent for U.S. Senators and Representatives, 59 percent for bankers, and 70 percent for small business proprietors.

Some indication of the behavior identified with labor leaders may be seen from the characterizations of them that most Americans endorse. In December 1976, Harris reported strong majorities—between 64 and 76 percent—agreeing with statements saying that union leaders have ties to organized crime and that they have "used their union positions to benefit themselves financially." Almost three fifths, 59 percent, said that "most union leaders have become arrogant and no longer represent the workers in their unions." Yankelovich, Skelly & White found in 1978 that a majority of a national cross section (55 percent) believed that union leaders are "generally immoral and unethical," compared to only 29 percent who felt that this was not true. Similarly, in March 1979, Roper reported that when asked what proportion of labor leaders use "union funds for their own personal expenses," 56 percent replied "most" or "fairly many." Union members agreed with the general public in this perception, some 54 percent describing many or most of their leaders as misusing union funds. And as reported in Table 6-1, more people believe that bribery and payoffs are widespread among labor officials than among business executives or Congressmen.

The complexity of the American view of unions and their leadership is brought out clearly in reactions to statements about unions presented by Harris to a national cross section in December 1976 (see Table 7-4). What is striking in Table 7-4 is that a majority of the public—indeed, quite a substantial majority—agrees with *every* pro-union statement and *every* anti-union statement. Unions are clearly seen as "needed," "legitimate," "good forces," protective of employees' interests, and socially progressive. But they are also seen as too powerful and their leaders as arrogant, abusive, self-serving, and corrupt.

Roper reported similarly mixed attitudes in two surveys taken in August 1977 and again in August 1981. On the one hand, 61 percent in the first poll, and 63 percent in the second, agreed that "unions have made employers more responsible about employees' welfare, even in companies that don't have unions." Only 31 percent in 1977 and 35 percent four years later took the position that "unions served a useful purpose once, but they've outgrown their usefulness." On the other hand, a majority, 56 percent in the

TABLE 7–4
Sentiments Toward Unions

	Agree	Disagree	Not Sure
		Percentage	
Pro-Union Statements			
"When unions were first started they were needed because workers were being exploited by low wages, long hours, and bad working conditions."	96	1	3
"In many industries, unions are needed so the legitimate complaints and grievances of workers can be heard and action taken on them."	85	7	8
"Labor unions are as much a part of our democratic system as private companies, farm groups, and other organized parts of American society."	80	7	13
"Most unions in the U.S. have been good forces, working for such things as national health insurance, higher employment compensation, better Social Security, minimum wage laws, and other desirable social needs."	76	10	14
"If there were no unions, most employers would quickly move to exploit their employees."	59	25	16
"Most unions stand for helping less privileged people get a better break."	59	25	16
Anti-Union Statements			
"Many union leaders have used their union positions to benefit themselves financially."	76	10	14
"Many union leaders have known ties with racketeers and organized crime."	64	13	23
"Unions have become too powerful and should be restricted in the abuse of their power by law."	63	25	12
"Most union leaders have become arrogant and no longer represent the workers in their unions."	59	24	17
"Many union leaders have abused union pension funds."	59	15	26

Source: Harris Survey, December 1976.

earlier survey and 54 percent in the latter, agreed that "many union leaders are crooked," while 56 percent in 1977 and 60 percent in 1981 felt that "unreasonable demands by labor unions make the cost of living go up more than it needs to."

Conclusion

The evidence is quite clear from a large number of surveys that the public views labor in contrasting lights. First, significant majorities see unions as legitimate forces in a democratic society, important in preventing the exploitation of their members and in serving the interests of the less privileged. Although the majority voicing approval of trade unions has declined steadily since the mid-1960s, unions have still won public approval in the most recent polls on the subject, which were taken in August 1981 at a time of high inflation. On the other hand, unions are resented for a number of reasons. Like business and government, labor unions are seen as powerful and essentially self-serving. Unions are perceived as worse than business and government in two respects: first, they are seen as giving low priority to the public interest and as working against the good of the whole society, and second, their leaders are believed to be exceptionally corrupt and unethical. In short, the principal virtue of unions is how well they serve the interests of their members. Their principal defect is that, by doing exactly that, unions seem to do little to benefit the public interest.

8

Government Regulation

"THE adversary relationship between government and business," that Ronald Reagan expressed so much concern about in January 1981 has been most evident in the area of government regulation. The effort of the federal government to circumscribe business activity has a long history, reaching deep into the nineteenth century. Farmers were particularly vocal in demanding that public authorities set limits on the activities of railroads, banks, and commodity marketing companies. Populists, Progressives, and Socialists joined in condemning the practices of big business in the years before World War I. Their criticisms produced controls on monopolies and utilities, anti-trust legislation, and legislation affecting conditions of work.

The Great Depression of the 1930s and the New Deal intensified the conflict between government and business, most notably through measures limiting the power of business in the area of labor relations. It was after World War II, however, that government regulation of business increased markedly. Regardless of whether Democrats or Republicans were in possession of the presidency, the number of federal regulations increased rapidly. Of the eight four-year presidential terms between 1949 and 1981, the pages in the *Federal Register,* a publication largely devoted to regulatory activity, increased by at least 24 percent during six of them. The only exceptions were Dwight D. Eisenhower's first term,

1953–57, and Lyndon B. Johnson's administration, 1965–69. The years shared by Richard Nixon and Gerald Ford, 1969–77, witnessed the largest post-war growth of the *Federal Register*—97 percent. It is noteworthy that the number of pages in the *Federal Register* increased by 167 percent in the sixteen years of Republican administration and by 114 percent during the sixteen years when the executive branch was presided over by Democrats.[1]

These changes, apparently unrelated to the manifest ideology of the two parties, were linked to the growth of public support for environmental protection, product safety controls, occupational safety, equal rights for women and minorities, and other reformist goals. In most cases, proponents of increased regulation made their case in terms of the need to control business, whose perceived greed for profits was in direct conflict with their conception of the public interest.

This increase in the regulatory activity of the federal government intensified the adversary relationship between business and government. Business leaders have argued that government regulation hinders their ability to operate efficiently, raises costs and prices, and inhibits the country's economic growth. Whatever the validity of these contentions, the public's readiness to accept the arguments for or against regulation basically reflects its confidence in either government or business, as President Reagan noted in his pre-inaugural essay. Given the fact that Americans have lost confidence in both institutions in recent years, it is a matter of some interest to find out how Americans react when it is a question of government *versus* business.

A Short History of Public Attitudes

A loosely comparable collection of polls dealing with the general question of government regulation of business is available from the mid-1930s through the present. It is difficult to come up with any reliable judgment about trends over this period, since the various polls posed quite different questions. Still, what is most striking about the results of these surveys is how little the evaluation of this issue has changed over forty years. All the studies

---

[1] Thomas Gale Moore, "The Democrats vs. the Republicans: A Quizzical Note," (unpublished paper, The Hoover Institution on War, Revolution, and Peace, Stanford, California, February, 1981).

indicate that a majority has consistently opposed *increased* regulation of business at any given moment. Most people have generally taken the position that the current amount of regulation was about right or too much. >

Thus, in September 1935, Gallup asked, "Do you think government regulation of business and industry should be increased?" The public said "no," 53 to 37 percent, even in the depths of the Great Depression. The results were similar in May 1940, when Gallup asked, "During the next four years do you think business should be regulated to a greater extent by the federal government?"—with the results this time 56 percent "no" to 27 percent "yes." However, the next question in the 1940 poll asked, "Do you think labor unions should be regulated to a greater extent by the federal government?" The answer with respect to unions was a resounding "yes," 62 to 20 percent. Indeed, the public has almost always favored greater regulation of labor unions.

A similar Gallup question asked in an October 1940 survey allowed three (somewhat different) responses instead of two: "During the next four years do you think there should be more or less regulation of business by the federal government than at present?" Twenty-two percent of the these respondents said they favored more regulation of business, a result close to the 27 percent who supported more regulation in the May 1940 survey. But this time, 41 percent replied that they were for less regulation, while 18 percent were coded as favoring the same amount of federal regulation of business. When the same question was asked with respect to labor unions, the balance of sentiment once again shifted: 44 percent called for more regulation of labor unions, 14 percent favored less, and 14 percent said that the amount of labor regulation should be kept the same.

World War II produced the most extensive government regulation the U.S. economy had ever experienced. How did the public react to this experience? In August 1945, a national survey taken by the *New York Herald Tribune* asked the following question:

> There have been all sorts of ideas suggested for things we should do in this country after the war, and we'd like to know how you feel about some of them. Do you think it is a good idea or not such a good idea to have less government regulation of business?

A majority, 54 percent, said that "it was a good idea" to have less government regulation of business, while only 26 percent said that this was "not such a good idea." Opposition to government regulation increased with socioeconomic status. Of those classified as "poor," 41 percent said that there should be less regulation. This figure increased to 55 percent among those identified as "lower middle," 70 percent of the "upper middle" respondents, and 76 percent of the "prosperous."

Indeed, it is not surprising that at the end of the war, people said they favored less government regulation of business, a position that most respondents probably interpreted as meaning less regulation than had been in effect during the war. But was regulation per se still unpopular? In September 1945, the National Opinion Research Center asked a question on government regulation in the context of a different time-frame: "During the next year or two, how much control do you think the government should have over business—do you think it should have more control than it had before Pearl Harbor, or should it have less?" In this case, 42 percent of the public favored more government control than there had been before Pearl Harbor, while only 20 percent favored less regulation and 22 percent said the same.

Thus, one gets the impression that Americans at the end of World War II wanted more government regulation of business than was the case in the 1930s but less regulation than during the war. The NORC survey asked an interesting follow-up question of the 42 percent who said they favored more control of business than was the case before the war: "What controls do you think the government should have now that it didn't have before Pearl Harbor?" The leading answer, given by 29 percent of those who favored greater regulation, was control of prices (price ceilings, the OPA, rent controls, etc.). An additional 17 percent replied that by greater government intervention, they meant control of strikes and labor unions, while 12 percent explained their answer as meaning control of both wages and prices. Thus, the form of "regulation" that grew in popularity during the war appears to have been government controls over wages and especially prices, not regulation of business competition or product quality.

Intermittently, between the end of the war and the general decline of confidence in the mid-1960s, different pollsters inquired —unfortunately with varying wordings—whether government regulation of business was excessive, about right, or inadequate. In 1948, the Roper organization found that 35 percent said regulation had been carried too far, 27 percent felt there was "the right amount," and 23 percent said more was needed. Four years later in 1952, a differently worded Roper question on the extent of regulation reported 49 percent saying "too much," 29 percent "about right," and only 7 percent, "not enough."

Then, in 1961 and 1962, the Gallup Poll asked, "Do you think the laws regulating (business corporations/labor unions) are too strict, or not strict enough?" The results are shown in Table 8-1. The findings of these polls may be viewed in different ways. First, if one discounts the variation in question wording between the Roper polls from 1948 and 1952 and Gallup's in 1961 and 1962, it appears that opposition to regulation may have declined between the Truman-Eisenhower period and the Kennedy era. In the early 1960s, few people, roughly one in ten, believed that business was overregulated, sharply down from the 49 percent who responded this way in 1952. But even under Kennedy, in 1961 and 1962, only a quarter felt there should be more controls. A plurality, around 39 percent, were presumably satisfied with the existing regulatory

TABLE 8–1

Attitudes Toward Regulation of Business and Labor, 1961–62

"Do you think the laws regulating business corporations are too strict, or not strict enough?"

	September 1961	June 1962
	Percentage	
Too strict	9	13
Not strict enough	26	27
About right	32	29
Don't know	33	31
Total	100	100

"Do you think the laws regulating labor unions are too strict, or not strict enough?"

	September 1961	June 1962
	Percentage	
Too strict	9	10
Not strict enough	42	48
About right	27	25
Don't know	22	17
Total	100	100

Source: Gallup.

legislation. On the other hand, there was considerably greater anti-labor sentiment, with close to half the public indicating that the laws dealing with unions were not strict enough.

During the 1970s, the proportion favoring an *increase* in government regulation of business continued to be a minority, although the pollsters who dealt most frequently with the issue—Harris, ORC, Yankelovich, Skelly & White (YSW), and Cambridge Reports, Inc. (CRI)—differed on how much support there was for an increase. Harris's and ORC's data suggest that the figure remained around 25 percent, CRI put it at closer to 30, while the Yankelovich firm reported a somewhat higher level of support for increasing regulation, about 40 percent. Harris asked on five occasions between 1974 and 1977: "In general, would you like to see government regulation of business increased, decreased, or kept about as it is?" On the average, 24 percent supported increased regulation, 28 percent favored having it decreased, and 38 percent were for keeping regulation "about as it is." The results from the five polls varied erratically and showed no clear trend.

A change in the public mood toward regulation of business began to be evident in polls taken toward the end of the decade by Cambridge Reports, ORC, and YSW. In the springs of 1978, 1979, and 1980, Cambridge Reports found an anti-regulatory trend in response to its argumentative question on the subject:

> In recent years, government regulation of all business has increased. Nearly everyone agrees that some regulation is needed, but some say there is now so much regulation it interferes with efficient business operation. Others say this regulation is needed to protect consumers. In your view, is there too much regulation of business or not enough?

Put this way, Cambridge found more people, 31 percent in 1978, 33 percent in 1979, and 42 percent in 1980, saying that there was "too much" regulation than the 27, 29, and 22 percent who replied that there was "not enough" in these three successive years; 25, 21, and 20 percent volunteered the answer that the existing amount of regulation was "about right" in 1978, 1979, and 1980. It is noteworthy that in the spring 1980 poll, support for the view that there is "too much" regulation equaled that for the two alternatives ("not enough" and "the right amount") combined. Cambridge returned to the subject of regulation in the summer of 1980, this time, however, wording its question somewhat differently: "In general, do you think there is too much, too little, or about the right amount of government regulation of business and industry?" In this case, the proportion replying "too much," 44 percent, was greater than the total of those saying too little, 16 percent, and the right amount, 23 percent, even though the latter response was now explicitly offered.

The *Los Angeles Times* used CRI's summer 1980 question in a national poll taken in March 1981 and reported a majority, 54 percent, saying there is "too much regulation," with 18 percent answering "too little" and 14 percent, "the right amount." A second March 1981 poll dealing with regulation, this one taken by Civic Service, gave respondents three comparable choices: "There is a need for more government regulation of business," "The present amount regulation is about right," or "There should be less government regulation." Put this way, slightly over 50 percent favored "less," 17 percent "more," and 23 percent said the present amount is "about right." And in July 1981, Harris reported overwhelming approval, 61 to 33 percent, for the statement: "After all the years that federal regulation of business has kept growing, we need drastic action . . . to cut it back."

Further evidence that opposition to regulation has been increasing as we enter the 1980s is contained in three polls taken by ORC between mid-year 1978 and December 1980 (see Table 8-2). The

TABLE 8–2

Attitudes Toward Regulation, 1978–80

"In general, what is your attitude toward the federal government's regulation of business? Do you think there is a need for more government regulation of business, is the present amount about right, or do you think there should be less government regulation of business?"

	June 1978	August 1979	December 1980
	Percentage		
Less regulation	43	47	54
Present amount	23	23	19
More regulation	25	24	19

Source: Opinion Research Corporation.
N for 1978: 1,008. N for 1979: 1,054. N for 1980: 1,452.

proportion favoring "less regulation" increased from 43 percent in 1978 to 54 percent in 1980. ⟩

In four surveys taken in 1966, 1970, 1977, and 1981, the Gallup Poll documented the change in sentiment toward regulation when it repeated a question asking whether respondents felt better or worse off "as a result of government control and regulation of the business practices of large corporations." In tandem with the findings of other pollsters, Gallup reported that regulation increased in popularity between 1966 and 1970. However, as shown in Table 8-3, those saying they were "worse off" as a result of regulation increased from 15 percent in 1970 to 26 percent in 1977 and 40 percent in 1981. In the most recent survey, for the first time more people claimed to be worse off rather than better off as a result of regulation, by the substantial margin of 40 to 24 percent—and this despite the fact that the Gallup question specifies regulation of the business practices of *large* corporations.

As might be expected, attitudes toward regulation correlate strongly with socioeconomic and political characteristics. The less privileged, manual workers, trade unionists, Democrats, and liberals have usually been more favorable to regulation. Table 8-4 shows the pattern in the 1981 *Los Angeles Times* poll.

However great the public's hostility to regulation became in the early 1980s most people still rejected *ending* government controls even when such controls were in a context stressing some of their adverse effects. In March 1981, Civic Service asked a national cross section to react to this statement:

TABLE 8–3
Personal Effects of Regulation, 1966–81

"Would you say that you, yourself, have been better off or worse off as a result of government control and regulation of the business practices of large corporations?"

	1966	1970	1977	1981
	Percentage			
Better off	37	43	28	24
Worse off	21	15	26	40
No difference	18	22	26	17
Don't know	24	20	20	19
Total	100	100	100	100

Source: Gallup.

TABLE 8–4

Correlates of Attitudes Toward Regulation

"In general, do you think there is too much, too little, or about the right amount of government regulation of business and industry?"

	Amount of Regulation is:		
	Too Much	The Right Amount	Too Little
		Percentage	
Total Sample	54	14	18
Education			
Less than high school	42	16	21
High school graduate	52	14	21
More than high school	65	14	12
Occupation			
Business owners	80	8	2
Managers	76	9	11
Executives	65	14	14
Farmers	68	10	5
Salespeople	69	15	8
Clerical workers	48	16	19
Technical workers	58	9	24
Skilled and semi-skilled workers	47	16	22
Unskilled workers	42	16	25
Union Membership			
Union member	44	14	25
Member in family	44	19	21
Non-union	59	14	16
Party Affiliation			
Republican	69	9	12
Independent	62	10	17
Democrat	44	20	22
Political Orientation			
Conservative	68	10	13
Middle of the road	50	15	20
Liberal	43	22	25

Source: Los Angeles Times Poll, March 1981.
N = 1,649.

People have said that government control is wrong and what we really need is to end all government control of industry. They say rules and controls cause inefficiency and waste and should be stopped. Do you think this is true or untrue?

In spite of the emphasis on inefficiency and waste, 35 percent said the statement was true and controls should be ended, while just over 50 percent were opposed to such a proposal. Clearly, many who favored a cutback in regulatory activity still saw a place for some controls.

Regulation in Particular Industries

Some surveys have probed sentiments about regulation in specific areas of business. The distinction between attitudes toward the general and the particular discussed earlier (Chapter 2) also applies here. Americans are more likely to approve of the government's role in regulating specific industries than they are in regulating business generally. Thus, in 1977, Harris gave respondents a list of thirty-two industries and asked whether they favored or opposed "regulation" of each. A majority or plurality favored regulating every single industry except one (newspapers). Harris polls taken in 1976 and 1977 found an average of 34 percent in favor of the existing amount of regulation, 14 percent in favor of decreased regulation, and an average of 38 percent in favor of increased controls for thirteen different types of business.

Cambridge Reports asked national cross sections to evaluate the amount of regulation for six industries in 1978 and for eight industries a year later. The average number replying "too much regulation" was 17 percent in 1978 and 17.5 in 1979. The proportion saying "not enough" was 36 percent the first year and 38 percent the second, while the average of those answering "the right amount" declined slightly, from 30 percent in 1978 to 27 percent in 1979. The range of those saying that particular industries were not regulated enough varied, in 1979, from 61 percent in the case of oil companies to 16 percent for department stores. Demand for more regulation was low for retailers (21 percent) and banks (26 percent), and high for chemical companies (49 percent), electric utilities (47 percent), and automobile and insurance companies (42 percent). What appears to differentiate industries for which there is substantial sentiment for greater regulation from other industries is the size of firms in the former category and the extent of their control of the market. Retailers, department stores, and, as we have seen repeatedly, banks, are perceived to be non-monopolistic service institutions and, hence, to require less regulation than other sectors of business.

The Roper poll asked about government regulation in five specific areas almost every year between 1974 and 1980. A plurality of respondents (38–46 percent) repeatedly said that the amount of government regulation of automobile safety has been "about right." Prescription drugs and interest rates charged by banks were felt to need more regulation; about equal percentages of the public said in each poll taken before 1980 that the amount of government regulation was either not enough or about right in those cases, with the proportion replying "not enough" increasing considerably in 1980. Not surprisingly, even more government action was favored to regulate the manufacture and sale of barbiturates and the honesty and accuracy of advertising. Around 60 percent said repeatedly that there is not enough government regulation in those areas. In no case—five subjects in six different Roper polls—did more than one quarter of the public say there is "too much" government regulation of these activities.

The public also came through in support of specific regulatory activities when asked by ORC in December 1980 to evaluate nine areas of consumer protection with which "government agencies are involved . . . whether you think the federal government is now doing too much, about the right amount, or too little to protect the consumer." As can be seen in Table 8-5, very few (an average of 10 percent) said too much; a plurality (47 percent on the average) replied "about the right amount," while an average of 37 percent felt the government is doing "too little." The areas where the public is most inclined to favor more regulation are truth in advertising and packaging, and prices. There is less concern, although still a great deal, about product reliability. The message in all these polls is that government control of business has become widely accepted, even though the concept of regulation in general is declining in popularity.

It is interesting to note that attitudes toward specific regulations appear almost uncorrelated with people's general feelings about regulation. In 1977, Gallup found that people who felt worse off as a result of regulation agreed with those who felt better off that regulations with respect to advertising claims, labeling, grading quality, and product safety were inadequate, while both groups tended to agree that packaging regulations were adequate (see Table 8-6).

In spite of considerable support for the current level of regulation, survey results suggest that the public is also ready to approve

231

TABLE 8–5
How the Public Rates Consumer Protection Activities by the Federal Government

"As you know, the federal government includes several regulatory agencies charged with protecting the American consumer. I'd like to ask you about some of the areas of consumer protection with which these government agencies are involved. For each area, please tell me whether you think the federal government is now doing too much, about the right amount, or too little to protect the consumer."

	Doing Too Much	Doing About The Right Amount	Doing Too Little
		Percentage	
Truthful and informative advertising	8	39	49
Tasteful and decent advertising	7	42	44
Packaging that is not deceptive	6	46	40
Products or services that are priced fairly	16	40	39
Fulfillment of product or service warranties and guarantees	8	50	35
Enough information for customers to make own purchasing decisions	8	51	35
Products or services that are dependable	11	51	32
Products or services that are safe	11	53	31
Vigorous and open competition with other companies	17	50	24
Average	10	47	37

Source: Opinion Research Corporation, 1980.
N = 1,011.

deregulation in specific areas. Thus, when asked in 1979 by Cambridge Reports, Inc., to react to an actual experience with deregulation by indicating whether the removal of "many of the regulations on the airline industry governing such things as fares and routes . . . has turned out to be a good thing or a bad thing," Americans overwhelmingly responded "good," by 58 to 11 percent. The survey then asked this question: "Currently, the federal government is considering removing the regulations on other industries, such as trucking and railroads. Do you generally favor or oppose removing the regulations on these industries?" A plurality, 44 percent, spoke in favor of such deregulation, while 25 percent opposed it.

TABLE 8–6

Attitudes Toward Specific Regulations, by
General Attitude Toward Regulation

Believe Regulations Are Inadequate with Respect to:	Of Those Who, As a Result of Government Regulation, Feel Personally:	
	Better Off	Worse Off
	Percentage	
Advertising Claims	72	72
Labeling	65	55
Grading Quality	63	58
Product Safety	68	58
Packaging	38	32

Source: Gallup, 1977.

Two years later in May/June 1981, Roper found continued support for the specifics of airline deregulation. When asked to react to the "deregulation of airline fares so that different airlines can charge different fares to the same place," 63 percent said the change had "generally worked in the public's interest," while 27 percent thought it had been "against the public's interest." Not surprisingly, the sample was less enthusiastic about "deregulation of airline routes, so that airlines can cover or not cover any routes they wish." The policy was approved by 47 percent to 37 percent.

Still, it cannot be concluded that this support for deregulation in the transportation industry implies a general public willingness to accept all such proposals. When President Reagan lifted federal controls on domestic crude oil shortly after taking office, an NBC News/Associated Press poll, taken in February 1981, found that 39 percent disapproved of the action, compared to 31 percent who supported the removal of controls. And, in May–June 1981, Roper found 46 percent opposed and 38 percent in favor of "deregulation of oil prices, so that the per barrel price of U.S. produced oil is not held down below that of foreign produced oil." The difference between the reactions to deregulation of the airline and oil industries probably reflects the effect on prices that followed the removal of controls in each case. In the case of air travel, deregulation was followed by many well-publicized, sizable reductions in air fares. When domestic oil prices were decontrolled, however, prices at the gas pumps quickly increased. Since the public recognizes both the assets and the liabilities of regulation, people may endorse

233

either more or less regulation depending on the justification offered. When greater regulation is explicitly justified by something the public dislikes about business—say, high prices, poor service, or policies that endanger consumer or worker health and safety—approval is likely to result. But if the cost and inefficiency of government or interference with the free enterprise system is brought into consideration, public sentiment is likely to reverse and a smaller amount of regulation will be favored.

Wage and Price Controls

One area in which a majority of the public has been generally supportive of increased regulation in recent years has been wage and price controls, presumably in response to high inflation rates. Gallup has frequently inquired of national cross sections: "Would you favor or oppose having the government bring back wage and price controls?" The support to opposition ratio was narrow in polls taken in December 1976 and February 1978, 44 percent to 40 or 41 percent. From May 1978 to June 1981, however, half or more have endorsed wage and price controls: 52 percent in May 1978, 57 percent in May 1979, 52 percent in September 1980, and 50 percent in June 1981.

The findings of the Harris, CBS News/*New York Times,* NBC News/Associated Press, and ABC News/*Washington Post* surveys corroborate those of Gallup. In five surveys taken in 1979 and 1980, Harris reported majorities of 51 to 57 percent in favor of "putting in a system of mandatory price and wage controls" rather than "continuing the present system of voluntary controls over price and wage increases." In April 1980, the CBS News/*New York Times* poll found that, by 59 to 34 percent, a majority felt that "to deal with our economic problems" they would favor "government-enforced limits on wage and price increases." Shortly after Ronald Reagan took office, the ABC News/*Washington Post* poll indicated in February 1981 that the public favored "having government bring back wage and price controls" by 53 to 38 percent.

Cambridge Reports, Inc., and Roper dealt with the issue somewhat differently. They inquired about prices and wages separately. CRI asked: "Do you favor or oppose complete controls on prices to fight inflation?" and "Do you favor or oppose complete controls on wages and salary increases to fight inflation?" In seven surveys taken in 1978 and 1979, they found an average of 47 percent in favor of controls on prices and 42 percent opposed, but an average of only 37 percent supported constraints on wage and salary increases while 52 percent opposed them. Similarly, Roper asked his respondents in October–November 1979 to choose between two proposals to control inflation: "freeze prices on all products and services even if it results in some shortages" or "freeze all salaries and wages even if it results in some injustices." A narrow majority backed a freeze in prices, while only one third favored a freeze in wages under the conditions specified.

Thus it appears that the public is much more sympathetic to controls on prices than on wages. Since everyone is a consumer and most people are employed (or depend directly on employed persons), this difference may simply reflect self-interest. It may also be a function of the popular belief, noted earlier, that wage increases can be absorbed by most business firms out of their "exorbitant" profits, with no need to raise prices. CRI also found higher support for both kinds of controls among lower income and less-well-educated respondents. But the gap between low- and high-status groups was much greater for wage controls than for price controls. Conservatives, though generally more opposed to government controls of any kind than liberals, were more inclined than liberals to back wage controls, presumably, according to CRI, "because conservatives feel wage controls would aid business at the expense of workers."

While Americans may approve of such controls, this does not necessarily mean they believe controls will actually work. In January 1980, NBC News found 53 to 37 percent approval for "a mandatory six-month freeze on prices, wages, interest rates, and profits." But when asked, "Do you think mandatory federal wage and price controls would succeed in controlling inflation?" the same cross section replied "no," by 51 to 34 percent. Roper found a similar pattern in a poll taken in March–April 1980. His sample approved "wage and price controls at the present time" by 49 to 41 percent. But when asked, "If wage and price controls were put on, do you think both wages and prices could pretty successfully be held at their present levels or do you think many people would find ways of getting around wage and price control?" only 15 percent believed the controls could be held. Fifty-nine percent said "people and business would get around controls," 11 percent felt that wages could be held but not prices, while 4 percent thought prices could be held but not wages. Here, once again, is the ambivalence many people feel about government regulation. They approve of it as the only means available to alleviate a problem, but they lack faith in its actual ability to accomplish the desired objective.

The Limits of Regulation and Deregulation

The public's ambivalence toward regulation is also a function of the fact that people approve of some of the consequences of government controls while opposing others. Thus, pollsters can obtain sharply divergent reactions depending on the purposes or effects specified in their questions.

Two statements that elicited strong responses in Cambridge Reports polls reveal something about the limits of pro- and anti-regulation sentiment. Americans agreed, 61 to 28 percent, with a statement offered in 1975 that "the way business is behaving, we need the government to keep an eye on them." On the other hand, the same respondents opposed regulation, 63 to 24 percent, when asked whether they favored or opposed "regulating individual firms as to what they can produce, how much they can charge, how much they can pay, and so on." The latter choice was presented again in 1976, 1977, and 1979. Regulation of this nature continued to be opposed by a consistent three fifths, while 20–25 percent endorsed it.

Similar variations in the way the public reacts to regulation showed up in the responses to questions posed by the CBS News/*New York Times,* Roger Seasonwein, and ORC polls. The first found large majorities disapproving of regulation when it was described as interference with "the free enterprise system." In January 1978 and again in November 1980, the CBS News/*New York Times* poll asked respondents to react to this statement: "The government has gone too far in regulating business and interfering with the free enterprise system." Presented in these terms, majorities rejected regulation by 58 to 31 percent in 1978 and by 65 to 27 percent in 1980.

A national poll taken by Roger Seasonwein in 1979 emphasized protection of the public and yielded considerable support for increasing regulation:

Government Regulation

> Is it your feeling that the federal government is doing more than it should, less than it should, or about the right amount to regulate major corporations in areas like product safety and other things that have to do with protecting the public?

This wording produced a plurality, 43 percent, in favor of more regulation, that is, of the view that the federal government is "doing less than it should"; 27 percent felt the government is "doing the right amount"; and only 22 percent complained of over-regulation, that the government is "doing more than it should." Seasonwein repeated the question later in the interview, asking the respondents to think "about economic conditions now and in the next year or so" and offering them the alternatives that "the federal government should be doing more, less, or about as it is now doing" to regulate business in order to protect the public. This time, the proportion favoring increased regulation reached a majority, 55 percent, with 22 percent calling for less regulation and 18 percent responding that the current amount was right. The specification that regulation is aimed at "protecting the public" clearly raises support for it considerably. And as noted earlier, an ORC poll taken in December 1980 found that almost two thirds agreed that "protecting consumer interests are so important that requirements cannot be too high."

These variations suggest a difference between two ideas of regulation. The reason we need regulation is that business "behaves badly"; it does all sorts of things that are against the public interest in order to make money. But when regulation is defined as telling possibly innocent firms how to operate—"what they can produce, how much they can charge, how much they can pay, and so on" —then Americans draw the line. Similarly, the responses to the CBS News/*New York Times* question point up the fact that the public does not want regulations that interfere with "free enterprise" or the operation of a competitive economy. But in responding to Seasonwein, the public favored controls to protect people in "areas like product safety." The ORC results show that people support restrictions to protect "consumer interests." Regulation is bad when it means telling people how to run their business. Regulation is good when it involves protecting the public interest from the "bad behavior" of businesspeople who charge high prices, pollute, and indulge in corruption.

The Government as Regulator

Most Americans still do not accept any inherent government expertise in running the economy. CRI polls taken in 1975, 1976, 1977, and 1979 included this statement:

> Some people say the government should become more involved in planning and managing the economy. Others say more government planning would only make the economy worse. Do you favor or oppose more government involvement in planning and managing?

The answer was "no" each time, by an average of 46 to 32 percent in the four polls. The fact that regulation is widely supported does not mean that most Americans have confidence in government planning and management. Americans still endorse free market economic values, particularly free enterprise and individual competition. They favor regulation not because they want the government to run the economy, but because they have become increasingly concerned with what they view as the "bad citizenship" of business—or, perhaps, because they have become increasingly sensitive to the social costs of traditional business practices. Regulation is aimed at ending these abuses, not at telling people how to run their affairs.

Americans clearly believe that business should be pressured to change its ways in the interest of consumers and workers. Hence, they repeatedly approve of regulations to reduce specific evils. But at the same time they reject what they view as an *excess* of regulation. A 1975 Harris question asked "whether there are too many federal agencies regulating business." The public answered yes: 59 percent said there are too many regulatory agencies, 5 percent felt that there are too few, and 16 percent replied "about the right number." The Harris poll included special samples of leadership groups. Not surprisingly, 76 percent of industry representatives said there were too many federal regulatory agencies. A little more surprisingly, 89 percent of state elected leaders also agreed with this view. More surprisingly still, 53 percent of regulatory officials said that there were too many regulatory agencies.

The Regulation of Big Business Abuses

If possible, the public would prefer dealing with abuses through noncoercive measures. This fact was evident in evaluations of the

238

following statement presented by the Opinion Research Corporation in 1978: "The best way for the government to regulate business and industry is by establishing goals and providing incentives instead of developing new rules and regulations." An overwhelming majority, 71 percent, preferred the techniques of goals and incentives, while only 18 percent supported new rules and regulations. As noted, when regulation is presented as an encroachment on free enterprise, public opinion turns decidedly negative.

Evidence for this interpretation is contained in the findings of a survey carried out in 1974 on behalf of the Advertising Council. This study examined in detail the sources of support for, and opposition to, regulation. The query began thus: "Now, I'd like to ask your opinion of government regulation of economic activities. Do you think that, at the present time, there is too much, just the right amount, or not enough government regulation?" Almost twice as many respondents gave the answer "not enough" (43 percent) as said "too much" (22 percent). Nineteen percent said we have "just the right amount" of regulation, while 13 percent gave qualified answers ("it all depends") and 3 percent said "don't know." This particular wording, "regulation of economic activities," rather than regulation of business, yielded the highest proportion favorable to greater regulation in any poll.

When respondents in this 1974 poll who favored more regulation were asked why they felt this way, their open-ended comments provide some clues as to what was bothering them. The most commonly stated reasons were monopolies, tax loopholes, excessive profits, and concentration of power, as well as the need, cited by 18 percent, to stabilize or freeze prices. In offering reasons for supporting greater regulation, what many respondents seem to have had in mind were abuses usually associated with "big business" and not with business generally or free enterprise.

Respondents who thought there was too much regulation of business commented most frequently that regulation favors big business over small business, protects monopolies, controls or limits competition, interferes with production and free enterprise, allows for price-fixing, and creates too much red tape. In other words, those who say that there is too much regulation defend their position by expressing the same values and priorities as those who say there is not enough regulation! Regulation is both advocated and criticized in the name of free enterprise and a competitive economy.

Accordingly, regulation of "big business" is considerably more popular than controls over "business." Harris asked about both in February and again in June 1976. He also inquired in the June poll whether regulation of "business" and "big business" should be increased or decreased. The responses are shown in Table 8-7. Americans in 1976 were opposed to federal regulation of "business" by a slight plurality, but they were decidedly favorable to federal regulation of "big business." In both polls, more respondents wanted to see a decrease than an increase in the regulation of "business," but the June 1976 poll showed more Americans favoring an increase than a decrease in the regulation of "big business"—more even than the percentage who favored keeping regulation of big business "about as it is."

TABLE 8–7
Attitudes Toward Government Regulation: Sources of Variation

	Favor	Oppose
	Percentage	
1. "In general, do you favor or oppose federal government regulation of business?"		
February 1976	35	50
June 1976	41	44
2. "In general, do you favor or oppose federal government regulation of *big* business?" *		
February 1976	48	39
June 1976	60	26

	Increased	Kept As Is	Decreased
	Percentage		
3. "In general, would you like to see federal government regulation of business increased, decreased, or kept about as it is?"			
February 1976	24	31	34
June 1976	18	44	25
4. "In general, would you like to see federal government regulation of *big* business increased, decreased, or kept about as it is?" *			
February 1976 (not asked)	—	—	—
June 1976	40	29	17

Source: Harris.
* Emphasis in questions.

The Harris poll went on to inquire why people wanted an increase in the regulation of big business. Their comments were similar to those reported in the Advertising Council survey. The reason most frequently given was that big business has too much power (14 percent made this comment) while 12 percent felt that regulation is needed to keep big business from fixing or raising prices; 9 percent said that big business is pushing small business out of the market; and 9 percent thought greater regulation is needed to promote competition and prevent monopolies. The objections cited in these comments—power, prices, and competition—are all criticisms that can be made of big business but not of small business. They are not criticisms of free enterprise or capitalism, but rather of practices that most people feel violate the principles of free enterprise and capitalism.

Areas for Regulation

This distinction also shows up when people are asked what specific business activities should be regulated. The June 1976 Harris survey asked respondents whether or not they favored federal "legislation or regulation" in a number of specific areas. The areas where respondents were most favorable to federal regulation were the following:

> Product safety standards (85 percent)
> Product quality standards (83 percent)
> Pollution controls (82 percent)
> Corruption, e.g., bribes, payoffs, illegal contributions (75 percent)
> Equal employment opportunities for women (72 percent)
> Equal employment opportunities for minorities (69 percent)
> Allowable price increases (54 percent)

In all of these areas, there have been widely publicized abuses linked to business power, or social problems associated with business activities. In each case, business was perceived to be doing something wrong, and regulation was seen as necessary to reform it. Interestingly, respondents were least sure about government "legislation and regulation" concerning "price increases business can charge."

There were a few areas on the Harris list for which respondents did not see any great need for federal regulation: "salaries paid top

241

executives" and "maximum profits a business can make" showed about equal numbers favoring and opposing regulation, while most respondents opposed regulation of "the amount of profits a business can make," "pay increases," and "dividends paid to stockholders." All these latter items on the list represent conventional business practices in a system of free enterprise; Americans see no particular reason why the federal government should "interfere" in any of these areas, even though as noted in Chapter 6, people are concerned about the size of profits and the way they are misused. In short, people want abuses, but not normal business activities, regulated by the government.

The Costs of Regulation

The public is critical of the effects of regulation on both the operation of business and the cost of products. Every year between 1975 and 1980, respondents were asked by Yankelovich, Skelly & White whether government regulation of business "increases inflation," "decreases inflation," or "does not affect inflation." About half the sample in all six polls said that government regulation increases inflation. Between a seventh and a fifth said that regulation has no effect on inflation, and 5 percent said that it actually decreases inflation. One reason why regulation is believed to increase inflation, endorsed by about four fifths of the respondents in all the surveys, is that "conforming to government standards involves extra spending for business." Comparable overwhelming majorities felt that these extra costs are passed on to consumers instead of being absorbed as reduced profits.

The same beliefs were reflected in some 1978 findings of the Opinion Research Corporation. Those interviewed agreed by 52 to 34 percent that "the cost of government regulation outweighs the benefits of such regulation"; by 69 to 18 percent that "federal regulations and requirements add to the cost of consumer products or services"; and by 51 to 37 percent that "the money that business spends meeting government requirements for environmental protection, health and safety, equal employment opportunities, etc., has significantly reduced the amount that business can invest in the expansion and modernization of plant and equipment." Yet these very respondents who were so aware of the negative economic effects of regulation said, by majorities or significant pluralities, that the increased costs are nevertheless worth it to protect workers and the public. (See Table 8-8.)

A fall 1979 Seasonwein study found that an overwhelming majority, 92 percent, was aware that regulation increases the cost of the average product; a majority felt it did so by more than 10 percent. Three fifths or more said that specific regulations dealing with pollution, worker protection, and consumer protection had the effect of increasing "the cost of the average product," but comparable majorities felt that these regulations should be made "more strict" than they are at present.

In December 1980, ORC updated its polls on government regulation and found that the belief that federal regulations add to consumer costs had increased from 69 percent in 1978 to 82 percent two years later. When requested to estimate how much product safety regulations add to consumer costs, 66 percent said "a great deal" or "a fair amount"—up from 55 percent two years earlier. But then, when asked, "Are the added costs of government regulation to ensure product or service safety worth it?" those interviewed in 1980 replied "yes," by 53 to 23 percent. The same respondents also agreed by 65 to 33 percent with the following statement: "Protecting consumer interests is so important that requirements and standards cannot be too high, and continuing improvements must be made regardless of cost."

Similarly, most Americans voiced a willingness in a September 1981 Harris poll to maintain strict air pollution controls, rather than bring down the costs of automobiles and power. The Harris question pitted health against costs in the following way:

The Clean Air Act does not permit the consideration of costs when setting standards for the protection of human health. The Reagan

Table 8–8
Costs vs. Benefits of Regulation

Are Costs Added by Regulation Worth It to:	Yes	No
	Percentage	
Protect workers' health and safety	52	12
Protect workers' pension plans	50	12
Ensure safety, dependability of products or services	47	15
Ensure equal employment opportunities	42	21
Protect the environment	42	19

Source: ORC poll, 1978.

Administration is considering asking Congress to require that pollution standards designed to protect human health be relaxed if the costs are too high. Do you favor or oppose relaxing pollution standards affecting human health if the costs are too high?

Put this way, 65 percent opposed relaxing standards while 32 percent favored doing so. When asked in the same poll, whether "given the costs involved in cleaning up the environment . . . you think Congress should make the Clean Air Act stricter than it is now, keep it about the same, or make it less strict," 29 percent replied "make it stricter," 51 percent said "keep it the same," and only 17 percent felt it should be made less strict. Significant majorities also opposed changes in the law that would postpone deadlines for automobile and electric companies to meet pollution standards or relax those standards.

Regulation to Protect Consumers

The issue of regulation specifically to protect and benefit consumers has been widely debated in recent years. In line with survey data bearing on all forms of regulation, those dealing with consumer protection indicate a fall-off in support for controls. Thus Roper found a decline in the proportion favoring a "major effort" by the government "to establish more controls to protect consumers on the products and services they buy" from 62 percent in 1975 to 51 percent in 1977 and to 43 percent in 1980. Still, six months after Ronald Reagan's election, in May-June 1981, Roper reported that only 17 percent felt that increased controls for consumer protection were "something not needing any particular government effort now," while 44 percent favored "a major effort" and 36 percent said there should be "some effort."

The sentiments underlying the belief in consumer protection were brought out in a comprehensive survey on the topic of consumerism carried out by the Harris poll on behalf of Sentry Insurance in December 1976. Many of the same questions were repeated two years later in a Harris update poll. The surveys clearly establish the fact that consumers feel they need some form of protection. When offered the statement, "Consumers don't need any help in looking after their own interests; they are quite able to do it themselves," only 24 percent of those queried in 1976 agreed, while a majority, 58 percent, disagreed.

The poll asked a number of questions about how things were perceived to have changed for consumers over the past ten years. Most people said that consumers "get a worse deal in the marketplace" than was the case ten years earlier (50 percent "worse" and 27 percent "better" in 1976, 52 and 28 percent in 1978). They believed that "the quality of most products and services has grown worse" (61 to 27 percent worse in 1976, 56 to 31 percent worse in 1978). They felt that "products do not last as long as they used to" (78 percent agreed in 1976, compared to only 18 percent who said either that products now last longer or that nothing has changed).

The public also reported in 1976 that it was "more difficult to get things repaired" (64 percent said "more difficult" compared to 30 percent who said "easier" or no change) and that "the difference between manufacturers' claims and how products actually perform" has increased (48 percent) rather than decreased (27 percent) or remained unchanged (15 percent). On the other hand, the public in 1976 felt that "labeling and information about products has gotten better" (70 percent) rather than worse (15 percent) or not changed (10 percent), and that "the safety of most products has improved" (60 percent) rather than grown worse (26 percent) or not changed (11 percent).

When asked how much such matters worried them personally as consumers—"a great deal," "somewhat," "a little bit," or "not at all"—increasing pluralities from 1976 to 1978 indicated a great deal of concern about "the poor quality of many products," "the failure of many companies to live up to claims in their advertising," "the poor quality of after-sales service and repairs," and "the feeling that many manufacturers don't care about you." Minorities of between 20 and 30 percent said such things worried them only a little bit or not at all.

The Consumer Movement

The 1976 Harris sample tended to be very favorable toward the consumer movement and credited it with whatever accomplishments had been obtained in the area of consumer protection. Respondents agreed, 77 to 8 percent, that "the consumer movement has kept industry and business on their toes" and, 69 to 10 percent, that "the consumer movement has helped a great deal to improve the quality and standards of the products and services people buy." When asked, "On balance, do you believe that the demands of the consumer movement have resulted in better quality products, worse quality products, or have made no difference in quality?" a majority, 57 percent, said that these demands have resulted in better quality products (28 percent said "no difference" and 5 percent, "worse"). The public consistently opposed every negative characterization of the consumer movement:

> "The consumer movement is a threat to our free enterprise system" (rejected 60 to 13 percent);
> "The consumer movement gives a one-sided and unfair picture of what industry and business do" (rejected 49 to 21 percent);
> "Most people in the consumer movement are more interested in attacking the free enterprise system than in helping the consumer" (rejected 47 to 24 percent);
> "The consumer movement seems to be running out of steam" (rejected 46 to 15 percent);
> "The activities of the consumer movement will inevitably lead to too much government control over our lives" (rejected 42 to 26 percent); and
> "The consumer movement makes a lot of charges against companies which aren't justified" (rejected 42 to 29 percent).

Most recent surveys also reveal positive attitudes toward the consumer movement. Early in 1980, the Harris poll asked a national cross section to evaluate seven institutions and groups "on the job they are doing to make our society acceptably safe." The "medical-scientific community" received the highest rating, 64 percent excellent or very good. They were followed by "environmental groups," 52 percent positive, and consumer groups, 50 percent positive. The "business community" was a poor fourth, with 34 percent positive. Governmental units followed, with "the federal government" at 29 percent and "state and local government" at 26 percent. The latter and the "insurance community," which also had a 26 percent positive rating, were at the bottom of the list.

Similar results were obtained by Cambridge Reports, Inc., in a poll taken in August 1980 that asked, in separate questions, whether each of five groups or institutions "represents your interests" on the issue of energy policy, and on environmental policy. "Scientific experts" and "Ralph Nader and other consumerists" received the most favorable judgments on both criteria, with around half of the respondents saying they represented their interests always or most of the time. Newspaper, television, and radio reporters were third, with close to two fifths expressing confidence in them, while "the AFL-CIO national labor organization" and "a group of business leaders" secured the lowest ratings as institutions representing the public's interests on these issues. The public is more inclined to trust scientific experts and environmental or consumer groups, who do not appear to be materially interested in policy outcomes, than self-oriented labor organizations and business groups.

These data attest to the high legitimacy of the consumer movement in the eyes of the public. Still, most Americans believe that the achievements of the consumer movement have been modest. When asked in the 1976 Harris survey, "Overall, do you feel that people active in the consumer movement have done a great deal of good, some good, some harm, or a great deal of harm?" two thirds replied "some good," while only 16 percent said "a great deal of good"; on the other hand, only 4 percent said the consumer movement has done either some or a great deal of harm, and another 4 percent said it had had no effect. The same pattern appeared when respondents were asked whether "consumers get a much better deal, a better deal, a worse deal, or a much worse deal because of the things the consumer movement has done." Sixty-five percent said that consumers get a better deal as a result of the consumer movement, while only 9 percent said "a much better deal"; 3 percent said "worse," and 12 percent said "things haven't changed."

The view that the achievements of the consumer movement have been modest is probably not a criticism of the movement. It more likely reflects the belief that the consumer movement has been relatively powerless in dealing with strong and influential adversaries. When asked, for instance, "On the whole, how much do you think business practices have changed as a result of the consumer movement?" 60 percent said "some but not a great deal" while 13 percent said "a great deal" and 17 percent, "not much." These figures match the previously noted assessment of the consumer movement itself: it has had some effect, but not a great deal.

Thus, the general public attitude toward the consumer movement is quite positive. The image of business activity on behalf of consumers, on the other hand, is negative. When asked in December 1980 by ORC what kind of job, "most major U.S. corporations are doing" in nine areas of consumer protection, including truthful advertising, fair prices, and safe and dependable products, the average positive response (excellent or good) was 31 percent. Consumers are perceived to suffer when there is any conflict between their interests and business profits. When offered the statement, "Business will do nothing much to help the consumer if that reduces profits significantly—unless it is forced to do so," Harris respondents in 1976 agreed by an overwhelming margin, 71 to 11 percent. Does the public believe that regulation is necessary to "force business to do so"? Generally speaking, yes. A substantial majority, 64 to 16 percent, agreed that "if companies were left to themselves and not regulated, the consumer would get a much worse deal."

A Consumer Protection Agency

On the question of the need for a new federal consumer protection agency, the 1976 Harris sample was favorable:

> Some people want the federal government to set up a new consumer protection agency. Those in favor argue that it will give consumers a bigger voice in shaping government decisions. Those who are against it say that we already have plenty of government agencies for protecting consumers. On balance, do you strongly favor, somewhat favor, somewhat oppose, or strongly oppose a new federal consumer protection agency?

A majority, 52 percent, favored a new agency (20 percent were strongly in favor and 32 percent, "somewhat" in favor); 34 percent were opposed (18 percent "somewhat" and 16 percent "strongly"). What is surprising about this answer is that the same respondents had been asked earlier whether "in the future, there should be more government regulation of business, less government regulation, or the same amount as there is now," and only 31 percent favored more government regulation of business (27 percent said there should be less and 30 percent said the same amount as now). And when asked, "On the whole, do you think businessmen's complaints about excessive government regulation of business are or are not justified?" the sample was about evenly divided, with a slight plurality, 39 percent, replying that business' complaints were justified and 35 percent saying they were not. More surprising still is the fact that the sample agreed, 46 to 24 percent, that "on the whole, government regulation has done more to help business than to protect the consumer." Americans seemed to approve of a new consumer protection agency despite their doubts about the effectiveness of government regulation.

Put briefly, government regulation represents an acceptable, but suspect, remedy. The public will accept a new federal agency for consumer protection, but there is an underlying fear that such a solution will only add to the power of government and create another layer of bureaucracy. Alternative solutions, when explicitly offered, are generally preferred. For instance, a May 1975 Harris poll asked, "All in all, do you favor or oppose a new consumer advocacy agency in the federal government?" The new agency was approved at that time as well, although by a thin margin—44 percent in favor, 41 percent opposed. (Democrats favored the new agency, 50 to 33 percent, while Republicans opposed it, 51 to 36 percent.) That question posed a choice between a new agency or no new agency. Another question in the same 1975 survey presented the choice differently:

> There are now efforts underway in Congress to establish an agency for consumer advocacy. This agency would take up and defend complaints and interests on behalf of consumers. Those in favor of setting up such an agency argue that it will give the consumer a larger voice in helping shape government decisions in the consumer purchasing area. Those who oppose setting up the agency argue that we already have plenty of government agencies to protect consumers, and it's just a matter of getting them to work better. Do you favor setting up an agency for consumer advocacy, or do you feel that already existing agencies can be made to do the job?

With the choice posed in this fashion, only 35 percent favored a new consumer agency, while 47 percent felt that "existing agencies can be made to do the job." What made the difference was the choice: support for a new agency rose when the choice was a new agency or nothing, but support declined when the choice was between a new agency and making existing agencies work better. The public prefers better existing bureaucracy over additional bureaucracy.

The importance of the way the alternatives are posed is also demonstrated by a 1975 Cambridge Reports poll on the same subject. Here again, the public first approved of a new consumer protection agency: "Recently there has been a proposal to create a federal consumer protection agency. People in favor say this is needed to help consumers. Opponents say it would be just another federal bureaucracy. Do you favor or oppose creating a consumer protection agency?" The sample favored such a new agency, 53 to 23 percent. But then quite a different choice was presented to them:

> There are two theories of how consumers can best be protected. One says that it is the free enterprise, competitive system, that is, that the best protection for the consumer comes from firms competing with each other for your business. The other theory says that this idea about free competition is nice, but it never works out in reality—that on the contrary, business gets together and devises ways to make a profit at the consumer's expense, in some cases by all the businesses getting together to fix prices and product quality. These people say the only answer is a strong government watchdog role to keep business honest. Which general position would you say you lean toward?

In spite of the fact that this question called attention to a generally held belief that business uses its power to exploit consumers, 56 percent endorsed free competition over "a strong government watchdog" (27 percent). These results were reiterated in a second 1975 CRI poll, when 75 percent of the sample said they favored "starting a federal consumer protection agency that would do nothing but protect consumers." But free competition was still favored over a government watchdog role, 53 to 34 percent. When CRI repeated the question in 1979, the margin of support for free enterprise was even higher, 56 to 26 percent. Competition is by far the preferred form of "regulation."

Substantial majorities in the Harris surveys also favored the free enterprise approach when they endorsed the following propositions:

	Agree	Disagree
	Percentage	
1. "Competition between products and services whereby the consumer buys the better product and services is the only way that consumer interests will be protected" (1975).	63	22
2. "Competition among companies is the best way to ensure better quality products and services" (1976).	72	13
3. "Competition among companies is the best way to make sure products are safe for the consumer" (1976).	58	23

In both of these surveys, it will be recalled, the respondents favored establishing a new consumer protection agency.

The public's conflicting values in this area also come across
clearly in two statements offered in the 1976 Harris survey. The
two appear to be inconsistent, and yet the public agreed with both
of them by about the same margin:

	Agree	Disagree
	Percentage	
1. "Adding another government bureaucracy, no matter how well intentioned, will lead to more red tape, spending more tax money, and won't give the consumer more protection."	62	23
2. "Such an agency is long overdue, for the individual consumer needs help in making his complaints heard and in getting better quality and safer products and services."	60	28

As noted earlier, the public supports improving the existing bureaucracy over creating a new bureaucracy. And it prefers free
enterprise and competition over bureaucracy altogether. But it will
accept a bureaucratic solution if that is the only one offered.

With Ronald Reagan in the White House, the issue of creating
a new consumer advocacy or protection agency is clearly moot.
The Administration is, in fact, beginning to reduce the activities
of the Consumer Product Safety Commission, a step that two polls
taken in August 1981 suggest is not popular. Thus Harris reported
that a national cross section rejected "cutting down the scope and
enforcement powers of the Consumer Product Safety Commission" by 59 to 32 percent. Roper found that only 7 percent of his
sample felt that the Commission "goes too far in regulating the
activities under its supervision," 24 percent said that it "doesn't go
far enough," 25 percent believed it was doing "the right amount,"
and 45 percent responded that they did not know enough to voice
an opinion.

Rejection of Restrictions on Choice

When questions ask about protecting people by means of gov-
ernment-imposed restrictions on consumer choice, the public re-

jects such proposals. Thus, in November 1977, Roger Seasonwein presented his respondents with a choice of either labeling or banning potentially harmful products:

> There is evidence that some products being sold today are dangerous to human health. Generally speaking, is it your feeling that most of these products should be taken off the market so that people cannot buy them, or do you feel most of these products should be available with labels that clearly spell out the risks to those who want to buy them?

Put this way, close to two thirds, 65 percent, chose the option of requiring labels that spell out risks, while 31 percent favored prohibiting such products from being sold.

A year later, Seasonwein inquired about ways of dealing with the risks involved in using saccharin and found that only 7 percent favored a ban on its use; a majority, 52 percent, opted for changing the regulations "so that the alleged risks are clearly spelled out by manufacturers," while 30 percent favored no such efforts. A similar question posed in 1979 about "sleeping aids" yielded comparable results, 11 percent in favor of taking them off the market, 57 percent for listing the dangers on the labels, and 23 percent for no action.

When Cambridge Reports, Inc., asked in 1978, "Do you think it is the responsibility of government to force people to reduce various risks and adopt safety procedures, or should the decision to reduce risks and adopt safety procedures be left pretty much to individual choice?" Americans opted by 48 to 39 percent for individual responsibility. When the same survey posed a more specific question concerning the wisdom of the government's restricting or discouraging "the sale and use of products it believes are hazardous to health" such as cigarettes, saccharin, solvents, and agricultural pesticides, the percentage who said "decisions on the use of such products should be left to consumers" was 56, as compared with 36 percent who favored efforts to restrict their sales. Similar sentiments were reflected in a 1980 ORC poll that asked a cross section to react to the statement, "The government should concentrate on educating the consumer to use products safely instead of banning products that might be used unsafely." The public agreed by 81 to 15 percent.

Criticism of government restriction on consumer *choice* does not mean that the public is turning against consumer *protection*. As noted earlier, a 1980 ORC survey also reported close to two thirds agreeing that "protecting consumer interests is so important" that regulatory standards cannot be too high, regardless of costs. The Roger Seasonwein poll found in 1975, 1977, and 1979 that only a tenth of the public felt there is "too much consumer protection by government." Majorities ranging from 59 percent in the two earlier studies to 55 percent in 1979 said that the government was doing too little to protect the consumer.

Who Should Protect Consumers?

In the 1976 Harris survey, respondents were asked to compare different sources of consumer protection, and a revealing pattern of preferences appeared. First, the sample was asked, "If (a certain regulatory agent) were given the main job of trying to regulate business and enforce standards of product quality and reliability, how effective do you think it would be—very effective, only somewhat effective, or not effective at all?" Four different regulatory agents were tested: industry (regulating itself), the federal government, "a group of people active in the consumer movement," and "consumers individually." Here is how the public ranked the "very effective" alternative for enforcing standards of product quality and reliability (each rated separately):

	"Very Effective"
	Percentage
Consumer activists	27
Consumers individually	20
Federal government	16
Industry	11

A second question inquired, "which *one* of these four groups—business, the federal government, consumer activists, or consumers individually—would you like to be primarily responsible for the job of seeing that consumers get a fair deal?" The answers showed the same rank-ordering:

	Would Like to See Each Agent "Primarily Responsible": Percentage
Consumer activists	29
Consumers individually	20
Federal government	19
Business	15

Government regulation is clearly not the "best" solution for consumer protection. Americans trust consumer activists and themselves ("consumers individually") more than government or business for this purpose. But they favor government *more* than business, presumably because government is a competing source of self-interest. Government regulation, in consumer protection, as in other areas, is not an ideal solution, but it is better than depending on self-interested institutions to control themselves.

Table 8-9, based on Gallup data, reveals, in conformity with the Roper findings reported earlier, that public opinion concerning consumer regulation followed the same trend during the 1970s as public opinion concerning regulation in general—namely, increasing opposition and criticism. But whereas the desire for less regulation in general had attained majority proportions by 1981, the proportion favoring less consumer regulation only reached 37 percent. A majority in 1981 continued to support the same amount of or more consumer regulation. As Andrew Kohut, president of the Gallup Poll, concluded:

TABLE 8-9
Attitudes Toward Consumer Regulation, 1970–81

"In your opinion, should there be more government regulation of consumer products and how they are sold, or less regulation than there is now?"

	1970	1977	1981
	Percentage		
More regulation	55	39	43
Less regulation	14	30	37
Same as now (volunteered)	17	17	8
Don't know	14	14	12
Total	100	100	100

Source: Gallup.

Longitudinal surveys suggest the public's appetite for regulation has lessened since the heydey of consumerism in the early 1970s, and the public is more than ever sensitive to the inefficiencies of the government sector. On the other hand [the public] certainly is willing to trade off a lot of red tape and even higher prices . . . when they feel a need for protection.[2]

Conclusion

Many Americans endorse government regulation in order to control big business and its potential for abuse. The only way big business and big labor can be restrained from abuse of power is to set against them the strength of a countervailing large institution. A 1976 ORC survey asked whether "government regulation is a good way of making business more responsive to ethical and moral considerations," and the public agreed, 52 to 36 percent. In 1975, National Family Opinion found an overwhelming majority (75 percent) in agreement with the statement, "In general, business will not do any more to control environmental problems than is ordered by law." And in November 1981, Roper found that 76 percent agreed that "government regulation makes the workplace much safer than it would be if corporations were left to their own devices," while only 18 percent disagreed. Asked another way in the same survey, 36 percent said that "most business is really concerned with problems of safety," while 60 percent felt that business worries "about these things only because the government forces it to."

On the other hand, as will be documented in Chapter 9, free enterprise remains a cherished value and the preferred solution for economic problems. All surveys show overwhelming majorities opposed to government takeover of big business. Even regulation, which is otherwise acceptable, loses support when "free enterprise" is posited as an explicit alternative. Thus, according to a 1981 *Time*/Yankelovich poll, 62 percent of the public endorsed the view that "government should stop regulating business and protecting the consumer and let the free enterprise system work."

The message in these results is that Americans do not trust big government any more than they trust big business or big labor.

[2] Andrew Kohut, text of remarks to *Opinion Outlook* conference, Washington, D.C. (May 14, 1981).

They distrust power and its potential for abuse in any setting, private or public. People feel strongly that big business is too powerful and that there are no informal or "personal" constraints on its abuse of power, as there are in the case of small business. The public is willing to endorse regulation as a solution that will curb the abuse of private power without giving too much power to big government. Solutions that are stronger than regulation—that is, remedies that give government even more control over business— are firmly rejected, as will be shown in the next chapter. What the public wants is not more power for big government, but a better *balance of power* between business and government.

9

Government Intervention and Free Enterprise

W HEN the public becomes cognizant of abuses of power by business, it turns to government as the only institution strong enough to correct them. Of the alternative actions government can take against business, regulation is a relatively moderate one, while divestiture and nationalization are more extreme approaches that challenge basic principles of free enterprise ideology. As we look at public attitudes toward government and business, the question arises: to what degree is the public willing to compromise its commitment to free enterprise in order to curb violations of the public trust by business? Where does it draw the line separating the proper roles of business and government?

Divestiture

"Divestiture"—breaking up large companies into smaller ones —has been advocated as a way of eliminating the monopolistic or oligopolistic control of an industry without creating permanent government involvement, as is the case with either regulation or nationalization. In effect, divestiture uses government power to restore competition and free enterprise, much in the manner of trust-busting in an earlier era. As reported earlier in Figure 1-4, support for divestiture, as reflected in agreement with the ORC statement, "For the good of the country, many of our largest companies ought to be broken up into smaller companies," increased steadily from 36 percent in 1967 to 57 percent in 1975 and remained in that range in 1977, 1979, and 1981.

Although the ORC surveys indicate that a majority has favored the general principle of divestiture since 1973, the only context in which the policy of divestiture has been widely discussed is the oil industry. Since the energy crisis of 1973–74, surveys have repeatedly tested public attitudes toward divestiture in that industry. Many of those polls have differentiated between "vertical" and "horizontal" divestiture. Vertical divestiture dissociates the various functions that a single company might perform within one industry, for instance, exploring for, transporting, and refining petroleum. Horizontal divestiture breaks up a single company that has diversified its interests into related (or unrelated) industries, such as an oil company that has entered the coal or nuclear energy business.

The Harris poll found widespread approval of divestiture for the oil industry in various surveys taken between 1975 and 1977. During 1976 and 1977, the public supported "breaking up the oil companies," without specifying whether vertically or horizontally, by an average of 50 to 31 percent in four polls. Harris also found comparably large majorities favoring vertical and horizontal divestiture tested separately in seven surveys conducted between 1975 and 1977.

Cambridge Reports, Inc., also inquired into public attitudes toward both types of divestiture in quarterly interviews with national cross sections between 1976 and 1980. Again, the policy was tested only for oil companies. The CRI results show sentiment shifting back and forth on both questions without much of a trend over these five years. As can be seen in Table 9-1, support for vertical divestiture was slightly higher on the average than support for horizontal divestiture; vertical divestiture averaged 39 percent for to 35 percent against, while the averages for horizontal divestiture were 37 percent for and 38 percent against. What is most striking about these responses is how little they varied over time. Support appeared to drop off a bit after the first period of drastic shortages, but the gas lines of mid-1979 did not seem to have much of an effect. With an issue as complicated as divestiture, and with such elaborate questions, a consistently even split in the answers suggests the possibility that many respondents are simply

258

TABLE 9–1

Attitudes Toward Divestiture in the Oil Industry, 1976–80

Horizontal Divestiture

"Some of our country's larger oil companies have acquired coal reserves in order to compete in the coal fuel supply business and have developed uranium mines to supply fuel to the nuclear power industry. Do you think having the oil companies expand their activities into other energy areas is good for America, or would you prefer to see the large oil companies prevented by the government from doing this?" ("favor" = prevent oil companies from doing this.)

Average for Quarterly Polls Each Year:	*Favor*	*Oppose*	*Don't Know*
		Percentage	
1976*	44	36	21
1977	36	41	24
1978	36	38	27
1979	34	39	28
1980	37	36	27
Average for all 19 polls	37	38	27

* Based on three polls in 1976. The wording of the question in two of them was slightly different from the one above.

Vertical Divestiture

"Some people say that the big oil companies should be broken up into smaller ones, each of which would handle a particular function like exploration, refining, transporting, or marketing oil and gas to customers. After the breakup of the big oil companies (called divestiture), each of the smaller companies could do one of these functions, but not all of them. In general, would you favor or oppose a program to break up all the large oil companies into smaller, unrelated companies?"

Average for Quarterly Polls Each Year:	*Favor*	*Oppose*	*Don't Know*
		Percentage	
1976	41	38	22
1977†	37	36	28
1978	38	34	28
1979	38	33	29
1980	39	33	28
Average for all 19 polls	39	33	27

Source: Cambridge Reports, Inc.
† Based on only three polls in 1977.

offering a random answer. (Note also the large proportion of "don't knows.")

Reasons For and Against Divestiture

What arguments underlie public attitudes concerning divestiture in the oil industry? Both Cambridge Reports, Inc., and the Harris poll asked respondents in late 1975 and early 1976 to indicate their agreement or disagreement with various reasons for and against breaking up the oil companies. The results are tabulated in Table 9-2.

TABLE 9–2
Agreement with Arguments for and against
Divestiture in the Oil Industry

	Source	Agree	Disagree
		Percentage	
Arguments Favoring Divestiture			
1. "Divestiture would reduce the power and influence of the large oil companies in the nation's political and economic life."	CRI	72	14
2. "More competition in the oil business would mean lower prices for the consumer."	H	68	16
3. "Divestiture would be a step in returning our economy back to smaller, more competitive units, in a sense, a return to the original idea of competitive free enterprise."	CRI	62	23
4. "Divestiture would create more jobs."	CRI	56	25
5. "Big oil companies have too much power over government and the economy, and should be broken up."	H	55	22
6. "Divestiture would help lower oil and gas prices to the consumer."	CRI	48	36
7. "Divestiture would punish the large oil companies for their activities of the last few years."	CRI	45	34
8. "The oil companies have behaved so badly, the way to punish them is to break them up."	H	30	44

Government Intervention and Free Enterprise

	Source	Agree	Disagree
		Percentage	

Arguments Against Divestiture

	Source	Agree	Disagree
1. "The big oil companies are more efficient than many small companies in doing the job of getting the oil out of the ground, refining it, transporting it, and marketing it to the public."	H	52	27
2. "Divestiture would hinder American companies' ability to compete with the large foreign oil companies."	CRI	42	37
3. "Breaking up the oil companies is wrong because they are the ones who can discover new sources of energy to ease the energy shortage."	H	40	43
4. "To develop more energy requires the highest skill and professional talent, which would be lost if the big oil companies were broken up."	H	38	39
5. "Divestiture would only punish the large oil companies who have been successful in the free enterprise system we all value and want to preserve."	CRI	36	42
6. "Divestiture would lower industry efficiency and raise prices eventually."	CRI	34	46
7. "Divestiture would hinder America's efforts at becoming more self-sufficient in energy in the years ahead."	CRI	32	46
8. "Divestiture would decrease jobs because the smaller firms would not be able to finance and conduct the large-scale exploration projects so much a part of today's oil business."	CRI	28	50
9. "Divestiture is a program of a certain element in the society who want to destroy the American economy as we know it."	CRI	22	56

Source: Harris, December 1975; Cambridge Reports, Inc., January 1976.
Key: H = Harris; CRI = Cambridge Reports, Inc.
Harris, N = 1,475; CRI, N = 1,500.

The most widely accepted arguments in favor of divestiture are *free enterprise* arguments: breaking up the big oil companies would reduce their "power and influence in the nation's political and economic life," it would return the economy "to smaller, more competitive units, . . . to the original idea of competitive free enterprise," and big oil companies should be broken up because they have "too much power over government and the economy." In both the Cambridge and Harris surveys, punitive reasons were the least widely accepted justifications for divestiture: "Divestiture would punish the large oil companies for their activities of the last few years," or "The oil companies have behaved so badly, the way to punish them is to break them up."

The argument that divestiture would lower fuel prices (Arguments 2 and 6 favoring in Table 9-2) seems to draw an inconsistent response, or so it appears until one inspects the statements more carefully. The Harris statement—"More competition in the oil business would mean lower prices for the consumer"—elicited widespread agreement (68 to 16 percent). But the CRI version— "Divestiture would help lower oil and gas prices to the consumer" —was substantially less popular (48 to 36 percent agreement). The Harris statement made no mention of divestiture directly, only by implication ("more competition"). Thus, the argument for divestiture in the oil industry appears to be more of an argument on principle—to restore free enterprise and curb the abuse of monopoly power—than one based on the anticipated benefits of such a policy.

On the other hand, the most widely accepted statements against divestiture are utilitarian—"The big oil companies are more efficient than small companies . . ." and "Divestiture would hinder American companies' ability to compete with foreign oil companies." Respondents in the CRI survey rejected criticisms of divestiture that were offered in the name of free enterprise—"Divestiture would only punish the large oil companies who have been successful in the free enterprise system we all value and want to preserve" (rejected 42 to 36 percent), and "Divestiture is a program of a certain element in the society who want to destroy the American economy as we know it" (rejected 56 to 22 percent). Americans appear to support divestiture because of their commitment to free enterprise, and not in spite of it.

The notion that divestiture will reduce prices seems to be less a cause of public support than a justification for it. In another CRI survey in 1976, a plurality of respondents said that if the oil companies were broken up, the price of gasoline and heating oil would go up (37 percent), rather than go down (24 percent) or stay the same (24 percent). The percentage who said prices would go up increased steadily as one moved along the seven-point scale from total support of, to total opposition to, divestiture (see Table 9-3).

In still another CRI survey taken in 1976, respondents were told, "One of the arguments made for breaking up the oil companies is that it will increase competition in the industry and this, in turn, will force prices to come down. Opponents of breaking up the oil companies say companies will be less efficient, will duplicate each other's efforts, and in the long run this will only cause prices to go up more. Which of these positions do you think is true?" The argument for divestiture and competition won over the argument for concentration and efficiency, 50 to 31 percent. The question revealed sharp differences by ideology and education. Liberals be-

TABLE 9–3

Anticipation of Price Increases by
Attitude Toward Divestiture

"Some people say that the big oil companies should be broken up into smaller ones, each of which would handle a particular function like exploration, refining, transporting, or marketing oil and gas to customers. After the breakup of the big oil companies (called divestiture) each of the smaller companies could do one of these functions, but not all of them. In general, would you favor or oppose a program to break up all of the large oil companies into smaller, unrelated companies? On a scale from one to seven where would you place yourself with regard to this question, if 'one' represents strong favor and 'seven' represents strong opposition?"

"If the oil companies were broken up, do you think the price of gasoline and heating oil would go up, go down, or stay the same?"

Attitude Toward the Divestiture of Oil Companies		Percentage Saying that Oil Prices Will Go Up with Divestiture
Totally favor divestiture:	1	15
	2	19
	3	26
Neutral on divestiture:	4	32
	5	49
	6	57
Totally oppose divestiture:	7	70

Source: Cambridge Reports, Inc., 1976.
N = 1,500.

lieved that divestiture and competition would bring prices down, 60 to 24 percent; moderates also felt this way, 51 to 31 percent; but conservatives were about equally divided on the issue, 43 percent saying that prices would be lower with smaller companies and more competition and 40 percent saying that divestiture would produce inefficiency and, therefore, higher prices.

From the standpoint of educational level, the first view was more prevalent among those with the least education, while the best educated were more likely to feel that big companies were more efficient, and divestiture, therefore, would lead to higher prices. The same held true in a 1975 ORC poll in which respondents were asked, "If the large oil companies were divided . . . , do you believe the price of gasoline would increase, decrease, or stay the same?" Those with less than 12 years of schooling said that prices would decrease rather than increase, 41 to 23 percent. High school graduates were split, 31 percent saying that gasoline prices would decrease and 30 percent saying that they would increase. The college educated felt that divestiture would lead to higher prices, by a margin of 40 to 27 percent. The effect of education persists even when views on oil industry divestiture are held constant, as can be seen in Table 9-4. The better educated on both sides of the issue are more likely to see oil industry divestiture as creating inefficiency and raising prices. Lower-status respondents are more likely to think that breaking up powerful monopolies will lower prices, no matter what their views on divestiture.

Thus, the prevailing argument in favor of divestiture is ideological (free enterprise). The principal argument against it is one of interest (it will raise prices). However, an opposing ideological

TABLE 9–4

Education and Opinion Concerning Price Increases with Divestiture

"If the large oil companies were divided . . . , do you believe the price of gasoline would increase, decrease, or stay the same?"

Educational Level	Total Sample	Supporters of Divestiture	Opponents of Divestiture
	Percentages Saying Prices Would Increase with Divestiture		
Less than 12 years	23	11	60
12 years	30	15	59
College	40	22	70

Source: ORC, 1975.

argument was raised in a 1976 CRI survey, and it appears to have been a convincing one. Respondents were asked, "Do you think that breaking up the oil companies would increase or decrease government involvement in the oil industry?" The sample felt that it would increase government involvement, 43 to 33 percent. The next question logically followed: "If this is true—that divestiture will increase government involvement in the oil industry—would you support divestiture or not?" The result was an even split, 36 percent saying that they would support divestiture even if it meant greater government involvement and 37 percent saying that they would not favor it. Thus, the introduction of "government involvement" as a condition associated with divestiture partially neutralizes the free enterprise argument for the policy.

Nationalization

"Nationalization," the assumption by the government of complete ownership and operation of a firm, is the most extreme form of government intervention. It is consistently rejected by the public as a direct violation of the principles of free enterprise. Comprehensive evidence on this point comes from Peter D. Hart Associates and Cambridge Reports, Inc., polls taken in 1975, the year when the country was badly affected by the mid-decade recession. Hart inquired whether respondents felt that "government ownership of all major companies" would "do more good than harm, or more harm than good." An overwhelming majority, 81 percent, replied that it would do more harm; only 13 percent said it would do more good.

CRI asked, "Some people have proposed nationalization—or government takeover—of particular industries which they feel have too much influence over U.S. life and should be controlled. Would you favor or oppose government takeover of any of the following industries?" Respondents were asked how they felt about nationalization of each of eight major industries. In every case, decisive majorities were opposed: television and radio networks (87 percent), automobiles (81 percent), banks (79 percent), steel (76 percent), telephone (72 percent), electric power (70 percent), railroads (67 percent), and oil (61 percent). Thirty-one percent favored nationalization of the oil industry, the highest figure for any industry listed.

In 1975, 1976, and 1977, Cambridge Reports, Inc., tapped atti-

265

tudes related to this issue when they asked respondents to react to another statement: "The way business is run we would be better off letting the government run everything." Less than one seventh favored the proposal, while three quarters opposed it in each survey. In 1981, when Civic Service repeated this question, they found only 4 percent in favor and 91 percent opposed. Harris also inquired in three surveys during 1974 and 1975 whether respondents favored "the federal government taking over and running most *big* businesses in this country." Even in this case, the results were decisive; only one tenth supported government ownership of big business, while over four fifths rejected the suggestion. When he repeated the question in 1979, Harris found that only 6 percent favored the proposal, while 92 percent opposed it. A year later, in 1980, the percentage in favor moved back up to 13, but 83 percent still rejected the idea of government taking over big business.

In the 1974 Harris survey—where over four fifths opposed nationalization of big business—a similar majority nonetheless agreed that "if left alone, big business would be greedy and selfish and would make profits at the expense of the public" and also that "if left unchecked, big business would stifle competition." Despite this, large majorities still opposed each of the following options for the federal government: "taking over and running big business" (rejected 83 to 11 percent), and "setting up model companies to compete with private companies as a kind of yardstick to measure the way big companies might be run" (rejected 64 to 26 percent). In 1980, the latter proposal was again turned down, by 61 to 35 percent.

Questions about varying degrees of federal intervention in the oil industry, the most unpopular of all major industries, afford the most revealing tests of support for nationalization and other forms of government control. The public—rightly or wrongly—associates the oil industry with monopolistic control, inflation, the energy crisis, foreign economic influence, and pollution. Yet there is still substantial sentiment for leaving oil companies under private control—albeit with substantial government regulation. The Roper poll posed a series of questions about the oil industry in February 1974, just after the country had experienced the oil embargo. Roper asked about a proposed "federal charter" for the oil companies:

It has been suggested that laws should be passed requiring oil companies to operate under a federal charter. Some people have said this would be a good thing because oil is an essential industry and a federal charter would give the government more control over the industry. Others have said it would be a bad thing because our system of government is based on free enterprise, and once government begins to control industry our whole system is undermined. How do you feel about this—do you think oil companies should be required to operate under a federal charter, or left to operate as private industries as they now do?

A majority of the public, 53 percent, said that the oil companies should be left to operate as private industries; just under one third, 31 percent, favored a "federal charter" as defined in the question.

Roper then went on to ask about nationalization more directly: "Another suggestion that has been made is that the government should set up and operate a government owned oil company that would operate in competition with the private oil companies. Do you think this is a good idea or not such a good idea?" Not surprisingly, sentiment toward this proposal was even more negative— 64 percent opposed, 23 percent in favor. Finally, Roper gave respondents a card listing four types of restrictions on oil company activities. Respondents were asked which, if any, "should be required by law of oil companies" (multiple responses were allowed). The two most popular proposals were the following: "There should be consumer representatives on the boards of directors of each company" (chosen by 38 percent), and "Oil companies should be required to conform to federal standards on prices and profits" (chosen by 37 percent). The less popular proposals were both forms of direct government interference in company management: "They should be required to get U.S. government approval on major contracts they make with foreign countries" (endorsed by 28 percent), and "There should be government representatives on the board of directors of each company" (chosen by 11 percent). None of these legal restrictions was endorsed by a majority of the public.

A proposal calling for the "nationalization of all the big oil companies" has been inquired about regularly from 1974 to 1980 by CRI. In this case, the figures show that between 43 and 49 percent have consistently opposed it, while 20 to 35 percent have favored it. It is significant that despite the steady and sharp increase in gasoline prices and the conviction, evidenced in many surveys, that the oil companies share a major part of the responsibility for that increase, there has been no steady upward trend in favor of the nationalization of the oil companies. In the spring of 1974, 32 percent supported government ownership and 52 percent opposed it. Six years later, in the fall of 1980—after the 1979 gas lines—32 percent were in favor and 47 percent were against. In between, support for nationalizing the big oil companies has dropped as low as 20 percent (the spring of 1975 and the spring of 1976) but has generally stood between 30 and 35 percent.

The continued opposition to government ownership of the oil companies can also be seen in surveys taken by Harris and Roper in the summer of 1979, just as the most recent gasoline crisis struck. Although two thirds of those interviewed by Harris in June felt that "the way major oil companies have behaved" is to blame for the gasoline shortage, the public opposed "a federal takeover of the oil industry" by a 68–27 percent majority, essentially the same distribution Harris reported three years earlier in 1976. A smaller but still sizable majority, 58 to 35, rejected "the federal government creating a government-owned and -operated oil corporation." Roper reported considerable opposition to nationalization in July 1979, in spite of the fact that 68 percent of his respondents felt that "there really isn't a shortage of gasoline and fuel oil and the big companies are holding it back for their own advantage." Offered the proposal that "the oil companies in this country should be nationalized—that is, be taken over and operated by the government . . . ," less than one quarter, 23 percent, favored such an idea, while 62 percent opposed it.

A poll taken by the *Washington Post* in January 1980 asked a national cross section to choose between two argumentative statements: A. "The government should take over the major oil firms because that wouldn't hurt us any more than the oil firms are hurting us now," or B. "A government takeover of the major oil firms would do nothing to reduce the energy crisis and might only make things worse." Three fifths, 59 percent, chose option B and rejected a government takeover, while 27.5 percent supported such an action. Thus, even the high price of gasoline and the widespread belief that much of the higher price is a result of exorbitant profit-taking have not induced the public to support nationalization of the oil industry.

This same pattern can be seen in the case of a different industry associated with the energy crisis: natural gas. In a 1975 survey, Cambridge Reports, Inc., asked whether people thought it was necessary to deregulate the price of natural gas in order to ensure an adequate supply; the public said "no," 43 to 23 percent. CRI then proposed that the U.S. government essentially go into competition with private industry in the production of natural gas: "Some people say that if the companies can't or won't produce gas at the regulated price, the government should step in and start producing gas at that price. Would you favor or oppose such an action?" The result was an even split, 39 percent in favor and 38 percent opposed. This proposal, it should be noted, is for government competition with private industry, not a government takeover. Moreover, the specified terms of the competition are that the government produce natural gas *at a lower price* than private industry. These stipulations obviously contributed to the relative popularity of this proposal. Further evidence to be shown below suggests that government competition without the specification of a lower price is not nearly so popular. Cambridge Reports, Inc., then asked an additional question of the 39 percent who favored government production of natural gas: "Would you favor this even if it meant the federal government taking over private business?" In this case, only 30 percent (of the 39 percent) continued to say yes, while 42 percent of them turned against the proposal and 28 percent said they were not sure. Clearly, a federal takeover of private industry is considered a much more extreme proposition.

The preference of Americans for private ownership also comes through in the replies to questions posed by Roper in a survey conducted for the American Enterprise Institute in November 1981, which dealt with government versus private ownership of telephones and the postal service. When asked about government ownership of telephones, 11 percent favored the proposal and 81 percent opposed it. Only 9 percent thought that the quality of telephone service would improve under public ownership, while 62 percent felt the cost would go up if the federal government took over. Conversely, 46 percent said that the quality of postal service would get better if it were handled by a private corporation, compared to 30 percent who felt it would stay the same and 18 percent who believed it would get worse.

Alternative Forms of Government Control of Business

The Roper Organization asked a question in its December 1977 survey that directly compares a number of alternative forms of government involvement in the business sector. Roper divided his sample into two random subsamples, labeled X and Y. Both half-samples were asked to look at a list of "different views as to the best way for people to get good quality products at reasonable prices from various large industries in this country." The only difference between the two half-samples was that the X-respondents were shown a list containing *four* options while the Y-respondents were shown a list of *six* options, the same four offered to the X-respondents plus two additional ones. Both half-samples were asked to choose the most appropriate option for each of four industries: steel, automobiles, chemicals, and oil. The results, as tabulated in Table 9-5, show the choices made for each industry by the X-respondents and the Y-respondents, respectively.

The four options offered in the X version of the question included: nationalization ("Have the government take over and run the whole industry"), a government-run competitive firm ("Have a government-run company to compete with the private companies"), divestiture ("break up the large companies into smaller ones"), and "keep the present system as it is."

The results show a clear rank-ordering of the four industries in terms of public confidence. The X sample was most satisfied with the automobile industry; just over half of the X respondents (52 percent) felt that it should be kept as is, while 37 percent desired some form of increased government intervention. The chemical industry ranked second in terms of public satisfaction, with 45 percent (of X respondents) approving the present system and 34 percent preferring a larger government role. Sentiment was about evenly divided in the case of steel, 44 percent to "keep the present system as it is" and 41 percent for greater government involvement. The oil industry was once again at the bottom of the list, with a majority (54 percent) in favor of stronger government action and 31 percent for keeping the present system.

Roper had asked the X version of this question earlier (in 1975 and 1976); the results of those polls showed that the responses for the four industries varied little over time. In each survey and for each industry, divestiture was the most popular of the three forms of government intervention offered. Relatively few respondents favored either nationalization or a government-run company; in 1977 these two "extreme" alternatives were chosen by a low of 10 percent (together) in the case of the automobile industry and a high of only 20 percent (together) in the case of oil (see Table 9-5, X sample). Support for divestiture as "the best way for people to

270

TABLE 9–5

Alternative Forms of Government Control of Business

"Here is a card listing 4 (X form)/6 (Y form) different views as to the best way for people to get good quality products at reasonable prices from various large industries in this country. Which *one* would you agree with for the steel industry? Which one would you agree with for the automobile industry? With which for the oil industry? And with which for the chemical industry?"

The "Best Way for People to Get Good Quality Products at Reasonable Prices" Would be to:	Automobile Industry		Chemical Industry		Steel Industry		Oil Industry	
	X form	Y form	X form	Y form	X form	Y form	X form	Y form
	Percentage							
(More Government Intervention)								
A. Have the government take over and run the whole industry	3	5	6	6	4	7	10	12
B. Have a government-run company to compete with the private companies	7	4	8	5	9	7	10	7
C. Break up the large companies into smaller ones	27	16	20	9	28	16	34	19
D.* Have more government control and regulation over private companies	—	14	—	15	—	12	—	16
(Sum of A + B + C + D)	(37)	(39)	(34)	(35)	(41)	(42)	(54)	(54)
(The Same or Less Government Intervention)								
E. Keep the present system as it is	52	32	45	31	44	23	31	16
F.* Have less government control and regulation over private companies	—	18	—	12	—	21	—	15
(Sum of E + F)	(52)	(50)	(45)	(43)	(44)	(44)	(31)	(31)
Don't Know	11	11	21	22	15	14	16	15
Totals	100	100	100	100	100	100	100	100

Source: 1977 Roper poll.

* Choices offered to Y-form respondents only.
X version, N = 934; Y version, N = 1,067.

get good quality products at reasonable prices" ranged from a low of 20 percent for the chemical industry to 34 percent for the oil industry in the 1977 survey.

The Y version of this question, which was asked for the first time in 1977, added one additional form of government intervention, namely, more regulation ("Have more government control and regulation over private companies"), plus the alternative of *reducing* government involvement ("Have less government control and regulation over private companies"). The six alternatives on the Y questionnaire have been grouped into those (four) choices representing more government intervention and the (two) options representing the same or less government involvement (see Table 9-5).

The most striking result in Table 9-5 is the similarity of responses in the two half-samples. Almost exactly the same percentages favored greater government intervention in each industry, whether three or four alternatives were given. And the sum of the percentages who, in the Y sample, wanted to keep the present system *or* reduce the role of government was almost exactly equal to the percentage of the X sample who preferred to keep the present system for each industry. The consistency of these patterns suggests that attitudes toward government intervention are quite stable, i.e., they are almost insensitive to changes in the format of the question.

What, then, was the effect of adding the two options to the Y questionnaire? In each case, the percentages who favored nationalization or a government-run company remained almost unchanged. Support for the new option (more government regulation) came almost entirely at the expense of divestiture. In the Y version, divestiture and regulation became the two most popular forms of government intervention, while the total preference for all forms of government intervention remained about the same. Support for *less* government regulation came, as one might expect, almost entirely at the expense of the most limited option in the X questionnaire, "Keep the present system as it is."

Roper repeated the new six-alternative Y version in December 1978 and again in December 1979, and secured very similar results. Support for nationalization and government-run competitive companies declined a bit, in tandem with slight increases in support for divestiture and more government regulation, i.e., changes *within* the sphere of increased government action. There was almost no change in the proportions favoring the present system or a reduction in government regulation.

Do the four industries inquired about by Roper represent extreme cases of the concentration of business power? The findings of a 1976 Harris survey of attitudes toward the regulation of fourteen industries indicate that the oil, chemical, steel, and automobile industries are not grossly unrepresentative of business as a whole, as far as public attitudes are concerned. On the average, 68 percent favored federal regulation of those four industries. This percentage hardly differed from the average of 67 percent who supported regulation of the other nine industries on Harris's list (drugs, food, utilities, airlines, banking, tire and rubber, cigarettes and tobacco, electrical appliances, and computers).

These results suggest that there are four basic positions concerning government involvement in the business sector:

1. A small minority of the public favors the most extreme forms of intervention, namely, nationalization and government-owned enterprise. Support for these approaches comes to no more than 20 percent in the case of the most unpopular industry, oil, and is considerably lower for the other industries. The minority support given to these positions is probably indicative of the limited extent of the public's willingness to challenge the principles of free enterprise directly.

2. A substantially larger proportion—between a quarter and a third of the public—favors a "moderate" form of government intervention, either divestiture or increased regulation. The shift of responses between the X and Y versions of the 1977 survey suggests that those who favor more regulation tend to choose divestiture as the next best alternative. What makes these two options "moderate" is not the amount of disruption they cause (divestiture is certainly more disruptive than creating a government-owned company); rather, they are "moderate" in the sense that they do not directly challenge the principles of free enterprise. Both regulation and divestiture may be interpreted as measures to restore free enterprise and curb the concentration of "monopoly power."

3. A plurality of the public in the case of all industries except oil favors the present system, which includes, for most industries, a substantial amount of government regulation.

4. A 10–20 percent minority prefers less government control and regulation than the present system provides.

Thus, in summary, the preponderance of public sentiment seems to be somewhere between the present system of government intervention and a "moderate" increase in that system, by means of either more regulation or divestiture. There are two minority fringe-groups: those who want to challenge free enterprise head on through nationalization, and those who want to reduce .the government's regulatory role. Government regulation appeals to many Americans today for the same reason that trust-busting appealed to an earlier generation; it uses government power to promote free enterprise and competition and to curb anti-social behavior by business. But the public today is far more concerned about the costs of excessive government power and increasingly alert to the possibility of anti-social behavior by government.

The Productivity Problem: A Cross-National Comparison

Regulation, divestiture, and nationalization are all anti-business policies. What about *pro-business* government intervention in the economy? Is the public willing to see the government step in to support or subsidize business when it is a question of protecting American industry from foreign competition?

Some recent surveys dealing with public attitudes toward economic growth and productivity shed light on what Americans perceive to be the proper relationship between government and business. These include the surveys carried out for the Union Carbide Corporation by Roger Seasonwein Associates in 1979 and by Cambridge Reports, Inc., in 1980, as well as a cross-national study, "Perspectives on Productivity," conducted in late 1980 and early 1981 by Louis Harris and Associates and Dr. Amitai Etzioni on behalf of the Sentry Insurance Company. Since the Sentry/Harris survey interviewed employees in five countries, it provides some evidence of how American attitudes diverge from those of people elsewhere on the role of the state in the economy.

How concerned is the American public about the problem of productivity in the U.S. economy? The data suggest that Americans regard productivity and economic growth as serious, but not calamitous, national problems. The 1979 Union Carbide/Seasonwein survey asked how much economic growth would be good for the United States. People did not rush to say they wanted the economy to grow "a great deal" or "a good deal"; a total of 41 percent gave these two strongest responses. About the same proportion, 42 percent, felt that "a fair amount" of economic growth would be sufficient. Only 13 percent said "not much" or "no growth" at all. The sample agreed, by majorities of three quarters or more, that economic growth produces many good effects (more jobs, higher wages). But comparable majorities also associated certain bad consequences with economic growth—higher taxes, higher prices, and more pollution and crowding.

In the 1981 Sentry/Harris survey, about one third of the public called declining productivity "one of the two or three most serious problems facing the nation in the 1980s." About half took the less alarmist view that declining productivity is "a serious problem for the next several years." Only 14 percent felt that the problem of declining productivity was "exaggerated." However, when asked to compare this country's current economic performance with that of most other industrial nations, 41 percent said we are doing better than other countries, compared with 29 percent who felt we are doing worse. This assessment was the reverse of the view held by the approximately 400 American business executives interviewed in the Sentry/Harris poll, who felt by a margin of 44 to 26 percent that the United States was doing worse than other nations.

Who is seen to be responsible for declining productivity in the United States? The Harris/Sentry survey asked respondents to evaluate "which groups on this list [of 16] are mainly responsible for this country's productivity not being better than it is?" Those cited most frequently were the federal government (61 percent), labor unions (52 percent), and major corporations (41 percent). Other government units, Congress (40 percent), state and local government (35 percent), and regulatory agencies (34 percent) came next, followed by "the work force" (27 percent). Small businesses were the group mentioned least often (4 percent).

Figure 9-1 reveals that the tendency to blame government for productivity problems was notably stronger in the United States than in the other four countries polled by Harris. Trade unions and "the work force" were much more widely held to blame in Britain and Australia, where problems with balky unions have been much more severe. American workers show more readiness than those elsewhere to blame *institutions* for their country's productivity problems; that means the federal government first and foremost, but labor and big business do not escape their share of the blame.

In the 1979 Union Carbide/Seasonwein survey, respondents were

FIGURE 9–1

Perceived Responsibility for Low Productivity: A Comparison among Five Nations

"Which groups on the list are mainly responsible for this country's productivity not being better than it is? Please name as many groups as you think have a major responsibility."

Figures show percentage of employees in each country who named each group.

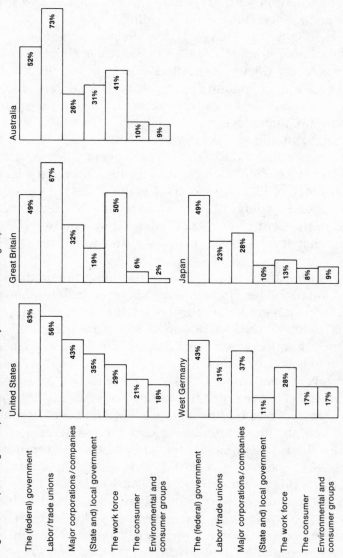

Source: Perspectives on Productivity: A Global View—survey conducted for Sentry Insurance by Louis Harris & Associates, Inc., and Dr. Amitai Etzioni, Director of the Center for Policy Research, Washington, D.C. Employees in Great Britain (N = 541), West Germany (492), Australia (799), and Japan (500) interviewed between December 10, 1980, and February 28, 1981, and employees drawn from a nationwide U.S. sample (N = 660) interviewed December 5, 28, 1980.

asked whether each in a list of factors was helping the nation's economic growth, holding down growth, or having little effect on growth. Major corporations were perceived, on balance, to be helping rather than hindering economic growth, 43 to 33 percent. Labor unions were felt to be hurting rather than helping growth, 49 to 28 percent. Government, however, was seen as the most harmful institution. The country's economic growth was believed to be held down rather than improved by the size of the federal government (54 to 12 percent), by government regulation (51 to 14 percent), by government spending (62 to 20 percent), and by the amount of taxes the average person pays (51 to 24 percent). Even environmental protection laws, which are otherwise popular, were perceived to be harmful to economic growth, 41 to 25 percent.

When asked by Harris about steps that could be taken to improve the nation's economic growth, both the public and the business executives put "cut government spending" at the top of the list (see Table 9-6). Business executives, however, gave much higher priority to measures that would increase investment. The public, on the other hand, was much more favorable than the executives to active government intervention in the economy, including not only regulation but also such ostensibly pro-business measures as retraining and relocating workers, financial aid to new companies and to failing industries, and public education about business and the economy. Forty percent of the public favored a "national economic plan," which received almost no support from the businesspeople polled.

When queried about policies business might undertake to stimulate economic growth (see also Table 9-6), the executives tended once again to place more confidence than the public in investment. The public, however, felt that it would be useful for business "to work closely with government to establish goals and priorities," a policy that business executives greeted with much less enthusiasm.

In the 1979 Union Carbide/Seasonwein survey, 43 percent of the public felt that government was doing less than it should "to regulate major corporations in areas like product safety and other things that have to do with protecting the public"; 55 percent thought the government should do more in this area. In other words, an adversary relationship between government and business is endorsed when the public has an interest in being protected. In the same survey, 50 percent felt the federal government was doing less than it should "to help business grow and create new jobs and products," and in response to a second question, 65 percent wanted government to do more in this regard. In this case, a cooperative relationship between government and business serves the public interest. In the absence of any countervailing claim on the public interest, the public perceives that interest to be served by having less government; 55 percent of the same sample said

TABLE 9–6

Steps Government and Business Should Take to Improve Economic Growth

A. Government

"I'm going to read some steps some people believe government should take to improve the country's economic growth. Please tell me how much of a contribution each one would make to improving economic growth—a major contribution, a minor contribution, or no contribution at all."

Steps to Improve Economic Growth	U.S. Public	U.S. Business Executives
	Percentage "A Major Contribution"	
Cut government spending	78	93
Encourage greater cooperation among business, labor, government, and social interest groups	59	51
Institute tax cuts	58	69
Provide financial incentives to business for new equipment and facilities	52	86
Provide financial incentives for increased consumer saving	52	71
Provide government funding to retrain and relocate workers in failing industries	49	14
Spend more to educate people to increase understanding of economic and business issues	47	27
Provide financial incentives to business for more spending on research and development	46	61
Develop a national industrial plan in which the government would determine where and how our resources are used	40	3
Give financial aid to new companies in growing industries	39	6
Relax environmental and safety regulations	37	57
Give financial aid to failing industries	25	1

B. Business

"I'm going to read you some steps some people believe business should take to improve the country's economic growth. Please tell me how much of a contribution each one should make to improving economic growth—a major contribution, a minor contribution, or no contribution at all."

Steps to Improve Economic Growth	U.S. Public	U.S. Business Executives
	Percentage "A Major Contribution"	
Give less emphasis to short-term profits and more emphasis to long-term growth	71	70
Spend more on research and development	68	87
Work closely with government to establish goals and priorities	58	35
Spend more on modern equipment and facilities	58	93
Spend more to develop and expand international sales	58	70

Source: *Perspectives on Productivity: A Global View* survey conducted for Sentry Insurance by Louis Harris & Associates, Inc., and Dr. Amitai Etzioni, Director of the Center for Policy Research, Washington, D.C. Interviews conducted December 1980–January 1981.
N = 1,205 American adults and 405 American business executives.

that the federal government and its programs should be cut back rather than left the same or expanded. To business executives, government is intrinsically bad. To the public, government is bad unless it can be seen to do some specific good.

The issue of national planning illustrates the basic disposition of Americans toward the role of government. In the Sentry/Harris survey, 45 percent of the American public favored less government planning and direction in the economy, compared with 49 percent who supported the same amount or more. In other words, opinion was about equally divided for and against planning. Among employees in the four other countries surveyed, government planning was much more widely accepted. Majorities ranging from 52 percent in Britain and 58 percent in West Germany to 67 percent in Japan and 76 percent in Australia opposed any reduction in government planning.

The American executives interviewed by Harris opposed government intervention even when presented as directly beneficial to business. By 66 to 32 percent, they rejected "government policies which channel investment into potential growth industries that cannot attract all the investment they need from the private sector." As Figure 9-2 shows, business executives were much more opposed than the general public to the notion that the government should bail out "important industries that are in severe financial trouble." A majority of them even opposed bailing out failing companies important to the national defense, a policy that the public

FIGURE 9–2

Attitudes Toward Government Bail-Outs of Corporations

"Do you think the government should bail out major companies in important industries that are in severe financial trouble, or should these companies be left to sink or swim on their own?"

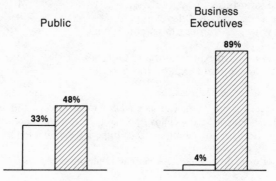

"Should failing companies be bailed out by government if they are important to the national defense?"

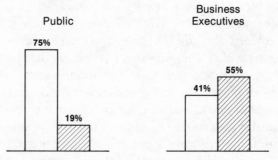

☐ Should bail them out

▨ Companies should not be bailed out

Source: Perspectives on Productivity: A Global View—survey conducted for Sentry Insurance by Louis Harris & Associates, Inc., and Dr. Amitai Etzioni, Director of the Center for Policy Research, Washington, D.C.

N = 1,205 Americans and 405 American business executives.

approved by four to one. Business executives do not want to replace an adversary government role with a supportive or collaborative one. They are opposed to all forms of government intervention, whether for ideological reasons or because government involvement, even when it is intended to help business, has usually been found to create distortions and inefficiencies.

The public is more flexible. By 49 to 34 percent, Harris's national sample felt that antitrust laws should be relaxed "to permit American companies to work together to compete more effectively in the world market." Not surprisingly, business executives also supported a relaxation of antitrust laws, 71 to 27 percent. But in the 1980 Union Carbide/Cambridge Reports survey, the public endorsed a government role that goes far beyond the level of intervention that business executives were willing to tolerate in the Sentry/Harris findings reported above:

> Some experts say that one of the major reasons Japanese industry has been able to compete so successfully with United States industry is that the Japanese government provides a great deal of help to Japanese business and industry. These experts say that the Japanese government protects vital industries in areas like defense, electronics, and construction, stimulates the growth of new industries and helps companies and workers in declining industries find new investment opportunities and jobs. These experts believe that similar kinds of programs will have to be set up in the U.S. if U.S. business and industry are to compete successfully with the Japanese in the years ahead. In general, do you tend to agree with this view or not?

By over two to one—55 to 25 percent—the American public agreed that such a program of massive government intervention would be necessary to make U.S. industry competitive.

The message of these surveys is that the public does not want the government to be either pro-business or anti-business in any uniform way. At most, it might be said that, as of 1981, Americans wanted the government to be *less anti-business* than in the past. But the kind of government-business relationship that people prefer depends upon the context:

• In some contexts—notably, regulation—the public prefers an *adversary* relationship between government and business, when it is put in terms of helping to accomplish specifically approved objectives, such as eliminating pollution or assuring safe products.

• For dealing with problems of productivity and economic growth, a basically *cooperative* relationship is seen as desirable.

• The public is willing to go further and endorse a *collaborative* relationship when it comes to protecting American jobs and American industry from foreign competition.

Americans tend to be pragmatic on these issues. They go about defining the proper relationship between government and business by first assessing what serves the public's interest best—and that interest varies from one situation to the next. The Sentry/Harris data reveal stronger ideological predispositions among American business executives, who are consistently more anti-government than the American public is (sometimes at their own expense), and among the working public in other major industrial countries, who consistently endorse a stronger role for the state than the American public is willing to tolerate. Americans are willing to be pragmatic about government and business, but not to the point of challenging the essential values of free enterprise.

The Legitimacy of Free Enterprise

When the issue of government intervention in the economy is rephrased in terms of socialism and free enterprise, public opinion takes on some predictable—and some unpredictable—qualities. Not surprisingly, there is very little public support for socialism as a concept. That limited support has come more from the ranks of the privileged than from the poorer sectors of American society, as we shall see. Conversely, as could be seen in many of the results already reported, the concept of free enterprise has a powerful appeal and is typically endorsed by over 90 percent of the population.

Socialism

The electoral strength of socialist parties in the United States has been below one percent in all presidential elections since the 1940s, a pattern also reflected in opinion polls that have inquired about attitudes toward socialism. When Cambridge Reports, Inc., asked early in 1976, "Would you favor or oppose introducing socialism in the U.S.?" only 10 percent replied that they would favor doing so, while 62 percent said they were opposed. Another 27 percent replied, "don't know." Civic Service repeated the CRI question six years later in March 1981 and found 12 percent in favor, 76 percent opposed, and 14 percent with no opinion.

The opposition to socialism and to nationalization demonstrated by polls taken since 1974 can be compared with public opinion on these issues during the 1930s. Although the Great Depression did not result in any permanent increase in support for radical political parties (both the Socialist and Communist parties secured considerably fewer votes in 1940 than in 1932), a much larger proportion of those polled during the 1930s and early 1940s endorsed socialism and government ownership than has been the case in recent years.

In 1942, the Roper-*Fortune* poll found that 25 percent felt that "some form of socialism would be a good thing . . . for the country as a whole," compared to 40 percent who said it would be a bad thing. This is the only survey conducted during or close to the 1930s that inquired about socialism explicitly, but the Roper-*Fortune* poll reported in 1936 that majorities supported public ownership of various utilities: electric lights (56 percent), gas (55 percent), telephones (50 percent), and trolleys and buses (49 percent). A Gallup survey conducted in 1937 found that 41 percent supported government ownership of banks, while 42 percent opposed the idea. In 1939, the Roper-*Fortune* poll reported that 34 percent favored government ownership of all or some of the railroads. Twenty-eight percent had similar sentiments about insurance companies, while 22 percent approved of nationalization of "the factories producing the essentials of life, like clothes, food, etc."

It is noteworthy that in the 1942, 1976, and 1981 surveys that inquired about "socialism," as distinct from the nationalization of industry, the most positive response was to be found among the more privileged. In 1942, Roper reported that 40 percent of executives interviewed said "socialism would be a good thing . . . for the country." In 1976, Cambridge Reports, Inc., found that college graduates were the most favorable to socialism; 20 percent endorsed socialism for the United States, compared to 8 percent among those with a high school education or less. Civic Service found that the occupational group most favorable to socialism in 1981 was professionals, 18 percent. In line with this finding, those with post-graduate education showed the highest support of all educational groupings, 17 percent. It is possible that socialism has been perceived by a significant minority of the well-to-do and the better educated as a way of improving the entire culture. Alternatively, since socialism has long been a scare-word in American society implying some sort of foreign and conspiratorial threat, lower-status groups may have reacted more negatively than the relatively sophisticated who have attended college.

The responses, however, to "nationalization"—a concrete socialist policy—have followed a more predictable class pattern. Whenever cross sections of the American public have been asked about nationalization generally or for specific industries, the less privileged have been more favorable than the well-to-do and the better educated. This pattern showed up during the Great Depression as well as in recent years. For example, Table 9-7 shows class differences in responses to a 1936 Gallup survey that inquired about government ownership of three industries: railroads, banks, and munitions. In all three cases, the lower the status or occupational level, the more likely people were to favor nationalization.

TABLE 9–7
Attitudes Toward Nationalization of Railroads, Banks, and the Munitions Industry, 1936

"Do you favor government ownership of the railroads?" "Do you favor government ownership of the banks?" "Do you favor government ownership of the war munitions industry?"

	Oppose All Three	Favor One or Two	Favor All Three
	Percentage*		
Total	22	50	29
Socioeconomic Status			
Average plus	33	50	17
Average	21	57.5	21.5
Poor	16.5	45	38.5
On relief	8	35	57
Occupation			
Professional	30	52	18
Business	28	57	15
Skilled	25	50	25
Unskilled	14	43	43
Unemployed	10	38	52

Source: AIPO Poll No. 60, December 9–29, 1936, calculated from data in the Roper Public Opinion Data Center.
* Percentages are based on "yes" or "no" only.
N = 2,659.

Free Enterprise

Although questions dealing with socialism per se are rare in U.S. opinion polls, many surveys have inquired about attitudes toward the free enterprise system. These invariably elicit a positive response from the great majority of Americans, even though, as has been shown, most people have important criticisms of the way business behaves. In March 1981, Civic Service reported that 79 percent agreed with the statement, "The private business system in the United States works better than any other system yet designed for industrial countries," while only 9 percent felt this was not the case.

Earlier surveys conducted by different polling groups also found strong support for the American economic system. In 1974, Roper asked respondents to check off which of thirteen national attributes they would consider "major causes of United States greatness." Sixty percent chose "our free enterprise system," less than the three quarters who cited our political institutions or the two thirds who named our natural resources, but much more than the 42 percent who specified "moral and religious beliefs" or the 22 percent who chose the absence of a "caste or class system." Strong support for free enterprise is also reflected in various studies by Yankelovich, Skelly & White. In surveys taken each spring since 1975, YSW found that over 90 percent agreed that "we must be ready to make sacrifices if necessary to preserve the free enterprise system." And in 1977, according to Yankelovich, the public rejected the comment, "The free enterprise system benefits the few," by 52 to 16 percent.

In 1976 and 1977, the Harris Survey asked respondents to react to a series of statements about the American economic system and free enterprise. Both polls found overwhelming majorities endorsing views that the American economic system works (see Table 9-8). Majorities of approximately two to one felt that the free enterprise system, "if left alone, except for federal regulations" can solve such problems as inflation and unemployment. Majorities of at least seven to one linked the American free enterprise system to high living standards, individual freedom, and advanced technology. By somewhat smaller but still decisive margins, the public described the free enterprise system as economically efficient and fair or equitable.

In four surveys, taken in 1975, 1976, 1977, and 1979, Cam-

TABLE 9–8

Statements about the American Economic System

Statements	1976			1977		
	Agree	Dis-agree	Not Sure	Agree	Dis-agree	Not Sure
	Percentage					
"For all of its faults, the American economic system still provides our people with the highest living standards in the world."	89	7	5	88	8	4
"Free enterprise for business also means freedom for the individual to choose where he works, where he lives, what he says."	86	5	9	79	10	11
"By allowing freedom of initiative and free enterprise, the American system produces the most advanced technology and know-how the world has known."	82	6	12	76	11	13
"The American free enterprise system is the most efficient economically the world has ever known."	69	13	18	62	20	18
"The business system, if regulated equitably by the federal government, can operate equitably for the vast majority of the people in this country." *	72	14	14	60	17	23
"If left alone, except for essential federal regulations, the free enterprise system can find ways to solve such problems as inflation and unemployment."	55	26	19	51	28	21

Source: The Harris Survey.
* In 1976, this statement was worded: "The business system, if regulated properly by the federal government, can be fair and prosperous for the vast majority of the people in this country."
N = 1,439 in 1976.
N = 1,625 in 1977.

bridge Reports, Inc., presented an argumentative question to samples of respondents: "Some people say that a free market economy is necessary for personal liberty and democracy and that if you take away the free market, we will lose liberty. Other people say the two aren't really related, and we can be free and democratic in any kind of economy. Is a free market economy essential to freedom?" Majorities of 54 percent in 1975, 59 percent in 1976, 60 percent in 1977 and 59 percent in 1979 replied that a free market economy is essential to freedom; between 15 and 19 percent said that such an economy is not essential to freedom, while 25 to 27 percent were not sure.

Striking evidence of the strength of free enterprise in American thinking may be seen in the results of a nationwide survey of American college and university faculty members conducted by Ladd and Lipset in the spring of 1977. By a variety of criteria, this group is one of the most liberal and Democratic in the country. A comparison of their views on many issues to those of other occupational groups indicates that college faculty invariably come out farther to the left.[1] However, no less than 81 percent of them agreed with the statement, "The private business system in the United States, for all its flaws, works better than any other system devised for advanced industrial society." Similarly, over two thirds, 69 percent, approved the view that "the growth of government in the U.S. now poses a threat to freedom and opportunity for individual initiative of the citizenry." When asked to rate various aspects of American society, fully 67 percent evaluated "the private business system" positively.[2]

Some of the underlying sentiments that lead Americans to favor free enterprise and to reject socialism or government control of the economy may be found in the responses to a series of questions posed by Roper in 1975 and 1978. These asked respondents to compare business and "federal agencies" on four criteria: efficiency, intelligence of management, quality of lower- and middle-level employees, and "contribution to people's lives." In each case, as evidenced by the data in Table 9-9, business was given a higher

[1] Everett C. Ladd, Jr., and Seymour Martin Lipset, *The Divided Academy: Professors and Politics* (New York: The Norton Library, 1976), pp. 25–26. See also Seymour Martin Lipset, "The Academic Mind at the Top: The Political Behavior and Values of Faculty Elites," *Public Opinion Quarterly* 46 (Summer 1982), pp. 143–68.

[2] Everett C. Ladd, Jr., and Seymour Martin Lipset, "Professors Found to be Liberal but not Radical," *The Chronicle of Higher Education* (January 16, 1978), p. 9.

TABLE 9–9
Comparisons Between Business and
Federal Agencies: Four Criteria

A. "Generally speaking, which do you think has the most intelligent people in top management positions—federal government agencies or business?"

B. "Generally speaking, which do you think is run more efficiently . . . ?"

C. "Which do you think attracts the best type of employee on middle and lower levels . . . ?"

D. "Which do you think contributes more to making people's lives better . . . ?"

	1975	1978
	Percentage	
A. Most intelligent people in top management		
Federal agencies	19	16
Business	60	58
Both equal (volunteered)	11	19
B. Run more efficiently		
Federal agencies	11	9
Business	72	71
Both equal (volunteered)	8	12
C. Attracts best type of employees on middle and lower levels		
Federal agencies	28	25
Business	51	52
Both equal (volunteered)	9	15
D. Contributes more to making people's lives better		
Federal agencies	31	25
Business	42	42
Both equal (volunteered)	13	23

Source: Roper.
1975, N = 2,000.
1978, N = 2,002.

rating than federal agencies. Business outranked federal agencies by a margin of eight to one on the criterion of efficiency. Business was even considered superior to federal agencies in terms of "contributing more to making people's lives better."

The same response pattern occurred in a November 1981 Roper survey that inquired whether "the phrase 'efficient and well-run' describes" different institutions. Only 20 percent said federal government was well-run, compared to 56 percent for "large business corporations" and 70 percent for "small business corporations."

Thus, one reason why free enterprise is highly valued is that private business is perceived to offer better standards of performance than the federal government. Business is believed to "work better" than government. Of course, this too may be partly an ideological sentiment rather than a product of actual experience.

Conclusion

If most Americans are critical of many practices they associate with business, they remain strongly committed to the value of a competitive free enterprise system. They would like to make business more responsive to the public interest, but unlike large segments of the polity in Europe, Australia, and Japan, here only a small minority favor any form of state socialism or public ownership. Although the state has developed adversary relations with business, particularly in efforts to regulate it, most Americans are more fearful of state power than of business power and see the state as more wasteful and inefficient than private enterprise.

The belief of many businesspeople that the American state has become more powerful and intrusive is valid from a historical point of view. Viewed in comparative terms, however, it is noteworthy that there are few other industrialized nations in which business is more legitimate or less threatened by public opinion. As noted, the United States is the only economically developed society without an effective socialist, communist, or labor party, and unions are weaker here than in most other industrialized countries. Both the socialist and trade union appeal have declined in the United States as compared to the past. High taxation, which so disturbs business here, still leaves the United States behind every other industrialized nation except Japan in the proportion of the Gross Domestic Product absorbed in taxes.[3] Although it is difficult to get precise estimates of total public spending on social welfare, the available evidence also indicates that few other countries devote as low a proportion of their national income to this purpose as the United States.[4]

What has made business particularly vulnerable to public criti-

[3] *Revenue Statistics of OECD Member Countries, 1965–1978* (Paris: OECD, 1979), p. 83.

[4] Harold Wilensky, *The "New Corporatism," Centralization and the Welfare State* (Beverly Hills, California: Sage Publications, 1976), p. 11.

cism is the continued growth of large corporations. Americans fear concentrated power, whether in the state or in the economy. And following a classic American tradition, they seek to restrain self-interested power through checks and balances. Much as they support the continuation of a divided and internally conflicted government, they also favor conflict among the state, business, and labor unions. These conceptions may be naive and they may produce inefficient economic policies, but they do not imply a rejection of free enterprise or a failure to appreciate the role of business or trade unions in sustaining the American standard of living.

10

The Social and Political Bases of Attitudes Toward Business, Labor, and Government

OUR analysis thus far has dealt with trends of public confidence in institutions and public opinion on a number of specific policy issues relating to business, labor, and government. We have examined changing levels of trust in institutions over time, the impact of aggregate economic conditions, and the public's assessment of the claims of business, labor, and government for its sympathy and approval. We will now examine the nature of the public's attitudes in more detail. As shown in Chapter 4, confidence in institutions generally is difficult to describe in demographic terms. Instead, different institutions tend to be favored by different categories of the population, as seen in Table 4-2. This chapter seeks to identify the social and political bases of support for, and opposition to, the three major institutions.

Attitudes toward business, government, and labor are at the heart of the "New Deal system" of partisanship that has characterized American politics since the 1930s. The Depression was a period of intense polarization between business and labor, and popular responses to this conflict tended to be structured along class lines: higher-status Americans were more favorable to business, lower-status Americans more supportive of labor unions. When Franklin

D. Roosevelt endorsed the Wagner Act in 1935, he committed the power of the federal government—and the Democratic Party—to the side of labor, reversing the pro-business bias of the federal government during the previous Republican era. Moreover, the New Deal initiated an array of social welfare programs that were generally redistributive in nature. Thus the traditional bias of Democrats and "Old Left" liberals has been pro-union, pro-government (or at least pro-federal government), and anti-business, while the corresponding bias of Republicans and traditional conservatives has been anti-union, pro-business, and opposed to the expansion of federal power—positions that are dominant again in the early 1980s.

The 1970s: Continuity and Change

Do these historical patterns continue to hold up in public opinion data from the 1970s? Earlier, in Table 4-2, there was some evidence that they do. Table 10-1, which uses data from the combined 1973–77 NORC General Social Surveys, displays the relationships in more detail. In this table, confidence in major companies and in organized labor is broken down by two indicators of social class (education and the occupational status of the head of household) and by two political measures, partisanship and ideology. (The NORC surveys did not include a question on overall confidence in government. Instead, the confidence series gauged trust only in specific parts of the federal government—the executive branch, Congress, the Supreme Court, and the military. Other data will be introduced shortly to measure trust in government more broadly.)

Support for business does rise with education, while that for organized labor falls. But the effect is modest at best (correlations of .08 and −.15, respectively). The proportion expressing "a great deal of confidence" in the leaders of major companies increased from 23 percent among those respondents who did not finish high school to 25 percent among high school graduates and 33 percent among those with college degrees. But even among the grade school-educated, more people said they have "a great deal of confidence" in business leaders than gave the negative response, "hardly any." In the case of the leaders of organized labor, high confidence fell from 16 percent among those who did not complete high school

TABLE 10–1

Confidence in the Leaders of Major Companies and Organized Labor by Education, Occupational Status, Partisanship, and Ideology

"As far as the people running (major companies/organized labor) are concerned, would you say you have a great deal of confidence, only some confidence, or hardly any confidence at all in them?"

	Major Companies		Organized Labor		
	A Great Deal	Hardly Any	A Great Deal	Hardly Any	N
	Percentage				
Education					
Grade school	23	18	21	26	1,293
Some high school	23	17	16	26	1,380
High school graduate	25	15	14	27	2,485
Some college	28	17	12	32	1,233
College graduate	33	14	6	38	1,058
Occupational status (head of household)					
Professional, technical	24	16	10	30	1,701
Managers, officials	37	13	10	40	997
Clerical, sales	25	13	11	28	1,359
Skilled workers	28	18	19	29	837
Semi-skilled workers	22	19	22	24	1,419
Unskilled, service	22	17	15	23	981
Partisanship					
Democrats	23	18	19	22	3,125
Independents	24	18	10	32	2,525
Republicans	35	10	10	37	1,630
Ideology[a]					
Extremely liberal	15	43	17	25	135
Liberal	22	22	18	25	734
Slightly liberal	19	19	13	27	800
Moderate	24	16	14	28	2,241
Slightly conservative	30	13	11	36	922
Conservative	34	14	13	36	677
Extremely conservative	38	18	10	44	136
All respondents (1973–77 combined)	26	16	14	29	7,449

Source: NORC, 1973–77 General Social Surveys.
a: 1974–77 only.

to 14 percent among high school graduates and 6 percent among those who had completed college. But those with "hardly any" confidence in labor leaders outnumbered those with "a great deal of confidence" at all levels of education.

The differences by occupational status are also small but confirm the traditional pattern. In blue-collar households, 24 percent of those polled expressed "a great deal of confidence" in the leaders of major companies. Among white-collar respondents, the figure was slightly higher, 28 percent. Similarly, high confidence in the leaders of organized labor fell from 19 percent among blue-collar respondents to 11 percent among white-collar interviewees. Table 10-1 reveals that business received the strongest support from those in households headed by "managers, officials, and proprietors," i.e., mostly businesspeople. Professional and technical-level people, the highest status white-collar occupational group, were not particularly pro-business, however. The strongest support for organized labor came from blue-collar households headed by semi-skilled workers, who are the most heavily unionized sector of the work-force. Conversely, the strongest anti-labor feeling was located among the business group.

The partisanship and ideology measures both showed greater support for business on the right and for labor on the left. Over a third of Republicans, but only 23 percent of Democrats, expressed "a great deal of confidence" in the people in charge of major companies. On the other hand, 37 percent of Republicans, but only 22 percent of Democrats, said they felt "hardly any" confidence in labor leaders. Interestingly, Independents were almost the same as Democrats in their feelings about business, but they were quite close to Republicans in their opinions about organized labor.

Conservatives were more pro-business than liberals; one third of the former, but only one fifth of the latter, had high esteem for the leaders of major companies. Approval of labor leaders rose slightly among liberals, but the figure never got very high. Even among those on the far left, the proportion expressing "a great deal of confidence" in people running organized labor never reached 20 percent. Strong anti-business sentiment (almost three to one negative) could be found only among those who described themselves as "extreme liberals," two percent of the electorate. By contrast, attitudes toward labor were slightly negative among liberals, two-to-one negative among moderates, and three- or four-to-one negative among conservatives.

Thus, the overall configurations in Table 10-1 reveal continuity with the New Deal pattern: support for business is greater among high status groups and on the political right, while support for labor is greater on the left and at lower status levels. But the differences are not very great, at least by these measures, and the general result—higher confidence in business than in labor—overrides just about all group variations. Even Democrats show higher approval of business than they do of organized labor.

There is good reason to believe that these correlations with social class and politics have been weakening since the 1930s. The intensity of labor-management conflict as a political issue has certainly declined. A new generation has grown up since World War II for whom the memories of the Depression and the New Deal are entirely second-hand and remote from their personal experience. Thus, less intense polarization over business, labor, and government, as reflected in Table 10-1, may be a consequence of the passage of time. The more recent political conflicts of the 1960s—over civil rights, the Vietnam War, and social and cultural radicalism—were not primarily economic in nature. Where government and labor were perceived positively by the Old Left of the 1930s, the New Left and New Politics liberals of the 1960s and 1970s were not particularly attracted to either: the New Left campaigned against the policies of the federal government under both Democratic and Republican administrations (although the principal target of New Left opposition was not those administrations' economic policies). The labor movement, characterized negatively by the stigma of a "hard-hat" mentality, has been considered unreliable and even reactionary by liberals on racial and foreign policy issues. In turn, many of the "backlash" votes for various right-wing candidates, from George Wallace to Ronald Reagan, were lower-status in origin and came from traditionally Democratic sectors of the population.[1]

Labor and government are no longer unambiguously positive to liberals in the early 1980s, while the New Left and the larger New Politics movement drew their support primarily from the professional upper middle class and the young. In the 1980 Presidential primaries, many affluent, well-educated, and student liberals preferred John Anderson to Edward Kennedy. Kennedy espoused the traditional liberal positions of social welfare spending, big government, and support for organized labor, while Anderson was a purer New Politics candidate, fiscally conservative and uncommitted to

[1] Seymour Martin Lipset and Earl Raab, *The Politics of Unreason: Right-wing Extremism in America, 1790–1977,* expanded ed. (Chicago: University of Chicago Press, 1977), pp. 378–402, 521–30.

labor unions but liberal on social and foreign policy issues. But while liberals may have lost some of their traditional enthusiasm for labor and government, there is no reason to believe they have become more favorable toward business. Most likely, the trend has been away from all three—that is, increasingly suspicious of, and hostile to, all concentrations of power.

Other research has found direct evidence of declining class differences over economic and political issues. After having reviewed a large body of survey data from the 1930s to the 1960s, Everett Ladd concluded: "This composite picture shows that on regulation of business and unions, social welfare programs, and the like, higher status groups were notably further apart from lower status groups in the New Deal and immediate post New Deal years than in the 1950s and early 1960s."[2] For instance, Ladd found class differences of 30 to 40 percentage points on questions eliciting approval or disapproval of trade unionism in the 1930s and 1940s, but "by the late 1950s and early 1960s, roughly similar pro-con questions on unionism showed relatively narrow inter-class variations."[3] Whereas the professional-managerial and manual worker classes were 35 points apart in endorsing less government regulation of business in 1940, a similar question asked in 1961 showed almost no class difference.[4]

Schlozman and Verba compared the relationship between class and attitudes on economic issues in their 1976 survey of the U.S. metropolitan work force with that found in a 1939 Roper survey for *Fortune* magazine. The 1976 data showed little or no class differences on economic policies among younger respondents but pronounced class differences among older ones. A direct comparison of class differences in 1939 and 1976 revealed a substantial attenuation over time. In 1976, the survey data showed little variation between white-collar, blue-collar, and even unemployed workers in their attitudes toward "action by the government to end unemployment; taxing the rich to help the poor; ending unemployment even if it means that the government will assign jobs; ending unemployment even if it means the end of the capitalist system; and a government program to limit income." Differences

[2] Everett C. Ladd, Jr., with Charles D. Hadley, *Transformations of the American Party System,* 2nd ed. (New York: W. W. Norton, 1978), p. 110.

[3] Ladd, *Transformations,* p. 109.

[4] Ladd, *Transformations,* p. 109 (Table 2-2).

between blue-collar and upper white-collar workers averaged less than two percentage points on these five issues in 1976, whereas on similar questions asked in 1939, the average difference was 18 points.[5]

The NORC data in Table 10-2 reveal a pattern similar to that found by Schlozman and Verba in their 1976 survey. The table shows class and party differences in confidence within age cohorts. In each case, the weakest differences can be found among the youngest respondents, those between eighteen and thirty years of age when they were interviewed. Class and party differences were generally stronger among older respondents. For example, young blue-collar workers were only 4 percent more likely to express "a great deal of confidence" in organized labor than young white-collar employees (16 percent of the former group, compared with 12 percent of the latter). Among people over sixty, the class difference was 12 points; 23 percent of the older blue-collar group, but only 11 percent of the older white-collar respondents, indicated strong trust in labor leaders.

Similarly in the case of major companies, class differences became stronger as age increased. Indeed, Table 10-2 shows almost no class differences among young persons in their feelings about the leaders of major companies. Younger people of every class tended to be negative toward them. The age difference was especially pronounced in the middle class, that is, among white-collar and college-educated interviewees, with the young quite anti-business and the old relatively favorable.

It is well known that younger Americans tend to reject party self-identification and to describe themselves as political Independents. In addition, as Table 10-2 shows, young Democrats and Republicans are somewhat less polarized in their attitudes toward business and labor than older partisans. For instance, young Democrats were only 5 percent more likely to express high confidence in labor leaders than young Republicans. The party difference among partisans over sixty was 14 points. Younger Republicans tended to be less pro-business than older Republicans, while younger Democrats were less pro-labor than older Democrats. These patterns support the notion that business-versus-labor conflicts are

---

[5] Kay Lehman Schlozman and Sidney Verba, *Injury to Insult* (Cambridge, Mass.: Harvard University Press, 1979), pp. 217–22.

TABLE 10-2

Confidence in the Leaders of Major Companies and Organized Labor by Education, Occupational Status, and Partisanship, Controlling for Age

Those Expressing "A Great Deal of Confidence" in the Leaders of:	Less Than High School Graduate	High School Graduate	College	Difference[a]	Blue Collar	White Collar	Difference[b]	Democrats	Independents	Republicans	Difference[c]
					Percentage						
Major companies											
Age: 18 to 30 years	21	21	20	− 1	20	20	0	19	20	26	+ 7
31 to 44 years	18	24	30	+12	20	28	+ 8	22	23	34	+12
45 to 60 years	26	31	42	+16	29	35	+ 6	27	30	42	+15
Over 60 years	24	30	38	+14	25	31	+ 6	22	28	35	+13
Organized labor											
Age: 18 to 30 years	17	16	10	− 7	16	12	− 4	16	13	11	− 5
31 to 44 years	15	12	8	− 7	16	8	− 8	16	8	8	− 8
45 to 60 years	20	12	10	−10	20	10	−10	21	10	10	−11
Over 60 years	19	13	10	− 9	23	11	−12	24	8	10	−14
N											
Age: 18 to 30 years	416	803	863	—	.850	1,218	—	755	959	309	—
31 to 44 years	496	725	646	—	775	1,073	—	786	654	370	—
45 to 60 years	767	643	469	—	855	976	—	844	551	453	—
Over 60 years	987	304	303	—	752	771	—	735	349	489	—

Source: NORC, 1973–77 General Social Surveys.

[a] College minus less than high school graduate.
[b] White collar minus blue collar.
[c] Republicans minus Democrats.

most salient to older partisans who grew up during the New Deal.

Another piece of evidence suggesting declining class division comes from the Opinion Research Corporation's index of public approval of large companies, measured every two years since 1959. (The six items comprising this index were shown in Figure 1-4). In reporting the results of their 1977 survey, ORC compared the correlates of "high" and "low" approval of large companies for 1967 and 1977. The results are displayed in Table 10-3.

Within every class and age category, as in the public at large, anti-business sentiment increased between 1967 and 1977. But the shift was not uniform. The fall-off in support for large companies was greater among the college-educated than among the grade-school educated; pro-business sentiment on the ORC index fell by 22 points at the college level but by only 10 points at the grade-school level. (The rate of decline in the population as a whole was 16 percent.) The increase in anti-business feeling between 1967 and 1977 was particularly strong among those under thirty: from 37 to 65 percent "low approval" of large companies, or an increase of 28 percent, compared with 20 percent for the population as a whole. Thus, the data in Table 10-3 suggest that by 1977 business had lost most support among young, high-status, and well-educated Americans.

The result has been a noticeable reduction of class and age differences. In 1967, the college-educated came out 23 percent more pro-business than the grade-school educated on the ORC index. In 1977, the difference by education had fallen to 21 percentage points. The gap between professional-managerial respondents and blue-collar workers remained about the same both years (17–16 points), but that may be attributable in part to the use of a coding scheme that grouped professionals and managers together. (Recall that Table 10-1 revealed a notable difference between these two "upper middle class" groups in their feelings about business.) Finally, in 1967, people under thirty years of age were 31 percentage points more favorable to business than those over sixty. In 1977, the age gap had virtually disappeared (4 points). Any small remaining pro-business margin among the young was undoubtedly a consequence of their higher status and education. As Table 10-2 already demonstrated, when either education or occupation is held constant, the young turn out to be consistently more anti-business than the old.

TABLE 10-3

Public Approval of Large Companies, by Education, Occupation, and Age

	1967			1977			Change 1967-77[b]
	High Approval	Low Approval	Margin[a]	High Approval	Low Approval	Margin[a]	
		Percentage					
Education							
Less than 12 years	12	60	(−48)	4	71	(−67)	−19
High school graduate	20	43	(−23)	7	66	(−59)	−36
College	34	35	(−1)	12	58	(−46)	−45
Occupation							
Professional, managerial	27	39	(−12)	11	55	(−44)	−32
White collar	23	42	(−19)	9	63	(−54)	−35
Blue collar	18	47	(−29)	7	67	(−60)	−31
Age							
18 to 29 years	23	37	(−14)	7	65	(−58)	−44
30 to 39 years	22	42	(−20)	6	63	(−57)	−37
40 to 59 years	19	51	(−32)	8	65	(−57)	−25
60 years and over	14	59	(−45)	9	71	(−62)	−17
All	20	46	(−26)	8	66	(−58)	−32

Source: Opinion Research Corporation, 1967 and 1977.

[a] "High" minus "Low."

[b] Average of change in percentage "High Approval" minus change in percentage "Low Approval," 1967 to 1977.

Note: Approval is measured by ORC's composite scale of responses to the six agree/disagree statements shown in Figure 1-4.

Business, Labor, and Government: Attitude Scales

In order to compare the social and political bases of support for business, labor, and government more systematically, attitude scales showing favorability toward each were constructed using data from the 1976 American National Election Survey administered by the Center for Political Studies at the University of Michigan. The sample for this survey was a cross section of the American electorate (citizens, age 18 and over) taken at the time of the 1976 Presidential election; 2,248 respondents were interviewed in October and November 1976, just before the election on November 3rd. Most were interviewed a second time shortly after the election, in November and December 1976 or January 1977.[6]

This survey included a set of parallel questions eliciting attitudes toward "big business," "labor unions," "businessmen," and "workingmen":

- Does each of the following groups have "too much influence," "just about the right amount of influence," or "too little influence" in American life and politics: big business, businessmen, labor unions, and workingmen?
- How "cool" or "warm" did respondents feel toward big business, businessmen, labor unions, and workingmen, as measured by ratings on a "feeling thermometer" that ran from zero degrees (coldest) to 100 degrees (warmest)?
- Did interviewees feel "particularly close to" businessmen and to workingmen as "people who are most like you in their ideas and interests and feelings about things"?

These questions were factor analyzed in order to construct composite scales summarizing attitudes toward business and labor. Such scales are useful because they tend to cancel out peculiar variations in response patterns caused by the wording of individual questions.

The factor analysis confirmed the assumption that feelings about big business and businesspeople were positively intercorrelated; the same was true for attitudes toward labor unions and workingmen. The responses to the five questions about big business and businessmen defined a pro-business scale, while the five questions concerning labor unions and workingmen defined a scale of

[6] The data for the 1976 survey were obtained from the Inter-University Consortium for Political and Social Research, Ann Arbor, Michigan. Neither the ICPSR nor the Center for Political Studies bears any responsibility for the analysis presented here.

support for labor. Of course, as one would expect from the earlier analyses in this book, the absolute level of approval for "big business" was quite different from that for "businessmen." The same was true for "labor unions" and "workingmen." The factor analysis simply confirms the fact that attitudes toward the objects in each pair are positively correlated, for example, that people who are more favorable toward businessmen are also relatively more favorable toward big business.

Here is how the public perceived the amount of influence in American life and politics of each of these groups:

	Those Saying:	
	"Too Much Influence"	"Too Little Influence"
	Percentage	
"Big business"	77	3
"Labor unions"	64	5
"Businessmen"	33	11
"Workingmen"	4	53

As discussed earlier in Chapters 6 and 7, Americans definitely feel that big business and labor unions have "too much influence" in American life and politics. But when the question shifts from institutions to individuals, perceived influence falls dramatically. A majority feels that businessmen have "just about the right amount of influence" in American life and politics, while a comparable number feels that workingmen have "too little influence." The principal distinction here is between institutions and individuals. A secondary difference is that *big* business is perceived to be more influential than labor unions, and businessmen are seen as considerably more influential than workingmen.

When these same objects are compared using the feeling thermometer, the order changes slightly:

	Those Expressing:	
	Warm Feelings (51–100 Degrees)	Cool Feelings (0–49 Degrees)
	Percentage	
"Workingmen"	88	1
"Businessmen"	61	14
"Big business"	35	38
"Labor unions"	32	41

A plurality of Americans in 1976 expressed hostile feelings about both big business and labor unions, with unions slightly less popular than big business. A clear majority of Americans felt "warm" toward both businessmen and workingmen. Only 14 percent of the sample expressed any degree of adverse feelings toward businessmen, and a scant 1 percent were negative toward workingmen.

Finally, when the sample was asked whether they felt "particularly close to" certain groups as "people who are most like you in their ideas and interests and feelings about things," a majority felt close to workingmen (56 percent), whereas only one in five reported this kind of personal identification with businessmen. While the image of the latter is certainly not negative, most Americans identify with the "workingman" image—possibly because most people, including white-collar employees and professionals, see themselves as "working" for a living. Undoubtedly, the high level of sympathy for workingmen is not based on class feeling but on democratic and populist sentiment. Still, the single most important difference in popularity and approval is between businessmen and workingmen as *individuals* and big business and labor unions as *institutions*.

Ten questions relating to confidence in government were extracted from the 1976 survey and analyzed separately. A factor analysis revealed that three were weakly related to the other seven and tended to form a separate dimension of political trust. The two sets of questions are shown in Table 10-4, Part I and Part II.

The questions in Part I of Table 10-4 concern confidence in government. They include the four that were traced over time in Figure 1-1:

- whether people in the government waste "quite a lot" of tax money (in 1976, three out of four respondents felt that they did);
- whether the government in Washington can be trusted "to do what is right" most of the time (two thirds did not think so in 1976);
- whether the government is run "by a few big interests looking out for themselves" rather than for "the benefit of all the people" (two thirds thought so);
- whether "quite a few" government officials are crooked (about half thought they were).

These are precisely the "mistrusting" attitudes that have been increasing at a rapid rate since the mid-1960s, as shown in Chapter 1.

303

TABLE 10–4

Attitudes Toward Government, by Education

	Did Not Finish High School	High School Graduate	Attended College	All
	Percentage of Sample: 32	*Percentage of Sample: 36*	*Percentage of Sample: 32*	
		Percentage		
I. Confidence in Government				
"Do you think that people in the government waste a lot of the money we pay in taxes, waste some of it, or don't waste very much of it?"				
Waste a lot of it	71	76	75	74
Waste some, or not much of it	22	23	23	23
"How much of the time do you think you can trust the government in Washington to do what is right—just about always, most of the time, or only some of the time?"				
Always, or most of the time	22	33	40	30
Only some of the time	66	65	58	62
"Would you say the government is pretty much run by a few big interests looking out for themselves or that it is run for the benefit of all the people?"				
For a few big interests	69	67	63	66
For all the people	20	25	27	24
"Do you feel that almost all of the people running the government are smart people, or do you think that quite a few of them don't seem to know what they are doing?"				
Almost all smart people	35	45	51	44
Don't know what they're doing	55	49	44	49

"Do you think that quite a few of the people running the government are crooked, not very many are, or do you think hardly any of them are crooked?"

Quite a few are crooked	47	44	35	41
Not very many/hardly any	42	53	63	53

"Over the years, how much attention do you feel the government pays to what the people think when it decides what to do—a good deal, some, or not much?"

A good deal/some	52	66	76	65
Not much	43	33	23	33

"How good a job is being done for the country as a whole by the federal government in Washington?"

Very poor/poor job	22	22	21	16
Fair job	49	51	44	69
Good/very good job	15	21	22	15

II. Confidence in the Political System

"Some people believe a change in our whole form of government is needed to solve the problems facing our country, while others feel no real change is necessary. Do you think a big change is needed in our form of government, or should it be kept pretty much as it is?"

Need a big change	28	23	21	24
Kept as is	34	44	54	44

"I'm going to read you a pair of statements about our form of government, and I'd like you to tell me which one you agree with more. Would you say . . . ."

"I am proud of many things about our form of government," or	64	77	86	76
"I can't find much in our form of government to be proud of."	27	18	11	19

TABLE 10-4 (Cont)

Attitudes Toward Government, by Education

	Did Not Finish High School	High School Graduate	Attended College	All
	Percentage of Sample: 32	Percentage of Sample: 36	Percentage of Sample: 32	
	Percentage			
"There has been some talk recently about how people have lost faith and confidence in the government in Washington. Do you think this lack of trust in the government is just because of individuals in office or is there something more seriously wrong with government in general and the way it operates?"				
Just individuals in office	55	66	64	62
Something wrong with government in general	31	27	30	29
III. Power of Government				
"What is your feeling—do you think the government is getting too powerful or do you think the government is not getting too strong?"				
Getting too powerful	39	50	59	68
Not getting too strong	19	19	22	27
"How much influence and power should the federal government in Washington have?"				
Much less/less influence and power	30	47	63	30
Same amount as now	28	30	24	30
More/much more influence and power	25	15	10	9

"There is much concern about the rapid rise in medical and hospital costs. Some feel there should be a government insurance plan which would cover all medical and hospital expenses. Others feel that medical expenses should be paid by individuals, and through private insurance like Blue Cross. . . . Where would you place yourself on this scale, or haven't you thought much about this?"

Government health insurance (positions 1–3 on scale)	39	32	35	42
Private health insurance (positions 5–7 on scale)	25	37	41	41

"Some people feel that the government in Washington should see to it that every person has a job and a good standard of living. . . . Others think the government should just let each person get ahead on his own. . . . And, of course, some other people have opinions somewhere in between. . . . Where would you place yourself on this scale, or haven't you thought much about this?"

Government guarantee job and standard of living (positions 1–3 on scale)	23	14	17	29
Let each get ahead on his own (positions 5–7 on scale)	26	42	53	47

Source: University of Michigan, Center for Political Studies, 1976 U.S. National Election Study. $N = 2,248$.

307

One additional "political trust" question, asked for the first time in the 1976 survey, was highly correlated with the others and was therefore included in the confidence in government scale, namely, the rating of "how good a job you feel the federal government in Washington is doing for the country as a whole." Three quarters of the 1976 sample rated the federal government as doing no better than a "fair" job, that is, between 0 and 4 on an eight-point scale. Another item from the 1976 survey was included in the confidence in government scale but given less weight, because it showed a weaker logical and and statistical relationship to the concept being measured. This item concerned whether "almost all of the people running the government" are smart (44 percent agreed) or whether "public officials don't seem to know what they are doing" (49 percent concurred). This query not only produced a more even division than those cited above, but it was only moderately correlated with the other measures of confidence. Very likely, many people who express low confidence in government still feel that government officials are "smart people" who "know what they are doing"; the public's lack of *confidence* is not necessarily seen as stemming from a lack of *competence,* and questions inquiring about the latter are not very good measures of the former.

The second set of political trust questions, listed in Part II of Table 10-4, differs from the "confidence in government" questions both in substance and in the nature of the public's response. These questions ask for feelings about the political system itself, about "our form of government" rather than its actual operation and the people running it. As noted in Chapter 1, the public has been strongly positive in its evaluation of the political system, despite intensely negative sentiments about the way the government is run. Three quarters of the 1976 sample said they were "proud of many things about our form of government," while only 19 percent said they could not "find much in our form of government to be proud of." Almost two thirds felt that their lack of trust in government was attributable to "the individuals in office" rather than to "something seriously wrong with government in general and the way it operates." And when asked whether "a big change is needed in our form of government," 44 percent thought it should be kept as it is; an additional 26 percent offered the response that some change is needed, while only 24 percent felt that a "big change" is necessary "to solve the problems facing our country."

As indicated in Chapter 1, even though by 1976 confidence in government had reached just about the lowest point since the late 1950s, most Americans continued to say that they were proud of our form of government. Their lack of confidence was clearly directed at the people running those institutions. A comparable distinction was noted between the high level of public confidence in the free enterprise system and the low level of confidence in big business and large corporations. Americans may be very critical of the performance of their institutions, but they maintain faith in the system itself. In order to keep these two concepts distinct, separate scales were constructed for "confidence in government" (the Part I questions) and "confidence in the political system" (the Part II questions).

Four additional government-related questions were added to the analysis for purposes of comparison. These items, constituting Part III of Table 10-4, included the following:

- Is the government "getting too powerful"? (68 percent thought so)
- Should the federal government have more influence and power or less? (18 percent said "more" and 52 percent said "less")
- Should we have private or government health insurance? (35 percent favored government health insurance and 34 percent favored private plans)
- Should the government in Washington "see to it that every person has a job and a good standard of living" (18 percent chose this response), or should the government "just let each person get ahead on his own" (preferred by 41 percent)?

These questions do not deal with confidence in government. Rather, they inquire about the *power of government,* particularly the balance between public and private power. They measure beliefs about what the government should and should not do, how much power it should have in relation to the private sector, and the status of the "New Deal system" of public power and social welfare spending. According to the responses reported in Table 10-4, Part III, it does not appear that the public in 1976 wanted a more powerful government or had a significantly greater degree of confidence in public over private power.

With this material, five scales were constructed:

A. attitudes toward business,
B. attitudes toward labor,

and attitudes toward government, specifically:

C. confidence in government,
D. confidence in the political system, and
E. attitudes toward the power of government.

Each respondent was given a numerical score on the five scales. The scores were standardized so that zero represents the average respondent in the sample. A score of +100 is one standard deviation more "positive" (pro-business, pro-labor, high confidence in government, etc.) than the average. A score of −100 is one standard deviation less favorable than average on the attitude in question. Thus, a positive score does not necessarily mean absolutely favorable to business, labor, or government, but only *relatively* favorable, compared, that is, to "the average American," as polled in 1976 by the Michigan Center for Political Studies.

Socioeconomic Status and Attitudes Toward Business, Labor, and Government

Figure 10-1 shows the five attitude scales broken down by respondents' education. For each scale, average scores are compared for respondents with less than twelve years of education, for high school graduates, and for those who went to college.

Figure 10-1 (A and B) reveals that feelings toward business and labor are not symmetrical in their relationship to education; that is, as education increases, attitudes toward labor decline markedly while those toward business fall and then rise. There is no apparent correlation between education and favorability toward business, but there is a very strong one between education and positive sentiments toward labor: the mean score on the labor scale decreased from a positive 35 among the non-high-school graduates, to 7 (just about the sample mean) among high school graduates, to −39 among those who attended college. The college-educated have relatively negative sentiments about unions, but their attitudes toward business are not comparably positive. The same is true for the poorly educated, who have relatively positive opinions about labor and workers but whose feelings about business and businessmen are not markedly negative. These findings vary slightly from those seen earlier in Table 10-1. In that table, confidence in the leaders of "major companies" rose with education, but the

310

FIGURE 10–1
Attitudes Toward Business, Labor, and Government, by Education
(Mean Factor Scores)

A. Business

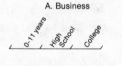

B. Labor

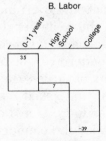

C. Confidence in Government

D. Confidence in the Political System

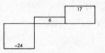

E. Power of Government

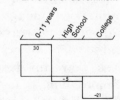

Source: Center for Political Studies, University of Michigan, 1976 American National Election Survey.
N = 2,248.

effect was not strong (gamma correlation of .08). The correlation between education and confidence in labor leaders was somewhat stronger (−.15). Thus, the negative linkage between education and support for labor seems to hold up. In the case of business, however, the relationship with education appears to be weak and inconsistent.

An interesting reversal occurs in the case of attitudes toward government. All three government scales are moderately related to education, although in different directions. Confidence in government and in the political system both *rise* with education (Figures 10-1-C and 10-1-D). On the other hand, support for a more powerful federal government *declines* with education (Figure 10-1-E). While the poorly educated are the most cynical and distrustful about government and have the least faith in our political system, the well-educated are the most opposed to the principle of an active, powerful government.

This pattern can be observed for various questions in the three government scales, as shown in Table 10-4. For instance, the question that asked respondents to rate "the job . . . being done for the country as a whole by the federal government in Washington" tapped the confidence, not the power, dimension. Poorly educated people were least likely to give the federal government a "good" or "very good" job rating. They were also the most likely to favor changes in our political system; only one third of those who had not finished high school thought that the political system should be "kept pretty much as it is," compared with a majority of the college-educated.

But when asked, "How much influence and power should the federal government in Washington have?"—clearly a "power" question—the college-educated were considerably more likely to endorse *less* power and influence. Among those who did not graduate from high school, about equal percentages favored a less powerful (30 percent) and a more powerful (25 percent) federal government, while a less powerful federal government was supported by a margin of more than six to one among the college-educated. Similarly on other "power" questions, the college-educated were the most likely to favor private rather than government health insurance and to believe that the government should "just let each person get ahead on his own" rather than guarantee every citizen a job and a good standard of living. On "confidence" questions, however, the college-educated were the least likely to say that public officials are crooked or incompetent or that those who run the government pay little attention to what the people think. The well-educated also showed the greatest pride and confidence in the political system itself.

Are these relationships truly the effect of education, or do they reflect some more specific attribute of social status? Figure 10-2 breaks the five scales down by the occupational status of the head of each respondent's household. Blue-collar and white-collar households are subdivided as in Table 10-1:

FIGURE 10–2

Attitudes Toward Business, Labor, and Government, by
Occupational Status

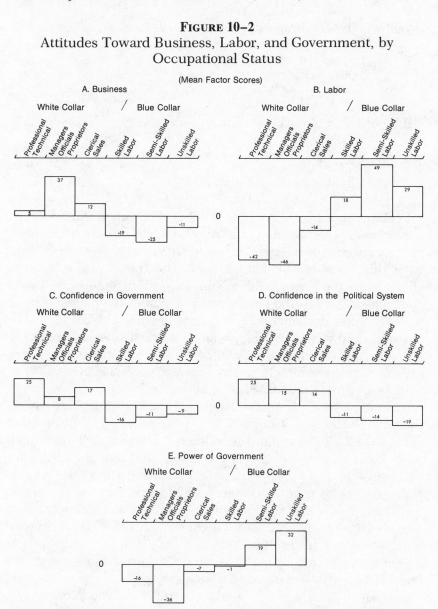

(Mean Factor Scores)

A. Business

B. Labor

C. Confidence in Government

D. Confidence in the Political System

E. Power of Government

Source: Center for Political Studies, University of Michigan, 1976 American National Election Survey.

N = 2,248.

White collar (non-manual)

> Professional and technical workers
> Managers, officials, and proprietors
> Clerical and sales employees

Blue collar (manual)

> Skilled workers, craftsmen, and foremen
> Semi-skilled workers
> Unskilled and service workers

Feelings about labor in Figure 10-2-B continue to show a strong relationship with social status. All blue-collar groups were more pro-labor than average, and all white-collar ones were more anti-labor than average. Skilled workers—the "elite" of the working class—were the least pro-labor subgroup among manuals. Clerical and sales workers—the lowest status group in the middle class—were the most pro-labor subgroup among nonmanuals. The manual subgroup most favorable to labor was not unskilled workers, however, even though the unskilled are the lowest in status. Labor unions were considerably better regarded by semi-skilled workers, that is, operatives and assembly-line workers among whom union organization has historically been most successful. Similarly on the non-manual side, labor was least popular among the subgroup of "managers, officials, and proprietors," the category into which most businesspeople fall. Both of these findings are consistent with those in Table 10-1, where confidence in the leaders of "organized labor" was broken down by occupational status. Generally, it is fair to conclude that *sympathy for labor is a function of social and economic status:* as status rises, sympathy for "labor unions" and "workingmen" tends to decline.

Attitudes toward business exhibit a weaker and less consistent relationship with occupational status. As in Table 10-1, business was most popular among "managers, officials, and proprietors." Business was favored least by highly unionized semi-skilled workers. Feelings about business seem to be related more to specific occupational groups—businesspeople and unionized workers—than to socioeconomic status in a generalized way. In Figure 10-2-A, as in Table 10-1, the best educated and highest status group in the occupational structure—professionals and technical workers—were hardly more pro-business than average (mean score of 5 on the

314

pro-business scale), whereas this group was considerably below average in its sympathy for labor (mean score of −42). Similarly, unskilled laborers, the least educated and lowest status group, were only slightly more negative toward business than average (mean score of −11), whereas they were considerably higher than average in their feelings about labor unions (mean score of 29). In Table 10-1, the correlation between occupational status and confidence in business leaders (.06) was weaker than the relationship between occupation and confidence in the leaders of organized labor (−.13).

Thus, as indicated earlier, attitudes toward business and labor, when broken down by either education or occupational status, are not symmetrical. The college educated were −39 on the labor scale but only +7 on the business scale. Those with less than a high school education scored +35 in their attitudes toward labor but were also slightly positive, +4, in their feelings about business. Support for business is conspicuously weak among the highest status and best-educated nonmanuals, namely, professionals, for whom business values show no noticeable appeal.

The government scales continue to show diverse relationships with socioeconomic status. Confidence in government (Figure 10-2-C) and confidence in the political system (Figure 10-2-D) were both above average among middle class respondents (i.e., those living in nonmanual households) and below average in working-class (manual) households. But manuals were the most likely to favor an active and powerful government (Figure 10-2-E). Figure 10-2 confirms what was noted in Figure 10-1, namely, that political trust is weakest in lower status groups, who are the very ones that benefit most from federal social welfare programs and government policies. But less privileged respondents continue to follow the New Deal tradition of being relatively strong in their support for a powerful and active government. Apparently the collapse of confidence in public leadership has occurred fastest among the poor and the poorly educated despite their continuing relative preference for strong government. It is undoubtedly in the interest of lower status groups to support government programs. But at the same time, they display the greatest cynicism about political authority—possibly because of their experiences and frustrations.

The position of professionals and technical specialists should also be noted. Like other nonmanuals, this group was above average in political trust and below average in support for government power. In fact, professionals, the best-educated occupational stratum, showed the highest levels of confidence in government and in the political system. But they were not as strongly opposed to government power as the managerial group (a mean score of -16 for the professional-technical category compared to -36 for managers, officials, and proprietors). Professionals tend to distort simple linear correlations between socioeconomic status and attitudes toward both government and business. Their attitudes are unusually "liberal"—less anti-government and less pro-business than other high-status groups. They are no different from managers, officials, and proprietors, however, in their lack of sympathy for labor. Thus, if the views of professionals reflect some measure of upper-class liberalism, that liberalism seems to apply to business and government but not to labor.

The Political Bases of Attitudes Toward Business, Labor, and Government

Figure 10-3 breaks down attitudes toward business, labor, and government by ideological self-classification. The 1976 respondents were asked to identify themselves on a seven-point scale, from "extremely liberal" to "extremely conservative." One third of the sample said that they "didn't know" what their ideological views were or that they "hadn't thought much about it"; an additional quarter positioned themselves at the mid-point on the seven-point scale, as "moderate, middle-of-the-road." Thus, over half the sample in 1976—58 percent—could not be identified as either liberal or conservative. Sixteen percent chose one of the three left positions, "extremely liberal" (1 percent), "liberal" (17 percent), or "slightly liberal" (8 percent). Twenty-five percent chose a position at the right end, "extremely conservative" (2 percent), "conservative" (11 percent), or "slightly conservative" (12 percent).

The NORC results for 1973–77, as displayed in Table 10-1, showed a more even balance between liberals and conservatives: 29 percent liberal, 31 percent conservative, and 40 percent "moderate, middle-of-the-road" or "don't know." The NORC question did not screen out respondents who had not thought much about their ideological views. Apparently, when respondents who say they "haven't thought much about it" are forced to classify them-

FIGURE 10–3

Attitudes Toward Business, Labor, and Government, by Ideology

(Mean Factor Scores)

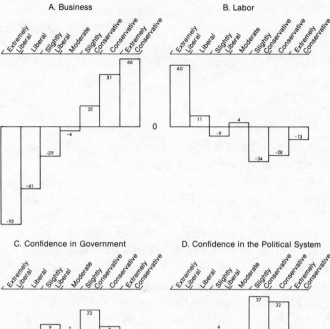

A. Business

B. Labor

C. Confidence in Government

D. Confidence in the Political System

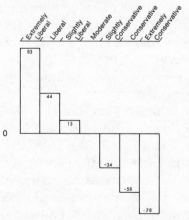

E. Power of Government

Source: Center for Political Studies, University of Michigan, 1976 American National Election Survey.

N = 2,248.

317

selves, liberals outdraw conservatives from this category by about two to one. In both the CPS and NORC versions, however, a plurality of respondents refused to identify their views as either liberal or conservative. In Figure 10-3, the "moderate" category includes all those who chose the middle position (4 on the CPS scale) or who said they "didn't know" or "hadn't thought about" their ideological views.

Attitudes Toward Business and Labor

The relationship between ideology and support for business and labor is again not symmetrical. Pro-union attitudes were slightly higher among liberals than among conservatives, but the overall differences were not great. Conservatives were moderately anti-labor. Most liberals were not very favorable to organized labor, except for those at the far left. Relatively strong support for labor was apparent only among the 1 percent of the electorate who, in 1976, classified themselves as "extreme liberals." On the other hand, the relationship between ideology and pro-business sentiment is considerably stronger and more consistent: pro-business sentiment increases regularly as one moves step by step along the ideology scale from left to right. The "extreme liberals," who were strongly pro-labor (mean score of $+60$), were also strongly anti-business (-95). The "liberals" and those "slightly liberal" were not particularly pro- or anti-labor (mean scores of $+11$ and -9, respectively) but were relatively hostile to business (mean scores of -61 and -29). The "moderates," who included a majority of the sample, were just about average in their feelings about business (mean of -4) as well as labor ($+4$). As one moves to the right, pro-business sentiment increases from an average of $+20$ among "slight conservatives," to $+51$ among "conservatives," to $+66$ among "extreme conservatives."

By comparison, in Table 10-1 presented earlier, the relative pro-labor enthusiasm of those at the extreme left does not appear as strongly as it does in Figure 10-3. Moreover, the extreme right in Table 10-1 is more anti-labor than the comparable group in Figure 10-3. The difference may be attributable to the questions involved. In Table 10-1, support for labor is measured by confidence in "the people running organized labor"; conservatives are quite hostile to labor leaders, and liberals are not particularly warm toward them. The pro-labor scale in Figure 10-3 tests sentiments about "labor unions" and "workingmen" generally, and not labor leaders. This broader reference may modify the antagonism of the far right (which sees itself as a populist force), while appealing to the "class consciousness" of the far left.

The relationships with ideology in Figure 10-3 are essentially the reverse of the relationships with socioeconomic status in Figures 10-1 and 10-2. Attitudes toward labor were found to be a strong function of education and occupation, while opinions about business were only weakly related to status characteristics. In Figure 10-3, on the other hand, feelings about business show a strong relationship with ideology, while the labor scale is only moderately related to left-right placement. *Attitudes toward labor thus appear to be primarily status-related, while feelings about business—"big business," "businessmen"—have a powerful ideological cast.*

Figure 10-4 illustrates this effect in terms of individual survey questions rather than the composite factor scores. One query used in constructing the scales asked whether specific groups—"big business," "businessmen," "labor unions," and "workingmen"— had "too much influence in American life and politics." Figure 10-4 shows the percentage across the ideological categories who felt that each of these groups had too much influence. In the case of "big business" and "businessmen," that percentage declines steadily as one moves from left to right. About 90 percent of liberals, 76 percent of moderates, and about 70 percent of conservatives said that "big business" has too much influence in American life and politics. This view was expressed by a strong majority— over 65 percent—of every ideological category, including "extreme conservatives." On the other hand, the percentage who said that "businessmen have too much influence" fell from 67 percent of extreme liberals, to about 45 percent of moderate liberals, 32 percent of moderates, 28 percent of moderate conservatives, and 19 percent of extreme conservatives. Even though criticism of businessmen was always much lower than hostility to big business, the two "business" lines in Figure 10-4 tend to move parallel to each other across the ideological spectrum.

Figure 10-4 reveals what kind of information is captured by the composite scales in Figure 10-3 and what is missed by them. The scales point up the strong relationship with ideology. But they lose the distinction between "big business" and "businessmen," which was stressed throughout the earlier analysis. That difference can be easily recovered in Figure 10-4: although "businessmen" and

FIGURE 10–4
Perceived Influence of Specific Business and Labor Groups, by Ideology

"Some people think that certain groups have too much influence in American life and politics, while other people feel that certain groups don't have as much influence as they deserve. Here are three statements about how much influence a group might have. For each group I read to you, just tell me the number of the statement that best says how you feel."

1. Too much influence
2. Just about the right amount of influence
3. Too little influence

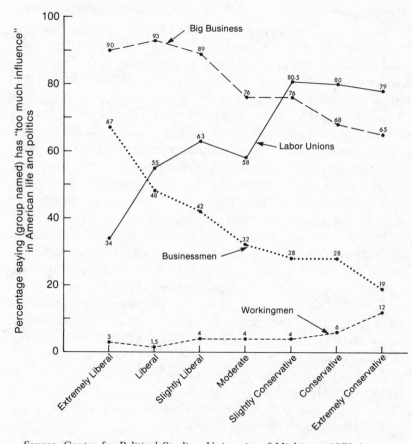

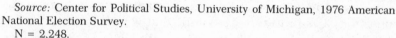

Source: Center for Political Studies, University of Michigan, 1976 American National Election Survey.
N = 2,248.

"big business" elicited similar ideological responses, antagonism to "big business" was stronger in every ideological group. The percentage saying that "big business" had too much influence was, on the average, 45 percent higher in every category than the percentage saying the same thing about "businessmen."

The same pattern holds true for "labor unions" and "working-men." Criticism of both tends to increase from left to right, but no more than 12 percent in any category—and only 5 percent overall —said that "workingmen have too much influence in American life and politics." On the other hand, a majority of every category except extreme liberals felt that "labor unions" have too much influence.

Attitudes Toward Government

How is confidence in government related to ideology? Figure 10-3 suggests that attitudes toward government are quite dispa-rate ideologically. Confidence in government (Figure 10-3-C) is lowest at both ends of the ideology scale, among extreme liberals and extreme conservatives. Mistrust of government has long been characteristic of conservatives, but by 1976, after disenchantment with the policies of the Democrats under Lyndon Johnson and of the Republicans under Richard Nixon and Gerald Ford, liberals expressed similar attitudes of disaffection, although with consid-erably less intensity than the extreme right.

Confidence in the political system, (Figure 10-3-D) shows a somewhat stronger left-right orientation: attachment to the politi-cal system rises as one moves from the far left to the moderate right. Those who call themselves "slightly conservative" or "con-servative" exhibit the highest faith in our political institutions. But these positive feelings reverse on the extreme right, whose adher-ents apparently have reservations about the soundness of our sys-tem. Both confidence scales show (a) a tendency for political trust to increase from the left to the moderate right, and (b) some de-gree of "curvilinearity," with confidence falling off on the far left and the far right. The left-right effect is stronger in the case of the political system, whereas the curvilinear pattern shows up more clearly in reactions to the way the government is run.

The finding that confidence in 1976 was relatively low on the left and relatively high on the moderate right may simply reflect partisanship, that is, the fact that the Ford Administration was in office at that time. But the curvilinear pattern does suggest some ideological basis for disaffection from government. Ideologues of the far left and the far right may resent the pragmatism and compromise—the absence of "principle"—inherent in the political process of a democracy, and this resentment may be expressed as a lack of trust in political leaders.

The sharpest ideological response appears when the power of government is at issue. Support for a powerful and active federal government is still very much a left-versus-right phenomenon; the left favors it and the right opposes it. The left wants the government to do more (regulation, health insurance, social welfare spending) and the right wants the government to do less. This is hardly news to anyone who has followed political debate in the United States over the past fifty years. The point is that this orientation—the choice between "laissez faire" and "welfare state" philosophies—is quite different from the mistrust of government that has been increasing so alarmingly for the past sixteen years.

The differences among the various attitudes toward government can be illustrated by once again turning to questions from the original survey. Figure 10-5 shows one question from each of the three government-related scales broken down by ideology. The question relating to power of government asked whether "the government is getting too powerful" (Figure 10-5-C). The percentage saying "no" declined consistently from left to right, from a high of 39 percent among extreme liberals to a low of 11 percent among extreme conservatives. The question on confidence in government asked respondents to rate "the job being done for the country as a whole by the federal government in Washington" (Figure 10-5-A). In this case, no linear relationship with ideology appears. The percentage who gave the federal government a "good" or "very good" rating was highest among moderate conservatives (30.5 percent) and lowest at both extremes of the left-right spectrum, 14 percent among extreme conservatives and 19 percent among extreme liberals.

The curvilinear pattern also shows up in responses to the item measuring confidence in the political system (Figure 10-5-B). Interviewees were asked whether the lack of trust in government is "just because of the individuals in office," or whether "there is something more seriously wrong with government in general and the way it operates." The percentage saying "something is wrong with government in general" was highest on the left, 38 percent.

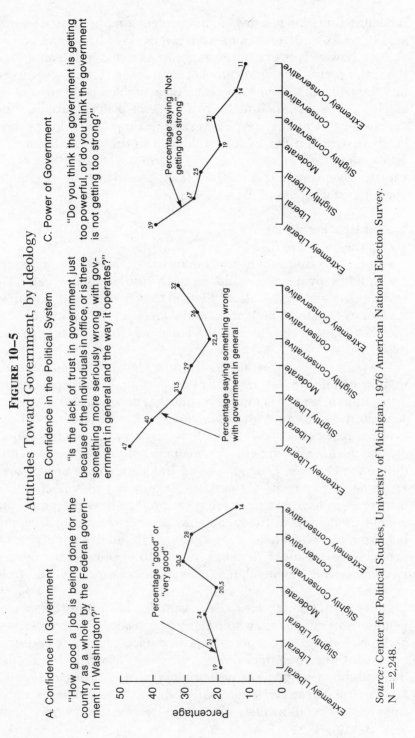

FIGURE 10–5

Attitudes Toward Government, by Ideology

A. Confidence in Government

"How good a job is being done for the country as a whole by the Federal government in Washington?"

B. Confidence in the Political System

"Is the lack of trust in government just because of the individuals in office, or is there something more seriously wrong with government in general and the way it operates?"

C. Power of Government

"Do you think the government is getting too powerful, or do you think the government is not getting too strong?"

Source: Center for Political Studies, University of Michigan, 1976 American National Election Survey. N = 2,248.

It declined steadily to a low of 22.5 percent among those who were slightly conservative. Among conservatives and extreme conservatives, however, the figure rose again. As noted in the analysis of the factor scores, both indicators of confidence (in the government and the political system) suggest a measurable loss of trust at the ideological extremes. But the two types of political trust are not symmetrical. Confidence in government drops to its lowest level on the extreme right, while confidence in the political system is weakest on the far left. The right concentrates its antipathy on the way the government is run. The left appears to have deeper doubts about the soundness of the system itself.

The Impact of Partisanship

Figure 10-6 breaks down attitudes toward business, labor, and government by ideology and partisanship simultaneously. The seven-point ideology scale of Figure 10-3 is collapsed into three categories (liberals, moderates, and conservatives). These are further divided into self-described Democrats, Republicans, and Independents.

The pattern of support for business in Figure 10-6 reiterates the finding of Figure 10-3 that there is a strong liberal-conservative orientation in attitudes toward business, a difference that holds up separately for Republicans, Democrats, and Independents. There is also a party effect, over and above ideology. Democrats tended to have the lowest sympathy for business, although there was little difference between Democrats and Independents *with the same ideology*. Republicans showed the strongest partisan effect: all categories of Republicans were more pro-business than any category of Democrats or Independents. In other words, the least pro-business class of Republicans, liberal Republicans, was more favorable to business than the most pro-business categories of Democrats and Independents (conservative Democrats and Independents).

Thus, party and ideology affect attitudes toward business independently of one another. Republican partisanship increases support for business across all categories of ideology, while conservatism has the same effect among all groups of partisans. Both of these findings confirm *the profoundly political nature of the public's attitudes toward business:* feelings about business divide Americans simultaneously along "old" partisan lines and "new"

FIGURE 10–6
Attitudes Toward Business, Labor, and Government, by Ideology and Partisanship
(Mean Factor Scores)

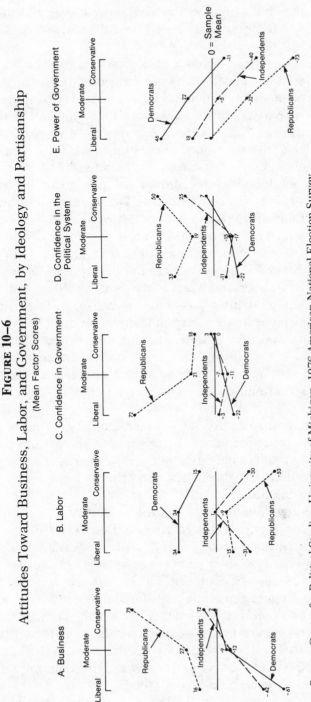

Source: Center for Political Studies, University of Michigan, 1976 American National Election Survey.
N = 2,248.
Key: Liberals (1, 2, and 3 on 7-point ideology scale).
Moderates (4 or "Don't know" on scale).
Conservatives (5, 6, and 7 on scale).

325

liberal-conservative lines. Ideological differences over business reinforce the "old" Republican-Democratic differences that date from the New Deal.

The traditional partisan difference also shows up in the case of labor (see Figure 10-6). All categories of Democrats were relatively sympathetic to labor, while Independents and Republicans were less favorable. The party variations in Figure 10-6 substantiate the pattern noted earlier in Table 10-1: Democrats and Independents tend to be similar in their attitudes toward business, with Republicans distinctively more pro-business. On the other hand, Republicans and Independents exhibit similar feelings about unions, while a pro-labor attitude distinguishes Democratic partisans. Sympathy for either business or labor continues to be an identifying mark of partisanship in the United States.

Figure 10-6 also reveals an interesting split among self-described liberals. Liberal Democrats were the most pro-labor group in the electorate, but liberal Independents were surprisingly negative in their feelings about labor—more negative, in fact, than any group except conservative Republicans. The split between liberal Democrats and liberal Independents suggests a division between the "old left" and the "new left." Liberal Independents are significantly younger and better educated than liberal Democrats. It appears that one of the substantive issues dividing the older and younger segments of the left is their attitude toward the labor movement. Sympathy for labor unions and "workingmen" has not been conspicuous in the younger, more affluent, and better-educated generation of liberals; their sympathies lie more with disadvantaged minorities, whom they often think of as a target of discrimination by organized labor.

Confidence in government again shows a complex relationship with ideology (see Figure 10-6-C). Among Democrats, faith in government was weakest among self-described liberals. Among Republicans, it was lowest among conservatives. These sentiments may bear some relationship to ideological activism within each party. The Republican right and the Democratic left both define themselves as protest movements against the centrist tendencies in their respective parties—including the most recent administrations of their respective parties, as of 1976. On the other hand, confidence in the political system was highest among self-described conservatives in both parties (see Figure 10-6-D).

With ideology held constant as in Figure 10-6, it becomes clear that all categories of Republicans in 1976, including conservative Republicans, expressed relatively high confidence in the government and in the political system. Their party was then in office, and apparently even highly generalized questions about the political system touched off a partisan response. Republicans "trusted" those who were running the federal government and felt better about the political system than Independents and Democrats did because, at the time of the 1976 survey, Republicans were running the federal government. (Those Republicans most unhappy with the way the government was being run were the conservatives, but they were still happier than conservative Democrats and Independents.) Apparently, the respondents in the 1976 survey did not take seriously the introductory admonition that interviewers were instructed to read to them just before the sequence of "political trust" questions: "These ideas don't refer to Democrats or Republicans in particular, but just to the government in general."

Finally, attitudes toward the power of government sort themselves out neatly by both ideology and partisanship. Figure 10-6-E shows three parallel lines, one for Democrats, one for Independents, and one for Republicans. Within each partisan group, moderates were more pro-government than conservatives and liberals were more pro-government than moderates. Within each ideological category, Independents were more pro-government than Republicans and Democrats were more pro-government than Independents. The difference between liberals and conservatives, controlling for party identification, averaged 63 points. The difference between Democrats and Republicans, controlling for ideology, averaged 53 points. Like attitudes toward business, therefore, sentiments about the power of government are both partisan and ideological. The consistency of the difference among Democrats, Independents, and Republicans in Figure 10-6-E suggests that this traditional issue of contention between Democrats and Republicans has remained strong; orientations toward government power and activism continue to define each party's support.

Summary

Attitudes toward business, government, and labor revealed very different patterns in the 1976 electorate:

1. Sympathy for business was deeply ideological and political. Anti-business sentiment was strongest among Democrats and liberals. Each appeared to perceive "business" as a reactionary force, although possibly for different reasons.

2. Attitudes toward labor were primarily a function of socioeconomic status, as defined by education and occupation. The residue of the New Deal partisan alignment continued to affect the electorate in that Democrats showed consistently greater sympathy for labor. But the beliefs of the younger, more Independent left have apparently tended to counteract rather than reinforce the traditional pro-labor bias of the left.

3. Political trust is a more complex attitude. There seems to be a significant partisan effect; Republicans were more "trusting" of the federal government and more confident of the political system in 1976, when their party was in office. The ideological effect, however, is mixed. Extreme liberals and extreme conservatives have both tended to be low in political trust, with extreme conservatives most distrustful of politicians and extreme liberals harboring the strongest reservations about the political system itself. Generally, political trust was highest in 1976 among moderate conservatives, a fact that probably also reflects the nature of the administration in office at that time; Ford's was a moderately conservative administration. Finally, political trust is also differentiated by status. Confidence in government and in the political system were weakest among the poorly educated and those lowest in social status.

4. On the other hand, the poor and the poorly educated were the most favorable toward a powerful and active government. Attitudes concerning the power of government were also deeply political. Unlike confidence in government, support for the welfare state increased consistently with left partisanship (Democratic) and left ideology (liberal).

5. The analyses contained in Figures 10-1 through 10-6 suggest that the link between lower socioeconomic status and liberal attitudes remains strong, at least in terms of economic issues. (We did not examine racial attitudes, social and cultural issues, or foreign policy, which are matters on which liberals and lower-status Americans sometimes part company.) But there is some evidence that upper-middle-class liberalism, even on economic issues, has tended to invert the traditional status-politics relationship, as Ev-

328

erett Ladd has argued.[7] For example, the highest status occupational group, professionals, was more liberal in its feelings toward business and government than other nonmanuals. This relative liberalism among professionals, however, did not apply to labor unions. A second example is the split between liberal Democrats and liberal Independents in their attitudes toward organized labor. Liberal Independents were notably unsympathetic to labor, and this group is known to be young, well-educated, and strongly influenced by New Politics attitudes.

We are struck by the fact that orientations toward business and toward the power of government (i.e., the welfare state) have almost exactly opposite correlates. The left, including both liberals and Democrats, are anti-business and pro-welfare-state, while the right, including both conservatives and Republicans, are pro-business and anti-welfare-state. Ideological conflict, as of 1976, seemed to be cast primarily in terms of *business versus government*, and not business versus labor.

A Further Inquiry into Political Trust

The trend of increasing political distrust has been widely noted by survey researchers and political scientists, but there is disagreement over what it signifies. Arthur H. Miller argued in 1974, based on an analysis of political trust data from 1964 to 1970, that "a situation of widespread, basic discontent and political alienation exists in the U.S. today."[8] He attributed that discontent to "dissatisfaction with the policy alternatives that have been offered as solutions to contemporary problems," pointing to the fact that political distrust was greatest among those with systematically right-wing and left-wing policy preferences across a wide range of issues.[9]

[7] Ladd, *Transformations,* pp. 211–28.

[8] Arthur H. Miller, "Political Issues and Trust in Government, 1964–1970," *American Political Science Review* 68 (September 1974), p. 951. See also James S. House and William M. Mason, "Political Alienation in America, 1952–1968," *American Sociological Review* 40 (April 1975), pp. 123–47, and Jack Citrin, Herbert McClosky, J. Merrill Shanks, and Paul M. Sniderman, "Personal and Political Sources of Political Alienation," *British Journal of Political Science* 5 (January 1975), pp. 1–31.

[9] Miller, "Political Issues," p. 970; see pp. 955–63 for an examination of policy preferences and their relation to political cynicism.

Critics of such analyses, however, have called attention to the highly partisan nature of political distrust. Those who are opposed to the incumbent administration—supporters of the "out" party, for instance—tend to be more distrustful of government than those who back the incumbent administration. The relationship reverses when the government changes hands, i.e., supporters of the formerly "out" party become more trusting. Between 1976 and 1978, Democrats became more trusting and Republicans more distrusting of government.[10] Such findings suggest that political distrust may not signify a basic sense of alienation but rather the normal antagonism between political "ins" and "outs." Moreover, as noted in Chapter 1, trust in the political system has remained quite high, even as trust in political leaders has plummeted. Jack Citrin has pointed out that "the burgeoning ranks of the politically cynical may include many who are verbalizing a casual and ritualistic negativism rather than an enduring sense of estrangement that influences their beliefs and actions."[11]

Figure 10-7 compares three different indicators of political trust from the Center for Political Studies 1976 national election survey —confidence in government and in the political system as defined above, plus approval of the incumbent (Ford) administration.[12] Unlike the factor scores in earlier figures, the scales in Figure 10-7 show *absolute* levels of political trust broken down by partisanship and ideology. (Each question was scored from -1, the least trusting response, to $+1$, the most trusting response; the scores were then summed and averaged.)

As expected, approval of the Ford Administration increased with Republican partisanship. But so did confidence in government and in the political system, as reported earlier, even though neither set of questions included any explicit partisan references. The

[10] Warren E. Miller, "Crisis of Confidence II: Misreading the Public Pulse," *Public Opinion* 2 (October/November 1979), pp. 14–15.

[11] Jack Citrin, "Comment: The Political Relevance of Trust in Government," *American Political Science Review* 68 (September 1974), p. 975.

[12] Approval of the Ford Administration was measured by three questions: (1) "Do you approve or disapprove of the way Mr. Ford is handling his job as President?" (59 percent approved, 31 percent disapproved); (2) "Thinking about the steps that should have been taken to fight inflation, would you say that the government has been doing a good job, only fair, or a poor job?" (12 percent said good, 60 percent only fair, and 26 percent poor); and (3) "Now how about the government's economic policy dealing with unemployment—would you say that the government has been doing a good job, only fair, or a poor job?" (12 percent said good, 56 percent only fair, and 28 percent poor).

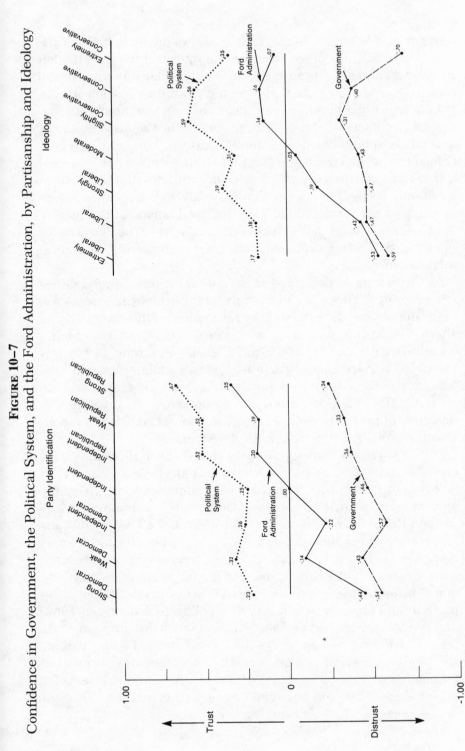

FIGURE 10-7

Confidence in Government, the Political System, and the Ford Administration, by Partisanship and Ideology

Source: Center for Political Studies, University of Michigan, 1976 American National Election Survey. N = 2,248.

curvilinear relationship with ideology shows up again here for the two "systemic" indicators: those on the right and those on the left had less confidence in government and less faith in our political system than those closer to the center. Both the ideological component identified by Miller, and taken to be a symptom of fundamental discontent, and the partisan component identified by Citrin, and taken to be indicative of normal partisan antipathy, are confirmed by the data. So is the fact that attitudes toward the political system are consistently positive while attitudes toward government and political leaders are consistently negative across every category of partisanship and ideology. Evaluations of the incumbent administration fell in between and were either positive or negative, depending on the respondent's partisan and ideological inclinations.

As Citrin argues, political distrust appears to have several different meanings. Those low in trust include " 'ritualistic cynics' and partisans of the 'outs' as well as respondents who see no viable alternative to the incumbent authorities and reject the ongoing constitutional order."[13] In 1976, for example, strong Democrats probably included many "partisan cynics," while "alienated cynics" were likely to have been prevalent on both the far left and the far right. "Ritualistic cynicism" shows up across the board, in the tendency of people in every category to express contempt for politicians (as distinct from the political system).

Still, it is not without significance that political distrust has increased since 1964 in every partisan and ideological group. That is shown in Figure 10-8. The changes of administration are readily apparent: between 1960 and 1962 Democrats became more trusting and Republicans less so; between 1968 and 1970 Republicans and conservatives moved up in trust and Democrats and liberals down; and between 1976 and 1978 Democrats once again became more trusting than Republicans. But the overall impression is one of a continuing slide from the mid-1960s to the late 1970s: every partisan and ideological category was politically trusting in 1964, and every category had become, on balance, distrusting ten years later. The timing and pattern of the changes varied with partisanship and ideology; at certain periods, Democrats and liberals lost faith faster than Republicans and conservatives, and vice versa for other periods. But the outcome has never been reversed; confidence, once lost, has not been regained.

[13] Citrin, "Comment," p. 978.

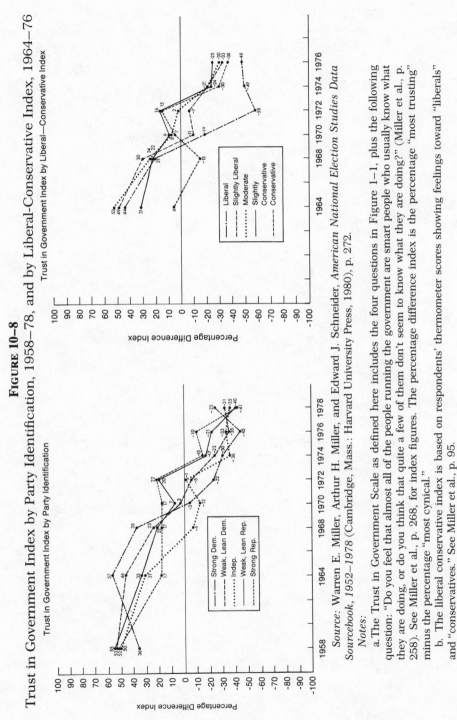

FIGURE 10-8

Trust in Government Index by Party Identification, 1958–78, and by Liberal-Conservative Index, 1964–76

Trust in Government Index by Party Identification

Trust in Government Index by Liberal—Conservative Index

Source: Warren E. Miller, Arthur H. Miller, and Edward J. Schneider, *American National Election Studies Data Sourcebook, 1952–1978* (Cambridge, Mass.: Harvard University Press, 1980), p. 272.

Notes:

a. The Trust in Government Scale as defined here includes the four questions in Figure 1–1, plus the following question: "Do you feel that almost all of the people running the government are smart people who usually know what they are doing, or do you think that quite a few of them don't seem to know what they are doing?" (Miller et al., p. 258). See Miller et al., p. 268, for index figures. The percentage difference index is the percentage "most trusting" minus the percentage "most cynical."

b. The liberal conservative index is based on respondents' thermometer scores showing feelings toward "liberals" and "conservatives." See Miller et al., p. 95.

Part III

Causes and Consequences

11

The Effects of "Malaise"

How has the decline of confidence affected the functioning of our political and economic institutions? This is a difficult question to answer in any precisely quantifiable way. Some effects have been direct and behavioral (the way people vote, for instance), a number have been inferred (such as declining membership in labor unions), while others depend on the beliefs and perceptions of the observer. As was pointed out in a study of the problem of confidence in the federal government,

> Not only have the trends in trust and confidence been hard to explain statistically, but the research has not been done to show the *effect* of a loss of confidence. In other words, we all have a sense that the trends should not be ignored, but we are hard put to say exactly what they mean—what are the consequences of loss in confidence for the leaders or for the institutions in question.[1]

Thus, we now consider what the consequences for government, labor, and business may be.

Consequences for Government

Political leaders themselves have often claimed that the public's diminishing confidence in government has made it more difficult

[1] Tom W. Smith, D. Garth Taylor, with Nancy A. Mathiowetz, "Public Opinion and Public Regard for the Federal Government," in C. Weiss and A. Barton, eds., *Making Bureaucracies Work* (London: Sage Publications, 1980), p. 38 (italics in original).

for them to govern. President Jimmy Carter presented this argument most dramatically in his speech to the nation on July 15, 1979. As noted earlier, he argued then that the "crisis of confidence" shown by the polls constituted a threat to the very survival of the nation. He pointed to "a growing disrespect for government and for churches and for schools, the news media and other institutions . . ." and emphasized that "the gap between our citizens and our government has never been so wide."[2]

In a follow-up speech the next day discussing the energy problem, the President went on to blame that situation on the crisis of confidence:

> We're coming to understand that the reasons for our energy crisis go beyond gas lines and wasteful habits, to a loss of confidence that divides us and threatens us and which for years, too many years, has prevented Presidents and the Congress and a great nation from acting courageously to meet this energy challenge.[3]

Mr. Carter's belief that such sentiments led to political immobility may have been based on his inability to get key groups in the country, particularly Congress, to support his programs. As he interpreted the situation in 1979, the loss of faith in national institutions made it almost impossible to convince people to compromise their self-interests and go down what he called on July 15th "the path of common purpose." Instead, as a result of growing cynicism, he said, individuals and groups were emphasizing their "narrow interests, ending in chaos and immobility."

The President's concern over the public's mood may also have been related to the fact that his job rating in the opinion polls had fallen more precipitously from 1977 to mid-summer 1979 than had been the case for any other President since polling on the subject began in 1945.[4] The President chose to place the blame for this decline and for his failure to achieve various legislative objectives on the negative and cynical mood of the people.

In 1980, two leading congressional figures, Chairman of the House Rules Committee Richard Bolling and Senator Henry Jack-

---

[2] "Transcript of President's Address to Country on Energy Problems," *New York Times,* July 16, 1979, p. 10.

[3] "Transcript of President's Address to the National Association of Counties in Kansas City," *New York Times,* July 17, 1979, p. A-14.

[4] "Countdown to Election: Presidential Popularity," *National Journal* 11 (October 20, 1979), p. 1729.

son of Washington, also called attention to the public mood. In mid-February, Representative Bolling discussed the need "to stem a tide of public alienation with government," which he believed was "sapping the nation's strength." In calling for a new bipartisan "Hoover Commission" to study government operations and propose "sweeping reorganization," he pointed "to a series of recent polls reporting public frustration and disillusionment with the present governmental process" and "widespread popular alienation." In early May, in an observation described by a journalist as "borrowed from Carter's own words . . . last July," Senator Jackson said: "I have never seen such a malaise on the American scene."[5]

But the evidence is that most Americans doubted the validity of Jimmy Carter's complaint that he was unable to govern effectively because of the public's loss of confidence. In fact, the public tended to believe that Carter had gotten the cause-and-effect relationship backwards: it was not that leaders could not govern because the people had no confidence in them, but rather that people had lost confidence in government because of ineffective political leadership.

A CBS News/*New York Times* poll offered alternative explanations for the "crisis of confidence" in a question asked in November 1979: "Some people say there is a crisis of confidence in the country—that is, the people lack confidence in themselves and their future. Others say there is a crisis, but that it is a crisis of confidence in the elected officials. And others say there is no crisis at all. How about you?" Almost everyone polled thought there was a crisis of confidence, but only 19 percent felt that the cause lay with the public itself. Sixty-five percent said responsibility for the crisis rested with "elected officials." Similarly, in an earlier (July–August 1979) poll taken by the Opinion Research Corporation, two thirds of those interviewed said they agreed with President Carter's assertion that the country was experiencing a crisis of confidence. But among those who believed there was a crisis, 82 percent felt it was because "people have lost confidence in their government"; only 10 percent accepted the argument that it was because "people have lost confidence in themselves."

[5] Richard L. Strout, "US Rep. Bolling Wants New 'Hoover Commission,' " *Christian Science Monitor*, February 12, 1980, p. 41. Saul Friedman, "Rising Discontent Faces Carter as He Emerges From the White House," *San Francisco Sunday Examiner and Chronicle*, May 4, 1980, p. A-19.

The Decline in Participation

Thus, it is not clear that the falloff of public faith in institutional leadership has undermined the capacity of our national leaders to govern—except to the degree that, like Carter, our leaders believe it is so and, therefore, make that belief into a self-fulfilling prophecy. There is one area of public *behavior,* however, where it is plausible to argue that declining political trust has had an effect: the proportion of the U.S. voting-age population actually casting a ballot in Presidential elections has been gradually declining since 1960. The data show a participation rate of 62.8 percent in 1960, 61.9 percent in 1964, 60.9 percent in 1968, and then a sharp drop to 55.5 percent in 1972 (when 18-to-20-year-olds were first enfranchised), 54.4 percent in 1976, and 54.0 percent in 1980. This decline in voting turnout roughly paralleled the collapse of trust in political leaders, although the former trend was not as rapid or as intense as the latter. These data suggest that increasing voter abstention may be related to the loss of confidence in political leaders, but research on the subject has produced inconsistent findings.

A study by James Wright analyzing national survey data collected by the University of Michigan Center for Political Studies (CPS) between 1956 and 1968 reported that "a clear and unambiguous characteristic of the politically alienated is that they participate less."[6] Those high in alienation voted less, were less interested, were less likely to expose themselves to politically relevant events or information through the media, and attended fewer political rallies.[7] Robert Gilmour's and Robert Lamb's analysis of the same subject based on the 1972 CPS poll also reported that those high in alienation were least likely to have cast a ballot, or to have tried to influence the way others voted.[8] Using data from the 1960 to 1976 CPS Presidential election surveys, Howard Reiter found that "in the 1970s nonvoters were more likely than voters at all income levels to express dissatisfaction with the political system."[9]

[6] James D. Wright, *The Dissent of the Governed. Alienation and Democracy in America* (New York: Academic Press, 1976), p. 251.

[7] Wright, *Dissent of the Governed,* p. 230.

[8] Robert S. Gilmour and Robert L. Lamb, *Political Alienation in Contemporary America* (New York: St. Martin's Press, 1975), p. 182.

[9] Howard L. Reiter, "Why Is Turnout Down?" *Public Opinion Quarterly* 43 (Fall 1979), p. 297.

Most measures of a sense of "political inefficacy" are strongly correlated with nonvoting. Thus, according to surveys, people who believe that they have no say in what the government does, that public officials do not care what they think, that they understand very little of what is going on in politics and government, and so forth, are not very likely to turn out to vote. Political inefficacy is also strongly correlated with education: the lower the level of formal education, the less politically efficacious a person is likely to feel. This is because the sense of efficacy is partly a *self*-image, an evaluation of one's own competence to understand issues and play a role in political life. For example, the view that "people like me have no say in what the government does"—a typical efficacy measure—is as much an evaluation of the self ("people like me") as it is an evaluation of the system. It is not surprising that the poorly educated, having relatively low self-esteem, also display a relatively low sense of political competence. Education largely accounts for the observed relationship between political efficacy and voter turnout. It is, therefore, difficult to conclude that political inefficacy, in and of itself, is a cause of declining voter turnout.

On the other hand, the political trust measures reported in Figure 1-1 (at the beginning of this book) do *not* seem to affect turnout in any consistent way. Jack Citrin's analysis of the relationship between "trust in government" and voter participation found no correlation between the two.[10] Similar results were reported by a CBS News/*New York Times* postelection survey taken in November 1976, which concluded that "the nonvoters scarcely differed from the voters on a broad range of questions designed to measure dissatisfaction and distrust." Voters, however, were much more likely than nonvoters in the CBS/*Times* survey to have a high sense of political efficacy and to feel that they could personally affect political conditions by their vote.[11] Our own examination of the 1976 CPS election survey revealed no relationship between political distrust and nonvoting, even when controls were applied for education, age, and partisanship.

In some studies, political alienation is measured by such beliefs as: "It makes no difference whether or not people participate in government" and "The choices offered by elections are meaning-

[10] Jack Citrin, "Comment: The Political Relevance of Trust in Government," *American Political Science Review* 68 (September 1974), pp. 982–84.

[11] Robert Reinhold, "Poll Links Sense of Powerlessness, Not Disillusionment, to Low Vote," *New York Times*, November 16, 1976, p. 33.

less." It is not surprising that these questions correlate with voter turnout: they measure attitudes toward the act of participation itself. People who take part in politics are more likely to say that such activity is meaningful than people who do not participate.

Political dissatisfaction and distrust, however, are not attitudes toward the act of participation. They focus on incumbent authorities and the way the government is being run. Why are dissatisfaction and distrust not correlated with nonvoting? Two reasons may be suggested. One is that they are not as strongly correlated with education as a sense of political efficacy is. Political dissatisfaction and distrust are sentiments evaluating the system and its leadership, not the self, and so the education-bias of such attitudes is weaker. Secondly, as indicated in Chapter 10, political distrust demonstrates a marked relationship with both partisanship and ideology. Those who support the party out of power tend to be more distrustful and dissatisfied. Political distrust also tends to be strongest at the ideological extremes, both left and right, as Arthur Miller has shown and as our analysis has verified. Strong partisans and ideologues are more—not less—likely to vote. They have the strongest views about politics, including discontent over the way things are being run, and they express those views at the polls. Thus, one must differentiate between the *personal* sentiments of alienation and inefficacy and *political* sentiments of distrust and dissatisfaction. The former are strongly related to abstention from the polls; the latter are not.

The Tax Revolt

Distrust of government does appear to be related to the most potent single attack on government in recent years, namely, the tax revolt. Taxation became a major issue in American politics as a result of the passage in June 1978 of California's Proposition 13, which mandated a substantial cut in that state's property taxes. The available survey evidence indicates that support for Proposition 13-type measures and for major income tax cuts is correlated with political distrust; David Sears reported such findings from a 1978 survey of California voters.[12] Tom Smith and Garth Taylor, using data from the 1976 and 1977 NORC General Social Surveys,

[12] David O. Sears, "The Jarvis Amendment: Self-Interest or Symbolic Politics" (Unpublished paper, Department of Political Science, University of California, Los Angeles, 1978).

found that people who had less confidence in the executive branch of the federal government were more likely to feel that their income taxes were too high.[13] The Center for Political Studies 1978 Congressional election survey revealed similar results. As Arthur Miller of CPS reports:

> Political cynicism was more strongly related with support for cutting federal taxes by one third than was the level of family income or how well off financially the respondent was this year compared with last year. Among those respondents who were distrusting of government, 40 percent favored cutting federal taxes by one third even if it meant a reduction in military spending or services such as health and education. By comparison, only 17 percent of trusting individuals favored such a cut in taxes.[14]

The possibility exists that the relationship between lack of trust in government and support for the tax revolt is a spurious one. Both may simply reflect ideological conservatism. Moreover, in 1978, when the two above-mentioned surveys were taken, the Democrats were in power in both Washington and California. Therefore, Republican partisanship may have generated distrust of government as well as anti-tax sentiment. To test for the possibility of a spurious correlation, we examined the relationship between trust in government and support for the tax revolt in the 1978 CPS survey controlling first for ideology, then for partisanship. As Table 11-1 shows, within each ideological and partisan category those low in political trust on a three-item scale were significantly more supportive of a Proposition 13-type measure in their state and more favorable toward cutting federal income taxes by at least one third. (We purposefully excluded the question asking whether public officials waste a lot of tax money from our three-item political trust scale, since that question was too close in meaning to the tax revolt itself.) Thus, the evidence indicates that the loss of confidence in government contributed to the success of the tax revolt, independently of ideology or partisanship.

"Waste in government" was the key phrase in the Proposition 13 campaign in California. Mervin Field of the California Poll re-

[13] Smith and Taylor, with Mathiowetz, "Public Opinion and Public Regard," pp. 60–61.

[14] Arthur Miller, "The Institutional Focus of Political Distrust" (Paper presented at the Annual Meeting of the American Political Science Association, Washington, D.C., August 31–September 3, 1979), p. 48.

TABLE 11–1
Trust in Government and the Tax Revolt, 1978

I

"If you had the chance, would you vote for or against a measure similar to Proposition 13 in your state?"

Trust in Government Scale[a]	All	By Ideology			By Party		
		Liberals	Moderates	Conservatives	Democrats	Independents	Republicans
		Percentage Who Would Vote for It					
Low	60	58	58	65	60	60	60
Mod/High	48	48	43	56	46	48	52
All	54	53	51	61	53	55	57

II

"Federal income taxes should be cut at least one third even if it means reducing military spending and cutting down on government services such as health and education."

Trust in Government Scale[a]	All	By Ideology			By Party		
		Liberals	Moderates	Conservatives	Democrats	Independents	Republicans
		Percentage Who Agree					
Low	32	30	29	38	32	31	33
Mod/High	21	23	19	22	20	21	23
All	27	26	25	31	26	27	29

Source: University of Michigan, Center for Political Studies, 1978 American National Election Study.
N = 2,304.
[a] Trust in Government Scale:
1. "How much of the time do you think you can trust the government in Washington to do what is right—always, most of the time, or only some of the time?"
2. "Would you say the government is pretty much run by a few big interests or that it is run for the benefit of all the people?"
3. "Do you think that quite a few of the people running the government are crooked, not very many are, or hardly any of them are?"

ported that the main comment made by proponents of Proposition 13, other than "Taxes are too high," was, "The time has come to cut government costs, waste, and inefficiency." Field noted that prior to election day, the California public believed that a cut of 10 percent in tax revenues could be accomplished without any decline in state and local government services. And three quarters of

Californians who voted for the proposition, according to the *Los Angeles Times*/KNXT-TV News election-day poll, said that they did not think public services would be reduced as a result of Proposition 13.

The magnitude of the problem of government waste as seen by most Americans is evident in the responses Gallup obtained from a question posed in 1978, 1979, and 1981: "Of every tax dollar that goes to the federal government in Washington, D.C. [the government of this state or your local government] how many cents would you say are wasted?" The replies for each year were quite similar. In the case of the federal government, the median in each year was almost half, 48 cents; for state governments it was less, 29 cents in 1979, 32 cents in 1978, and 29 cents in 1981; while for local authorities, it was 23 cents in 1979, 25 cents in 1978, and 23 cents in 1981. These estimates of government waste correspond to variations in confidence in each level of government. The closer the unit is to the people, the lower the estimate of waste and the higher the confidence. Still, a belief that state and local governments waste from a quarter to a third of their revenues reflects little faith even in their competence, while the judgment that the federal government wastes almost half of all the money it raises in taxes indicates disastrously low faith in the efficiency or integrity of our national leadership. It is also striking to note that there were literally no differences in estimates of government waste associated with income, occupational status, race, or age.

What Proposition 13 supporters had in mind can be seen in their answers to a question asked in a *Los Angeles Times* follow-up survey taken three weeks after the vote: "Now that Proposition 13 has passed, which one of the following things do you think will be the final, lasting result: government services will be cut back permanently, other taxes will be raised to make up the difference, the gap will be closed by cutting out waste and inefficiency, or none of these will happen—they'll find other money somewhere else?" Only 5 percent of those favorable to Proposition 13 said "the final, lasting result" would be government services cut back permanently. Twenty-six percent said that other taxes would be raised, and 18 percent said "they'll find other money somewhere else." The most popular answer among Proposition 13 supporters—45 percent of them, to be exact—was that "the gap will be closed by cutting out waste and inefficiency," with no need to reduce services or raise other taxes.

The national public holds similar views. After the passage of

Proposition 13, an overwhelming majority of Americans (89 to 5 percent in an ABC News/Harris poll) interpreted the California vote as "a strong protest that people running the government will have to respond to by trimming a lot of waste from government spending." A Yankelovich survey taken in October 1978 found that 69 percent agreed that "it is possible to cut taxes without decreasing services if the government becomes more efficient." In February 1979, 71 percent of those interviewed in an NBC News poll felt that "the federal budget could be balanced just by reducing waste and inefficiency."

Support for Government Programs

Despite strongly felt complaints about government waste, Americans continue to approve of the things that government does for them. The desire for government to intervene in beneficent ways has not diminished. The Gallup poll reported that, in 1960, 63 percent agreed that "the government in Washington ought to see to it that everybody who wants to work has a job." In 1978, the CBS News/*New York Times* poll found that 74 percent—including 70 percent of those who described themselves as "conservative"—approved that mandate for government, in response to the same question. In a survey taken in the fall of 1980, Research and Forecasts reported that Americans agreed by 69 to 25 percent that "the government ought to make sure everyone has a good standard of living." Over three fifths of Republicans (62 percent) and conservatives (64 percent) felt that way.

In a report on a Roper survey conducted in June 1978, just after the passage of Proposition 13, Albert and Susan Cantril noted that "a general consensus exists that it is appropriate for the federal government to create jobs for the unemployed." Almost two thirds, 64 percent, felt that the government should "provide a job that pays a base wage so that a person can get along."[15] In 1960, about 64 percent of the public endorsed the proposal that "the government ought to help people to get doctors and hospital care at low cost." By 1978, 81 percent of those interviewed by the CBS News/ *New York Times* poll agreed. In the fall of 1976, CPS asked a national sample whether they thought "government should spend

[15] Albert H. and Susan D. Cantril, *Unemployment, Government and the American People* (Washington, D.C.: Public Research, 1978), pp. 90–91.

less even if it means cutting back on health and education." Only 21 percent favored spending less under such circumstances, while 75 percent opposed the cut.

The election of Ronald Reagan in November 1980 raises doubts about our contention that the American public continues to approve of the things that government does for them. In his budget message to the Congress on February 18, 1981, President Reagan submitted a program that he described as "aimed at reducing the growth in government spending and taxing." The President concluded his address with a direct attack on the welfare state: "The taxing power of government," he said, "must not be used to regulate the economy or bring about social change. We've tried that and surely we must be able to see it doesn't work. Spending by government must be limited to those functions which are the proper province of government."

But the President may be surprised to learn what the public still thinks is "the proper province of government." An ABC News/ *Washington Post* poll taken just after the President's speech asked people whether they thought federal government spending in several general areas should be "increased, decreased, or left about the same." Predictably, almost three quarters favored increasing government spending on military programs and on fighting crime. But 49 percent supported *more* government spending on health care and on helping "the poor," while 43 percent endorsed more government spending for education. Only 12 to 15 percent felt that government spending should be reduced in any of these areas.

The ABC/*Post* poll also asked people how they felt about spending cuts in fourteen specific programs, including child day-care, synthetic fuels, unemployment insurance, aid to the arts, food stamps, Medicaid, Medicare, student loans, public television, and the postal service. The answers ranged from 4 percent who favored a curtailment in expenditures for Medicare to 49 percent who favored a decrease in spending for food stamps. In other words, a majority did not approve spending cuts in any specific program. But when asked a few minutes later whether they approved or disapproved of the spending cuts proposed by the Reagan Administration, the margin of support was an overwhelming 72 to 21 percent. The reason, apparently, was that by 64 to 28 percent, this cross section felt that Reagan's economic program— "including spending cuts in almost all the programs just mentioned"—would help bring about an end to inflation.

These findings are consistent with previous polls showing support for increased government spending in many specific areas alongside the view that government spending in general should be cut back. In this respect, the election of Ronald Reagan was not a significant break with the past.

In January 1979, for example, the ABC News/Harris poll found that majorities would oppose a major cutback in federal spending if that meant less spending for aid to the elderly, handicapped, and poor (78 percent), health care (75 percent), education (73 percent), defense (62 percent), environmental protection (52 percent), and help for the unemployed (54 percent). Yet 69 percent of those interviewed favored a major cutback in federal government spending in principle.

Those seeking to reduce the scope of government and the impact of federal expenditures on inflation often have advocated a constitutional amendment that would require a balanced budget. Support for such an amendment has grown, in tandem with the rapid hike in the inflation rate, to the point where Gallup found in February 1980 that almost four fifths backed such an amendment. But equal or larger majorities of the same cross section wanted "to maintain or increase government spending for medical and health care (89 percent), programs to reduce water pollution (87 percent), farm price supports (71 percent)," etc. Even in the case of food stamps for poor people, 67 percent of all registered voters favored maintaining or increasing federal expenditures, compared with only 25 percent who wanted them reduced and 6 percent who preferred to end them entirely.[16]

In March 1980, the *New York Times*/CBS News poll found direct evidence that the public favors "a smaller government." A majority, 54 percent, approved "a smaller government providing fewer services," compared to 32 percent who opted for "a bigger government providing more services." But by a plurality of 46 to 43 percent, the same sample supported "national health insurance, financed by tax money, and paying for most forms of health care." And only 28 percent said that "government spending on *domestic* programs should be decreased." Three fifths favored keeping domestic spending at the same level (38 percent) or increasing it (22 percent). Only 8 percent supported cutting back on military and defense programs, while 60 percent endorsed increases and 24 percent wanted to keep the same level.

[16] "Newsweek Poll on the Issues," *Newsweek*, March 3, 1979, p. 27.

The Effects of "Malaise"

Early in 1980, the Center for Political Studies (CPS) and the National Opinion Research Center (NORC) asked the same question bearing on a trade-off between government services and spending cuts:

> Some people think the government should provide fewer services, even in areas such as health and education, in order to reduce spending. Other people feel it is important for the government to continue the services it now provides, even if it means no reduction in spending. Where would you place yourself in this [seven-point] scale, or haven't you thought about it?

The scale ran from 1 ("government should provide many fewer services and reduce spending a lot") to 7 ("government should continue to provide services with no reduction in spending"). CPS found in its January-February 1980 poll that 24 percent opted for cutting services and spending, points one to three (6 percent placed themselves at point one); 15 percent took the neutral middle position, point four; 44 percent preferred maintaining services without expenditure cuts, points five to seven (16 percent at point seven); and 17 percent said they had no opinion. Two months later, NORC secured strikingly similar results: 28 percent endorsed cutting services and spending (with 8 percent at point one); 19 percent were in the middle; 42 percent favored maintaining services without spending cuts (16 percent at point seven); and 12 percent took no position. Maintaining services was preferred over spending cuts by a 20-point margin in the CPS poll and by a 14-point margin in the NORC poll—almost two years after Proposition 13 and a few months before Reagan was elected President.

Well into 1981, the polls showed that the public wanted to cut spending generally but opposed cuts in programs designed to aid the aged, the sick, the poor, the handicapped, the unemployed, and the disadvantaged. The popularity of spending cuts in principle is mostly explained by the public's preoccupation with inflation. By March 1981, a Gallup poll indicated that 73 percent of the public named inflation as the most important problem facing the country, the largest proportion ever; fewer than 10 percent named any other problem. And, as indicated earlier, wasteful spending by the federal government has been increasingly targeted as the cause of inflation since the mid-1970s.

The tax revolt and the attack on government spending were

precipitated by the interaction of two trends: the collapse of confidence in government beginning in the mid-1960s and the hyperinflation of the late 1970s. The two together produced "the anti-government rebellion" of 1978–80, including the tax revolt and the election of a conservative Republican government. Nevertheless, there is little evidence that Americans have turned against the idea that the government should support social welfare, provide needed services, help disadvantaged groups, and protect citizens from economic and social adversity. Americans seem to have developed an irreversible commitment to basic government welfare programs, just as they did, finally, to social security. A poll conducted for *Money* magazine early in 1981 by Yankelovich, Skelly & White indicated "a strong strain of support for social programs that help people who need it most—the poor and the elderly." Those polled, for instance, opposed by a two-to-one margin slowing down the rate of increase in such widely distributed government benefits as social security, civil service retirement, veterans' pensions, education, and medical programs. In the ABC News/ *Washington Post* poll taken just after President Reagan's economic address to Congress in February 1981, the same national cross section that approved the President's proposed spending cuts by over three to one was asked whether or not they agreed with the following proposition: "The government should work to substantially reduce the income gap between rich and poor." They very definitely agreed, by 64 to 31 percent. That too, it seems, is accepted by the American public as "the proper province of government."

Although all the polls taken in the spring and summer of 1981 reported that the large majority supported President Reagan's economic program and that his popularity and approval ratings were extremely high, Gallup found that the proportion who expressed concern that Ronald Reagan "would cut needed social programs" had increased from 27 percent in September 1980 to 44 percent in April 1981. We do not agree, therefore, with those conservatives who saw the tax revolt as signifying a massive shift of public sentiment to the right or as an attack on the welfare state.

But we also do not agree with Senator George McGovern, who said after the Proposition 13 vote that Californians had displayed "degrading hedonism that tells them to ask what they can take from the needy." The tax revolt was an expression of general frustration against what the public views as the abuse of power by government. As has been amply documented in this book, abuse of power is associated by the public with all powerful and self-interested institutions, including, most notably, government, business, and labor. Both Governor Edmund G. Brown, Jr., of California and Senator Edward M. Kennedy of Massachusetts have remarked on separate occasions that the frustration and resentment behind the tax revolt could be channeled against big business as easily as big government. We have reason to suspect that they are right, although we would warn that it could also be directed against "powerful labor unions."

Can Confidence in Government Be Regained?

What, if anything, can be done to improve confidence in government? Americans have not turned against the political system itself. They still see it as fundamentally good. The problem in their eyes lies in inadequate, inept, and even corrupt leadership. Such sentiments suggest that any effort to change the low level of confidence in government must focus, not on changing public attitudes as President Carter proposed in his July 1979 speech, but in making government more responsive and effective in dealing with the key problems of society. As Arthur Miller has pointed out:

> Current distrust of authorities and institutions does not necessarily mean that citizens want a change in the basic democratic form of government. On the contrary, their discontent means that government is perceived as functioning in a manner which deviates from their normative expectations of honesty, competence, efficiency, equity and responsiveness.[17]

In other words, the problem is not primarily attitudinal. It is essentially substantive. More intelligent and skillful leadership and more effective government are necessary before confidence in government can be restored. The problem is, they may not be sufficient. That is because a number of important interests in our society have a stake in maintaining public doubts about government. These interests include the press and especially the broadcast media, which, it will be argued below, have found that "bad news" is more effective than "good news" in competing for the attention of the mass audience. Politicians may also try to foster a defeatist attitude

---

[17] Arthur Miller, "Institutional Focus of Political Distrust," p. 47.

as a form of self-justification: "I haven't done particularly well in solving the nation's problems because they are complex and beyond the control of *any* political leader." Finally, if the ideological polarization of our two major parties continues—Democrats to the left, Republicans to the right—they will be less and less likely to find areas of consensus, to agree on solutions, or to accept each other's apparent successes.

Even if things do get better, we are saying, the political system has developed certain inhibitions against spreading the news that it is really so; indeed, certain groups may have an incentive to sustain the belief that things are worse than they really are. As Warren Miller has put it, "The continuing sense of malaise may also flow from the rather pervasive mood of concern, if not pessimism, that has been consistently conveyed both by the elected leaders and by the articulate, self-selected activists and spokespersons for various causes over recent years."[18] Thus, in order for the trends in political confidence to reverse, things will not just have to get better; they will have to get better in such a clear and palpable way that the public will pay no attention to the inevitable voices of cynicism and disbelief.

Consequences for Labor

A second major institution for which trust has been very low is the labor movement. In the Harris-NORC confidence ratings from 1966 through 1981, "the people running organized labor" averaged the lowest confidence rating of any institution tested; only 15 percent, on the average, expressed "a great deal of confidence" in labor leaders. Labor leaders usually ranked below business and political leaders except during the Watergate period, when the executive branch slipped to last place, and during the 1974–75 recession, when both business and government dropped.

The public does continue to accept the basic legitimacy of labor unions, as shown in Chapter 7. They also believe that unions are good for their members. Thus, when Fingerhut/Granados Opinion Research asked in 1977 whether members of labor unions were "better off, worse off, or no different as a result of being a union

---

[18] Warren Miller, "Misreading the Public Pulse," *Public Opinion* 2 (October/November 1979), p. 60.

member," the overwhelming consensus, even among respondents from non-union households, was that they were better off (p. 353).

The Effects of Low Confidence in Labor

Have unions been affected by the loss of public confidence in them during the 1960s and 1970s? The evidence on union membership and the results of union elections held by the National Labor Relations Board suggests that they may have been.

Except for the immediate postwar period, union membership as a percentage of the nonagricultural labor force reached a high in 1954, when it stood at 35 percent. The favorability rating for labor unions was also very high at that time; the Gallup poll for 1953 shows 75 percent approving of labor unions. Union membership as a percentage of the nonagricultural labor force fell off slightly over the next five years, to 33 percent in 1957, the year in which the Gallup approval rating reached an all-time high of 76 percent. Unions' percentage of the labor force began to decline steadily after that. It was at 30 percent in 1961, 27 percent in 1969, 25.5 percent in 1975, and 24 percent in 1978, 23 percent in 1979, and 21 percent in 1980, the latest figure available.[19] From 1967 to 1980, the percentage belonging to unions and the percentage of the population favorable to unions were going down together.

Another indicator of the appeal of unions to American workers is the ability of labor organizations to win elections supervised by the National Labor Relations Board. This trend also seems to reflect a reduced faith in labor unions. In 1940, unions won 77 percent of organizing elections; in 1945, 83 percent resulted in union victories; in 1950, 74.5; in 1960, 59 percent; the figures stayed at 60 percent in 1965 and 61 percent in 1966. The proportion of union victories then began to fall, down to 55 percent in 1970, 50 percent in 1974, and less than half after that: 48 percent in 1975, 46 percent in 1977, and 45 percent in 1979 and 1980. The decline once again coincides with the period of diminishing public confidence.

The right-to-work issue illustrates well the public's ambivalence toward labor unions and the effects of the declining confidence trends. Business-sponsored polls on the "right to work" generally

[19] U.S., Department of Labor, Bureau of Labor Statistics, *Handbook of Labor Statistics 1978* (Washington, D.C.: U.S. Government Printing Office, 1979), p. 507. Additional data supplied by U.S. Bureau of Labor Statistics.

emphasize the principle of coercion and show that the public dis-
approves of any measure that forces workers to join a union as a
condition of employment. Union-commissoned questions on this
issue almost always stress the principle of fairness: "Do you think
it's fair for people to receive benefits from an organization such as
a labor union without paying any of the costs of getting those
benefits?" The public's answer, given in 1977 to a poll taken by
Fingerhut/Granados for the AFL/CIO, was "of course not," 74 to
15 percent. When the issue is put in a relatively unbiased way, as
it was in a 1978 survey taken by Cambridge Survey Research for
the American Retail Federation, the public is more closely divided
over the issue: "Some people say that if a majority of employees of
a firm or factory want to have a labor union, then every employee
should have to pay dues to the union since the union will be
representing them. Do you agree with this idea or not?" The answers were 46 percent "no" and 39 percent "yes."

Generally speaking, the evidence in Chapter 7 showed that the
public agrees *in principle* with many anti-union positions. They
oppose measures that give unions more power or to make it easier
for unions to organize and recruit members, particularly if those
measures are depicted in any way as coercive. On the other hand,
people are quite aware of the potential for abuses of power by
employers, and they think unions should have legal protection in
such cases. The public does not want to see unions destroyed or
to tip the balance of power decisively in favor of business. That is
why, *in practice,* the public usually votes against right-to-work
laws when they appear on the ballot; the unions manage to depict
these laws, not as matters of principle, but as issues of survival.

Support for unions may also be related to the fact that labor as
an institution gets more credit than business for supporting socially progressive causes. In 1977 Fingerhut/Granados asked, "Over
the years, which group—the national labor unions or the large
business organizations—do you think have most supported" each
policy in a list of social reforms and programs. Labor was seen as
more supportive of the minimum wage (77 percent said labor, 9
percent said business), full employment (61 percent labor, 14 per-
cent business), Social Security (57 percent labor, 15 percent business), better housing (51 percent labor, 15 percent business),
Medicare (46 percent labor, 13 percent business), civil rights legislation (45 percent labor, 15 percent business), lower fuel prices
(45 percent labor, 18 percent business), closing tax loopholes (40

percent labor, 16 percent business), and aid to education (38 percent labor, 22 percent business). This social commitment, assiduously cultivated by the labor movement over the years, has clearly paid off in public recognition. But the image of social commitment does not hide labor's equally visible faults—primary among them, the disreputable image of labor's leadership.

Union Leadership

One of the most serious problems for labor is the sharp discrepancy between the public's view of labor *leaders* on the one hand and labor unions and workers on the other. We have reviewed evidence of the resoundingly negative public view of labor leaders. As noted in Chapter 7, when Gallup, in 1981, asked about the honesty and ethical standards of people in twenty-four different occupational groups, labor leaders came out twenty-third on the list. Business executives did considerably better (p. 217). In April 1981, the *Los Angeles Times* poll asked a national cross section to give their impression of "labor leaders" and of "businessmen or women." Labor leaders were judged negatively, 47 percent unfavorable to 41 percent favorable, while business people were approved of by 80 to 12.

It should be noted, however, that union leaders are not perceived as particularly representative of their members. A 1978 Cambridge Reports, Inc., poll asked, "Do you think the average union leader represents the members of his union well or not?" A plurality of 43 percent replied "no," compared to 31 percent who answered "yes." Respondents from union households were evenly divided on this question: 40 percent "yes" and 39 percent "no." But nonunion respondents, who comprise more than two thirds of the public, said "no," 45 to 27 percent.

Union leaders are seriously bothered by these criticisms. An article published in 1980 reporting on the views of a group of new international union presidents who have succeeded to the AFL-CIO executive council since 1977 (fully one third of the council's thirty-three members) noted: "What most concerns this new generation of union leaders is labor's recent decline in public opinion. Polls show it has fallen to an all-time low. Says DeConcini of the Bakery Workers: 'Our people are working full time trying to help other people, and yet our image is down at the bottom of the ladder.'" These leaders urged "a nationwide advertising campaign to promote a better view of labor unions."[20] In February 1981, the executive council "reactivated a long-dormant public relations committee to monitor what many unions feel is unfair media treatment of unions and to suggest tactics for improving labor's tattered image, which has ranked in some opinion polls near that of used-car salesmen."[21]

To deal with this problem, the United Automobile Workers, the International Association of Machinists, and the American Federation of Teachers decided to set up a large number of "low power" television stations in order, according to UAW President Douglas Fraser, to "better communicate with our members and the general public."[22] Other unions such as the International Ladies Garment Workers, the Brotherhood of Carpenters, the Communications Workers of America, and the American Federation of State, County, and Municipal Employees now advertise regularly on television.

It is difficult to argue that labor unions can change their low status by publicity campaigns. As we have seen, although their position in the public eye declined during the 1970s, organized labor has been close to the bottom in all the surveys taken to measure institutional trust over the years. Union leaders and members are not likely to seek popularity at the expense of economic bargaining power. Probably the best thing they can do is remind the public of labor's reputation of concern for the social welfare, at least in noneconomic areas. As William Konyha, president of the Carpenters' Union, has suggested, "The general public has to realize that if it had not been for the labor movement, we wouldn't have such things as Social Security, unemployment insurance, and worker's compensation."[23]

On the other hand, the new leadership of the labor movement proposes to enhance its strength by taking actions that may further alienate the nonunion public. Most notable are the growing number of union mergers in recent years, a trend that does nothing to dispel the public's concern over the apparent concentration of power within the union movement. "Almost every one of the newer union presidents is considering a merger with another union,"

[20] "Rush of New People to Top Union Jobs," *U.S. News and World Report,* February 28, 1980, pp. 101–2.
[21] "Can Low-Power TV Shine the UAW Image?" *Business Week* (March 16, 1981), p. 32.
[22] "Can Low-Power TV Shine the UAW Image?," p. 32.
[23] "Rush of New People to Top Union Jobs," p. 102.

according to one report, while AFL-CIO President Lane Kirkland "encourages mergers to strengthen smaller unions."[24]

The results of the opinion polls suggest that unions should do more than they have done to police their internal operations and to reduce the widespread impression that corruption and lack of democracy characterize their internal governance. But Lane Kirkland, with the support of the newer members of the federation's council, has invited the Teamsters' union—expelled in 1957 on charges of corruption—to rejoin the AFL-CIO. *U.S. News and World Report* indicates that most recently elected union presidents believe that George Meany made a mistake in expelling the Teamsters from the federation. "Advocates of reaffiliation note that the Teamsters are not the only union charged with corruption. . . . 'The Teamsters are cooperating with us in our strike,' says Goss of the Oil Workers. 'I don't ask a guy who's helping me whether he's been indicted.' "[25] Public relations campaigns to counter deeply held ideological biases or impressions stemming from perceptions of reality are not likely to have much effect, particularly since union leaders are apparently not prepared to change the behavior that appears to substantiate those beliefs.

Consequences for Business

It is even more difficult to identify the effects of "the crisis of confidence" on the business sector than it was for government and labor. Business leaders are certainly aware of their decline in public esteem, and they show evidence of being deeply concerned about what they view as the misunderstanding of their activities by the public. In a December 1976 survey for the Sentry Insurance Company, the Harris poll asked a sample of senior business managers the following open-ended question: "What do you think is the one most important change that is needed in the relationship between business and society in the United States?" The answers most frequently mentioned, by a majority of 52 percent, were coded collectively as, "The public should have a better understanding of the role and economics of business." The second most common category was "better communication, understanding, and cooper-

[24] "Rush of New People."
[25] "Rush of New People."

ation between business and consumers," mentioned by 37 percent. The third category, cited by 18 percent, included responses suggesting that "business must win the confidence, trust and credibility of the public." Behavioral changes by business were rarely proposed; for example, only 5 percent replied "truth in advertising, honesty and clarity of product information," 4 percent said "business should be more responsive to consumer needs," and 3 percent recommended "improved quality, serviceability, and safety of products." Thus, both business and labor leaders, like President Carter, believe that the problem of the public's decline in confidence in them lies in the minds of the public and not in their own behavior.

These replies, like those of the political and labor leaders above, reflect the anxieties produced by the evidence of negative judgments about business reported by the pollsters. The commissioning of many of the surveys cited here is a product of these concerns. Many major corporations have spent considerable sums to find out what the public thinks of business or big business in general and of their industry or their firm in particular. Many corporate executives are convinced that government policies designed to limit their freedom to act reflect public antagonism, and, hence, they look for ways to improve their public image. Their publications and private statements often place the blame for what they perceive as the public's misunderstanding of business, and particularly the public's exaggerated estimates of profits, on misinformation provided by a left-leaning intelligentsia, a liberal press, hostile bureaucrats, and irresponsible politicians seeking to gain popularity by stirring up populist resentment.

The Question of Social Responsibility

Although the decline of confidence has been very broad, business clearly has its own special problems that may be more difficult to solve than those facing other institutions. It is significant that between 1966 and 1981, confidence in the leaders of major companies fell farther and faster than confidence in the leaders of any other major institution. In 1966, the leaders of business ranked above the average confidence level expressed in institutional leaders. In 1971, confidence in business leaders was precisely average. Since 1972, business leaders have remained below average in confidence, although they continue to outrank government and labor unions. What is there specifically about business that troubles the American people?

We have found two attributes of business that are viewed very negatively by the public and considered sources of undesirable behavior and anti-social effects. First of all, there is the fact that business is perceived to be motivated exclusively by considerations of self-interest. Whatever social benefits accrue from business activity—and these are readily acknowledged by the public—are felt to be incidental to business' main purpose, that of securing maximum profits. The second factor is more properly associated with big business, although it undoubtedly affects feelings about business in general, namely, the concentration of an enormous amount of power through the ownership and control of economic resources.

These two considerations lead many to conclude that business does things that are against the interests of society. The issue is not the activities or reputation of specific firms or industries, but rather a generalized feeling that business puts profits ahead of human concerns and that it lacks compassion and social responsibility. Moreover, the public believes that business cannot avoid responsibility for larger social developments. Its obvious wealth and power are enough to convince most Americans that business has a significant impact on public policy. Household heads polled by *U.S. News and World Report* in late 1977 had almost no doubt that "large companies have major influence on government agencies," a statement they agreed with by a margin of ten to one.

Currently, a number of the problems that have faced the country are seen as related to the activities of business: unemployment; inflation; the energy shortage; shoddy consumer products, or at least ones that are not as good or as efficient as they could be; problems of pollution in its various forms; and, to a lesser but still significant degree, concerns about employee welfare and safety on the job. What these issues have in common is that, when survey respondents are asked about them, large numbers, usually majorities, favor *more* government regulation to ameliorate or solve each of them. The public does not believe that these problems will be solved by the operation of the invisible hand of the free market. Despite the public's inherent distrust of big government, there are specific areas in which people feel that it is worth the risk of giving government more power in order to curb the even worse abuses of big business.

It would seem, then, that business is expected to demonstrate its social responsibility in *these* areas more than in such fields as political reform or cultural improvement. Several reasons may be offered for this judgment:

1. These are matters for which business is held specifically responsible. Attacking other problems will probably not do much to enhance the reputation of business so long as these issues remain salient to the public.

2. These are relatively noncontroversial issues. Almost everyone, including business people, voices concern about inflation, unemployment, consumer protection, environmental protection, job safety, and energy independence.

3. These are tasks that business can reasonably be described as competent to deal with; that is, they are subject to technological and administrative solutions, while most other political and social problems are not.

All of this does not mean that most Americans hold business solely or even primarily, responsible for these problems. Thus, as has been shown, labor and government share the blame for inflation along with business. Indeed, labor is seen as responsible because unions pursue their self-interest with little concern for the effect of wage increases on the price structure. The greatest amount of blame for inflation is reserved for government because of high taxes, excessive spending, and costly regulations. Unemployment is also regarded as a government-induced problem. The tax revolt of the late 1970s was an effort by the voters to intervene directly to reduce the price they pay for government services. The energy crisis, to take another example, is blamed on government and the Arab nations as well as the oil companies.

Poor products, environmental pollution, and lack of safety on the job, on the other hand, are problems directly attributed to business. When government is criticized in these cases, the complaint is usually over its lack of action rather than some specific policy or abuse causing the problem. But regardless of which institutions are held responsible for particular difficulties, an overwhelming majority of the public supports government intervention to force business and other groups to be more socially responsible, to act more in the public interest. In this context, business power is seen not only as a cause of these problems but also as an obstacle to implementing necessary regulatory actions.

The policy conclusions that flow from the public's attitudes are ambivalent and even paradoxical. If people want to eliminate ills by increasing government regulation, they also see big government as a source of major social problems and they are decidedly hostile to bureaucracy and higher taxes. They also recognize that regulation has certain negative effects on the economy, such as raising prices. Many people state that in principle they are opposed to increasing government regulation, and a growing number favor a reduction of existing regulations. However, when asked what should be done to solve specific problems, the same people often endorse continued or increased government regulation by substantial majorities. Similarly, the public sees free enterprise as responsible for the high standard of living in this country and even as a necessary condition for political freedom. The public wants business to do well, but it also wants it to curb its anti-social behavior. Since big business in particular is far removed from control by individual citizens, there is especially strong sentiment in favor of government control where big business is the target.

Can Educational Campaigns Save Business?

As was evident in the comments of the senior executives reported above, many in the business world believe that a major source of diminished confidence in business is the lack of accurate knowledge about business activity, particularly exaggerated notions about how much profit the average firm receives. People who share this view would have business support an extensive "educational" campaign designed to inform the public better, on the assumption that more knowledge will produce a more positive attitude. Advocates of such a program point to the results of surveys supposedly demonstrating that persons who are well informed about the economy are generally more favorable to business than the less knowledgeable or those who have not studied economics.

This causal attribution is highly questionable, however. It is based on efforts to differentiate between questions that measure "economic knowledge" and those that reflect "attitudes." One major conclusion of the report of a 1975 survey conducted by the Corporate Marketing Research Section of the du Pont Company for the Business Roundtable is that "not only is there a relationship between . . . 'economic knowledge' and 'attitudes toward business' but attitudes toward business may improve as understanding of economics increases." The report presents tables that appear to

361

support this generalization. The imputed causal relationship between knowledge and attitudes in this and other studies becomes somewhat doubtful, however, when one looks closely at the questions purporting to test "knowledge." The distinction between knowledge and attitudes is often not clear. For most "knowledge" questions, the "correct" answer, it turns out, is also a pro-business answer. A person who is biased against business or who favors a government interventionist position might very well give the "wrong" answer to the following indicators of supposedly factual knowledge, as defined by the du Pont researchers:

- "One of the problems businesses face today is finding enough capital so that they can expand and grow" ("true" graded as the correct answer);
- "A good way to curb inflation is for the government to reduce unemployment" (false);
- "Of the total money taken in by manufacturing companies, more goes to the stockholders in dividends than to the workers in wages and salaries" (false);
- "One of the causes of our inflation is that people are being laid off" (false);
- "Workers in the U.S. earn more than in other countries because the equipment and machinery they use allows them to produce more than workers in other countries" (true);
- "The surest way to raise the country's standard of living in the long run is to limit profits and increase wages" (false);
- "The main function of competition is to prevent large firms from driving small ones out of business" (false);
- "Government control over corporate profits would lead to fewer new and improved products for consumers" (true);
- "Competition is wasteful because it means too many companies are making the same thing" (false);
- "An unprofitable company is usually a poor place to work" (true);
- "Our standard of living is higher than in other countries because our level of productivity is higher" (true); and
- "The most likely result of increased investment in machinery and equipment for a company would be an increase in cost of products to consumers" (false).

Perhaps each of these "knowledge" questions has an unambiguously "correct" answer, but one would suspect that many liberal and socialist economists would give a number of "incorrect" answers.

Indeed, the report of the du Pont survey results suggests that ideology influences answers to both "attitude" and "knowledge."

On the set of items classified in the report as "attitudes," self-described liberals were, predictably, more critical of business than self-described conservatives. Thus, liberals were less likely than conservatives to agree that "most companies charge fair prices for their products" (52 percent agreement among conservatives, 31.5 percent among liberals). And conservatives were more likely than liberals to disagree that "the men who run the country's biggest companies really cannot be trusted" (51 percent of conservatives and 38 percent of liberals disagreed).

However, conservatives were also more likely than liberals to give "correct" answers to the "knowledge" questions. For example, almost half of the conservatives and one third of the liberals gave the "correct" answer, i.e., "false," to the statement, "A good way to curb inflation is for the government to reduce unemployment." A majority of conservatives, 56 percent, compared to 41 percent of liberals, chose the "right" response, "deficit spending by the government," to the question, "Which one of the following [four] activities does most to raise the prices of goods and services?" In fact, conservatives were more likely than liberals to give the "correct" reply to thirty of the thirty-six so-called "economic knowledge" items in the du Pont survey. In general, the "attitude" questions displayed the same demographic and political correlates as the "knowledge" questions. The more liberal, the less well-educated, the less well-to-do, union members, and those who had never studied economics were (a) less sympathetic to business on the "attitude" tests, and (b) less likely to answer the "knowledge" questions correctly.

The contamination was apparently introduced by the selection of the questions. Items appear to have been classified as "knowledge" or "attitude" indicators wholly on a judgmental basis. No statistical techniques were used to demonstrate the uniqueness and validity of the two sets of items. (Factor analysis and other scaling procedures have been widely used for this purpose.) Thus, a statement such as "the surest way to raise the country's standard of living in the long run is to limit profits and increase wages" undoubtedly taps political views and not simply "information." The same is true for most of the other "knowledge" questions in this survey. It is likely that pro-business "attitudes" and "knowledge" about business—as measured by these tests—are both determined by ideological predispositions, precisely the sort of convictions not readily modified by educational campaigns.

The purported impact of educational campaigns on attitudes toward business remains unproved. Even if a correlation were found between uncontaminated measures of knowledge and pro-business attitudes, the causal sequence would remain unclear unless some sort of quasi-experiment were devised to see whether people's attitudes *change* after they are exposed to factual information.

Educational campaigns ought not to be considered worthless, however. Such efforts can be used to correct errors of fact and understanding at the elite level, that is, among those whose positions enable them to influence public policy. But there are two reasons to suspect that the impact of educational campaigns on pro-business attitudes at the mass level will be slight. One is the fact that, over time, institutions have been shown to gain and lose esteem more or less in tandem with each other. Specific information about any one institution is likely to be a very weak force for counteracting broad and general social trends that are based on a perception of conditions in general.

The second problem is that, across the population, feelings about business are related to basic ideological convictions. The political left has been anti-business since at least the Progressive era, and recent events appear to have increased its anti-business bias. Any effort to "educate" business opponents into a more sympathetic attitude is likely to run up against deeply felt ideological predispositions. Many apparent misperceptions about business may actually be anti-business attitudes that no amount of factual information is likely to dispel. As noted earlier in the discussion of profits, those critical of business systematically overestimate profit margins. It is not likely that more accurate information about profit margins will change their minds about business.

In any case, information coming from clearly self-interested sources is distrusted by the public. Yankelovich, Skelly & White documented the cynicism or gullibility of most Americans when they inquired in 1976 and 1978 about the credibility of a number of opinion sources: "Every day we all hear different points of view from different people and institutions. We are interested in knowing how often you believe what each of them says." The least believable source inquired about was "public issue ads" (an average of 8 percent of the public always or usually believed such advertisements, while 51.5 percent seldom or never believed them). Corporate executives and union leaders also were not found credible by significant pluralities. Ralph Nader, on the other hand, was the source most likely to be accepted (44.5 percent found him always or usually believable, while 19 percent said they seldom or never believed him). Television commentators and newspapers were also viewed positively, with close to two fifths believing them most of the time, compared to less than one fifth who did not. Credibility, in other words, is a strong function of perceived self-interest.

Direct Efforts to Improve the Image of Business

Many big business firms have undertaken direct efforts to improve the image of their company or industry. Some firms have greatly enlarged their programs of corporate giving to the arts and to charities, including the sponsorship of touring companies and prestigious cultural events on radio and television. Others have concentrated on conveying the message that large companies share the same concerns as the public. Advertisements by oil companies often promote the idea that they are strongly committed to environmentalism, conservation, and reduction of the country's dependence on foreign oil. The fundamental problem remains, however, the credibility of the sources. The Shell Oil Company's "Come to Shell for Answers" campaign has generally been regarded as one of the more successful efforts, mostly because the program actually "paid off" by offering helpful consumer information to motorists. Episodes like the Love Canal incident in 1979 brought similar responses from the chemical industry—corporate advertising explaining the benefits of chemical discoveries in everyday life and proclaiming the commitment of companies like du Pont, Dow, and Monsanto to environmental protection and safety.

A private report entitled "Coping with a Hostile Environment: Public Affairs Responses by the U.S. Oil Industry" noted in November 1980 that

> . . . corporate advertising, as distinct from product advertising, and in particular that segment of corporate advertising commonly called "issue" or "advocacy" advertising, is definitely a growth industry in the U.S. A 1979 survey by the Association of National Advertisers found that (a) more companies are using corporate advertising and there is greater continuity in their use, compared to the association's previous survey in 1977; (b) there is an increase in the number of users discussing public issues in their advertising; (c) expenditures on corporate advertising are rising in real terms; and (d) target audi-

ences are widening, and increasingly include not only narrow target groups but large segments of the public or even the entire adult population.

The report found that corporate image advertising probably can be effective only over a long period of time and with a big budget. Issue advertising may be effective with small target audiences but is of dubious value with mass audiences. Evidence of the effectiveness of corporate advertising is, in fact, scanty, according to the report. As noted above in the Yankelovich surveys on credibility, only a tiny minority of the public said they found "public issue ads" credible. Moreover, firms are still faced with difficult unresolved legal questions about the meaning and application of the "fairness doctrine" in broadcasting and the boundary between advertising and political expression. Nevertheless, the report concludes, "for corporate communications this is the way things are moving."

Can big business really modify its image? Business leaders, like the leaders of other institutions, need to recognize that they have been caught in a downdraft that has swept across the entire social landscape, so that public confidence in business can hardly be separated from that in other institutions. Only if major social changes generate a renewal of public confidence can business and other institutions expect to rise significantly in the esteem of most Americans. So long as alienation remains as pervasive as it was throughout the 1970s, however, business leaders cannot hope to regain the lofty pinnacles of confidence they enjoyed in earlier years. Even the resurgence of optimism occasioned by Ronald Reagan's accession to the presidency in 1981 had little effect on confidence in business and no apparent impact on broader confidence levels (see Tables 2-1, 2-2, and 2-3). If anything, confidence in non-governmental institutions declined in 1981.

This is not to say that corporations (or labor unions) can do nothing about their loss of public trust. The negative image of business institutions does bear some relationship to their actual behavior. This can be seen in the public's differentiation of specific firms and industries and in the variations in the level of confidence expressed in them over time. Thus, the oil companies suffered a severe loss of confidence after the 1973 price increases. The extensive public relations campaigns described above have done little to modify this adverse impression, since prices continued to rise and were believed to be mainly under the control of the oil companies themselves. Similarly, nuclear power companies fell very low in public esteem after the Three Mile Island incident, as did the chemical industry after the Love Canal revelations.

Banks, on the other hand, once the targets of extreme hostility from Populists and left-wing groups, have tended in recent years to be the single most popular business institution. It is difficult to discern exactly what changed the image of banks, but, as noted earlier, we believe that the public no longer sees banks primarily as creditors and property foreclosers—a perception that, in decades past, was particularly salient to rural Americans, who lived mostly in debt. Although the majority of the public still borrows money and often pays high interest in order to buy homes, people view banks today as service institutions. The banks on every corner are no longer viewed as usurers and monopolists exploiting the people but as agencies serving the public's needs. The data do, however, show a noticeable slippage in the reputation of the banking industry in the last few years, possibly as a result of the dramatic increases in interest rates that borrowers had to pay at the end of the 1970s and the early 1980s.

The Historical Record

In asking whether we can anticipate any major upswing of confidence in business, a review of past changes may give some indication of what is possible in the future. Public opinion data do not exist for any period before the mid-1930s, but a quantitative content analysis of attitudes toward business as they were expressed in major journals between 1880 and 1940 provides some evidence of the shifts that occurred over that sixty-year period. Louis Galombos, the author of the study, reports that the prosperous 1880s were characterized by relatively positive attitudes, although negative ones grew toward the end of the decade. The high point of anti-business (i.e., anti-trust) sentiment "occurred during the severe depression of the mid-nineties."[26]

A crisis of authority emerged in the 1890s as a consequence of "bitter struggles over political, economic and organizational issues." Leaders of major corporations were blamed for many social

[26] Louis Galombos, *The Public Image of Big Business in America, 1880–1949* (Baltimore: Johns Hopkins University Press, 1975), p. 255.

problems, including the severe economic depression of that decade. The pre–World-War-I Progressive Era, which witnessed major legislative changes aimed at controlling or breaking up trusts and monopolies, was also a period of steady economic growth and a rising standard of living. With the latter came more widespread public acceptance of the large corporation. In fact, the striking conclusion of the Galombos study is that the large business corporation acquired increasing legitimacy between the Progressive Era and the 1930s.

> Increasingly, [people] bought goods from companies, not octopuses; they worked for firms, not trusts. By 1919 they viewed these businesses in a relatively impersonal light. . . .
> Middle class Americans first became very angry with the large corporation and then slowly came to tolerate it. . . . Accommodation began in the 1890's, continued through the Progressive Era and the First World War, and lasted well into the 1920's.[27]

Following the Depression and World War II, public opinion data reveal a steady growth in the legitimacy of all institutions and of business in particular. A detailed review of attitudes toward big business, based on opinion data collected by the Survey Research Center in 1950, found that attitudes toward big business had become quite positive, with large corporations having gained considerable support as employers, creators of jobs, and producers of valuable services and wealth.[28] As noted earlier, these favorable feelings toward business specifically and toward the social and political system in general continued and even increased through the early 1960s, only to collapse during the ensuing period of social conflict and political polarization.

Public trust remained on a generally downward slope during the troubled 1970s, reaching a low point during the mid-decade recession and declining even further during the hyperinflation of 1978–81. Business shared fully in these trends, reaching its lowest confidence levels to date in the Harris polls of September 1974 and November 1980, when only 16 percent of the public expressed "a great deal of confidence" in the leaders of major companies (continuing at this low level in September 1981.) The Gallup and ORC

[27] Galombos, *Public Image of Big Business,* pp. 261, 265.
[28] Burton K. Fisher and Stephen B. Withey, *Big Business as People See It* (Ann Arbor, Michigan: Survey Research Center, University of Michigan, 1951).

polls also show a downward trend for "big business" (Gallup) and "large companies" (ORC) from 1975 to 1980–81. In 1981, ORC's index of anti-business sentiment (Figure 1-5) revealed the highest level of antipathy toward large companies in twenty-two years, following a temporary improvement in 1977.

The only good news for business has been of a rather special kind: the public's hostility to *government* grew so fast at the end of the decade that it produced a relative upswing in support for business. In tandem with the widely publicized "tax revolt," increasing proportions of the public supported reductions in business taxes and increased tax incentives for investment. Less government regulation of business was winning majority support in the polls for the first time in 1980 and 1981. The implication of these trends is that support for business has not been going up because of any surge of confidence in business itself. Rather, business has been the principal beneficiary of the public's anti-government mood. The improvement in public attitudes toward business are most visible in questions involving regulation, taxation, government control, blame for inflation, and relative power—that is, in questions where business is judged vis-à-vis the state.

Anti-Business Policies in Other Countries

The fact is that both anti-business sentiment and policies are less severe in the United States than in most industrial democracies (Japan being the principal exception). In other industrial countries, the prevailing pattern is for a major part of the political spectrum to be occupied by parties that are at least formally anticapitalist and committed to ending the private business system. Given the alternations in power characteristic of most democracies, it seems likely that, in most of these countries, the socialists alone or in alliance with other parties will eventually come to power, as they have at various times in Austria, Britain, France, Germany, Scandinavia, and elsewhere. With a large proportion of the population accepting some variant of a socialist ideology, the nonsocialist parties have also come to accept economic doctrines and policies that are much more statist than anything advanced by the major political groups in the United States. Thus, socialist François Mitterrand was elected President of France in 1981, running on a platform that promised to nationalize eleven major industries in an economy that already included many government-owned companies that had been established or nationalized by non-socialist governments.

A political scientist, John Clayton Thomas, systematically coded the positions of fifty-four political parties in twelve industrial nations from the 1870s to the 1960s, and subsequently updated his work for ten nations for the 1971–76 period. He found increasing "patterns of convergence" between leftist and non-leftist parties over the decades. But even more significantly, the non-leftist parties changed their policy positions; they moved leftward toward increased acceptance of the welfare-planning state more dramatically than the left and labor groups shifted to the right. The two exceptions to this pattern in the most recent period have been the Republicans in the United States and British Tories under Margaret Thatcher.[29]

Taxes are significantly higher in most of Europe than they are in the United States, a much larger proportion of the economy is nationalized, and social-welfare benefits are greater. American businessmen would regard as intolerable the forms of taxation and government intervention that exist today under conservative and non-socialist rule in Britain and Norway.

These conclusions are reinforced by the findings of the Harris/Sentry Insurance surveys conducted from December 1980 to February 1981 in five countries, the United States, Great Britain, Australia, West Germany, and Japan, discussed earlier in Chapter 9. Samples of American employees and of business executives showed up repeatedly as more likely than their peers in other countries to oppose government planning and direction of the economy and to favor "a free market economy . . . [as] the best way to achieve economic growth." Thus, when asked, "Do you think the economy would perform better with more government planning and direction, less government planning and direction, or just about the same amount that we have now?" 90 percent of American business executives responded "less," compared to 50 percent of the British, 49 percent of Australians, 39 percent of West Germans, and 30 percent of Japanese executives. Similarly, on questions addressed to executives in the three English-speaking countries,

[29] John Clayton Thomas, *The Decline of Ideology in Western Political Parties: A Study of Changing Policy Orientations* (Beverly Hills, California: Sage Publications, 1974), pp. 13, 26, 44–46; "The Changing Nature of Partisan Divisions in the West: Trends in Domestic Policy Orientations in Ten Party Systems," *European Journal of Political Research* 7 (December 1979), pp. 403–6.

the Americans were more favorable to cuts in government spending (93 percent) than the British (75 percent) or the Australians (55 percent); more supportive of "an across-the-board tax cut" (69 percent) than the British (30 percent) or the Australians (44 percent); and more favorable to relaxing environmental and safety standards (57 percent) than the British (7 percent) or the Australians (13 percent). The American corporate leaders were also less disposed to providing "government funding to retrain and relocate workers in failing industries" (14 percent) than their British (37 percent) or Australian (54 percent) peers, or to channeling "investment into potential growth industries that cannot attract all the investment they need from the private sector," (32 percent) than British (66 percent) or Australian (75 percent) executives.

American Attitudes and Politics

The future of American business depends in some part on whether American society for the next generation continues to resemble its past or moves toward more European types of political, economic, and social arrangements. To go the latter route would probably require that the Democratic Party and the American labor movement become much more committed to socialism and social democratic policies and manifest more opposition to business than they ever have done. It is true that, beginning in the 1930s, both the Democrats and the labor movement moved toward the acceptance of what can be described as social democratic, welfare-state orientations, and that this constituted a decisive break with the antistatist policies previously supported by these groups. As a result of the Depression and subsequent political changes, the American public and almost all of its leaders came to accept social-welfare programs and government interventions that differed greatly from earlier policies. The period since World War II has been characterized by an increased reliance on regulatory agencies to remedy social ills.

The fact remains, however, that the United States has not had a well-developed socialist movement or social democratic party. At most, the Democratic party offered economic protection. In 1980, however, the social welfare liberalism inherited from the New Deal no longer implied economic protection to most voters; it meant "big government." The Democrats' resounding defeat at the polls that year led many party leaders to express open doubts about even

371

the modest welfare-state consensus that had held the party to-gether since the 1930s. The Democratic National Committee sub-sequently selected a national party chairman who was himself a businessman and banker and who expressed a desire to reorient the party in a pro-business direction. These sentiments were echoed in 1981 by the senior Democratic figure in Congress, House Speaker Thomas P. ("Tip") O'Neill, who criticized the Democratic party for minimizing the influence of businesspeople and accepting too much guidance from (presumably left-leaning) academics.

The fundamental opposition to business today does not come from its traditional enemy, organized labor, with which it shares a commitment to economic growth and support for traditional social and cultural values. The spearhead of the attack on business has come from the New Politics liberal left, the intelligentsia, and af-fluent college-educated professionals who are basically critical of the materialistic emphasis in society, which they see as fostered by business. The intelligentsia are primarily concerned with the culture, values, and environment of society, and not with the econ-omy as such. They regard business as crass, materialistic, and uninterested in improving society. In this context, the majority of the labor movement sometimes finds itself at odds with both busi-ness and the intelligentsia. On the one hand, unionists are com-mitted to a traditional conflict with business, as they seek to maximize income and improve working conditions. On the other hand, they also take exception to the cultural values espoused by the intelligentsia as these bear on economic growth, education, the family, sex, law and order, authority, national defense, and patriotism. (It should be noted that a minority within the labor movement, mainly in white-collar and professional unions and unions in which socialists hold leadership posts, does endorse the social values of the New Politics intelligentsia.)

In a curious way, the views of the New Politics intelligentsia are comparable to those of the old aristocracy of European society. The aristocratic ruling classes of Europe, whose power derived from their ownership of land and who dominated cultural, reli-gious, and political life, frowned upon the materialistic values of the emerging capitalist class of 19th- and early 20th-century Europe. They also rejected the claims for equal rights by the un-derprivileged, particularly those presented by trade unionists and socialists. The aristocracy favored state intervention and welfare legislation both to protect the poor and to enhance the moral atmosphere of their society. Capitalism has never achieved the legitimacy in once-aristocratic Europe that it has in the United States, which lacks Europe's upper-class inheritance of feudal and aristocratic values. Hence, American businesspeople have a tradition of public leadership, high status, and social recognition that the business class rarely acquired elsewhere. Although the position of business corporations in the United States was under attack prior to World War I by the American labor and Progressive movements, as Galombos has documented, this challenge to the power of business really did not affect the basic status of businesspeople. The public, then as now, seemed to disapprove of the behavior of big businesspeople but did not question the legitimacy of their function. The challenge from the intelligentsia today, however, may be more fundamental in that it involves a disdain for the role and status of business in American society. Business is under attack because social responsibility is only an incidental function and not a basic motivation of business activity.

The so-called New Right movement is pro-business on many issues and would seem to be a useful ally for the corporate community. Yet the new breed of conservatives shares the same intense moralism and disdain for "interest politics" as the New Politics liberals (with whom they also share a base of support that is predominantly affluent and upper middle class). The New Right is better described as ideologically committed to free enterprise than as politically concerned with the interests of the business community. Its practical alliances with business are often motivated more by hostility to government (as in the case of regulation) or to labor (as with labor law reform) than by a desire to protect business. Ideologues of the New Right have parted company with business on such issues as trade with Communist countries (the grain embargo), protectionism for American industry (import quotas on Japanese automobiles), and government aid to failing American companies (the Chrysler and Lockheed loan guarantees). The New Right is, in fact, widely distrusted by the business community, and with good reason. A basic suspicion of business values and a fundamentally moralistic view of politics are as characteristic of the New Right as they are of the New Left.

Ideology aside, a considerable body of evidence suggests that the expectations that many Americans hold for their society and its key institutions have changed. Such changes are reflected in the consumer, environmental, and women's rights movements.

These changes entail a heightened demand for social responsibility on the part of powerful institutions. To regain confidence in such a context, business and other key institutions must not only "deliver the goods" in terms of economic prosperity, but they must also manifest some degree of commitment to the public interest, as conceived by a better educated, more socially conscious public.

12

Is There a Legitimacy Crisis?

IMPLICIT in the decline of public confidence in institutions is a potential crisis of legitimacy. Severe critics of the American system believe that the decline shown by the polls is a manifestation of a much deeper loss of institutional legitimacy that has resulted from basic flaws in the structure of our society. Others claim that the negativism in the polls represents a casual and ritualistic cynicism. The notion that the legitimacy of our institutional order has been seriously eroded seems, in their view, drastic and premature. The evidence we have presented could be used to buttress both interpretations. Our final task is to evaluate the evidence and assess the overall seriousness of its implications.

We have argued throughout this book that a number of "real events"—a sequence of negative experiences first in the political and social realm and later in the economy—are the key to understanding the decline of confidence. In conclusion, we seek to delve further into the effects of these events. Do they represent structural defects endemic to our institutional order, or can they be attributed, at least in part, to changes in our communications system—particularly the new prominence of the broadcast media—that exacerbate the impact of events and stimulate a more critical and cynical posture on the part of the American public? In either case, how deeply affected is the legitimacy of our institutional order?

375

Concern about Legitimacy

One effect of declining confidence in leaders is status insecurity. An elite that is not esteemed by the public will probably feel anxious about its own authority. In fact, many institutional leaders in this country feel that they are disliked, or at least not sufficiently respected, by the public.

The leaders' response, as we have seen, is a sometimes obsessive concern with their public image. For example, intellectuals, who are, of course, more self-analytical than any other group, have long complained that most Americans are anti-intellectual and that the country exhibits little regard for their work, a phenomenon supposedly reflected in the fact that most of them earn less than people in other elite occupations. Many lawyers are equally convinced that they are regarded as unprincipled "shysters" who will do anything to make money. Physicians worry that there is a general view that they place their own income and comfort above the needs of their patients. Both the legal and medical professions see these views reflected in popular support for regulating their activities.

Labor leaders point to the widespread impression that they are corrupt and that their unions act against the public interest; as a result, they believe that their political influence and membership are lower than they should be. Business executives are also convinced that there is generalized hostility toward them, that politicians are able to win votes by campaigning against them, and that excessive government regulations and harsh business taxation are a direct result of their low public esteem. Teachers are sensitive to the public's complaint that they do a poor job. Civil servants are sure they are perceived as inefficient, offensive, and less capable than employees in private industry. And politicians, who are subject to constant scrutiny by the public, the media, and each other, are especially disturbed by the invidious reputation of their profession.

Sensitivity to Criticism

Why do American elites have such a pervasive sense that they lack respect? While the polls certainly demonstrate a loss of public esteem for almost all institutional leaders over the last fifteen years, the historic evidence suggests that sensitivity to public image is by no means a new phenomenon among American elites. Foreign travelers in America from the early nineteenth century to the present have been struck by the extent to which Americans at all levels have been "other-directed," to use David Riesman's perceptive phrase; that is, Americans are typically more concerned than Europeans with the way others react to them. One summary of the writings of English travelers from 1785 to 1835 makes note of a repeatedly mentioned characteristic, "the acute sensitiveness to opinion that the average American revealed."[1] Francis Grund, a German aristocrat, wrote in the 1830s that

> . . . nothing can excite the contempt of an educated European more than the continual fears and apprehensions in which even the "most enlightened citizens" of the United States seem to live with regard to their next neighbors, lest their actions, principles, opinions, and beliefs should be condemned by their fellow creatures.[2]

This sensitivity to criticism on the part of American elites reflects the strength of egalitarian values and democratic institutions in the United States. Many upper-class visitors saw a threat to genuine individuality and creativity as a consequence of the concern of American leaders to be popular. They believed that the source of this behavior was an open class system. As one analyst of various travelers' writings states,

> One reason why the English are blunt and abrupt about their rights . . . is because class lines are more sharply drawn there. Within these limits, one is likely to develop the habit of demanding his dues. He insists on his prerogatives all the more because they are narrowly defined. When an English writer (Jowett) says, "We are not nearly so much afraid of one another as you are in the States," he expressed this truth.[3]

Max Weber, after a visit to America in the early 1900s, noted the high degree of "submission to general opinion" in America, "to a degree unknown in Germany"; he explained the phenomenon as

---

[1] Jane L. Mesick, *The English Traveller in America 1785–1835* (New York: Columbia University Press, 1922), p. 301.

[2] Francis J. Grund, *Aristocracy in America* (New York: Harper Torchbooks, 1959), p. 162; also pp. 52 and 157.

[3] J. G. Brooks, *As Others See Us* (New York: Macmillan, 1908), p. 97.

a result of an imprecise status structure linked to the absence of inherited class status.[4]

Suspicion of Power

A related consequence of this country's egalitarianism and democratic values is the absence of deference for elites and the recurrent waves of populist attacks on various leadership groups. Although most Americans hold the country's basic institutions in high regard, they have almost always found much to object to in the way these institutions operate and in the performance of their leaders. The public suspects that unchecked power will be abused by self-interested power-holders. The strong fear that the Revolutionary generation had of an all-powerful state led the Founding Fathers to set up an elaborate system of checks and balances, designed to inhibit governmental power. Political authority was deliberately divided among the President, the two houses of Congress, the Supreme Court, and the states, so that the various units could counter each other and reduce the potential for abuses of power.

Americans also exhibit suspicion of private concentrations of power in business and labor organizations. They assume the worst, or the possibility of the worst, from the leaders of all powerful institutions, whether public or private. Indeed, the public has shown a tendency to personalize social problems, that is, to attribute them to inept leaders and corrupt power-holders. At its worst, this conception has made Americans unusually receptive to conspiratorial theories. The Populists in the 1890s attacked the Eastern financial interests and monopolists who threatened the "honest" farmer. During the 1930s, the isolationists launched investigations of the munitions manufacturers who purportedly had conspired to lead the United States into World War I. Franklin D. Roosevelt attacked the "economic royalists" who were selfishly impeding the New Deal. Following World War II, Senator Joseph McCarthy and others linked the decline of American influence abroad to the supposed activities of Communist conspirators within the U.S. government. This instinctive public mistrust of power-holders has a positive side, however; people lose faith in leaders

---

[4] H. H. Gerth and C. Wright Mills, eds., *From Max Weber: Essays in Sociology* (New York: Oxford University Press, 1946), p. 188.

much more easily than they lose confidence in the system. All the indicators that we have examined show that, while the public has been growing increasingly critical of the performance of major institutions, there has been no significant decline in the legitimacy ascribed to the underlying political and economic systems.

The source of the suspicion of power, as Robert Lynd has emphasized, is

> ... the traditional identification of power with dominance—riveted home in popular thought by the most widely quoted of all statements about power: Lord Acton's dictum that "power corrupts"—[which] renders public reference to organized power in a society professing democratic values furtive and its use awkward. Liberal democracy has, accordingly, tended to resolve the problem of power by quantitative limitation of its use.[5]

Such sentiments help to explain the seemingly contradictory opinions reported by the pollsters. Most people describe government actions to control or regulate private activities as inefficient, often corrupt, and overly costly; yet when "push comes to shove," they still want the government to regulate business, labor, and other private organizations. They are highly critical of the behavior of labor leaders and see their organizations as acting against the public interest; yet they approve of labor unions and repeatedly say that without unions, workers would be unduly exploited by business. They regard big business as excessively powerful and, therefore, in need of regulation by the government to protect the public and in need of counterbalancing by unions to protect employees. But they overwhelmingly oppose proposals to nationalize large companies, even the highly unpopular oil companies, and strongly support the system of competitive free enterprise. They believe that business, including big business, has played a key role in fostering national growth and job opportunities.

The public tends to favor two approaches to curbing potential abuses of power. One was initially devised for the political system by the Founding Fathers, namely, conflict among powerful interests. In most areas of institutional life, private as well as public, Americans place their faith in a theory of countervailing power, or

---

[5] Robert S. Lynd, "Power in American Society as Resource and Problem," in Arthur Kornhauser, ed., *Problems of Power in American Democracy* (Detroit, Michigan: Wayne State University Press, 1959), p. 5. Acton actually said, "Power tends to corrupt, and absolute power corrupts absolutely."

checks and balances as it is popularly known. The public prefers institutionalized conflict, regulation, labor-management strife, and hamstrung government to alternative arrangements that allow a single powerful interest to dominate—even though these conflicts may raise costs, inhibit effective action to solve problems, and retard economic growth. Evidence of such beliefs in the political realm can be seen in the public's response to a question asked by Civic Service in February 1980:

> Some people say that when a President and a Congress are of opposite political parties it gives balance to our government . . . Others say that with the problems we face, we need a President and Congress to be of the same political party to enact laws efficiently and quickly. Do you agree or disagree . . . the President and Congress should be of the same party to enact laws efficiently and quickly?

The national cross section rejected this view, 51 to 36 percent, preferring instead a situation of divided party control that increases the chances for disagreement between the executive and legislative branches and, therefore, inaction. This response reflects a continuity in the American value system. Americans believe in countervailing constraints on all centers of power, not just the state. Hence the more power inherent in an institution or its leaders, the more suspected or feared it is.

Fearing and suspecting power, the public prefers smaller rather than larger institutions—the second approach to controlling potential abuses of power. People favor small business and would like to see large corporations broken up wherever possible. Similarly, they express a preference for smaller labor unions, although this idea has never become a serious policy issue. In the area of government, the public is more favorably disposed toward state government than toward the federal government and toward local government more than state government. As we have noted, the association of "bigness" with "badness" comes up again and again in the data.

One reason labor has tended to be less popular than business, we would argue, is that labor is viewed as more monopolistic and less differentiated than business. The concentration of power within the labor movement is more obvious than in the case of business. The public tends to approve of the specific functions that labor unions perform on behalf of their members. But they disapprove of the concentrated power of the labor movement as a whole. Similarly, they oppose those sectors of business that can be identified as large, impersonal, and monopolistic.

Sentiments critical of powerful institutions do not necessarily stem from negative personal experiences with these institutions. That was the message of a Survey Research Center study that argued that "people actually organize their cognitions both at a pragmatic empirical level, and at a more general ideological level. Ideologically, they may be against large public bureaucracies; pragmatically, they are all for them."[6] Persons who had direct dealings with government agencies, both federal and state, were found to be satisfied with their "bureaucratic encounters" and to believe that they had been treated well. Such judgments are in sharp contrast with general evaluations of government agencies, which reveal low levels of confidence in them and considerable criticism of their efficiency and reliability.

> [The difference] is marked . . . on the parallel questions of problem solution where 71 percent of the clients report successful outcome in their own case whereas only 30 percent give the government office good marks on being able to take care of problems generally. It is also marked in reports of fairness, 80 percent in personal encounters compared to 42 percent in general evaluation. Considerate treatment was indicated by 77 percent for their own experiences, and by 39 percent for government offices in general. While 72 percent of clients thought the agency had functioned efficiently for them, respondents were rather evenly divided in responding positively or negatively on how most agencies functioned in general with respect to prompt services and avoiding errors.[7]

The ABC News/Harris survey found striking differences in responses to three polls taken in 1978 that asked people to "rate the job Congress has done" and to "rate the job your own Congressman here in this district has been doing." Less than one third, 31 percent, judged Congress positively ("excellent" or "pretty good") in the three surveys, while 64 percent gave it a negative rating ("only fair" or "poor"). "Your own Congressman," however, was evaluated positively by almost half, 48 percent, and negatively by

[6] Daniel Katz, Barbara A. Gutek, Robert L. Kahn, and Eugenia Barton, *Bureaucratic Encounters* (Ann Arbor, Michigan: Institute for Social Research, University of Michigan, 1975), p. 178.

[7] Katz et al., *Bureaucratic Encounters*, p. 120.

41 percent, on the average. The public reacted similarly when asked in 1980 by Civic Service whether "most Congressmen" and "my Congressman" are "for sale to the highest contributors to their campaigns." A majority, 56 percent, felt that most members of Congress "are for sale," but only one third, 34 percent, believed the statement applied to their own Representative.

The same disparities appear in people's reactions to nongovernmental institutions. Thus, as noted earlier, in 1975 the Gallup poll asked people to evaluate the business that employed them, big business, and business in general. Only one third indicated a positive level of confidence ("a great deal" or "quite a lot") in "big business," while 48 percent gave comparable responses about "business." When asked about "the company or business you work for," however, favorable judgments rose to two thirds, 67 percent. Polls taken of attitudes toward physicians and attorneys also reveal that respondents are much more favorable about the qualities of the doctor or lawyer with whom they have dealt than with the medical or legal professions as a whole. The general point is that people are more positive about their direct relations with representatives of an institution than about the institution itself. It would not seem likely, therefore, that personal experiences are a valid explanation for institutional distrust.

It would appear that the invidious sentiments expressed about large organizations reflect a general anti-elitist, anti-power ideology much more than a sense of personal maltreatment. Americans apparently believe that uncontrolled, self-oriented power will always be used against the public interest, and that those in charge, if not watched closely, will act to benefit themselves—at the expense of the public if they are politicians, against the interests of consumers and their own employees if they are corporation executives, and against the interests of the community and even their own members if they are union leaders. The public feels that businesspeople, union leaders, and politicians will act in a socially responsible way only when the public interest coincides with their own self-interest, that is, when there is something in it for them.

This suspicion of power is our basic explanation of the trends and patterns identified in the confidence data. The experiences of the late 1960s and the early 1970s—an unpopular war, social protest, racial polarization, and scandal in high places—served to confirm and intensify the fear that the people "running things" were abusing the public trust. Thus, one of our important findings is that the collapse of confidence was general, that it applied to a whole range of institutions and not just business or government. Institutions outside of government shared in the general downturn of confidence even if they did not actually lead the trend. The period of the most rapid increase in alienation and cynicism was 1965 to 1972. Events since that time—Watergate and other scandals, the energy crisis, recession, and inflation—have done nothing to reverse the trend; rather, faith in institutions tended to move down gradually in the 1970s and at the start of the 1980s to a level much lower than that of the 1960s.

Suspicion of power also helps to explain why business, labor, and government have been among the lowest-rated institutions in terms of public confidence, with business usually faring somewhat better than the other two. The evidence suggests that it is the self-interested quality of business, labor, and government and the fact that they represent visible concentrations of power that turn public opinion against them. The institutions that consistently do best in confidence ratings are those most clearly identified as altruistic: science, medicine, education, the military, and religion. Professionals in these fields are not highly regarded simply because of their "expertise"; lawyers, after all, are experts, but they tend to be ranked relatively low. What lawyers share with businesspeople, labor leaders, and politicians is the essentially nonaltruistic, self-interested nature of their profession—or so they are perceived. Lawyers, businesspeople, labor leaders, and politicians are "just in it for themselves," while the public holds scientists, doctors, clergymen, military leaders, and educators in much higher regard as people who appear to be willing to sacrifice their own interests for the well-being of others and whose financial reward is incidental to the true motivation of their work. Americans do admire hard work, enterprise, and inventiveness—the Thomas Edison and Henry Ford images—but they do not believe that these characteristics apply to the typical business executive in the modern large corporation. Businesspeople are seen as exploiting the needs of others in order to serve their own purpose, which is to make money. Thus, social goals are perceived to be incidental to the work of the business executive and not his or her central motivation.

In the end, therefore, the concern among American elites about their esteem is well-founded. But it is not entirely attributable to their behavior; the simple fact that elites have power makes them

383

a source of suspicion and distrust to the American people. There are, however, conditions in which elite behavior can alter public beliefs and counter the perception that all types of leaders are invariably self-interested. People will always be suspicious of the motives of businesspeople, labor leaders, and politicians, but they do not rule out the possibility that statesmen, innovators, and champions of working people might ascend to positions of power in the American system. There are few signs that the quality of our institutional leadership has been improving in such directions in recent years—in fact, events would seem to provide evidence to the contrary. Still one aspect of the American belief system sustains optimism, and that is the continuing high legitimacy of the country's institutional order itself.

Optimism about the System

Those who speak for the interests of business, labor, and government have tended to argue one of two extreme positions: either that the crisis of confidence is not real, or that it is fundamental and systemic. Our conclusion is that the decline of confidence has both real and superficial aspects. It is real because the American public is intensely dissatisfied with the performance of their institutions. It is also to some extent superficial because Americans have not yet reached the point of rejecting those institutions. As Everett Ladd has written: "Available data surely do not sustain the argument that the U.S. has experienced any sort of legitimacy crisis—or that the country is at the beginning of one."[8] Nor is there any evidence to suggest that Americans feel there are fundamental defects in their systems of democratic government or free enterprise.

Factors That Reinforce Legitimacy

Our analysis suggests three attributes of the American belief system that have sustained the legitimacy of the country's institutional structure. One is the distinction in the public mind between the (admirable) functions performed by our institutions and

[8] Everett Ladd, "The Polls: The Question of Confidence," *Public Opinion Quarterly* 40 (Winter 1976–77), p. 552.

the (not so admirable) behavior of the leaders and members of those institutions necessary for those institutions to work. Competition and self-interest are indispensable for both democratic politics and a free enterprise economy. But the public does not feel constrained, out of devotion to democracy and free enterprise, to admire the self-interested pursuit of profit and power. This discrepancy may be illogical, but it is deeply embedded in American values. It also implies that our institutions are valued for reasons unrelated to the kind of behavior that makes them work. The political and economic systems are approved of because they result in freedom and prosperity. Profit-seeking and power-grasping are the price that must be paid to obtain those objectives. But such undesirable behavior by the leaders and members of institutions does not discredit the essential legitimacy of the institutions themselves.

Some direct indication that the public differentiates between the leaders of institutions and the health of the system itself was provided by the Roper poll of February 1981, discussed earlier, which elicited evaluations of the soundness of the political system, the system of business and industry, and the system of organized labor. The same poll inquired about confidence in business, labor, and political leaders. The leadership question offered respondents three choices: a great deal of confidence, a fair amount, and not much. As in the Harris and NORC polls, relatively few expressed a great deal of confidence in institutional leaders: 16 percent in the case of political leaders, 16 percent for business leaders, and 7 percent for labor leaders. (The poll was taken during Ronald Reagan's first month in office.) But fully 67 percent of the same respondents rated our political system as basically sound, while 64 percent felt the same way about our system of business and industry. Only 45 percent thought our system of organized labor was basically sound, but this was still considerably higher than the percentage who voiced high confidence in labor leaders.

The failure of the majority to express a great deal of confidence in the leaders of key institutions clearly does not mean that most Americans believe the institutions have failed or that they require fundamental change or reform. Rather, most Americans continue to feel positively about the basic character of the country's political and business institutions, while entertaining serious doubts about their performance.

A second stabilizing factor has been the American people's continued optimism about their own personal situations. We reviewed evidence in Chapter 5 showing that Americans have been much more positive in evaluating their own personal situations than in judging the state of affairs in the country as a whole. Moreover, a pattern of optimism about both has been the rule, with the exception of the explosive inflationary period of 1978–79 when optimism about the future of the country temporarily vanished. Even the experience of unemployment does not appear to shake the public's belief in the American dream of greater opportunity for each generation.

In December 1978, almost three quarters (74 percent) of the respondents in an ABC News/Harris poll said that they had "a great deal of confidence in this country." But only 28 percent indicated that they had "a great deal of confidence in the President." A few months later, in February 1979, the ABC News/Harris poll found an average of 23 percent—the lowest figure ever —expressing "a great deal of confidence" in the people running ten different institutions. By October 1979, after a summer of gasoline lines and Jimmy Carter's "malaise" speech, confidence in the President had fallen to only 16 percent. But in the same October poll, Harris found evidence that "Americans display abundant confidence in their country and themselves," to wit:

- a substantial 73 percent reported "a great deal of confidence in this country," almost unchanged from December 1978;
- 65 percent expressed "a great deal of confidence" in the ability of the American people to work out their problems;
- the highest level of confidence was indicated for people's faith in themselves, as 81 percent expressed "a great deal of confidence" in their own ability to work out their own problems.

NORC administered its General Social Surveys every year between 1972 and 1980 (except 1979), thus producing a series that spans the period of severe economic decline following the late-1973 oil crisis. As noted, this data series shows no significant change in people's reported happiness with their marriages, their health, their work, or their lives as a whole. The surveys find only a slight decline in people's satisfaction with their financial condition, from 33 percent "pretty well satisfied" in 1972 to 29 percent expressing the same sentiment in 1980.[9]

[9] Figures reported in *Public Opinion* 3 (August/September 1980), p. 31.

Is There a Legitimacy Crisis?

Table 12-1 reports the results of an ABC News/Harris poll taken in September 1979, when national "malaise" and Presidential disapproval were extremely high. Harris listed "some things some people believe have made America great" and asked respondents to indicate whether they thought each of them would be "a major factor, a minor factor, or hardly a factor at all" in continuing to make America great. Table 12-1 reveals no noticeable lapse of faith in "factors making America great" in 1979, as compared with 1977, the first year of Jimmy Carter's presidency, when the question was first asked. Feelings remained overwhelmingly positive with respect to America's democratic political system, technological and industrial know-how, hard-working and highly-motivated people, responsive government, and even its "outstanding political leaders." In fact, optimism about many of these items as "major factors in continuing to make America great" actually went up a bit from 1977 to 1979, although the average level of faith in institutions expressed in the confidence surveys dropped sharply in this period (see Table 2-1). Interestingly, the items thought of as least likely to contribute to America's greatness were heavy government spending for social programs, government regulation of industry, and "welcoming refugees from all over the world." This last factor elicited considerable pride in the 1977 survey but then collapsed in popularity in 1979, in the wake of the large numbers of Indo-Chinese and Cuban refugees entering the country.

Overall, then, we would concur with the conclusion reached by Potomac Associates in their 1976 report on "trust and confidence in the American system," that Americans have "cast a critical eye on various institutions within their society. . . . but they see themselves and their system in strongly positive terms, certainly a sign of health which pessimists would do well to recognize."[10] The Survey Research Center's study of *Bureaucratic Encounters* also concluded that "system support is strong":

> Many people express distrust of national political leaders and speak almost in cliches about the relative inefficiency of government, but they expect to find the local offices open and functioning when they need unemployment compensation or reach the age of retirement. Moreover, there is support for the nation and its symbols at the most

[10] Francis E. Rourke, Lloyd Free, and William Watts, *Trust and Confidence in the American System* (Washington, D.C.: Potomac Associates, 1976), pp. 26–27.

Table 12–1

Factors Making America Great

"Now I'm going to read you some things some people believe have made America great. Looking ahead to the next 25 years, for each item I read, tell me if you think it will be a major factor in continuing to make America great, a minor factor, or hardly a factor at all."

	Major Factor	Minor Factor	Hardly a Factor at All	Not Sure
	Percentage			
Scientific research				
1979	89	8	1	2
1977	91	4	1	4
Industrial know-how				
1979	80	15	2	3
1977	80	14	2	4
Hard-working people				
1979	79	17	3	1
1977	76	17	4	3
Rich natural resources				
1979	79	15	4	2
1977	77	15	4	4
A government that responds to the people's needs				
1979	78	15	5	2
1977	70	18	7	5
Skill at organizing production				
1979	74	18	3	5
1977	71	19	3	7
Democracy as its political system				
1979	74	15	5	6
1977	72	17	4	7
Technological genius				
1979	73	18	4	5
1977	78	12	3	7
A highly motivated labor force				
1979	72	17	5	6
1977	64	22	6	8
Giving every race and creed an equal chance to get ahead				
1979	70	23	5	2
1977	70	21	6	3
The availability of money to expand industry				
1979	69	23	4	4
1977	71	18	4	7
Free, unlimited education to all qualified				
1979	67	23	8	2
1977	75	16	4	5

Is There a Legitimacy Crisis?

	Major Factor	Minor Factor	Hardly a Factor at All	Not Sure
	Percentage			
Outstanding political leaders				
1979	62	23	12	3
1977	51	28	15	6
A talent for selling and marketing things				
1979	60	29	6	5
1977	61	25	8	6
Freedom of thought in the universities				
1979	60	27	8	5
1977	67	21	7	5
Having industry and business under private control				
1979	59	25	8	8
1977	58	23	9	10
Deep religious beliefs				
1979	57	29	11	3
1977	61	22	12	5
Advertising				
1979	41	40	14	5
1977	49	32	12	7
Heavy government spending for social programs				
1979	31	38	24	7
1977	x	x	x	x
Having a government which regulates industry				
1979	27	36	28	9
1977	36	32	19	13
Welcoming refugees from all over the world				
1979	24	34	34	8
1977	53	30	10	7

Source: ABC News/Harris Survey, September 1979.
N = 1,520 for 1977.
N = 1,514 for 1979.
x = Not asked.

general level. The problems of erosion seem to involve the intermediate levels of system support [i.e., confidence in government leadership].[11]

The same study looked for disaffection in certain specific groups: women, blacks, young people, and the socially and economically deprived. While people in these categories did not show a high

[11] Katz et al., *Bureaucratic Encounters*, pp. 187–88.

degree of system support, "we found little evidence for a serious condition of alienation in any of these groups."[12]

Daniel Yankelovich called attention to a similar phenomenon in an effort to explain why in spite of the "rising tide of disaffection in America," it has not led to a European-style pattern of *ressentiment,* of the kind of deep-rooted "negative feelings in relationship to authority" that can produce violent reactions. He suggests as an explanation the fact that many "people who are most critical of the government, who express the keenest mistrust, the greatest political alienation, and the most social resentment, nonetheless profess to be contented, productive, secure and fulfilled in their private lives." He noted that at the height of the Watergate scandal,

> ... the opinion surveys showed that almost 90 percent of the public felt things were going badly in the country. Yet when people were asked about their private and public lives, the same overwhelming 90 percent majority stated that everything was going very well indeed in their personal lives. ...
>
> In 1975, eight out of ten American families reported that they were doing quite well personally. ... In the midst of the worst economic setback since the 1930s, a majority of families expressed keen satisfaction with such crucial aspects of their private lives as their confidence in handling personal problems, the pleasures and cohesiveness of family live, the enjoyment they get out of life, their ability to derive from life what they feel they are entitled to, and their progress in getting ahead and achieving success.[13]

And Yankelovich went on to conclude that "as long as most people feel reasonably comfortable in their personal lives and are able to cope, political stability will be sustained and *ressentiment* will be kept at bay."[14]

The third factor helping to sustain the legitimacy of the country's institutions is the public's belief that, since failures of the system are the fault of incompetent power-holders, the situation can be greatly improved by changing the incumbent authorities. The cure for a government and an economy that are performing poorly is a change of leadership—brought about by the democratic process. In September 1979, a decisive 73 to 21 percent majority in an ABC News/Harris poll felt that "there is nothing wrong with this country that good leadership couldn't cure." In the same poll,

[12] Katz et al., *Bureaucratic Encounters,* p. 188.

[13] Daniel Yankelovich, "The Status of *Ressentiment* in America," *Social Research* 42 (Winter 1975), pp. 761–65, 767–68.

[14] Yankelovich, "The Status of *Ressentiment* in America," p. 777.

86 percent felt that the quality of life in this country would be better "if the federal government were more accountable to the public for its decisions," rather than worse (3 percent) or "not much different" (8 percent). Seventy-one percent thought things would be better "if business were more accountable to the public for its decisions" (5 percent thought things would be worse in that case and 19 percent said it would not make much difference).

The view that a change of leadership would improve the country's situation applied with particular force to President Carter. In October 1979, Gallup asked people to name the most important problem facing the nation. Respondents were then asked, "How confident are you that President Carter can deal with this problem?" Only 30 percent thought President Carter could handle the problem they named. People were then asked, "How confident are you that any President can deal with this problem?" Almost twice as many, 59 percent, were confident that the problem they named could be dealt with by a competent chief executive.

Given the conviction that we have a good system run by bad or inadequate people, hope seems to spring eternal in the public breast. In October 1978, the ABC News/Harris survey came up with the following findings:

- By a massive 84-10 percent, voters were convinced that we did not have a federal government "which is almost wholly free of corruption and pay-offs." But by 48-45 percent, they also believed that it was possible to have such a state of affairs.
- By 69-18 percent, a majority said that the best people are not attracted to serve in public life. However, by 68-22 percent, voters were convinced that this situation could change for the better.
- By 61-26 percent, a majority denied that we had a federal government in which "the good of the country is placed above special interests." Nonetheless, a 76-16 percent majority believed that the attainment of such a government was possible.
- By 59-24 percent, voters did not feel that "government is the most exciting place to work" these days. But by 57-27 percent, a comparable majority thought that the public sector could be made exciting and interesting again.
- By 51-36 percent, voters did not agree that "most public officials are dedicated to helping the country rather than being out for themselves." But by 77-16 percent, they were convinced that it was possible to get a government made up of dedicated officials.
- By 48-38 percent, a plurality held the view that the country lacks public officials who really care what happens to the people. Yet, by 81-12 percent, a big majority thought it was possible to find such men and women.

As Harris went on to note in commenting on the findings of this and other surveys:

> It is evident that the American people have not given up hope for a better federal government and better people to lead it. In fact, despite the shock waves that have visited the public over the past 15 years, including assassinations, the Vietnam War, Watergate, continuing high inflation and unemployment, as well as leadership which held out high promise only to fall short, there has never been much evidence that most people have gone sour on the system itself and have finally concluded that it is unworkable.
>
> To the contrary, the constant search over the past years has been precisely to find the kind of leadership that can make the system work. People have not lost faith that somehow they will find that high calibre of public official.[15]

The Reagan Effect

Given this trend of public opinion about our national leadership during the Carter administration, the election of Ronald Reagan in November 1980 had a predictably restorative effect. The ABC News/Harris survey interviewed a national sample a few days after the November 4th vote. When that sample was compared with those interviewed in May and September 1980, the results showed greater optimism about the economy. Fewer Americans thought that, over the next six months, unemployment would be rising steadily, the cost of living would be going up as fast as it had been, the cost of food would be rising faster than before, people would be postponing major purchases, or the average family would have a harder time making ends meet. (Despite increasing optimism, however, pluralities or majorities still thought each of these things was "not very likely.") There was no evidence of increasing optimism, however, on either interest rates or OPEC oil prices in the postelection poll, possibly because those situations are not thought to be controlled directly by the President.

The CBS News/*New York Times* poll asked a national sample immediately after Reagan's inauguration in January 1981 what they thought was the most important problem facing the country and whether they thought President Reagan would be able to do something about it. In stark contrast to the results obtained when

---

[15] Louis Harris, "Despite Skepticism, Voters Say Government Can Be Made to Work," *The Harris Survey* (November 13, 1978), p. 1.

Gallup asked the same question about President Carter in October 1979, 66 percent now thought President Reagan would be able to do something about the problem that most concerned them. The CBS/*Times* post-inaugural poll went on to ask whether President Reagan would or would not be able to solve a number of specific problems facing the country. The results are shown in Table 12-2.

At the time of Reagan's inauguration, Americans were clearly optimistic about the new President's ability to strengthen the country's position in the world and to bring the federal government under control (reduce the size and influence of the federal government, clean up the welfare system). On the other hand, the public showed no exaggerated optimism about Reagan's prospects in the economic area. An overwhelming two-thirds majority felt that Reagan would *not* be able to stop inflation or to balance the budget and cut taxes at the same time. A majority did not think he would be able to balance the budget at all in the next four years, and the public was only slightly optimistic that the new President would be able to reduce unemployment or cut federal taxes "to any real extent." Most of those who said that Reagan could not accomplish these objectives felt that no President could do so, that the problem was "beyond *any* President's control."

Several of the same questions had been asked by CBS News and the *New York Times* four years earlier, at the time of Jimmy Carter's taking office in January 1977. Table 12-2 reveals that, by and large, the expectations of the American people at the time of Carter's inauguration were repeated four years later. They had felt that Jimmy Carter would clean up the welfare system and reduce unemployment, but they did not think he would be able to balance the federal budget or stop inflation. Where comparisons are available in Table 12-2, the similarities in the expectations for Reagan and for Carter are striking. In fact, in January 1977 and again in January 1981, the CBS News/*New York Times* poll asked people whether they were "generally optimistic or pessimistic" about the next four years with either Carter or Reagan as President. The results in both polls were exactly the same—69 percent optimistic, 13 percent pessimistic, and 18 percent not sure. It is clear that the public gives an incoming President the benefit of the doubt. Moreover, the election of a new President has the effect of renewing national confidence. Even if the country's major economic prob-

393

TABLE 12-2

Expectations for Carter, Reagan, and "Any President"

	January 1981 "Do you think Ronald Reagan will or will not be able to . . ."		January 1977 "Do you think Jimmy Carter will or will not be able to . . ."		January 1981 (If answer for Reagan was "will not" or "no opinion") "Do you think it's possible for any President to . . . or is that something beyond any President's control?"	
	Will	Will Not	Will	Will Not	Possible	Beyond Control
	Percentage					
. . . significantly strengthen the country's military defenses?"	88	6	—	—	—	—
. . . see to it that the United States is respected by other nations?"	87	7	—	—	—	—
. . . reduce the size of the Federal government?"	58	31	—	—	26	58
. . . clean up the welfare system?"	58	33	47	35	32	57

394

... reduce the amount of influence the Federal government has on people's lives?"	50	36	—	—	20	68
... reduce unemployment to any real extent?"	50	40	53	33	32	58
... cut Federal taxes to any real extent?"	47	42	—	—	26	65
... negotiate a treaty with the Soviet Union to reduce nuclear weapons?"[a]	37	49	30	40	—	—
... balance the Federal budget within the next four years?"	37	55	34	50	10	81
... balance the budget and cut income taxes at the same time?"	25	66	—	—	—	—
... keep prices from going up all the time?"	25	66	22	63	18	75

Source: CBS News/New York Times Poll, January 26–29, 1981.

N = 1,512.

[a] Wording of this question in January 1977 was "negotiate a treaty with the Russians to cut back on military weapons."

"—" Not asked.

lems are not expected to be solved, things are expected to get better.

The renewal of optimism can also be seen in Figure 12-1, which is based on a *Washington Post*/ABC News poll taken in February 1981. The public saw the state of the economy and their own financial situations as having deteriorated in the previous year. But the data showed a surge of optimism about the future, an improvement of over one full ladder step in the coming year for people's own financial situations and an improvement of almost *two* ladder steps for the nation's economy. As in the past, people continued to rate their own financial situations as better than the condition of the economy as a whole. What they seemed to expect for the future was that the country would begin to catch up to their own personal sense of well-being; in other words, that the news about the economy would be good.

Causes of Alienation and Cynicism

Research Findings

In the conclusion to his quantitative analysis of trends in confidence during the 1960s, James Wright notes that the attitudes of political trust and efficacy are not established early in life and, therefore, do not form a reservoir of "diffuse support" in the population that is relatively insensitive to political and social events. Rather, he emphasizes

> . . . efficacy and trust, far from being independent of outputs, seem to be rather sensitive to them: Their level appears to rise and fall *precisely* in response to those "disappointments" against which the reservoir of diffuse support is supposed to protect the system. . . . However well-inculcated these orientations may be in the early years, they can be quickly unlearned as they become discordant with the realities of adult political life.[16]

Using a two-wave panel survey of young adults and their parents taken in 1965 and 1973, Gregory Markus also found that political cynicism was sensitive to events and to positions on the major

[16] James D. Wright, *The Dissent of the Governed: Alienation and Democracy in America* (New York: Academic Press, 1976), p. 196.

Figure 12–1

Ladder-Scale Ratings, Your Financial Situation, and the State of the Nation's Economy, February 1981

Question: "Please try to picture a scale from zero to 10 where zero means the economy is in very bad shape, 10 means the economy is in very good shape, and 5 means the economy is neither particularly bad nor good. If you could choose any number between zero and 10, . . .

A. How would you rate the state of the nation's economy today?
B. How would you rate the state of the economy one year ago?
C. And what do you expect the state of the economy to be one year from now?

"Again, please picture a scale from zero to 10 where zero means your financial situation is in very bad shape, 10 means your financial situation is in very good shape, etc. . . ."

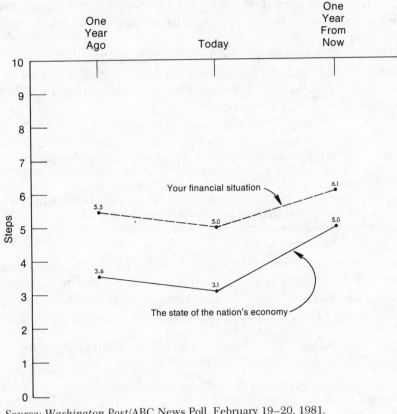

Mean Ratings for "Your Financial Situation"
and "the State of the Nation's Economy"

Source: *Washington Post*/ABC News Poll, February 19–20, 1981.
N = 1,205.

issues of the day: "The evidence indicates that a capacity for life-long political learning exists, and historical occurrences may influence basic political attitudes throughout the life cycle."[17] A study by Anne Statham Macke correlated time-series data on political alienation (1952–72) with (1) actual and perceived economic conditions, (2) situations conducive to "social discontent" (war, low church attendance, and a high proportion of young adults in the population), and (3) direct indicators of governmental performance (Presidential approval and disagreement between the President and Congress, as measured by the percentage of bills passed by the House of Representatives that had been backed by the President). She found that "alienation decreases as social discontent decreases, as economic conditions improve, and as government officials perform their jobs well."[18] Alienation is a direct response to conditions that are conducive to social, economic, and political discontent, in other words, to social changes, economic conditions, and events.

In an article analyzing "The Effects of Watergate upon Confidence in Social Institutions," Albert Bergesen and Mark Warr argued that the decline of confidence in the political arena quickly spread to other social institutions:

> The imagery here is the ripple effect, with the crisis of Watergate the stone thrown into a calm pond. The resultant crisis in confidence is represented by the waves or ripples the stone generates. It first appears at the center of the social system—the executive branch— and then moves in concentric circles through social space. The harder the stone is thrown (the greater the threat), the further the ripple extends (the more social institutions drop in confidence).[19]

Nie, Verba, and Petrocik's study of "The Changing American Voter" tried to disentangle the *sequence* of changes in political orientations that occurred between 1956 and 1972. They found, first, a "sharp rise" in political interest and involvement at the time

[17] Gregory B. Markus, "The Political Environment and the Dynamics of Public Attitudes: A Panel Study," *American Journal of Political Science* 23 (May 1979), p. 338.

[18] Anne Statham Macke, "Trends in Aggregate-Level Political Alienation," *The Sociological Quarterly* 20 (Winter 1979), pp. 77–87.

[19] Albert Bergesen and Mark Warr, "A Crisis in the Moral Order: The Effects of Watergate upon Confidence in Social Institutions," in Robert Wuthnow, ed., *The Religious Dimension: New Directions in Quantitative Research* (New York: Academic Press, 1979), p. 290.

of the 1960 election, followed in 1964 by a sudden increase in ideological polarization and in the consistency of political attitudes. The authors speculate that "the Kennedy years aroused citizen interest; the Goldwater candidacy crystallized the issue positions of that more interested citizenry."[20] And, in the late 1960s, after these two initial changes had occurred, political cynicism and disenchantment with government began to accelerate. The authors hypothesized that increased political interest might lead to an increased consistency of political attitudes, and that such increased consistency might in turn produce dissatisfaction with government. The first relationship turned out to be supported by the data: the consistency of political attitudes was found to have risen fastest among people whose level of political interest had increased most. The second relationship, however, was not supported by the data. During the late 1960s, dissatisfaction grew among *all* segments of the public, left, right, and center, and not only—or even primarily—among those with strong or consistent ideological views.[21]

A Response to Events

We suggest that the increase in political dissatisfaction was not a cognitive or ideological change; it was rather a response to events, and to the perception of events, primarily in the political sphere. The vast majority of the population was not unhappy because government policy did not correspond to their ideological predispositions. They were unhappy because political leadership was proving ineffective in dealing with massive social and political problems, like war, race relations, and the economy.

It is important to reemphasize that the decline of confidence in institutions and their leaders after 1965 initially flowed from disastrous events in the political system rather than in the economy. The growth in alienation toward established institutions, including business and labor, did not stem from specific complaints about the malfeasances of corporations or trade unions. Rather, the sequence of crises that began with the Kennedy assassination and continued through the Vietnam War, the various protest movements, Watergate, exposés of corruption in high places, and violence in American cities, all served to enhance the impression of

[20] Norman H. Nie, Sidney Verba, and John B. Petrocik, *The Changing American Voter* (Cambridge, Massachusetts: Harvard University Press, 1976), p. 283.
[21] Nie, Verba, and Petrocik, *The Changing American Voter*, pp. 284–88.

many Americans that our system was not under control. All major sources of power, particularly but not exclusively government, labor, and business, were affected by this negative assessment. Each time things quieted down momentarily, the poll data suggest that the public began to regain confidence. That happened in 1972 and early 1973, but it was soon followed by Watergate, the energy crisis, and the mid-decade recession. Another upswing occurred in 1977 when Jimmy Carter was elected, only to shift downward within a year as the country was again faced with reversals in the economy. A similar resilience characterized public opinion in the aftermath of the Reagan election in 1980, only to show signs of rapid decline toward the end of 1981 and throughout 1982 as the economic news turned bad.

James L. Sundquist has labeled the problem, aptly, a "crisis of competence" rather than a "crisis of confidence."

> A succession of adverse events has produced a generalized feeling about government far more negative than was the case fifteen or twenty years ago—the malaise about which Carter spoke. . . . The people expect the government to control events. After all, candidates for office keep promising that it can do so. They go on insisting that elections make a difference. So each time an election does not, it adds to the disillusionment.[22]

The question may be raised as to whether the events of the period in which confidence declined *had* to be interpreted negatively. The late 1960s witnessed a country deeply divided about the wisdom of sending American troops to fight in Vietnam. The eventual outcome was a triumph for the anti-war movement. Lyndon Johnson's withdrawal from the Presidential race and the ending of the war could easily be viewed as examples of the democratic system at work. Opponents of the war, though subject to harassment, were basically able to present their case and eventually to win majority support for the view that the Vietnam War was a catastrophic mistake.

The second major adverse event, Watergate, also resulted in a triumph for the system, as an irresponsible President who violated

[22] James L. Sundquist, "The Crisis of Competence in Government," in Joseph A. Pechman, ed., *Setting National Priorities: Agenda for the 1980s* (Washington, D.C.: The Brookings Institution, 1980), pp. 534–35.

the law was driven from office. The system, operating through investigative journalism and Congressional hearings, subsequently produced exposures of malfeasance by intelligence agencies and by American companies operating abroad. The result was legislation designed to curtail sharply the power of private and public agencies to engage in such activities. Few other democratic nations, if any, allow private organizations and parliamentary bodies as much access to the details of government activity as the United States does. That makes Americans more aware of improper behavior on the part of their leaders, but it also enables an outraged public to take remedial action.

The conflicts of the 1960s also fostered the growth of a variety of mass movements and citizen's action groups in the fields of race relations, women's rights, gay rights, consumer protection, environmental protection, and others. These groups exposed a variety of gross social inequities. But again, they were able to secure legislative and administrative remedies and to affect public values and behavior. From the viewpoints of these movements, much remains to be done in these and other areas; but their existence and success indicate that our democratic system works.

Hence, it is not obvious that the period from 1965 to 1980 had to have been seen as a period in which the American system, particularly its political component, failed. To the contrary, the era can be viewed as one that demonstrated that the system was responsive. To some extent, the growth of complaints about the system reflects the fact that most of the period was one of "rising expectations," that the American public generally, and various subgroups, became more sensitive to social concerns and more determined to enlarge their rights and improve their situations. Spokespersons for aggrieved groups have an incentive to emphasize the continuing defects of our society and government, not the improvements made and victories won; to call attention to the latter would run the risk of reducing the pressure for further gains. As noted earlier, the increase in group conflict that occurred in the late 1960s had the effect of increasing the volume of criticism of institutions and reducing confidence in them. Ironically, the growth of political activity, which helped to fulfill the promise of the American Creed, intensified the feeling among those on the left particularly that the system was not delivering the goods, that it was not sufficiently responsive.

Perceptions of Events

The public's reaction to events really amounts to a response to events as they are *perceived*. There is some evidence to suggest that confidence is more responsive to subjective perceptions than to objective conditions. In the Macke study of trends in alienation, the author found that objective economic indicators showed little correlation with political alienation between 1952 and 1972. "The effects of *perceived* economic conditions, however,"—as measured by subjective expectations concerning unemployment and prices —were "quite large and in the expected direction."[23]

It is not surprising that economic effects were mostly subjective, given the fact that the economy remained prosperous during the period covered by Macke's research. Another study by Donald Kinder focused on the period between 1972 and 1978, i.e., the years of the economic downturn of the 1970s. Kinder correlated presidential popularity with two types of indicators of economic conditions: "pocketbook economic discontents," that is, people's sense of financial well-being and their experiences with unemployment, and what he labeled "sociotropic economic judgments," their evaluation of the economic condition of the country as a whole and the economic performance of the government. Kinder's finding was that "sociotropic judgments" had the stronger and more consistent impact on presidential job ratings. People exhibit a "bending toward the social," as opposed to the purely personal, in making political judgments. Even in a period of severe economic decline such as the 1970s, Kinder found that "in evaluating the president, citizens seem to pay principal attention to the nation's economic predicament, and comparatively little to their own."[24] They do not ask "How are things going for me personally?" but "How are things going for the country?" when making political judgments.

This finding is consistent with the data presented earlier in this chapter and in Chapter 5 showing that people's assessment of their own personal well-being remained high, even while their confidence in institutions and their optimism about the country as a whole were deteriorating. Confidence in institutions seems to be more a social than a personal judgment. People's assessment of the situation in the country is to a considerable extent indepen-

[23] Macke, "Trends in Aggregate-Level Political Alienation," p. 82.
[24] Donald R. Kinder, "Presidents, Prosperity, and Public Opinion," *Public Opinion Quarterly* 45 (Spring 1981), p. 17.

dent of their judgment of how things are going in their own lives —even including their own economic well-being. The obvious question is, where do "sociotropic" judgments come from? How are assessments of the conditions of society and the quality of leadership made? Are such judgments reliable?

The Impact of the Media

One major source—perhaps *the* major source—of information concerning the condition of the country is, of course, the mass media. Recent research has found strong and direct links between political cynicism and exposure to negative information in the media. Michael Robinson developed a theory of "videomalaise" linking political distrust and cynicism to public affairs programming on television. Using an experimental design, Robinson found that exposure to a controversial CBS News television documentary that was critical of military policy, "The Selling of the Pentagon," lowered viewers' sense of political self-confidence. He also used survey evidence to demonstrate that reliance on television as a source of news increased "(a) social distrust, (b) political cynicism, (c) political inefficacy, (d) partisan disloyalty, and (e) third party viability."[25]

Note the evidence in Table 12-3 from Robinson's study. A sense of political efficacy is a strong function of education; the percentage who score *low* on the efficacy scale declines sharply with education. But media use has an independent impact on efficacy: among people at each educational level, the greater the dependence on television as the primary source of political information, the lower the sense of political efficacy (that is, the larger the proportion scoring "low" on the efficacy scale).

A later study by Miller, Goldenberg, and Erbring took this line of analysis one step further by looking at the relationship between political trust and efficacy and the actual *content* of news stories. Their finding was that exposure to a greater degree of political criticism in the newspapers led to lower levels of political efficacy and, even more markedly, to lower levels of political trust. They measured "degree of criticism" in different newspapers, not in terms of how critical of government policy or leadership the news-

[25] Michael J. Robinson, "Public Affairs Television and the Growth of Political Malaise: The Case of 'The Selling of the Pentagon,'" *American Political Science Review* 70 (March 1976), p. 425.

TABLE 12–3

Political Efficacy by Media Use, Controlling for Education, 1968

Education	Primary Source of Political Information		
	Television Only	Television Principally	Other News Media
	Percentage Low on Political Efficacy Index		
Grade school	82	74	64
High school	48	41	36
Some college	46	26	24
College graduate	25	18	14

Source: Michael J. Robinson, "Public Affairs Television and the Growth of Political Malaise: The Case of 'The Selling of the Pentagon,'" *American Political Science Review* 70 (March 1976), p. 418. Data are from the University of Michigan, Survey Research Center, 1968. American National Election Study. N = 1,113.

paper was, but in terms of how frequently the newspaper reported *any* negative statements about officeholders, institutions, parties, and policies. "Degree of criticism" meant the tendency to report political conflict and controversy. The authors concluded that "the presentation of news in a manner that conveys a high degree of political conflict or criticism leads to a sense of distrust and inefficacy among newspaper readers."[26]

They found that the effect of critical information on political *trust* was stronger than the effect on political *efficacy*. Efficacy reflects normative beliefs about the legitimacy of institutional arrangements and the responsiveness of government ("I don't think public officials care much what people like me think"). Trust measures performance more than legitimacy ("Do you think the people in the government waste a lot of the money we pay in taxes . . . ?").

One implication of these findings is that political distrust may have increased after 1965 because the gross level of "criticism" rose, that is, there was a greater amount of conflict and controversy to report. This is consistent with the Nie, Verba, and Petrocik finding that ideological polarization increased in 1964, just prior to the massive decline of confidence in institutions. Conflicts among social groups, racial groups, political parties, branches of govern-

[26] Arthur H. Miller, Edie N. Goldenberg, and Lutz Erbring, "Type-Set Politics: Impact of Newspapers on Public Confidence," *American Political Science Review* 73 (March 1979), p. 77.

ment, and interest groups became more intense and had the effect of raising the total volume of "critical information" reaching newspaper readers and television watchers. If conflict and controversy represent "bad news," then the amount of "bad news" no doubt increased, with the likely effects identified in the research just reported. Moreover, for reasons already discussed, interest group leaders had an incentive to maintain a high level of "criticism" even when progress was being made and battles won, simply because negative information continued to justify their position.

Robinson took this argument one step further. He argued that there was not only more "conflict and controversy" to report, but that television news in particular has an inherent bias toward reporting negative and critical information. In other words, "video-malaise" was as much the product of the medium as of the message. Here is his description of this effect:

> The highly credible television news organizations have been compelled to bombard the American television audience with interpretive, sensational, aggressive, and anti-institutional news items. This content reaches and holds a unique audience, larger and more volatile than that attracted by any other medium. Many of the members of this unique audience are inadvertent to it. These inadvertent viewers tend to lack political sophistication: they cannot cope well with the type of news and information that the networks provide. But because the networks are too credible to be dismissed in their messages, these viewers respond to the content by growing more cynical, more frustrated, more despairing; they become increasingly less enamored of their social and political institutions.[27]

Robinson sees a kind of Gresham's law operating in television news reporting: the bad news drives out the good.

Thus the biases of the news media, particularly television, may have exacerbated the impression of a negative turn of events. The special impact of television is that it delivers the news to a much larger and "inadvertent" audience than was the case before television, when only a limited segment of the population chose to follow news about politics and government.

When people read newspapers and magazines, they edit the information by skipping over articles about subjects they are not interested in. Television news watchers, however, are exposed to everything.

[27] Robinson, "Public Affairs Television," p. 426.

It is undeniably true that the quantity of "bad news" has been great in recent years, and the media have had a duty to report it. But television seems to display a proclivity for reporting "bad news," especially scandals, conflict, and controversy, all of which make "good video." Still, the fact remains that events did take a decidedly negative turn after 1964. Public life was marked by greater conflict and contentiousness, and there was seldom a sustained period of good news to report in either the domestic or foreign spheres. The country, as President Carter complained, became harder to govern. But the problem has emerged in part because our Presidents since 1964 have been unable to convince the nation that they had the ability to lead. Three Presidents, Franklin D. Roosevelt, Harry S Truman and John F. Kennedy, apparently were able to convey the impression, at least in retrospect, that they had the situation under control and were leading the country effectively. In a survey taken in late 1979, the Gallup Poll inquired, "Of all the Presidents we have ever had, who do you wish were President today?" Kennedy and Roosevelt headed the list, with Truman third. Younger persons, those under 45, preferred Kennedy, while older ones named Roosevelt. Few mentioned any of the four most recent Presidents, Johnson, Nixon, Ford, or Carter.

Similar results were obtained by a March 1980 CBS News/*New York Times* poll that inquired: "Looking back on past Presidents, living or dead, which *one* of them would you want to have running this country today?" This time, Truman placed second, following Kennedy, with Roosevelt a close third. Johnson, Nixon, and Ford were each cited by only 2 or 3 percent, while only 1 percent preferred Carter. When asked for the reasons behind their choice, the three most commonly mentioned were "handled government, domestic problems" (30 percent), "strong, decisive" (17 percent), and "leadership" (9 percent). The public definitely feels—in retrospect—that we used to have better leaders than we do now.

The Impact of National Decline

In concluding this book, we do not want to leave the reader with the impression that the problems facing the country are solely or primarily a result of the way the media handle the news or are the possibly fortuitous consequences of our having had a series of inadequate Presidents. There have been changes for the worse in the American condition and people are responding to an awareness of them. There is simply less for the country to feel confident about. Internationally, the power and influence of the United States have declined since the Vietnam War. That monumental disaster was followed by a change in the relative power positions of the United States and the Soviet Union, which the public became conscious of in the mid-1970s. Support for large increases in the military budget and fearfulness over the possible outbreak of World War III both grew considerably as a result. More important, perhaps, for a long-range interpretation of the public's malaise has been the steadily increasing anxiety about the nation's economic future, the possibility that the energy crisis may bring an end to economic growth and its consequent improvements in the standard of living, the acceptance by sizable majorities of the view that inflation cannot be permanently brought under control, and, more recently, concern about high rates of unemployment.

These opinions correspond to reality, for not only did the rate of inflation reach its highest point in post–World-War-II history in 1978–81, while unemployment, in 1981–82, climbed to the highest levels since the war, but the 1970s were also characterized by a falloff in the rate of economic growth, from an average of 4.3 percent per year between 1960 and 1969 down to 2.8 percent per year between 1969 and 1978. During 1978 and 1979, growth in gross labor productivity was halted. Daniel Yankelovich and Bernard Lefkowitz have effectively described the way these developments affected the country's mood:

> From an expectation of steady growth, ever increasing abundance, continuing improvement in the individual's standard of living, stable prices, and jobs for all who want to work, the majority has shifted grounds to expect economic instability: recession, depression, continued inflation, joblessness, and shortages. . . .
>
> The individual's perception of ever narrowing limits is most clearly expressed in the response to two survey statements. One is: "Our current standard of living may be the highest we can hope for." In 1979, a 67 percent cross section of Americans agreed entirely or in part with that statement. The other statement is: "Americans should get used to the fact that our wealth is limited and most of us are not likely to become better off than we are now." In 1979, 62% of the American public agreed with that statement. Moreover, such agreement is virtually uniform across all demographic groupings. . . .

> An impressive 72% of the public concur with the view: "We are
> fast coming to a turning point in our history where the 'land of plenty'
> is becoming the land of want."[28]

Yankelovich and Lefkowitz go on to summarize the main concerns of Americans as revealed in the polls: "a scarcity of essential
resources; mounting personal debt; unjustified corporate profits;
the high cost of medical treatment; hazardous working conditions;
deterioration of the environment; excessive and wasteful government spending; and the dangers posed by certain forms of technology, particularly nuclear energy." But, as they also emphasize,
"One concern that always tops the list is inflation. . . . After a decade of rising inflation rates, most Americans don't believe they
can win the battle against inflation."[29]

The 1979 Seasonwein-Union Carbide survey reaffirmed these
findings that Americans are pessimistic about the prospects for
economic growth in the future. When asked for their opinion about
developments in the next five years, a plurality, 46 percent, anticipated "not too much" or "no growth" during the first half of the
1980s, 29 percent said the economy would grow "a fair amount,"
while only 19 percent expected a great deal or a good deal of
growth. When asked in an open-ended question about the consequences of "no growth," almost half, 48 percent, volunteered the
answer, "unemployment," while 25 percent said "decreased buy-
ing power" or a "lower standard of living." Given these views, it is
not surprising that 61 percent of this sample also held the view
that things are going "pretty badly" or "very badly" in the country.

The issues on the public's mind are obviously real ones. The
responses of government and other major institutions have not
convinced most people that the situation is under control. Yet, as
we have seen, in spite of their pessimism, Americans do feel that
things can be improved with the right leadership. The malaise that
so troubled Jimmy Carter may actually have the effect of raising
public support for new policies. That appeared to have happened
with the election of Ronald Reagan: the public in the first half of

[28] Daniel Yankelovich and Bernard Lefkowitz, "The Public Debate on Growth: Preparing for Resolution" (Mitchell Award Paper, presented at the Third Biennial Woodlands Conference on Growth Policy, The Woodlands, Texas, October 28–31, 1979),
pp. 5, 19–20, 26.

[29] Yankelovich and Lefkowitz, "The Public Debate on Growth," p. 47.

1981 expressed doubts about the wisdom of many of Reagan's specific economic proposals, but overall support for the new Administration's program remained high, presumably because people were impressed by the fact that leadership was being shown and a comprehensive solution was finally being proposed to combat inflation. Not surprisingly, support for Reagan and his economic program declined sharply in 1982 in tandem with a rapidly worsening economic situation. This decline, predictably, brought about renewed criticism of governmental and economic institutions. Most disturbing was the fact that throughout 1982 evaluations of his performance as President fell below those given to each elected President since Dwight D. Eisenhower in polls taken at the same point in their administrations. Still, such a change in response to circumstances does not contradict the evidence from the first two years of the new Administration that, following fifteen years of frustration and setbacks, the American people have not lost their capacity for optimism.

The principal reason, as we have noted, is that Americans still believe in the legitimacy and vitality of the American system. What bothers the public is the apparent growth of concentrations of power and the cynical, self-interested abuse of power by government, business, and labor leaders, developments that, among other things, appear to cause inflation, lower growth rates, and other problems. Accurately or not, most people continue to see these developments as aberrations, not as structural problems. There is still an enormous reservoir of trust in the basic economic and political order. In March and November 1981, two polls taken by Civic Service and Roper reported that 90–92 percent said that the United States is "the very best place in the world to live;" 80–81 percent felt that "the United States has a special role to play in the world today," rather than being "pretty much like other countries"; and 78–81 percent answered that they were "extremely proud . . . to be an American." And although, as noted in Chapter 5, black Americans have exhibited high levels of resentment toward Ronald Reagan and have felt particularly neglected by the changes he has proposed, the great majority of them have also remained positive about the promise of America. As Everett Ladd, reporting on the March study noted: "76 percent of black respondents nationally stated . . . that they thought the United States had a special role to play in the world; 86 percent said the U.S. is the best place in the world to live; and 64 percent were 'extremely proud' to be Americans, while 29 percent said 'somewhat proud' and only 5 percent 'not proud at all.' "[30]

In the spring of 1982, the initial results of a major international survey undertaken to compare fundamental values in different countries were released. Gallup International had conducted parallel surveys in eleven countries in 1981 on behalf of the European Value Systems Study Group and the Value Systems Study Group of the Americas. The surveys included Gallup's confidence question (see Table 2-2) for the same ten institutions in each country: the police, the armed forces, the legal system, the educational system, the churches or organized religion, the press, labor unions, major companies, the civil service, and the parliament or Congress. Confidence in business ("major companies") was higher in the United States than in all the other countries. The overall level of confidence turned out to be higher in the United States than in any other country surveyed except Ireland. After Ireland and the United States came Britain, Denmark, Spain, West Germany, Belgium, Holland, France, Japan, and Italy, in that order. Thus, it appears that while U.S. confidence levels have certainly been declining, Americans still show more faith in their institutional order than the citizens of almost every other major country in the free world.

One reason why most Americans still feel positive about the country is that, in spite of all the troubles the country has gone through, the overwhelming majority say that things have gone well for them in their lifetime and that they are doing better than their parents did. The *Washington Post* asked a national sample in April 1980 to react to the statement, "Think of your parents when they were your age—would you say you are better off financially than they were or not?" Eighty-eight percent replied better off, compared to 10 percent who said they were worse off. Continued high rates of inflation led growing numbers of people to report that their real income or standard of living was declining, but still at the end of March 1981, when the *Washington Post*/ABC News poll repeated the question, 65 percent said they were better off financially than their parents, compared to 35 percent who said

[30] Everett Carll Ladd, "The American 'Sense of Nation,' 1981," in Martin Christadler, ed., *Political Culture in the United States in the Seventies: Continuity and Change* (Frankfurt Am Main: Zentrum fuer Nordamerika-Forschung, Johann Wolfgang Goethe-Universitaet, 1981), pp. 14a–f, 16.

they were not. Perhaps even more indicative of the public's positive state of mind is the way a *Washington Post* cross section responded in February 1980 to the choice between two statements: "All in all, I'd have to say that life has been unfair to me—or—All in all, I've had my share of good breaks." Overwhelmingly, by 85 to 6 percent, the interviewees felt that they had experienced their "share of good breaks." The persistent disparity between public pessimism and personal optimism has, we feel, contributed in no small measure to the ability of our institutions to withstand the growth of cynicism and distrust.

Yet, we must report that as this book goes to press, the "malaise" that characterized most of the Carter years did not lift during the first year of the Reagan Administration. Although confidence in "the White House" and the "executive branch" were higher in Harris's September 1981 survey than in the last confidence poll conducted during Carter's presidency, the ratings were nevertheless lower than in confidence surveys taken during Carter's first year in office. More significant, however, is the fact that in 1981, unlike 1977, increased confidence in the presidency did not carry over to other institutions. The Harris, Gallup, and ORC polls reported a continuing decline in the average level of confidence for non-political institutions in 1981. By the fall of 1982, with unemployment over 10 percent, confidence in the leaders of ten institutions had reached the lowest level ever recorded in any survey, averaging 21 percent in the Harris poll. And, as noted earlier, by the end of Reagan's first year in office, the public turned on him, disapproving of his record in office, and feeling that he had been unable to improve the economy. Disapproval accelerated during his second year, and the Republicans experienced substantial losses in the 1982 midterm elections. Seemingly, Americans look for a quick fix to their problems.

Although we have pointed to evidence that Americans retain faith in their social system, it would be wrong not to indicate our belief that the situation is much more *brittle* than it was at the end of the 1920s, just before the Great Depression, or in 1965, immediately preceding the unrest occasioned by the Vietnam War and the outbreak of racial tension. These two troubled eras, each of which resulted in a decline of faith in institutions, followed periods of high legitimacy. The United States enters the 1980s, however, with a lower reserve of confidence in the ability of its institutional leaders to deal with the problems of the polity, the society, and the economy than at any time in this century. As a result of the strains produced by the experiences of the last fifteen years, our institutional structure is less resilient than in the past. Should the 1980s be characterized by a major crisis, the outcome could very well be substantial support for movements seeking to change the system in a fundamental way. Serious setbacks in the economy or in foreign policy, accompanied by a failure of leadership, would raise greater risks of a loss of legitimacy now than at any time in this century. Although the evidence on the surface seems reassuring, there are disturbing signs of deep and serious discontent.

Index of
Poll Results

ABC News/Harris Survey; *see also*
  Harris Survey; ABC News/
  Washington Post Poll
  1977: 387–389
  1978: 346, 381–382, 386
  1979: 348, 386–391
ABC News/*Washington Post* Poll;
  see also ABC News/Harris
  Survey; *Washington Post* Poll
  1981: 150, 213, 234, 347, 350,
  397, 410–411
Advertising Council
  1974: 239
American Council on Education
  1977: 287
Associated Press Poll, *see* NBC
  News/Associated Press Poll

Cambridge Reports, Inc. (CRI)
  1974: 25, 131–132, 136,
  140–143, 267–268
  1974–81: 140–141, 146–148, 267
  1975: 25, 115, 131–133, 136,
  140–143, 170, 236, 238, 250,
  260–262, 265–266, 268–269,
  287
  1976: 25, 86, 115, 131–132, 136,
  140–143, 170, 174–176, 185,
  189, 202, 207, 209, 214, 236,
  238, 258–259, 260–264, 266,
  268, 282–283, 287
  1977: 115, 131–132, 135–136,
  143, 145, 170, 171, 236, 238,
  258–259, 266, 287

  1978: 131–132, 136, 139, 143,
  166, 191, 202, 207, 211, 215,
  226, 230, 235, 252, 258–259,
  355
  1979: 65–66, 131–132, 136–139,
  143, 175, 226, 230, 232, 235–
  236, 238, 250, 258–259, 287
  1980: 131–134, 136, 143, 226–
  227, 246–247, 258–259, 268,
  281
  1981: 131–132, 134, 143
Cambridge Survey Research, Inc.
  1978: 354
CBS News/*New York Times* Poll
  1976: 341
  1977: 153, 393–395
  1978: 236, 346
  1979: 129, 149, 339
  1980: 153, 234, 236, 348, 406
  1981: 153–154, 211, 392–395
Center for Political Studies, *see*
  Survey Research Center
Civic Service, Inc.
  1980: 92–96, 380, 382
  1981: 204, 227, 229–230, 266,
  283, 285, 409–410

E. I. du Pont de Nemours and
  Company
  1975: 361, 363

Fingerhut/Granados Opinion
  Research
  1977: 202, 354–355

415

Gallup Poll
  1935: 223
  1936: 203, 284
  1937: 203, 283
  1939: 203
  1940: 203, 223
  1941: 203, 215
  1947: 203
  1949: 203
  1950: 113
  1953: 203, 353
  1956: 112
  1957: 203, 216, 353
  1959: 203
  1960: 346
  1961: 203, 225
  1962: 203, 225
  1963: 112, 203
  1963–71: 113–114
  1965: 39, 203, 206, 210
  1966: 228
  1967: 203, 208
  1968: 208, 212
  1970: 228–229, 234
  1973: 57, 203
  1975: 57, 71–72, 382
  1976: 216–217, 234
  1977: 57, 71, 90, 112, 208, 216–
    217, 228, 233, 254
  1978: 128, 203, 233, 345
  1979: 57–58, 126–127, 203, 234,
    345, 391, 406
  1980: 57–58, 82–83, 150, 234,
    348, 350
  1981: 39, 57–58, 71, 150, 203–
    204, 208, 216–217, 228, 234,
    254–255, 345, 349–350
  1982: 410
General Electric Company
  1973: 179

Harris Survey; *see also* ABC News/
  Harris Survey
  1966: 41–42, 47–48, 50, 54, 56,
    63–64, 68–69, 111
  1966–81: 200, 352
  1967: 42, 48, 50, 54, 56, 63–64,
    68
  1970: 201–202
  1971: 48, 50–51, 54, 56, 63–64,
    68
  1972: 48, 50–51, 54, 56, 63–64,
    68, 166

  1973: 45, 48, 50–51, 54, 56, 63–
    64, 68, 82
  1974: 45, 49–51, 54, 56, 63–64,
    68, 201–202, 226, 266, 368
  1974–77: 226
  1975: 43, 49–50, 54, 56, 63–64,
    68, 201–202, 238, 249–250,
    260–262, 266
  1976: 45, 49–50, 54, 56, 63–64,
    68, 83, 170, 185, 189–190, 194,
    202, 218–219, 230, 240–241,
    244–248, 250–251, 253–254,
    258, 260–262, 268, 273, 285–
    286, 357–358
  1977: 45, 49–50, 54, 56, 63–64,
    68, 84, 90, 111, 165–166, 189,
    226, 230, 258, 285–286
  1978: 45, 49–50, 54, 56, 63–64,
    68, 111, 245
  1979: 45, 49–50, 52, 54, 56, 63–
    64, 68, 234, 266, 268
  1980: 45, 49–50, 52–54, 56, 63–
    64, 68, 70, 111, 167, 234, 246,
    266, 370–371
  1981: 50, 53–56, 63–64, 68–69,
    165, 167–168, 200, 204, 227,
    251, 275–281, 368, 370–371
  1982: 53, 411
Hart, Peter D., Research Associates,
  Inc., *see* Peter D. Hart Research
  Associates, Inc.

Institute for International Social
  Research
  1959: 131–136, 138, 142, 156
  1959–64: 141
  1964: 131–132, 136, 142, 157

Los Angeles Times Poll
  1978: 344–345
  1980: 200, 213
  1981: 204, 213, 227, 229, 355

National Family Opinion
  1975: 165, 177–178, 180–181,
    202, 255
National Opinion Research Center
  (NORC), University of Chicago
  1945: 224
  1966: 114
  1972: 112, 386
  1972–80: 114–115, 127

1973: 45, 48, 50, 54, 56, 63–64, 68, 110, 291–295, 297–298, 316
1973–77: 98–107, 117–125,128
1973–80: 352
1974: 45, 48, 50–51, 54, 56, 63–64, 68, 110, 112, 127, 291–295, 297–298, 316
1974–77: 106
1975: 45, 49–50, 54, 56, 63–64, 68, 127, 291–295, 297–298, 316
1976: 45, 49–50, 52, 54, 56, 63–64, 68, 110, 291–295, 297–298, 316
1977: 45, 49–50, 52, 54, 56, 63–64, 68, 110–124, 291, 297–298, 316
1978: 45, 49–50, 54, 56, 63–64, 68, 124, 127
1979: 45
1980: 45, 49–50, 52, 56, 63–64, 68, 70, 110, 127, 349, 386
1982: 53
NBC News Poll; *see also* NBC News/Associated Press Poll
1978: 213
1979: 346
1980: 213, 235
NBC News/Associated Press Poll; *see also* NBC News Poll
1979: 127
1980: 153
1981: 154, 233
New York Times Poll, *see* CBS News/*New York Times* Poll

Opinion Research Corporation (ORC)
1959: 29–30, 33–34, 36, 38, 258, 299
1961: 29–30, 33, 36, 38, 258, 299
1961–69: 116
1963: 30, 33, 36, 38, 258, 299
1965: 29–31, 33, 35–39, 258, 299
1967: 30, 33, 35–38, 181–182, 258, 299, 300
1969: 30, 33, 35–38, 181–182, 258, 299
1971: 30, 33, 35–38, 181–182, 258, 299
1971–81: 177

1973: 30–33, 36–38, 113, 170–171, 180–182, 258, 299
1973–79: 116
1974: 88
1975: 30–33, 36–38, 60, 78, 113, 171, 181–182, 217–218, 258, 264, 299
1976: 191, 255, 258
1977: 30–31, 33–39, 59–60, 78, 113, 182, 190, 217–218, 258, 299, 300
1978: 212, 227–228, 239, 242–243
1979: 30–33, 59–61, 78, 171, 180–182, 191, 212, 214, 217–218, 229, 258, 299, 339
1980: 227–228, 231–232, 237, 243, 248, 252–253
1981: 30–34, 59–61, 78, 177–178, 217–218, 258, 299
Opinion Research Survey
1980: 203, 205

Penn + Schoen Associates
1980: 207–208
Peter D. Hart Research Associates, Inc.
1975: 170, 265
Potomac Associates
1971: 131, 136, 142, 157
1971–72: 143
1972: 131, 136, 142
1976: 149–150
Procter & Gamble Company
1975: 81–82, 179, 181, 209

Research & Forecasts, Inc.
1980: 346
Roger Seasonwein Poll
1975: 167, 253
1977: 252–253
1978: 167, 191, 252
1979: 88, 171, 189, 214–215, 237, 243, 252–253, 274–275, 277–279, 408
Roper Organization
1939: 152–153
1942: 283
1948: 224–225
1952: 225
1960: 346
1971–80: 128
1973: 87

Roper Organization (*cont.*)
1974: 27–28, 87, 231, 266–267, 285
1974–80: 231
1975: 167, 171–173, 177, 200, 214–216, 244, 288
1976: 165, 167, 171, 189, 201
1977: 28, 87, 172–173, 177, 200–201, 211, 214–215, 218, 244, 269–272
1978: 137, 150, 165, 167, 187, 193–194, 207–208, 216, 235, 288, 346
1979: 167, 171–172, 177, 187, 193, 218, 235, 268
1980: 84–85, 174, 192, 201, 231, 235, 244
1981: 28, 165, 171, 208, 216, 218, 233, 244, 251, 255, 269, 288, 385, 409

Seasonwein, Roger, Poll, *see* Roger Seasonwein Poll
Survey Research Center (SRC)/ Center for Political Studies (CPS), University of Michigan
1947–59: 116
1952: 21–22, 26
1954: 21
1955: 21–22, 26, 115
1957: 111
1958: 16–17, 33–34, 115
1958–78: 333
1959: 16
1960: 16, 21–22, 26, 115
1960–69: 116
1961: 16
1962: 16, 115
1963: 16
1964: 16–17, 19, 21–24, 26, 33, 109, 115
1965: 16, 25
1966: 16, 19, 21, 109
1967: 16
1968: 16–17, 21–22, 24–26, 33, 109, 404
1968–72: 113
1969: 16
1970: 16–19, 21–23, 25, 33
1970–79: 116
1971: 16–17, 109
1972: 17–19, 21–22, 25–27, 33, 109, 128–129, 210

1973: 73, 109
1974: 17–19, 21–22, 24–25, 32–33, 109
1975: 381
1976: 17–19, 21–22, 25–28, 33, 206–207, 209–210, 302–327, 329–331, 346–347
1978: 17–19, 21–26, 33, 79, 343–344
1980: 17–18, 22–26, 32–34, 116, 209, 349
1981: 116, 150

U.S. News and World Report
1975: 178, 212, 217
1976: 151
1977: 178, 180–181, 212, 217, 359

Washington Post Poll; *see also* ABC News/*Washington Post* Poll
1980: 268, 410–411

Yankelovich, Skelly & White, Inc. (YSW); *see also* Yankelovich, Skelly & White/*Time* Magazine Poll
1968: 182–183
1969: 182–183
1970: 182–183
1971: 183
1972: 182–183
1973: 182–183
1974: 182–183
1974–75: 129
1975: 182–183, 242, 285
1976: 15, 178, 182–183, 242, 285, 364–365
1977: 15, 168, 182–183, 188, 242, 285
1977–80: 178, 207
1978: 166, 172, 183, 186, 194, 218, 242, 285, 346, 364–365
1979: 183, 201, 242, 285, 407–408
1980: 183, 242, 285
1981: 183, 285, 350
Yankelovich, Skelly & White/*Time* Magazine; *see also* Yankelovich, Skelly & White, Inc.
1981: 255

General
Index

ABC News/Harris polls; *see also*
    Harris polls, ABC News/
    Washington Post polls;
    Index of Poll Results
  on confidence in nation, 386–392,
    396
  on Congress, 381–382
  on government spending, 346,
    348
ABC News/*Washington Post* polls;
    see also ABC News/Harris polls;
    Washington Post polls; Index of
    Poll Results
  on blacks, expectations of, 151
  on confidence in institutions, 58–
    59
  on financial satisfaction, 396, 397,
    411
  on government regulation, 234
  on government spending, 347,
    350
  on inflation, 213–214
Abscam scandals, 173
Adams, Abigail, 1–2
Adams, John, 1–2
Advertising, 231, 233
  corporate image, 365–366
  executives, 201, 217
Advertising Council survey, on
    government regulation, 239,
    241; *see also* Index of Poll
    Results

Age, confidence in institutions and,
    101, 122–124
Air controllers' strike, 204
Airline industry, 186–198, 232,
    233
Alcoa Corporation, 35–38
Alienation, 3, 110–111, 329, 330,
    340–342
  causes of, 396–412
Almond, Gabriel, 19
Aluminum industry, 35–38
American Council on Education,
    287; *see also* Index of Poll
    Results
American Enterprise Institute,
    269
American Federation of Labor/
    Congress of Industrial
    Organizations (AFL/CIO), 205–
    206, 247, 354, 355, 357
American Federation of State,
    County, and Municipal
    Employees, 356
American Federation of Teachers,
    356
American National Election Survey
    (1976), 301–310, 313, 317,
    320, 323, 325, 330–331
American National Election Survey
    (1978), 343, 344
American Retail Federation, 354
American Revolution, 1–2

American Telephone and Telegraph
Company, 35, 39
Amoco Oil Company, 35–37, 39
Anderson, John, 295
Andrews, Frank M., 129n
Anomia, 110, 119
Armed forces, see Military
Associated Press, see NBC News/
Associated Press polls
Australia, 370–371
Austria, 369
Automobile industry, 35–38, 186–
198, 230, 231
  alternative forms of government
  control of, 270–273

Banking industry, 57, 60, 61, 71, 72,
74, 75, 77–79, 83–84, 184,
186–198, 217, 218, 230, 231,
284, 367
Barton, Eugenia, 381n
Belgium, 410
Bergesen, Albert, 398
Blacks
  confidence in institutions, 100–
  101, 122–123
  expectations for future, 149–151
  financial satisfaction, 116–117
  on state of nation, 409–410
Bolling, Richard, 338–339
Borrowing, 120–121
Brooks, J. G., 377n
Brotherhood of Carpenters, 356
Brown, Edmund G., 351
Building contractors, 217
Business, 163–198; see also
  Government regulation;
  Industries; Labor unions;
  Legitimacy
  comparison of anti-government
  and anti-business sentiment,
  32–34
  confidence in foreign countries,
  369–371
  consequences of decline in
  confidence in, 357–374
  direct efforts to improve image of,
  365–367
  disdain for money-making and,
  174–176
  educational campaigns, 361–365
  ethical practices, 77–79, 164

future of, 371–374
history of confidence levels, 367–
369
inflation and, 211–215
job opportunities, 165, 166
labor unions, attitudes toward,
39–40
leaders, 172–173, 215, 217, 218
morality and self-interest issue,
169–172
power issue, 164
profits, attitudes toward, see
Profits
small vs. big companies, 39–40,
86, 164
social and political bases of
attitudes toward, 291–334
technical and economic
accomplishments, 164–165
trends in attitudes toward, 29–32
Business Roundtable, 361
Butler, David, 101n

Cambridge Reports, Inc. (CRI)
polls, 25, 257; see also Index of
Poll Results
on attitudes toward business,
174–175
classification of respondent types,
144–148
on concentration of power in
industries, 185, 189
on consumer protection, 246,
249–252
on divestiture, 258–263
favorability ratings of industries,
191
on financial satisfaction, 115,
116
on free enterprise, 285, 287
on government regulation, 226,
230, 232, 234, 236, 238
on inflation, 65–66
on labor unions, 215, 354, 355
on morality and self-interest in
business, 170, 171
on personal satisfaction, 130–134,
166
on productivity and economic
growth, 274, 281
on small vs. big companies, 86
on socialism, 282, 283

on state of economy, 141
on state of nation, 136, 138
on wage and price controls,
178
Cambridge Survey Research, Inc.
polls, *see* Index of Poll Results
Campbell's Soup, 39
Cantril, Albert H., 137, 139, 150,
346
Cantril, Hadley, 130
Cantril, Susan D., 137, 139, 150,
346
*Capitalism, Socialism, and
Democracy* (Schumpeter), 80
Car salesmen, 217
Carnegie, Andrew, 176
Carter, Jimmy, 19, 406, 408
confidence in presidency, 25, 28,
31, 52, 53, 55, 59, 153, 158,
393–395, 406, 411
"malaise" speech (July 1979), 9,
13, 18, 139, 156, 338, 339
CBS News/*New York Times* polls,
58; *see also* Index of Poll
Results
on Carter administration, 393–
395
classification of respondent types,
149
on crisis of confidence, 339
on financial satisfaction, 129
on government regulation, 234,
236, 237
on government spending, 346,
348
on inflation, 153
on labor unions, 206–207, 211
on presidents, 406
on Reagan administration, 392–
395
on voter participation, 341
Center for Political Studies (CPS) of
the University of Michigan
polls, 16, 18n, 19, 24, 27, 28,
32
American National Election
Survey (1976), 301–310, 313,
317, 320, 323, 325, 330–331
American National Election
Survey (1978), 343, 344
on government spending, 343,
346–347, 349
on labor unions, 204, 206

on voter participation, 340
on workingmen, 209, 210
Checks and balances, 6, 379–380
Chemical industry, 35–38, 186–
198, 230
alternative forms of government
control of, 270–273
image, efforts to improve, 365
Chrysler Corporation, 39
Cigarette and tobacco industry,
186–198, 251
Citizen's duty, 25, 26–27
Citrin, Jack, 13–14, 329n, 330, 332,
341
Civic Service, Inc., polls, 91–95; *see
also* Index of Poll Results
on Congress, 382
on free enterprise, 285
on government regulation, 227,
228
on labor unions, 204
on nationalization, 266
on political power, 380
on socialism, 282–283
on state of nation, 409
Civil Rights, 295
Clean Air Act, 243–244
Clergy, 217, 383
College teachers, 217
Communications Workers of
America, 356
Competition, 88
Computer industry, 186–198
Congress, confidence in, 42–55, 57,
58, 60, 62–64, 67–73, 75, 77–
79, 98–99, 123–124, 217, 292,
381–382
Conservatives, 159, 235, 294, 316–
321, 323–327, 329, 333, 344,
363, 373
Consumer movement, 245–248
Consumer Product Safety
Commission, 251
Consumer protection, 232, 233,
243–255, 401
Converse, Philip E., 20, 22, 109n
Corporate Marketing Research
Section of the du Pont
Company, 361–363
Corruption, 173, 174, 216, 218,
241
Crisis of authority, 1–2
Criticism, sensitivity to, 376–378

Cynicism, 16–18, 375
  causes of, 396–412

Democrats, 103–106, 124–125,
  221–222, 230, 292, 294, 295,
  297, 298, 321, 324–332, 343,
  344, 371–372
Denmark, 410
Department stores, 230
Deregulation, 232–233
Differentiated quality of public
  confidence, 159
Divestiture, 257–265, 270–273
Doctors, *see* Medical profession
Dotson, Jean D., 109*n*
Dow Chemical Corporation, 35–38
Drug industry, 186–198, 231

E. I. du Pont de Nemours and
  Company, 35–38, 361–363; *see
  also* Index of Poll Results
Eastman Kodak Company, 36
Easton, David, 159
Ebony, 150–151
Economic growth, 274–282, 407,
  408
Economy; *see also* Inflation
  confidence and, 61–66
  impact on personal satisfaction,
  139–154
Edison, Thomas, 176
Education
  attitudes toward business, labor,
  and government by, 99–101,
  120–123, 292–293, 298–299,
  304–307, 310–312, 315, 316,
  319, 328
  confidence in leaders of, 42–44,
  45*n*, 46–55, 57, 58, 60, 63, 64,
  67–79, 383
  political efficacy and, 19–20
  voter participation and, 341
Efficacy, political, 19–24
Eisenhower, Dwight D., 221
Electrical equipment and applicance
  industry, 35–38, 186–198
Energy crisis, 359, 360, 400, 407
Engineers, 217
Environmental pollution, 359, 360
Environmental protection, 222, 401
Equal rights, 222, 241
Erbring, Lutz, 403–404
Ethical practices, 74–81, 216–217

Etzioni, Amitai, 274–276, 279,
  280
European Value Systems Study
  Group, 410
Executive branch, 42–44, 46–57,
  59, 61–64, 67–73, 82–83, 87,
  122–124
Exxon Corporation, 35–39

Factor analysis, 363
Favorability ratings of industries,
  190–193, 195–196
Federal agency and department
  heads, 201
Federal bureaucracy, 75, 76
Federal government, *see*
  Government
Federal Register, 221–222
Field, Mervin, 343–344
Financial satisfaction, 114–117,
  118, 127, 129, 386, 396, 397,
  402, 410–411
Fingerhut/Granados Opinion
  Research poll, on labor unions,
  202, 352–354
Firms, *see* Industries
Fisher, Burton K., 368*n*
Food industry, 35–38, 186–198
Ford, Gerald, 51–52, 222, 321, 330–
  331, 406
Ford Motor Company, 35–39
France, 369–370, 410
Fraser, Douglas, 356
Free, Lloyd A., 130, 134–135, 387*n*
Free enterprise, 71–72, 255, 361
  divestiture and, 262, 264
  legitimacy of, 282–289
Free Speech Movement, 16
Future, expectations for, 149–151

Gallup International, 410
Gallup polls; *see also* Index of Poll
  Results
  on attitudes toward business,
  368–369, 382
  on blacks, expectations of, 151
  on confidence in institutions, 55,
  57–59, 61, 89–96, 411
  on consumer protection, 254
  on ethical practices, 78–79
  on government regulation, 223,
  225, 228, 231, 233, 234

on government spending, 346, 348, 350
on happiness, 112–113
on honesty and ethical standards, 216–217, 355
on inflation, 212, 349
on institutional leadership, 44, 70–72
on job satisfaction, 113–114
on labor unions, 39, 200–204, 206, 208, 216–217, 353, 355
on nationalization, 283, 284
on personal satisfaction, 126–128
on presidents, 62–63, 406
on state of nation, 126–128, 391
on workingmen, 210
Galombos, Louis, 367, 368, 373
General Electric Company, 36–39, 179; *see also* Index of Poll Results
General Foods Corporation, 39
General Motors Company, 35–39
General Telephone and Electronics Corporation, 39
Germany, 369, 370, 410
Gerth, H. H., 378n
Gilmour, Robert, 340
Goldenberg, Edie N., 403–404
Goodyear Tire and Rubber Company, 36
Government; *see also* Government intervention; Government regulation
citizen's duty, 25, 26–27
comparison of anti-business and anti-government sentiment, 32–34
Congress, 42–55, 57, 58, 60, 62–64, 67–73, 75, 77–79, 98–99, 123–124, 173–174, 217, 292, 381–382
consequences of decline in confidence in, 337–352
executive branch, 42–44, 46–57, 59, 61–64, 67–73, 82–83, 87, 122–124
inflation and, 211–215
perceived responsiveness, 24–26
political efficacy, 19–24
political system, confidence in, 27–29
social and political bases of attitudes toward, 291–334

Supreme Court, 42–44, 46–55, 57, 60, 63, 64, 67–75, 77–79, 98–99, 122–124, 292
trends in attitudes toward, 15, 16–19, 21
Government intervention, 257–290
alternative forms of, 269–274
divestiture, 257–265, 270–273
free enterprise, legitimacy of, 282–289
nationalization, 265–273, 283–284
pro-business, 274–282
Government regulation, 221–256, 369; *see also* Government intervention
consumer protection, 244–255
costs of, 242–244
history of attitudes toward, 222–230
limits of, 236–242
in particular industries, 230–234
wage and price controls, 234, 236
Great Britain, 369–371, 410
Great Depression, 4, 65, 221, 283, 284, 291, 295
Grund, Francis, 377
Gulf Oil Company, 36–38
Gulf of Tonkin crises, 16
Gutek, Barbara A., 381n

Happiness, 111–113, 117
Harris polls; *see also* ABC News/Harris polls; Index of Poll Results
on alienation, 110–111
on attitudes toward business, 165–168, 181, 357, 368, 370
on concentration of power in industries, 185–188, 194
on confidence in institutions, 82, 89–96, 411
on consumer protection, 244–251, 253
on divestiture, 258, 260–262
favorability ratings of industries, 190, 193, 195
on free enterprise, 285, 286
on government regulation, 226, 227, 230, 234, 238, 240–241, 243, 273
on inflation, 154

on institutional leadership, 41–59, 61–64, 67–70, 385
on labor unions, 39–40, 200–202, 204, 206, 218–219, 352
on nationalization, 266, 268
on productivity and economic growth, 274–277, 278–282
on small vs. big companies, 84
Hibbs, Douglas, 65
Hoag, Wendy J., 109*n*
Holland, 410
Honesty and efficiency contrast, 74–76
Honesty and ethical standards, 216–217
Horizontal divestiture, 258, 259
House, James S., 23*n*, 329*n*

IBM Corporation, 35, 36, 39
Ideology, 101–107, 122–125, 292–295, 316–329, 331–333, 364
Independents, 103–106, 294, 297, 298, 324–329, 331, 344
Industries, 34–39, 183–198
concentration of power issue, 184–189, 194
favorability ratings of, 190–193, 195–196
government regulation of, 230–234
overall ratings of, 196–198
Inflation, 34, 61–66, 153–158, 181, 349, 359, 360, 407, 408
effect of unions on, 211–215
effects of, 140–141, 145, 148–149
government regulation and, 242
Institute for International Social Research, 130–133, 136, 138, 143, 157; *see also* Index of Poll Results
Institutions, confidence in; *see also* Business; Government; Labor unions
alienation and, 110–111
economy and, 61–66
education and socioeconomic status and, 99–101, 120, 121–123
ethical practices, 75–81
financial satisfaction and, 114–117, 118
general index of, 97–99
happiness and, 111–113, 117

job satisfaction and, 113–114, 118
politics and ideology, 101–107, 122–125
psychological factors and, 108–120
rankings of, 67–73
size, perception of, 81–88
trust in others and, 108, 109–110, 118–120
Insurance industry, 217, 230
Interest rates, 367
International Association of Machinists, 356
International Ladies Garment Workers, 356
Inter-University Consortium for Political and Social Research (ICPSR), 301*n*
Ireland, 410
Italy, 410

Jackson, Henry, 338–339
Japan, 369, 370, 410
Job safety, 359, 360
Job satisfaction, 113–114, 118, 127
Johnson, Lyndon B., 16, 222, 321, 400, 406
Journalists, 217

Kahn, Robert L., 381*n*
Katz, Daniel, 381*n*
Kellogg Company, 39
Kennedy, Edmund M., 295, 351
Kennedy, John F., 399, 406
Kilpatrick, F. P., 130
Kinder, Donald, 402–403
Kirkland, Lane, 357
Kohut, Andrew, 254–255
Konyha, William, 356

Labeling, 252
Labor unions, 39–40, 98–99, 163–164, 199–220; *see also* Legitimacy
confidence rankings of, 67–73
consequences of decline in confidence in, 352–357
correlates of confidence in, 122–124
ethical practices, 77–79
high valuation, 201–205

honesty and efficiency contrast, 74

inflation and, 211–215

leaders, attitudes toward, 42–55, 57, 60, 63, 64, 172–173, 199–201, 215–220, 355–357

membership, ambivalence of, 205–206

membership rates, 353

power of, 87, 88, 206–209

social and political bases of attitudes toward, 291–333

workingmen, attitude toward, 209–211, 302, 303

Ladd, Everett C., Jr., 287, 296, 328–329, 384, 409–410

Laissez-faire philosophy, 322

Lamb, Robert, 340

Lane, Robert, 14–15

Law enforcement officials, confidence in, 83

Lefkowitz, Bernard, 152, 407–408

Legal profession, 60, 73–79, 382, 383

Legitimacy, 4–5

causes of alienation and cynicism, 396–412

factors reinforcing, 384–392

Reagan effect, 392–396

sensitivity to criticism, 376–378

suspicion of power, 378–384

Liberals, 235, 294–296, 316–320, 323, 325–329, 331–333, 344, 363, 372, 373

Life satisfaction, *see* Personal satisfaction

Lipset, Seymour Martin, xx*n*, 4*n*, 287, 295*n*

Local government, confidence in, 82–83

Los Angeles Times polls, 200, 345; *see also* Index of Poll Results

on government regulation, 227–9

on inflation, 212–213

on labor unions, 204, 355

Love Canal incident, 365, 367

Lynd, Robert, 379

Macke, Anne Statham, 398, 402

Major companies, confidence in leadership of, 30, 39–40, 42–44, 46–60, 62–64, 67–79, 81–82, 84–86, 88, 98–99, 122–123

Markus, George, 396, 398

Martin, Steven S., 23*n*

Mason, William M., 23*n*, 329*n*

Mathiowetz, Nancy A., 337*n*

McCarthy, Joseph, 378

McClosky, Herbert, 329*n*

McGee, William H., III, 109*n*

McGovern, George, 350

McWilliams, Wilson C., 173, 176

Meany, George, 357

Media, 107*n*

ethical practices, 77–79

honesty and efficiency contrast, 74–76

impact of, 403–406

Medical profession, 42–44, 46–55, 57, 60, 61, 63, 64, 67–75, 77–79, 201, 217, 382, 383

Mesick, Jane L., 377*n*

Military leaders, 42–44, 46–55, 57, 60, 62, 64, 67–75, 77–79, 122–124, 292, 383

Miller, Arthur H., 159*n*, 329, 332*n*, 342, 343, 351, 403–404

Miller, Warren E., 23*n*, 24, 330*n*, 332, 352

Mills, C. Wright, 378*n*

Minority rights, 15, 401

Mobil Oil Corporation, 35–38

Moderates, 293, 316–325, 327, 333, 344

Money magazine, 350

Monopoly, 88

Monsanto Company, Inc., 36–39

Moore, Thomas Gale, 222*n*

Morality, 169–172

Munitions industry, 284

Nader, Ralph, 364–365

Nation, confidence in, 126–128, 136, 138, 386–396, 409–410

National Family Opinion surveys, 166, 255; *see also* Index of Poll Results

on labor unions, 202

on profits, 177–178, 180, 181

National Labor Relations Board, 353

National Opinion Research Center (NORC), University of Chicago polls; *see also* Index of Poll Results

National Opinion (*cont.*)
  on confidence in institutions, 89–
    96, 98, 99, 105, 121–125, 292,
    293, 297, 298, 316, 385, 386
  on financial satisfaction, 115, 116,
    127
  on government regulation, 224
  on government spending, 349
  on happiness, 112, 117
  on institutional leadership, 41,
    44–59, 61–64, 67–70, 181
  on job satisfaction, 114, 118, 127
  on labor leadership, 39–40, 200
  on personal trust, 109–110
Nationalization, 265–273, 283–284
NBC News polls; *see also* NBC
    News/Associated Press polls;
    Index of Poll Results
  on government spending, 346
  on inflation, 212–213
NBC News/Associated Press polls;
    see also NBC News polls; Index
    of Poll Results
  on government regulation, 233–
    235
  on inflation, 153, 154
  on state of nation and personal
    satisfaction, 127
New Deal, 221, 291–292, 294–296,
    371
New Left, 295
New Politics movement, 295, 372,
    373
New Right movement, 373
New York Herald Tribune survey,
    on government regulation,
    223–224
New York Times, see CBS News/
    New York Times polls
Nie, Norman H., 104*n*, 398–399,
    404
Nixon, Richard M., 51–52, 222,
    321, 406

Occupational safety, 222
Occupational status, attitudes
    toward business, labor, and
    government by, 292–295, 298–
    299, 312–316, 319, 328
Oil and gasoline industry, 35–38,
    184, 186–198, 230, 233
  alternative forms of government
    control of, 270–273

attitudes toward divestiture in,
    259–265
  image, efforts to improve, 365
  nationalization of, 265–269
  price increases (1973), 366–367
Oil embargo, 158
O'Neill, Thomas P. ("Tip"), 372
Opinion Research Corporation
    (ORC) polls; *see also* Index of
    Poll Results
  on attitudes toward business, 29–
    34, 39, 175, 299–300, 368–369
  on confidence in institutions, 55,
    57–61, 411
  on consumer protection, 247–
    248, 253
  on crisis of confidence, 339
  on divestiture, 258, 264
  on ethical practices, 77–78
  favorability ratings of industries,
    190, 191, 196
  on financial satisfaction, 115–116
  on government regulation, 226–
    228, 231, 232, 236–238, 242,
    243
  on inflation, 212, 214
  on institutional leadership, 44,
    72–73, 172, 200, 217
  on morality and self-interest in
    business, 170–171
  on personal satisfaction, 113*n*
  on profits, 177, 178, 181–182
  on small vs. big corporation, 30,
    84, 85–86, 88
  on workingmen, 210
Opinion Research Survey polls, on
    labor unions, 205–206; *see also*
    Index of Poll Results
Opinion sources, credibility of, 364–
    365, 366
Optimism, 110, 118, 144–151, 386–
    387
  changes in pattern of, 135, 137–
    139
Organized labor, *see* Labor unions
Organized religion, *see* Religion

Partisanship, 101–107, 122–125,
    292–298, 324–333
Penn + Schoen poll, on labor
    unions, 207, 208; *see also* Index
    of Poll Results

Perceived responsiveness of government, 24–26
Perceptions of events, 402–403
Personal satisfaction, 113n, 118–121, 126–159, 386, 411
  economy, impact of, 139–154
  with self and nation, 126–129
  views of past, present, and future, 130–139
Personal trust, 108, 109–110, 118–121
Pessimistic pattern, 137–138, 142, 144–148
Peter D. Hart Research Associates, Inc., 170, 265; *see also* Index of Poll Results
Petrocik, John, 104n, 398–399, 404
Plotkin, Henry A., 174, 176
Police, 217
Political leaders, *see* Government
Political trust, 15, 16–19, 21, 329–333, 341, 403–404
Pollution controls, 241, 243, 244
Potomac Associates polls, 157, 387; *see also* Index of Poll Results
  on personal satisfaction, 130–133
  on state of economy, 143
  on state of nation, 136
Power, 206–209, 359, 409
  concentration of, 5, 6, 184–189, 194
  suspicion of, 378–384
Presidency, 62–63, 77–79, 406; *see also* Executive branch; *individual presidents*
Presidential election of 1964, 16
Presidential primaries, of 1980, 295
Press, confidence in, 42–57, 60, 63–65, 67–73, 123–125; *see also* Media
Price increases, 241
Problem issue ads, 364, 366
Pro-business government intervention, 274–282
Procter & Gamble Company poll, 81–83; *see also* Index of Poll Results
  on labor unions, 209
  on profits, 179–180, 181
Product safety, 222, 241
Productivity, attitudes toward, 274–282

Profits
  exaggerated perception of, 176–178
  high estimation and anti-business sentiment, 180–181
  public understanding of, 178–180
  trends in attitudes, 181–183
Progressive movements, 368, 373
Proposition 13, 342–346, 350
Protest era, 1–3
Psychological factors, influence on confidence in institutions, 108–120

Quaker Oats, 39

Raab, Earl, 295n
Racial disorder, 16
Railroads, 232, 284
RCA Corporation, 36
Reagan, Ronald, 295
  blacks, expectations of, 152
  confidence in presidency, 28, 31, 53, 58, 59, 61, 145, 153–154, 158, 163, 411
  economic program, 347, 350, 409
  on relationship of government and business, 221, 222
Realtors, 217
Recessions, 152, 153, 155, 158
Reinhold, Robert, 341n
Reiter, Howard, 340
Religion, confidence in leaders of, 42–55, 57, 58, 60, 63–65, 67–79, 123, 383
Republicans, 103–106, 124, 221–222, 292, 294, 297, 298, 321, 324–327, 330, 331, 333, 343, 344
Research & Forecasts, Inc., 346; *see also* Index of Poll Results
Resiliency of public confidence, 158–159
Retailers, 230
Reynolds Aluminum, 36–38
Riesman, David, 377
Right-to-work issue, 353–354
Robinson, Michael, 403, 404–405
Rockefeller, John D., 176
Roger Seasonwein polls; *see also* Index of Poll Results
  on attitudes toward business, 88, 167, 171

Robert Seasonwein (*cont.*)
on concentration of power in
industries, 189, 194
on consumer protection, 252, 253
on economic growth, 408
on favorability ratings of
industries, 191, 195
on government regulation, 236–
237, 243
on inflation, 214
on productivity and economic
growth, 274, 275, 277
Roosevelt, Franklin D., 292, 378,
406
Roper Organization polls; *see also*
Index of Poll Results
on alternative forms of
government control of business,
269–273
on American political system, 27–
28
on attitudes toward business,
165–167, 171, 172
on blacks, expectations of, 150–
151
on business, political, and labor
leaders, 172–173
on concentration of power in
industries, 185, 187, 194
on consumer protection, 244, 251
favorability ratings of industries,
192, 193, 196
on free enterprise, 285, 287–288
on government regulation, 224–
225, 231, 233–235
on government spending, 346
on inflation, 181
on labor unions, 200–201, 207–
208, 214–216, 218
on nationalization, 266–269
on personal satisfaction, 128
on profits, 177
on small vs. big companies, 81–
82, 84–88
on socialism, 283
on state of nation, 128, 137, 409
on wage and price controls, 178
Rourke, Francis E., 387*n*

Scandinavia, 369, 410
Schlozman, Kay Lehman, 151–152,
296–297
Schneider, Edward J., 332*n*

Schumpeter, Joseph, 80
Science, 98–99, 122–123, 383
Sears, David, 342
Sears, Roebuck and Company, 35,
36, 39
Self-interest, 80–81, 169–172, 359,
383, 409
Sensitivity to criticism, 376–378
Sentry Insurance Company, 244,
274–276, 279, 280, 282, 357,
370
Shanks, J. Merrill, 329*n*
Shell Oil Company, 35–39, 365
Shoddy products, 359, 360
Size, perception of, 81–88
Small business, 30, 39–40, 74–79,
81–82, 84–86, 88
Smith, Tom W., 44*n*, 46, 337*n*,
342–343
Sniderman, Paul M., 329*n*
Social class, 149, 150, 291, 295–
299, 314, 315, 328
Social democratic policies, 371
Social responsibility, 358–361
Socialism, 282–284, 369, 371
Socioeconomic status, influence on
confidence in institutions, 99–
101
Spain, 410
State government, confidence in,
82–83
Status insecurity, 376
Steady-staters, 144–148
Steel industry, 35–38, 186–198
alternative forms of government
control of, 270–273
Stock market, 60, 73, 77–79
Stokes, Donald, 101*n*
Strikes, 204, 211, 215
Strout, Richard L., 339*n*
Sundquist, James L., 400
Sunoco Corporation, 39
Supreme Court, 42–44, 46–55, 57,
60, 63, 64, 67–75, 77–79, 98–
99, 122–124, 292
Survey Research Center (SRC)
polls; *see also* Center for
Political Studies (CPS),
University of Michigan; Index
of Poll Results
on blacks, expectations of, 151
on business, 368
on confidence in institutions, 73

on financial satisfaction, 115–117
on government, 16, 32, 33, 381
on happiness, 111–112
on job satisfaction, 114
on personal satisfaction, 113*n*,
    128–129
on personal trust, 109–110
on state of nation, 128–129, 387,
    389

Tax revolt, 342–346, 360, 369
Taylor, D. Garth, 337*n*, 342–343
Taylor, Marsha, 123
Teamsters' Union, 357
Television, 403–406
    correlates of confidence in, 122–
    124
Temporary crisis outlook, 138–139,
    140, 144–148
Texaco Corporation, 35–39
Thatcher, Margaret, 370
Thomas, John Clayton, 370
Three Mile Island incident, 367
Tire and rubber industry, 35–38,
    186–198
Trucking industry, 232
Truman, Harry S, 406
Trust-busting, 257, 274
Trust in others, 108, 109–110, 118–
    120

Undertakers, 217
Unemployment, 61–66, 151–153,
    155–157, 359, 360, 407
    effects of, 140–141, 145, 148–149
Union Carbide Corporation, 35, 36,
    39, 274, 275, 277, 281, 408
United Automobile Workers, 356
U.S. News and World Report polls;
    see also Index of Poll Results
    on attitudes toward business, 85,
    168, 172, 359
    on confidence in institutions, 74–
    76
    on inflation, 212
    on labor leadership, 217
    on profits, 178, 180–181
U.S. Steel Corporation, 36
Universities, 2–3
Utilities, 184, 186–198, 230

Value Systems Study Group of the
    Americas, 410

Verba, Sidney, 19, 104*n*, 151–152,
    296–297, 398–399, 404
Vertical divestiture, 258, 259
Vietnam War, 1, 15, 16, 69, 295,
    399, 400, 407
Voter participation, 107*n*, 340–342

Wage and price controls, 178, 234–
    236
Wagner Act of 1935, 292
Wallace, George, 295
Warr, Mark, 398
Washington Post polls; *see also* ABC
    News/*Washington Post* polls;
    Index of Poll Results
    on nationalization, 268
    on state of union, 410
Watergate, 18, 27, 28, 32, 51, 158,
    352, 390, 399, 400–401
Watts, William, 130, 134–135,
    387*n*
Weber, Max, 377–378
Welfare state philosophy, 322
Westinghouse Corporation, 36–39
Wilensky, Harold, 289*n*
Withey, Stephen B., 129*n*, 368*n*
Workingmen, attitudes toward,
    209–211, 301–303, 314, 326
Wright, James, 340, 396

Xerox Corporation, 39

Yankelovich, Daniel, 15, 152, 390,
    407–408
Yankelovich, Skelly & White, Inc.
    (YSW) polls; *see also*
    Yankelovich, Skelly & White/
    Time Magazine poll; Index of
    Poll Results
    on attitude toward business, 166,
    168
    on business and labor leadership,
    79, 172
    on concentration of power in
    industries, 185, 186, 188, 194
    on credibility of opinion sources,
    364–365, 366
    on financial satisfaction, 129
    on free enterprise, 285
    on government regulation, 226,
    242, 255
    on government spending, 346,
    350

Yankelovich, Skelly & White, Inc.
(*cont.*)
on labor unions, 201, 207, 218
on profits, 178, 182

Yankelovich, Skelly & White/*Time*
Magazine poll; *see* Yankelovich,
Skelly & White, Inc., polls;
Index of Poll Results

About the Authors

Seymour Martin Lipset is the Caroline S. G. Munro Professor of Political Science, Professor of Sociology, and a Senior Fellow of the Hoover Institution on War, Revolution and Peace, Stanford University. He is also a co-editor of *Public Opinion* magazine. Before moving to Stanford in 1975, he was the George Markham Professor of Government and Sociology at Harvard University. He has also held positions at the University of California at Berkeley, Columbia University, and the University of Toronto.

Dr. Lipset has been elected to membership by the National Academy of Sciences, the American Philosophical Society, the National Academy of Education, and the American Academy of Arts and Sciences, of which he was vice-president for the Social Sciences from 1974–78. He served as president of the American Political Science Association for 1981–82, as president of the International Society of Political Psychology for 1979–80, and as chairperson of the Section on Economic and Social Sciences of the American Association for the Advancement of Sciences, for 1975–76. He is Vice-President of the International Political Science Association (1982–85) and has been elected to serve as President of the Sociological Research Association and of the World Association for Public Opinion Research.

He is the author or co-author of seventeen books, including *Agrarian Socialism, Union Democracy, Political Man, The First New Nation, The Divided Academy, Rebellion in the University,* and *The Politics of Unreason*. Translations of his works have appeared in twenty languages. He has received the Robert MacIver and the Gunnar Myrdal awards, and the Townsend Harris Medal. He has held fellowships awarded by the Guggenheim Foundation, the Social Science Research Council, and the Center for Advanced Study in the Behavioral Sciences.

William Schneider is a Resident Fellow at the American Enterprise Institute for Public Policy Research in Washington, D.C. He is also Senior Polling Consultant to the *National Journal,* Associate Editor of the *Baron Report,* and a political consultant associated with the *Los Angeles Times* and with Craver, Mathews, Smith & Company of Falls Church, Virginia.

About the Authors

Dr. Schneider received his Ph.D. in political science from Harvard University in 1971. He subsequently taught in the Department of Government at Harvard and was a Research Fellow at the Harvard Center for International Affairs. During 1976–77, he held a National Fellowship from the Hoover Institution on War, Revolution and Peace at Stanford University, and, in 1979, became a Visiting Fellow there. He spent 1980 in the office of Senator Daniel Patrick Moynihan of New York as an International Affairs Fellow of the Council on Foreign Relations. Since 1981 he has been a Senior Research Fellow (by courtesy) of the Hoover Institution.

Dr. Schneider has published many scholarly and popular articles dealing with American public opinion and voting behavior. He is currently working on a new book, *The Radical Center: New Directions in American Politics,* to be published in 1984.

PROGRAM FOR STUDIES OF
THE MODERN CORPORATION
Graduate School of Business, Columbia University

PUBLICATIONS

FRANCIS JOSEPH AGUILAR
Scanning the Business Environment

MELVIN ANSHEN
Corporate Strategies for Social Performance

MELVIN ANSHEN, *editor*
Managing the Socially Responsible Corporation

HERMAN W. BEVIS
Corporate Financial Reporting in a Competitive Economy

COURTNEY C. BROWN
Beyond the Bottom Line

COURTNEY C. BROWN
Putting the Corporate Board to Work

COURTNEY C. BROWN, *editor*
World Business: Promise and Problems

YALE BROZEN
Concentration, Mergers, and Public Policy

NEIL W. CHAMBERLAIN
Social Strategy and Corporate Structure

CHARLES DE HOGHTON, *editor*
The Company: Law, Structure, and Reform

RICHARD EELLS
The Corporation and the Arts

RICHARD EELLS
The Political Crisis of the Enterprise System

RICHARD EELLS, *editor*
International Business Philanthropy

RICHARD EELLS and CLARENCE WALTON, *editors*
Man in the City of the Future

JAMES C. EMERY
Organizational Planning and Control Systems: Theory and Technology

ALBERT S. GLICKMAN, CLIFFORD P. HAHN, EDWIN A. FLEISHMAN, and BRENT BAXTER
Top Management Development and Succession: An Exploratory Study

NEIL H. JACOBY
Corporate Power and Social Responsibility

NEIL H. JACOBY
Multinational Oil: A Study in Industrial Dynamics

NEIL H. JACOBY, PETER NEHEMKIS, and RICHARD EELLS
Bribery and Extortion in World Business: A Study of Corporate Political Payments Abroad

SEYMOUR MARTIN LIPSET and WILLIAM SCHNEIDER
The Confidence Gap: Business, Labor, and Government in the Public Mind

JAY W. LORSCH
Product Innovation and Organization

IRA M. MILLSTEIN and SALEM M. KATSH
The Limits of Corporate Power: Existing Constraints on the Exercise of Corporate Discretion

KENNETH G. PATRICK
Perpetual Jeopardy—The Texas Gulf Sulphur Affair: A Chronicle of Achievement and Misadventure

KENNETH G. PATRICK and RICHARD EELLS
Education and the Business Dollar

IRVING PFEFFER, editor
The Financing of Small Business: A Current Assessment

STANLEY SALMEN
Duties of Administrators in Higher Education

GUNNAR K. SLETMO and ERNEST W. WILLIAMS, JR.
Liner Conferences in the Container Age: U.S. Policy at Sea

GEORGE A. STEINER
The New CEO

GEORGE A. STEINER
Top Management Planning

GEORGE A. STEINER and WILLIAM G. RYAN
Industrial Project Management

GEORGE A. STEINER and WARREN M. CANNON, editors
Multinational Corporate Planning

GUS TYLER
The Political Imperative: The Corporate Character of Unions

CLARENCE WALTON and RICHARD EELLS, editors
The Business System: Readings in Ideas and Concepts

*The colophon for this book
as for the other books of the
Program for Studies of the
Modern Corporation was
created by Theodore Roszak*